KU-608-036

TEMPERAMENT AND BEHAVIOR DISORDERS IN CHILDREN

Temperament
and
Behavior Disorders
in Children

ALEXANDER THOMAS, M.D.
Professor, Psychiatry
New York University
School of Medicine

STELLA CHESS, M.D.
Associate Professor, Psychiatry
New York University
School of Medicine

HERBERT G. BIRCH, M.D., PH.D.
Research Professor, Pediatrics
Albert Einstein College of Medicine

New York · NEW YORK UNIVERSITY PRESS

London · UNIVERSITY OF LONDON PRESS LIMITED

1968

© 1968 by New York University
Library of Congress Catalog Card Number: 68-13025
Manufactured in the United States of America

C. F. MOTT COLLEGE OF EDUCATION

PREFACE

Writing this book was a long but pleasant task for the authors, who have spent a considerable portion of their professional lives concerned with children and their problems. One of the frustrations of practical work is the absence of detailed information on children and their development before they are brought to clinical notice. The clinician, of course, seeks to reconstruct the past, but even the most elaborate and carefully bolstered reconstruction must leave him with the nagging doubt that the edifice may well be constructed of fancies joined together by the cement of strongly held theories. It was, therefore, most refreshing to be able to deal with clinical cases whose past histories were known and did not have to be inferred. The knowledge of the past helped to illuminate the present and to provide a new and hopefully sounder basis for understanding the developmental course of behavioral disturbance in children. The purpose of this book is to share this experience with our colleagues.

The task of conducting the longitudinal study which makes this report possible has been arduous, not only for ourselves, but for our many associates in the venture. It is only fitting that we acknowledge our indebtedness at this time. In the first place, we must give thanks to the parents who unstintingly gave of their time and energies to this study of their children. We are grateful, too, to the teachers and directors of nursery and elementary schools who inconvenienced themselves beyond the call of duty to make us welcome, to provide the opportunity to observe the children in school settings, and to submit to detailed interviews about their pupils.

Our co-workers were numerous, and all were consistently devoted to their tasks and responsibilities. We wish to thank the interviewers and observers, Sylvia Zuckerman, Hilda Meltzer, and Mimi Lewin; the scorers and data tabulators, Martha Roth, Ruth Sinreich, Beatrice Hyman, Mimi Korn, and Edith Pollack, who over the years devoted thousands of hours to the detailed task of behavioral classification; and the secretarial staff, Miriam Rosenberg, Helen Pauker, Ida Hafner, and Charlotte Bruskin, who prepared miles of records, organized schedules, and kept data in a form permitting ready availability and analysis.

Special thanks are due to Sophie Ladimer, clinical psychologist, who carried through the program of psychological testing and participated in a number of the data analyses, as well as to Marguerite Rosenberg, psychiatric social worker, whose responsibilities included participation in the psychiatric evaluations, in the selective analysis of the anterospective information, and in the follow-up of the clinical cases.

At another level, we wish to thank Dr. Sam Korn and Dr. Margaret E. Hertzig, who have functioned as our collaborators at all points and stages in the investigation. This book is as much theirs as it is ours. Special appreciation is due, too, to Dr. Michael Rutter who, during the course of a Nuffield traveling fellowship and thereafter, functioned as a most productive colleague and collaborator. In the most recent period, our work has been very much facilitated by the consultations on data analysis and statistical procedures provided by Dr. Jacob Cohen. Our deep thanks are also due to Drs. Lillian Robbins, Edwin Robbins, and Nettie Terestman, who took major responsibility for developing and organizing specific phases of data collection and analysis, and to Drs. Patricia Waly, Irving Dryman, and Jane Raph, who participated actively in a number of the data analyses.

The preparation of the text and its features of readability owe much to the editorial activities of Abby Hand and Janet Sillen. Segments that are obscure are entirely the responsibility of the authors.

The longitudinal study was initially aided financially by several private sources. Since 1960 the study has received major support from the National Institute of Mental Health (MH–3614), together with additional support from the National Institute of Child Health and Human Development (HD–00719), and the Association for Aid of Crippled Children. The views expressed in the volume are, of course, entirely the authors' and should in no way be construed as reflecting the opinions of any of the agencies that have given the study financial support.

Chapter XIII represents an expansion of a previously published paper, "Behavioral Development in Brain-Damaged Children," which appeared in the *Archives of General Psychiatry*, 11:6 (1964). Appreciation is extended to this journal for permission to incorporate portions of this paper in the present volume.

CONTENTS

TEMPERAMENT AND BEHAVIOR DISORDERS IN CHILDREN

1 | BEHAVIOR DISORDERS AND THE CONCEPT OF TEMPERAMENT

In the present volume we are concerned with examining certain of the factors which contribute to the development of behavior disorders in young children. The particular focus will be on the child's temperament and on the role it plays in the emergence and elaboration of behavior problems. Despite this focus, however, we will not and cannot consider temperament in isolation as the cause for disturbed development. Together with all serious workers in psychiatry and psychology we recognize that both normal development and disturbances in development, rather than being the products of any single factor, result from complex interactions between the child and his environment. Our concern with temperament and our divergence from other theories, therefore, do not derive from a disagreement with the concept of behavioral development as the consequence of the continuous interaction between an organism and its environment, but rather from a different view of the variables which are interacting.

Our concern with the role of temperament as an organismic contributor to the course of behavioral development is not new. Beginning over fifteen years ago, we came increasingly to be impressed with the contribution made to behavioral development by reactive characteristics of the child, particularly his pattern of temperamental organization. Our own clinical experience, as well as that of others,[1, 2, 3, 4, 5, 6] suggested that an exclusive concern with environmental influences could not explain the range and variability in developmental course exhibited by individual children. Nor could it explain the marked differences in the responses of children to similar patterns of parental attitudes, values, and child-care practices.[7, 8, 9, 10] It was evident, too, that parents frequently showed significant variations in their response patterns to their different children,[11] suggesting that the child's own characteristics as an individual could and did act as specific stimuli for the parent.

To test the validity of these personal and clinical impressions, we mounted a longitudinal study in 1956, the central aims of which were the objective definition of temperamental characteristics in children and the delineation of the contributions which such characteristics made to both normal and aberrant behavioral development. Although we started to study each child in our sample of 136 children during early infancy and so had no sound basis for predicting which child would develop in an

3

abnormal way, we anticipated that a sizable number of the children in the study population would develop behavioral disturbances. This indeed happened and made the present report possible.

Since the children were studied from early life onward, and both their temperaments and environments were repeatedly assessed, the data make it possible to deal with two issues of importance for child psychiatry: 1] the manner in which temperamental patterns influence the likelihood that a behavior disorder will develop, and 2] an anterospective view of the emergence of behavioral disturbance, together with the factors contributing to symptom formation and evolution.

Before entering upon the substance of this inquiry, it is of value to consider the place of our main variable, temperament, in the behavioral scheme. Temperament may best be viewed as a general term referring to the *how* of behavior. It differs from ability, which is concerned with the *what* and *how well* of behaving, and from motivation, which seeks to account for *why* a person does what he is doing. When we refer to temperament, we are concerned with the *way* in which an individual behaves. Two children may each eat skillfully or throw a ball with accuracy and have the same motives in so doing. Yet, they may differ with respect to the intensity with which they act, the rate at which they move, the mood which they express, the readiness with which they shift to a new activity, and the ease with which they will approach a new toy, situation, or playmate.

Thus, temperament is the *behavioral style* of the individual child— the *how* rather than the *what* (abilities and content) or *why* (motivations) of behavior. Temperament is a phenomenologic term used to describe the characteristic tempo, rhythmicity, adaptability, energy expenditure, mood, and focus of attention of a child, independently of the content of any specific behavior. A formal analysis of behavior into the *why,* the *what,* and the *how* has also been utilized by other workers, such as Guilford [12] and Cattell, [13] the latter of whom identifies "the three modalities of behavior traits" as: 1] "dynamic traits or interests . . . [including] basic drives plus acquired interests such as attitudes, sentiments," etc.; 2] "abilities, shown by how well the person makes his way to the accepted goals"; and 3] temperament, "definable by exclusion as those traits which are unaffected by incentive or complexity . . . like highstrungness, speed, energy and emotional reactivity, which common observation suggests are largely constitutional." [14]

Temperament is not immutable. Like any other characteristic of the organism, its features can undergo a developmental course that will be significantly affected by environmental circumstances. In this respect it is not different from height, weight, intellectual competence, or any other characteristic of the individual and, as is the case for all such characteristics, the initially identified pattern of the young child may

be relatively unchanged by environmental influences, or it may be reinforced and heightened, diminished, or otherwise modified during the
developmental course.

The need for studying the child's own characteristics and the contribution these might make to his psychological development were high-
lighted by the paucity of information available on temperament when
we began our longitudinal study in the mid-1950's.[15] The contribution
of other factors to the development of behavior disorders had been
examined through many lines of inquiry in the previous decades. Important insights had been provided by these studies on the role of
heredity, pre- and perinatal brain damage, biochemical and neuro-
physiological disturbances in development, unfavorable parental practices and attitudes, intrafamilial conflict, conditions of social stress and
deprivation, and distortions of the learning process involved in the
child's socialization. On the other hand, little attention had been paid to
the nature of the child's own characteristics as a reactive organism and
in particular to the possibility that the manner in which his individual
pattern of reactivity is organized may affect his development. It is true
that in 1937 Freud had asserted that "each individual ego is endowed
from the beginning with its own peculiar dispositions and tendencies," [16]
and that in the 1930's two pioneer workers in child development, Gesell [17] and Shirley,[18] had reported significant individual differences in the
behavioral characteristics of infants. Somewhat earlier, Pavlov and his
followers [19] had postulated the existence of congenitally determined
types of nervous systems as basic to the course of subsequent behavioral
development. They had classified different types of nervous systems
according to the balance between excitation and inhibition, and had
attempted to explain features of both normal and abnormal behavioral
states on this basis.

In the 1940's and 1950's, a number of studies appeared which reported observations of individual differences in infants and young children in specific, discrete areas of functioning such as motility,[20] perceptual responses,[21] sleeping and feeding patterns,[22] drive endowment,[23]
quality and intensity of emotional tone,[24] social responsiveness,[25] autonomic response patterns,[26, 27, 28] biochemical individuality,[29, 30] and electroencephalographic patterns.[31] These various reports emphasized that
individual differences appeared to be present at birth and are not determined by postnatal experience. Although studies of this kind provided
valuable data and leads for further investigation, they were too narrow
in focus to provide a basis for systematic and comprehensive understanding of behavioral individuality in early childhood, and of the significance
of such individuality for psychological development.[32]

A number of factors were responsible for the neglect of temperament as an area of investigation. Important among these was the general
disrepute of earlier constitutionalist views that had ascribed heredity and

constitution as causes for complex personality structures and elaborate psychopathological syndromes. It was our repeated experience in the early and mid-1950's to find most of our colleagues reproaching us for returning to an outdated and discredited constitutionalist position when we expressed the idea that individual organismic behavioral differences important for development might exist in young children. In a period when behavioral disturbance was most generally considered to be produced by the environment, to pay attention to the intrinsic characteristics of the reactor was viewed as a return to a static and almost Lombrosian constitutional typology. It was indeed the period of the "empty organism" for many workers and thinkers in psychiatry.

In spite of the prevailing atmosphere, however, a set of facts could not be neglected. These were: 1] the lack of simple relationship between environmental circumstances and their consequences; 2] individual differences in susceptibility to stresses and pressures; 3] differential responses to similar patterns of parental care. These facts could not be denied, and increasingly led a number of workers [33, 34, 35, 36, 37] to concern themselves with attributes of the individual as an organism which, in their view, could significantly contribute to his idiosyncratic responsiveness to environmental events. Different workers emphasized different attributes of the individual. Independent of the attribute stressed, the most important result of these studies was a rekindling of concern with, and interest in, the contributions which organismic individuality made to development.

This concern with the child's own characteristics as a force in development has accelerated sufficiently in the past few years so that currently there is a broad consensus among investigators in child psychiatry and child development that the consideration of both organismic and environmental factors, as well as their mutually interactive influences, is required for any comprehensive study of a child's normal or aberrant development.

However, there is still a need to convert agreement in principle to agreement in practice. For the child's individuality to be incorporated seriously into psychiatric theory and practice, detailed information on specific patternings of interaction between organismic and environmental factors in development is required. Such information can be obtained only from a longitudinal study that identifies temperamental patterns and follows the dynamics of the interaction of temperament and environment over a significant segment of the developmental course. Though such a study makes special demands for sample maintenance and long term devotion to data collection and analysis,[38, 39, 40, 41, 42] it is uniquely effective for the exploration of the relation between the early characteristics and the later development of the individual, and for the delineation of individual behavioral sequences. For most other questions, serial sampling of appropriate populations at different ages represents an entirely adequate and more efficient study design. For example, a determination of the types of behavior problems characteristic of children at different ages can be made by the simultaneous study of representative samples drawn from different age groups. If, however, one is concerned with developmental questions involving the relationship between specific attributes of the young child and the emergence of behavioral disturbance at an older age or with the identification of the factors leading to specific patterns of symptom formation and evolution, one is forced to study the same individual at more than one point in time—that is, to pursue a longitudinal investigation.

Furthermore, such a longitudinal study must be anterospectively oriented if the distortions of retrospective recall by parents or other reporters are to be minimized. The vast majority of investigations into the origins of behavior disorders in childhood have relied upon retrospective reports of events in early childhood obtained either from older children, from the parents of younger children, or from adults suffering from behavioral disturbances. For a number of decades, the assumption that retrospectively obtained histories of early childhood events, feelings, and fantasies represented a valid body of data on which to base theories of child development went virtually unquestioned. In recent years, however, this assumption has been challenged by the findings of several investigations that question the accuracy of mothers' retrospective reports on the early developmental histories of their children. Several studies, both from our own and other centers, have revealed significant distortions in the accuracy of such reports even when the child's development has been normal.[43, 44, 45] Wenar, in a recent review of these studies, has concluded that "A good deal of past research has leaned heavily on the slenderest of reeds. It may well be that mothers' histories mislead more often than they illuminate and, as yet, we are in a poor position to know when they are doing one or the other." [46]

If retrospective parental reporting of the child's normal development is unreliable, the unreliability will undoubtedly be even greater when the child presents a behavior disorder. In such cases, the inaccuracy of parental recall will be magnified by defensiveness, by the search for plausible explanations, or by the influence of popular theories about the causes of psychopathology. The accuracy of parental histories describing the development of behavior problems in their children was tested in our New York Longitudinal Study.[47] The parent's retrospective report of the child's behavioral development was compared with the information collected anterospectively in the course of the longitudinal study. Significant distortions of parental recall were found in one-third of the cases. The distortions included: 1] revisions of timing to make the sequence of events conform to prevalent theories of causation; 2] denial or minimization of the problem; and 3] inability to recall pertinent past behavior. Of additional interest was the lack of systematic relationship between the degree of internal consistency and fluency of the parent's retrospective report and the correlation of this report with the corresponding anterospective data.

It is true that the clinician must, on many occasions, utilize retrospective data obtained from patients and parents. He must evaluate the patient's problem and institute treatment on the basis of whatever data are available. In addition, the issues emphasized by a patient in his retrospective recall, even if factually inaccurate, may provide useful clues as to his significant concerns and preoccupations. On the other hand, the research worker has a different responsibility. His obligation is not immediate action or patient care, but the accumulation of pertinent and accurate data. In this task, retrospective histories, if utilized at all, must be evaluated with great caution.

The need for anterospective longitudinal studies in the investigation of the origins and evolution of behavior disorders in children has been recognized by a number of workers at Berkeley,[48] the Fels Institute,[49] Yale,[50] and Topeka.[51] Longitudinal studies at these centers have made a number of contributions to our knowledge of normal and aberrant behavioral development. The possible significance of temperamental characteristics of the child in interaction with parental functioning has been indicated. A lack of correlation between the child's patterns of psychodynamic defenses and the occurrence of behavioral dysfunction has been found. Symptoms typical of various age-periods have been tabulated, their vicissitudes over time traced, and correlations among different symptoms determined. However, each of these studies has been limited either by small sample size, which has not permitted generalization of the findings, or by the absence of systematic psychiatric evaluation of the children, which has severely restricted the possibility of categorizing the behavior disturbances and making meaningful correlations with the longitudinal data on behavioral development.

The identification of the limitations for interpretation intrinsic to earlier studies helped us to formulate the issues and problems with which we had to be concerned in our own longitudinal study. The problem was threefold:

1] Methods for studying temperament and for following a substantial number of children for a long period of time by these methods had to be developed.

2] A procedure for identifying children in the group who develop behavior disorders had to be established.

3] The conditions of care, environment, and stress confronting these children had to be determined and recorded. With these data it would be possible to determine the differential risks that attach to specific temperamental patterns and to study the temperamental characteristics and environmental features involved in the production of normal or disordered behavior.

Neither in theory nor in fact would we expect a one-to-one relation to exist between a specific pattern of temperament and the emergence of a behavior problem; temperament, in and of itself, does not produce a behavior disorder. We would anticipate that in any given group of children with a particular patterning of temperamental organization, certain of these children would develop behavior disorders and others would not. Hopefully, this variability in consequence could be identified as deriving from differences in the patterns of care and other environmental circumstances to which the children were exposed. However, we also would anticipate that given a uniform environment and set of stresses, certain patternings of temperament are more likely to result in behavior disorders than are others. We are therefore concerned with the identification of both the differential likelihoods for the development of disturbances that attach to different temperamental patterns, and the specific environmental factors that interact with each temperamental type to result in a pathologic consequence. These tasks have represented the major goals of the study and are reported in the present volume.

REFERENCES

1. H. R. Beiser, "Discrepancies in the Symptomatology of Parents and Children," *Jour. of Amer. Acad. Child Psychiat.*, 3:457 (1964).
2. L. B. Murphy, *The Widening World of Childhood* (New York: Basic Books, 1962).
3. S. K. Escalona, "Patterns of Infantile Experience and the Developmental Process," *Psychoanalytic Study of the Child*, 18:197 (1963).
4. W. Goldfarb, *Childhood Schizophrenia* (Cambridge: Harvard University Press, 1961).
5. L. Bender, "Childhood Schizophrenia," *Amer. Jour. Orthopsychiat.*, 17:40 (1947).
6. D. Levy, *Maternal Overprotection* (New York: Columbia University Press, 1943).
7. H. Orlansky, "Infant Care and Personality," *Psychol. Bull.*, 46:1 (1949).
8. H. Bruch, "Parent Education or the Illusion of Omnipotence," *Amer. Jour. Orthopsychiat.*, 24:723 (1954).
9. I. Stevenson, "Is the Human Personality More Plastic in Infancy and Childhood?," *Amer. Jour. Psychiat.*, 114:152 (1957).
10. E. H. Klatskin, E. B. Jackson, and L. C. Wilkin, "The Influence of Degree of Flexibility in Maternal Child Care Practices on Early Child Behavior," *Amer. Jour. Orthopsychiat.*, 26:79 (1956).
11. A. Thomas and Others, "The Developmental Dynamics of Primary Reaction Characteristics in Children," *Proceedings, Third World Congress of Psychiatry*, 1:722 (Montreal: University of Toronto Press, 1961).
12. J. P. Guilford, *Personality* (New York: McGraw-Hill, 1959).
13. R. B. Cattell, *Personality: A Systematic and Factual Study* (New York: McGraw-Hill, 1950).
14. *Ibid.*, p. 35.

15. H. L. Witner and R. Kotinsky, eds., "Personality in the Making," *Fact Finding Report of Mid-Century White House Conference on Children and Youth* (New York: Harper & Brothers, 1952).
16. S. Freud, "Analysis, Terminable and Interminable," *Collected Papers,* 5:316 (London: Hogarth Press, 1950).
17. A. Gesell and L. B. Ames, "Early Evidences of Individuality in the Human Infant," *J. Genetic Psychol.,* 47:339 (1937).
18. M. M. Shirley, *The First Two Years: A Study of Twenty-five Babies* (Minneapolis: University of Minnesota Press, 1931 and 1933).
19. I. P. Pavlov, *Conditioned Reflexes: An Investigation of the Physiological Activity of the Cerebral Cortex,* trans. and ed. G. V. Anrep (London: Oxford University Press, 1927).
20. M. Fries and P. Woolf, "Some Hypotheses on the Role of the Congenital Activity Type in Personality Development," *Psychoanalytic Study of the Child,* 8:48 (1953).
21. P. Bergman and S. Escalona, "Unusual Sensitivities in Very Young Children," *Psychoanalytic Study of the Child,* 3–4:33 (1949).
22. S. Escalona and Others, "Emotional Development in the First Year of Life," *Problems of Infancy and Childhood* (New York: Josiah Macy, Jr. Foundation, 1953), p. 11.
23. A. Alpert, P. W. Neubauer, and A. P. Weil, "Unusual Variation in Drive Endowment," *Psychoanalytic Study of the Child,* 11:125 (1956).
24. R. Meili, "A Longitudinal Study of Personality Development," *Dynamic Psychopathology in Childhood,* eds. L. Jessner and E. Pavenstedt (New York: Grune and Stratton, 1959), pp. 106–123. [This is a summary of a monographic report, "Anfange der Charakterentwicklung" (Bern: Hans Hunber, 1957)].
25. Gesell, *op. cit.*
26. W. H. Bridger and M. F. Reiser, "Psychophysiologic Studies of the Neonate," *Psychosomat. Med.,* 21:265 (1959).
27. H. J. Grossman and N. Y. Greenberg, "Psychosomatic Differentiation in Infancy," *Psychosomat. Med.,* 19:293 (1957).
28. J. B. Richmond and S. L. Lustman, "Autonomic Function in the Neonate," *Psychosomat. Med.,* 17:269 (1955).
29. I. A. Mirsky, "Psychoanalysis and the Biological Sciences," *Twenty Years of Psychoanalysis,* eds. F. Alexander and H. Ross (New York: W. W. Norton, 1953), pp. 155–76.
30. R. V. Williams, *Biochemical Individuality* (New York: John Wiley & Sons, 1956).
31. G. Walter, "Electroencephalographic Development of Children," *Discussion on Child Development,* I, eds. J. M. Tanner and B. Inhelder (New York: International Univ. Press, 1953), 132–60.
32. *See* A. Thomas and Others, "A Longitudinal Study of Primary Reaction Patterns in Children," *Comprehensive Psych.,* 1:103 (1960), for references to some of these studies.
33. Escalona, *op. cit.*
34. B. Fish, "The Prediction of Schizophrenia in Infancy," *Amer. Jour. of Psychiatry,* 121:768 (1965).
35. D. C. Ross, "Poor School Achievement: A Psychiatric Study and Classification," *Clinical Pediatrics,* 5:109 (1966).
36. W. H. Bridger and B. M. Birns, "Neonates' Behavioral and Autonomic Responses to Stress During Soothing," *Recent Advances in Biological Psychiat.,* V (New York: Plenum Press, 1963).

37. Goldfarb, *op. cit.*
38. A. L. Baldwin, "The Study of Child Behavior and Development," *Handbook of Research Methods in Child Development,* ed. P. H. Mussen (New York: John Wiley, 1960).
39. A. A. Stone and G. C. Onque, *Longitudinal Studies of Child Personality* (Cambridge: Harvard University Press, 1959).
40. W. Kessen, "Research Design in the Study of Developmental Problems," *Handbook of Research Methods in Child Development,* ed. P. H. Mussen (New York: John Wiley, 1960).
41. C. W. Harris, ed., *Problems in Measuring Change* (Madison: University of Wisconsin Press, 1963).
42. K. W. Schaie, "A General Model for the Study of Developmental Problems," *Psycholog. Bull.,* 64:92 (1965).
43. K. E. Goddard, A. Broder, and C. Wenar, "Reliability of Pediatric Histories: A Preliminary Report," *Pediatrics,* 28:1011 (1961).
44. E. A. Haggard, A. Brekstad, and A. G. Skard, "On the Reliability of the Anamnestic Interview," *Journal of Abnorm. Soc. Psychol.,* 61:311 (1960).
45. L. Robbins, "The Accuracy of Parental Recall of Aspects of Child Development and of Child Rearing Practices," *Journal of Abnormal Soc. Psychol.,* 66:261 (1963).
46. C. Wenar, "The Reliability of Developmental Histories," *Psychosomat. Med.,* 25:505 (1963).
47. S. Chess, A. Thomas, and H. G. Birch, "Distortions in Developmental Reporting Made by Parents of Behaviorally Disturbed Children," *Jour. of Amer. Acad. of Child Psychiat.,* 5:226 (1966).
48. J. W. McFarlane, W. Allen, and M. P. Honzik, *A Developmental Study of the Behavior Problems of Normal Children Between 24 Months and 14 Years* (Berkeley: University of California Press, 1962).
49. J. Kagan and H. A. Moss, *Birth to Maturity* (New York: John Wiley, 1962).
50. M. Kris, "The Use of Prediction in a Longitudinal Study," *Psychoanalytic Study of the Child,* 12:175 (1957).
51. Murphy, *op. cit.*

2 | THE BACKGROUND: THE NEW YORK LONGITUDINAL STUDY

To understand the findings on the interaction between temperament and environment in the development of behavior disorders, the longitudinal study from which the information has been drawn must be considered in detail.

The families whose children were selected for longitudinal study were of middle- or upper-middle-class background, resident in New York City or one of its surrounding suburbs, and willing to participate in a long-term study of the behavioral development of their children. The specific restrictions regarding social class and geographic limits were introduced in order to make the sample relatively homogeneous for background and to reduce, to some extent, social and geographical differences as a source for variance in behavioral development. In this way we would be better able to analyze individual differences in the children themselves. In March, 1956, the first of the families were enrolled. Enrollment was begun either shortly after a child had been born, or during the pregnancy of which the child was the product. The collection of cases was cumulative and was continued until 85 families were included in the study. Since for certain research purposes comparisons between siblings were to be made, subsequent children from enrolled families were included in the study sample. The cumulative collection of families was completed over a six-year period, with the 85 families contributing 141 children for study. Retention of the cases, on the whole, has been excellent. Over the twelve-year period, five children have been lost from the study because of long-distance changes in residence, and 136 of the original 141 children (96 per cent) are still being followed.

Forty-five of the 85 families have one child; 31 have two; 7 have three; and 2 families, four children enrolled in the study. The ages of these 136 children at the end of June 1966 showed the following distribution: forty were 10 years of age, twenty-five were 9, eighteen were 8, sixteen were 7, fifteen were 6, ten were 5 and twelve were 4 years old. Sex distribution was almost equal, with 69 boys and 67 girls in the total sample.

The study families are predominantly Jewish (78 per cent), with some Catholic (7 per cent), and Protestant (15 per cent) families. There is one Negro and one Chinese family. Almost all parents were born in the United States. Forty per cent of the mothers and 60 per cent

12

of the fathers had both college educations and postgraduate degrees, and only 9 per cent of the mothers and 8 per cent of the fathers had no college at all. With only three exceptions, all of the fathers worked either in one of the professions, or in business at a management or executive level. Eighty per cent of the mothers had occupations similar to the fathers, and the remaining 20 per cent had been employed as office workers or secretaries. At the time of the birth of the first child enrolled in the longitudinal study, half of the mothers were less than 31 years old, with an age range of 20 to 41 years. The median age of the fathers was 33.6 years; the youngest was 25 years and the oldest, 54 years of age. The length of marriage at the child's birth ranged from one to nineteen years, with half of the group married for at least 5.3 years.

The attitudes and expressed attachments of the parents to child-care practices showed marked homogeneity. This uniformity within the group was also evident in the responses of the parents on the Parental Attitude Research Instrument (PARI) administered to both parents when each child in the study population reached three years of age. However, the homogeneity of expressed attitudes was not duplicated in the actual child-care practices and patterns of parent-child interactions present within the families. Considerable variability existed with regard to child-care practices and made possible the study of different patterns of interaction between various types of parental functioning and different styles of temperamental organization in the children. In addition, although the parents showed uniformity in expressed child-care attitudes, they by no means revealed the same preferences for given patterns of temperament, nor showed similar tolerances for different temperamental styles in their children.

Expressed parental attitudes were permissive and child-centered. Emphasis was placed on the importance of identifying and satisfying the infant's needs. It was considered quite acceptable and even desirable for the father to participate actively in the care of the child, though the actual degree of paternal involvement varied widely from family to family. Spock's manual, *Baby and Child Care*,[1] was uniformly utilized as a source of child-rearing advice, though a number of the mothers felt free to diverge on occasions from its specific recommendations. The families had pediatricians who were also actively consulted by most of the parents for guidance in the routine care of the baby. The parent group as a whole was oriented toward the desirability of obtaining psychiatric advice and, if necessary, treatment for a child with deviant behavioral functioning.

With almost no exception, the mothers in this group expressed an acceptance of the self-demand approach to feeding. Approximately 50 per cent breast-fed their infants and offered supplementary bottle feedings. In most of these cases, the shift to the exclusive use of bottles was gradually accomplished during the first two to five months. Weaning from the bottle was started when the child was between five and eleven months of age. By the end of twenty-four months, more than 50 per cent of the children were completely weaned. Weaning of the remaining children was accomplished, with five exceptions, by the age of four years.

In toilet training a generally permissive approach was reported. The parents did not press vigorously for the establishment of early training. Only 20 per cent of the parents started training before the child was twelve months of age. Half of the group did not begin any systematic bowel or bladder training until the children were at least sixteen months old, and in most cases training was completed between eighteen and thirty-six months. However, in a few children training was not successfully completed until the fourth year.

Some of the mothers continued in their occupations following the birth of the child or resumed them on a full-time (5 per cent) or part-time (32 per cent) basis by the time the child was two years old. However, the working mothers all described the care of the children as their major responsibility.

Attendance at nursery school was considered a socially desirable experience for the child by almost all the parents, and 89 per cent of the children were enrolled in various private nursery schools at three or four years of age. Ten per cent started their school experience at the kindergarten level at five years, and one child began school with admission to the first grade at six years. The attendance at nursery school or kindergarten made it possible to gain information on each child's interaction with the broader environment including peer groups, teachers, and structured demands outside the home in addition to that obtained on his interaction with parents and other members of the family unit.

METHODS OF DATA COLLECTION

The detailed design of the study, including the techniques of sample maintenance, data collection, scoring of data for temperament, and other features of procedure for the first two years of life are discussed in detail in a previous publication.[2] At this point it is necessary to provide a brief synopsis of this earlier presentation, as well as to indicate the nature of the data obtained at later age-periods.

Data necessary to define the child's temperamental organization and to delineate his developmental course were obtained from several sources. The parents were interviewed at regular intervals regarding the characteristics of the child's behavior in the routine functions of daily living, his responses to any changes in these routines or in his environment, and his reactions to any special events or life situations. Information was obtained from the teacher regarding the child's initial adaptation to school and his overall functioning during each school year. Direct observations of his behavior in school were obtained at least once a year. Behavioral observations of the child's play and problem-solving activities were made during the administration of standard psychological tests at three and at six years of age.

Other data included: 1] measures of cognitive functioning at three and six years of age; 2] estimates of parental attitudes and child-care practices obtained when the child was three years old; 3] wherever indicated, additional psychometric tests, measures of perceptual functioning, and clinical psychiatric evaluations were made; 4] information from special pediatric or neurological studies, hospitalization, or treatment by psychiatrists or psychotherapists was gathered whenever such diagnostic or therapeutic procedures had been carried out.

In the collection of data on the child's behavioral characteristics, certain principles were strictly observed to insure the maximum validity, objectivity, and reliability of the information obtained:

1] The parent and teacher interviews focused on the details of daily living during feeding, play, sleep, etc. Behavior was described in factual descriptive terms with a concern not only for what the child did but *how* he did it. Statements as to the presumed meaning of the child's behavior were considered unsatisfactory for primary data. When such interpretative statements were made by a parent or teacher, the interviewer pressed for an actual description. Thus, to a parental report that "the baby hated his cereal," or that "he loved his bath," the question was always posed, "What did he do specifically that made you think he loved or hated it?" Similarly, if a teacher commented that "this child always gets angry if he doesn't get his way," she was asked to give several examples with detailed descriptions of the manner in which the anger was expressed. If a staff observer reported that a child "was afraid to ask the teacher for help," she was instructed to spell out in detail the incidents she had observed and describe the behavior she had interpreted as "fear."

2] Special emphasis was placed on the recording of a child's first response to a new stimulus and his subsequent reactions on re-exposure to the same stimulus until a consistent long-term response was established. Such stimuli might be simple, as the first bath or the introduction of a new food, or they might be complex, as the move to a new home, the introduction of a new person into the household, or the first contact with nursery school. The sequence of responses to new stimuli, demands, and situations, whether simple or complex, was found to give especially rich information on a child's individual temperamental pattern.

3] The contamination of the data collection by "halo effects" was avoided by using different staff members for different phases of the data collection for any specific child. Thus, the parent interviewer did not do the teacher interviews or direct observations, and the same staff member never did both the teacher interview and direct school observation on the same child.

4] Quality control of the interviews and observations was established by periodic checks of intra- and inter-interviewer and observer reliabilities. The item scoring of the behavior protocols also served as a continuous check on the quality and quantity of the data in each record. Interview protocol forms were revised when necessary to make them appropriate for succeeding age-periods and were pretested on samples of children not included in the longitudinal study.

A. Parent Interviews

To obtain detailed longitudinal behavioral information on a sufficiently large sample of children, a readily available and economical source of data is necessary. Parents represent just such a source because of their continued direct observation of the child. This could otherwise be duplicated only by an investigator living in the home. The crucial question, whether the parental reports represent valid reflections of the child's actual behavior, was answered by comparing these reports with direct observations of the child's behavior in the home. Twenty-three children, ranging in age from less than three to eighteen months or more, were drawn from the study population by case number to form the direct observation group. In eighteen of these cases, observations were made by two observers, neither of whom was aware of the data obtained by parental interview. The direct observations were each independent of the other and were separated by seven to fourteen days. Each observation occurred within two weeks of a parent interview. In the remaining five cases, only one observation was made within one week of the interview. The observation period was planned so that it would include a period of the day during which it would be possible to observe the child's behavior at feeding, sleeping, bathing, dressing, play, and elimination. Each observation lasted from two to three hours. Although no single period could be selected in which all phenomena were observable, the times chosen were ones in which most could be noted. In addition, the observers recorded the reaction of the children to themselves as strangers, both initially and throughout the course of the observation period. The observations were recorded as detailed behavioral descriptions.

The behavioral observations were scored for temperamental characteristics by the same criteria * as were the parent interviews, and preponderance for each category was determined. Comparisons of the scores of the direct observations with those of the parental interview showed agreement at the .01 level of confidence. The independent direct observations were in agreement with one another at the .05 level of

---

* The definitions of each temperamental category and the criteria for scoring are summarized later in this chapter.

confidence. Thus, each of the episodes of observation produced behavior protocols which agreed more fully with the overall characterization of the child derived from the parental interview than they did with one another. This should not be surprising, since immediate circumstances present at each instant of episodic observation would be expected to enhance the difference between short periods more than they would effect the interrelation between any single period and overall functioning. These findings permitted us to conclude that the data of the parent interview were a valid reflection of the child's behavior. In our judgment such accurate parental reporting is possible if descriptive factual information is requested and the behaviors to be described are not too remote in time.

The mean age of the children at the time of the first parental interview was 3.3 months, and well over half of the children were less than 2.5 months old. These interviews were conducted at three-month intervals during the first eighteen months of life, then at intervals of six months until five years of age, and yearly thereafter. The interviews focused on eliciting detailed factual descriptions of the behavior of the child in everyday life situations over the preceding time interval. In early childhood, the data were derived from the child's behavior during such activities as feeding, sleeping, dressing, bathing, nail cutting, handling, diaper-changing, dressing, and contact with people. Later interviews were also concentrated on the accumulation of detailed, factual, behavioral descriptions. At each age-stage, the range of questions was expanded to obtain behavioral information concerning the child's development and his utilization of new modes of functioning. For example, in contrast to the emphasis upon action in the earlier interviews, the later interviews focused attention on problem solving, characteristic patterns of learning, play preferences, social interactions and, most importantly, on the circumstances, form, and content of the child's adaptive behavior. Included, too, was the collection of data relevant to the development of the child's interest patterns and to his characteristic responses to success and failure.

B. School Observations and Teacher Interviews

Since the overwhelming majority (89 per cent) of the children attended nursery school, this first formal school experience was utilized as a source of direct observational data on the behavior of the child. In addition, the nursery school teachers were interviewed at two points in time. The first interview occurred during the period of the child's initial adaptation to the nursery school situation, and the second during the latter portion of the school year. If the child attended nursery school for more than a single year, both the behavioral observation and a single teacher interview were conducted each year. Similar observations and teacher interviews were conducted during the kindergarten and the first elementary school years.

The yearly nursery, kindergarten, and elementary school observations lasted one hour and, whenever possible, were scheduled for the indoor "free play" period or for some combination of "free play" and routinized activity. An hour was found to be long enough to provide a meaningful sequential picture of the child's behavior.

The observer had no previous knowledge of the child's history or behavior. She sat unobtrusively in a corner of the schoolroom. The child who was being observed had no knowledge that he was being studied either before, during, or following the period of observation. The observer noted the general and specific attributes of the setting and every observable verbal, motor, and gestural interaction of the child with materials, other children, and adults. All notations of behavior were made in concrete, descriptive terms. Inferences as to the meaning of the child's behavior were avoided. The observer recorded any failures to catch verbalizations or other behavior, together with any incidence of "noninteraction." For example, if the subject was off playing ball by himself while a whole group was involved in making Easter hats, the occurrence was described. Duration of sequences was also noted. The notes of the observation were edited on the same day, and dictated or written out in full soon after.

The teacher interview was conducted by an investigator other than the observer, one who also had no previous knowledge of the child. The interview was based upon a detailed questionnaire and took one and a half to two and a half hours to administer. It aimed at gathering descriptive details of the child's day-to-day behavior with respect to routine events (such as arrival, departure, dressing, eating, toileting, and resting), play activity (both structured and "free," solitary, parallel, and social), responses to people (peers and teachers), mood and emotional responses (instances of anger, fear, frustration, pleasure, and expressiveness). Questions focused also on the child's initial reactions and successive adaptation in each of these areas. The teachers seemed to find it relatively easy to give the necessary information because of its specific nature. Interviewers quoted verbatim evaluative or interpretative comments and probed for the concrete bases on which they rested. Where the source of the evaluative statements remained unclear or vague, it was so noted.

C. Behavioral Observations During Standard Test Situation

Psychological testing and direct behavioral observation were carried out when each child was three years old, and again when he was six years of age. In order to compare the direct observational data on the children studied, it was necessary to select a situation that was both standard in form and sufficiently diversified in content to permit the observation of a wide range of behavioral responses. These needs led to the utilization of standard intelligence testing (Stanford-Binet, Form L) as the nucleus of the observational situation. The children were tested at three and again at six years of age by a psychologist in a fully equipped children's playroom. The procedure was witnessed by an independent observer who kept a running written record of the child's behavior. The observer, in the room before the child entered, did not participate in the testing procedure. The duration of direct observation was usually at least one hour. It began with a warm-up period during which the child became acquainted with the examiner and the facilities of the playroom and was allowed free access to all toys. Whenever possible, the child was separated from his mother. This was followed by formal testing, which proceeded as far as the responsiveness of the child permitted. The final period, after the completion of testing, was one of free play on the part of the child and ended with his cleaning up and departing.

D. Parental Practices and Attitudes Interview

When the child was three years old, a special structured interview to elicit information regarding parental practices and attitudes was held with each mother and father separately but simultaneously. These interviews were conducted and taped by two staff members who had had no previous contact with the parents. Immediately after the interview, which lasted from one and a half to four hours, each parent filled out the Schaefer and Bell Parental Attitude Research Instrument (PARI). These interviews provided data regarding the style of parental practices, as well as information on the parents' attitudes toward the child, their family role, and their relationships.

DATA ANALYSIS

The data available on the 136 children made it possible to define the characteristics of each child's temperamental organization at various points in time as well as to relate them to his intra- and extrafamilial environmental circumstances and experiences.

A. Temperamental Characteristics

Nine categories of reactivity were established by an inductive content analysis of the parental interview protocols for the infancy period in the first twenty-two children studied. A three-point scale was established for each category. The categories, their definitions, and illustrative items of behavior under each one follow (a detailed description of the parent interview protocol and of the criteria and methods for scoring temperamental characteristics has been published elsewhere [3]):

1] ACTIVITY LEVEL

This category describes the level, tempo, and frequency with which a motor component is present in the child's functioning. In scoring, all data in the protocol concerned with motility were utilized. Some examples of representative behaviors that were scored as high activity are: "He moves a great deal in his sleep"; "I can't leave him on the bed or couch because he always wriggles off"; "He kicks and splashes so in the bath that I always have to mop up the floor afterward"; "Dressing him becomes a battle, he squirms so"; "He runs around so, that whenever we come in from the park I'm exhausted"; "He crawls all over the house"; and "Whenever I try to feed him he grabs for the spoon." Examples of low activity behaviors are: "In the bath he lies quietly and doesn't kick"; "In the morning he's still in the same place he was when he fell asleep. I don't think he moves at all during the night"; and "He can turn over, but he doesn't much."

2] RHYTHMICITY

This category was based upon the degree of rhythmicity or regularity of repetitive biological functions. Information concerning rest and activity, sleeping and waking, eating and appetite, and bowel and bladder function was utilized in the scoring.

A child's sleep-wake cycle was considered to be regular if he fell asleep at approximately the same time each night and awoke at approximately the same time each morning. The child's functioning was considered to be irregular if there was a marked difference in the time of retiring and arising from day to day.

Information concerning the rest and activity periods of the child was derived from the protocol data on napping behavior. The child was scored as regular if he napped for the same length of time each day, and irregular if no discernible time pattern of function was established.

Eating and appetite behavior was scored as regular if the protocol reported that the child demanded or accepted food readily at the same time each day and consumed approximately the same amount of food on corresponding diurnal occasions. The child was scored as irregular if his intake fluctuated widely on different days, or if he tended to eat at times which differed widely from day to day.

Bowel function was scored as regular if the protocol indicated that the number and time of evacuations were relatively constant from day to day, and irregular if the number and time were not readily predictable.

In all of these areas, behavior was considered variable if there was evidence in the protocol that the child had established a pattern of functioning, but that there was some deviation from this pattern on occasion. This designation stands in contrast to a score of irregular, which denoted the failure to establish even a partial pattern.

3] APPROACH OR WITHDRAWAL

This category describes the child's initial reaction to any new stimulus, be it food, people, places, toys, or procedures. A few examples of initial approach responses are: "He always smiles at a stranger"; "He loves new toys and he plays with one so much he often breaks it the first thing." Withdrawal responses are illustrated by: "When I gave him his orange juice the first time he made a face. He didn't cry but he didn't suck it as eagerly as he does milk"; "Whenever he sees a stranger he cries"; "When we went to the doctor's for the first time he started to cry in the waiting room and didn't stop until we got home again"; and "It takes him a long time to warm up to a new toy. He pushes it away and plays with something more familiar."

4] ADAPTABILITY

When considering adaptability, one is of necessity concerned with the sequential course of responses a child makes to new or altered situations. In contrast to the previous category, it is not with the initial response that one is concerned. Rather, emphasis is on the ease or difficulty with which the initial pattern of response can be modified in the direction desired by the parents or others. Examples of adaptive behavior may be found in the following excerpts from parental interviews: "He used to spit out cereal whenever I gave it to him, but now he takes it fairly well, although still not as well as fruit"; "Now when we go to the doctor's he doesn't start to cry till we undress him, and he even stops then if he can hold a toy"; "At first he used to hold himself perfectly stiff in the bath, but now he kicks a little and pats the water with his hand"; and "Every day for a week he'd go over to this stuffed lion someone gave him and say, 'I don't like it,' but today he started playing with it and now you'd think it was his best friend."

Nonadaptive behavior can be illustrated by the following examples: "During the summer she used to nap in her carriage outside, and now that it's cold I've tried to put her in the crib, but she screams so I have to take her out and wheel her up and down the hall before she falls asleep"; "Every time he sees the scissors he starts to scream and pull his hand away, so now I cut his nails when he's sleeping"; "Whenever I put his snowsuit and hat on he screams and struggles, and he doesn't stop crying till we're outside"; and "He doesn't like eggs and makes a face and turns his head away no matter how I cook them."

5] INTENSITY OF REACTION

In this category interest is directed to the energy content of the response, irrespective of its direction. A negative response may be as intense or as mild as a positive one. Scorable items for this category were provided by descriptions of behavior occurring in relation to external stimuli, to preelimination straining, to hunger, to repletion, to new foods, to attempts to control, to restraint, to diapering and dressing, to the bath, and to play and social contacts.

Examples of intense reactions are the following: "He cries loud and long whenever the sun shines in his eyes"; "Whenever she hears music she begins to laugh loudly and to jump up and down in time to it"; "When he is hungry he starts to cry, and this builds up to a scream, and we can't distract him by holding or playing with him"; "When she is full she spits the food out of her mouth and knocks the spoon away"; "The first time we gave him cereal he spit it out and started to cry"; "If we tell him 'no' he starts to cry"; "Dressing is such a problem, he wriggles around so, and when I hold him so that he can't move, he screams"; and "She loves her bath so, that as soon as she hears the water running she tries to climb into the tub even if she's still fully dressed."

Examples of mild responses are: "He squints at a bright light but doesn't cry"; "To a loud noise he jumps and startles a little, but he doesn't cry"; "If he's hungry, he starts to whimper a bit, but if you play with him he won't really cry"; "When she's had enough she turns her head away, and I know that it is time to stop"; "If he does not like a new food he just holds it in his mouth without swallowing and then lets it drool out"; "When we tell her 'no' she looks and smiles and then goes right on doing what she wants"; "Now it's a pleasure to dress him, he stands up when you tell him to, and holds still when he has to"; and "When other children take a toy away from him, he plays with something else; he doesn't try to get it back or cry."

6] THRESHOLD OF RESPONSIVENESS

This category refers to the level of extrinsic stimulation that is necessary to evoke a discernible response. The explicit form of response that occurs is irrelevant and may be of any quality, e.g., approaching or withdrawing, intense or mild. What is fundamental is the intensity of stimulus that has to be applied before a response of any kind can be elicited. The behaviors utilized were those concerning responses to sensory stimuli, environmental objects, and social contacts. We are also interested in the magnitude of difference between stimuli that must obtain before the child shows evidences of discrimination.

Examples of the types of descriptions that were scored in this category are the following: "You can shine a bright light in his eyes and he doesn't even blink, but if a door closes he startles and looks up." This would be scored as high threshold for visual and low threshold for auditory stimuli. "I can never tell if he's wet except by feeling him, but if he has a bowel movement he fusses and is cranky until I change him." The statement indicates high threshold with respect to wetness, but low threshold to the tactile complex associated with a bowel movement. "He loves fruit, but if I put even a little cereal in with it he won't eat it at all." This was scored as a low threshold response because it demonstrated the ability to discriminate small taste or textural differences. "He doesn't pay any attention to new people; he doesn't cry, but he doesn't respond to them, either." This is an example of a high threshold in the area of social relations, as contrasted with "He laughs and smiles at a stranger, and starts to cry if they don't play with him," a response scored as low threshold. "He always cries when he sees a man wearing a hat even if it's his father" is illustrative of effective discrimination to presence of a specific item of clothing and was scored as a low threshold response. "He makes himself at home anywhere, and runs around a strange house as if it were his," was scored as high threshold, while "He notices any little change. When we got new curtains for his room he spent a whole day crawling over to the window and pulling on them," received a low threshold score.

7] QUALITY OF MOOD

This category describes the amount of pleasant, joyful, friendly behavior as contrasted with unpleasant, crying, unfriendly behavior. Consequently, statements which indicated crying and unfriendly behavior were scored as negative mood, as in the following: "Whenever we put him to bed he cries for about five or ten minutes before falling asleep"; "He cries at almost every stranger, and those that he doesn't cry at he hits"; "I've tried to teach him not to knock down little girls and sit on them in the playground, so now he knocks them down and doesn't sit on them"; and "Every time he sees food he doesn't like he starts to fuss and whine until I take it off the table." Examples of positive mood statements are: "Whenever he sees me begin to warm his bottle he begins to smile and coo"; "He loves to look out of the window. He jumps up and down and laughs"; "He always smiles at a stranger"; and "If he's not laughing and smiling I know he's getting sick."

8] DISTRACTIBILITY

This category refers to the effectiveness of extraneous environmental stimuli in interfering with, or in altering the direction of, the ongoing behavior. If the course of a child who is crawling toward an electric light plug can be altered by presenting him with a toy truck, he would be considered distractible. If such efforts to alter his behavior are unsuccessful, he would be considered nondistractible. A child who is crying because he is hungry but stops when he is picked up, is distractible, as opposed to the child who continues to cry until he is fed.

9] ATTENTION SPAN AND PERSISTENCE

This category includes two subcategories which are related. By attention span is meant the length of time a particular activity is pursued. For example, if a two-year-old child engaged in water play poured water from one cup to another for half an hour, he would be scored as possessing a long attention span. If he engaged in this play activity for five minutes, his attention span would be considered short. The attention span can be measured with regard to self-initiated activities, such as the above example of water play, as well as to the child's participation in planned activities, such as listening to a story or listening to music. By persistence, we mean the child's maintaining of an activity in the face of obstacles to its continuation. Obstacles may be external. In the case of our child pouring water, if his mother comes along and says "no" and he continues to do it, he would be considered persistent. The obstacles may be much more directly related to the child's abilities. For example, the child who continually attempts to stand up although he always falls down would be scored as persistent, as would the child who continues to struggle with a toy he can't make perform properly without asking for help. The category, therefore, is an omnibus one which includes selectivity, persistence and, at a later age level, frustration tolerance.

Item scoring has been utilized, providing a specific item sum for each of the three points of the scale for each category. Interscorer reliability is high with 90 per cent level of agreement. To avoid contamination by halo effects, each protocol was scored for one attribute of temperament at a time, and no successive interviews of a given child were scored contiguously. A snip-analysis study found that whole protocol scoring was not significantly influenced by associated content.

All the behavioral records of each of the children have been found suitable for the scoring of the temperamental characteristics. These have included the parental interviews at each age period, the nursery school, kindergarten, and elementary school direct observations and teacher interviews, and the direct observations during the psychological test sessions at three and six years of age. The direct observations could not be scored for rhythmicity and adaptability, which measure behavioral characteristics occurring over time. Appropriate scoring criteria for the nine categories for each age period and source of data have been developed by content analyses of the first 20 records for each age or data source. Details of method and of interscorer reliability have been described elsewhere.[4]

B. *Other Behavioral Characteristics of the Child*

The behavioral data obtained from the school observations, teacher interviews, and observations during the standard test situations were found suitable not only for the categorization of temperament, but also for the delineation of other behavioral characteristics. These included degree of independence versus dependency, the nature of social functioning with peers and adults, play patterns and emotional expressiveness.

In addition, each test item on the Stanford-Binet test was considered to represent a concrete demand on the child for specific task performance, and the total test to represent a standard series of such demands presented in sequence. Each child's mode of response to demands for task performance was categorized by the scoring of his verbal and motor behavior during each test item of the Stanford-Binet test administered at three and six years. For each child it was possible to define the degree to which he actively engaged in the task demanded of him and the patterns of behavior exhibited when the child did not do what was demanded of him.*

C. Intellectual Functioning

The I.Q. of each child was determined at three and again at six years of age on the Stanford-Binet test, Form L. In those children for whom a satisfactory test performance was not obtained at three years, testing was repeated six months to a year later.

At both three and six years, the I.Q. scores of the group were normally distributed around a mean of 127, with a standard deviation of 12.1 at both years.

D. Parental Practices and Attitudes

Information on parental practices with and attitudes toward all the 136 children in the longitudinal study were derived from several sources.

The first source constituted the periodic interviews with the parents. During these interviews it was possible to gather systematic information on patterns of parental functioning as well as on behavioral characteristics of the child and special environmental events as they occurred within the family. In connection with any feature of the child's behavior, a sequence of questions was systematically pursued by the interviewer: What did the parent do? How did the child respond? What did the parent do with respect to the response? What did the child do subsequent to the parent's response? The data chain, therefore, contained an equal number of links which described parental practices and child behaviors. As an illustration, an extract may be presented from a parental interview which deals with the nighttime sleep behavior of a twenty-five-month-old girl:

"Isobel had begun to sleep through the night by the age of twenty-one months. Mother went to hospital one month later to deliver a baby boy. Isobel continued to sleep through night during her mother's hospitalization, but three nights after mother and baby brother came home she began to awaken once nightly and call for her mother. When

* The definition of these categories and the scoring criteria and techniques will be reported in detail in a monograph now in preparation.[5]

this happened, mother went to her, cuddled her, rocked her, and gave her a bottle. Isobel then went back to sleep. This went on, with occasional sleeping through, for about six weeks. Mother then tried to discourage this nighttime awakening by only talking to her and refusing to rock her or give her a bottle. However, the nighttime awakening continued and Isobel also began to climb out of bed before going to sleep. If her door was shut, she screamed. Whichever parent came, she wanted the other one and demanded to be taken downstairs. After a few nights of calling either parent she simply was placed back in bed by the parent who came. If door not shut, she came down or stood at top of stairs calling, 'I up.' Climbed out as many as three times. Parents became increasingly firm in insisting she stay in her room and after a few nights she quit getting up or calling immediately on being put to bed. Mother also told her that if she awoke in middle of night she could sing or talk to self but shouldn't call. When she did call during night, mother came. Isobel called several times each night. Finally, after about a week, mother spanked her one night when she had called for the fourth time. Mother told her at the same time that she wouldn't come into room even if Isobel cried. Isobel has not called at night since (for past two weeks), but has been heard talking and singing to herself during night on a number of occasions."

This data chain contains not only the consequences of the child's behavior in response to specifically defined and detailed environmental changes, but also the various child-care techniques employed by the mother in her attempts to modify the child's sleep pattern.

The second source of data was the special parental interview done when each child was three years old. These simultaneous but separate interviews of each parent-pair were focused on practices and attitudes. The practices elicited were those involved in general planning for the child and in the details of his care and management. The range of attitudes probed was broad and extended from the parents' views on specifics of child rearing, to their positions on sex role, marriage, parental role, and their aspirations and expectations for the future of the child and family. Supplementally, the PARI was administered but was found not to provide a basis for differentiating idiosyncratic parental attitudes within the group.*

Inductive analyses of the data obtained from these two sources provided the categories and ratings by which parental practices and attitudes were assessed. These categories correspond, in the main, to those utilized by many other investigators and clinicians. They include such items as permissiveness, consistency, strictness of discipline, approval of child and child's interests, protectiveness to child, liking for

* This finding is in agreement with the conclusions of other workers who have utilized the PARI.[6]

child, toleration of child's deviation, expectations for the child, attitude toward spouse, and agreement between parents.

Several general principles have been followed in the rating of these categories: 1] The assessment of attitudes and practices has been based on the direct statements by parents of their feelings and attitudes and on their detailed reports of behavior and practices. No attempt has been made to evaluate systematically any presumed underlying subjective states, due to the absence of reliable criteria for making such inferences. 2] Global judgments have been avoided, and ratings have been based on attitudes and practices in specific areas, and subcategory ratings were established to implement this approach. 3] Global psychopathological labels such as "rejecting," "hostile," "anxious," etc. have been avoided. 4] The ratings have been based on the parents' responses to the specific child, rather than on their statements of abstract or general attitudes.

A parent may state that he has no expectations of high educational status from his child and is concerned only that the youngster go as far as his interests take him. This is an expressed attitude. However, if in regular discussions with the child, the parent points out that it is unlikely that anyone with the youngster's intelligence would be happy in his adult life unless he gained the vocational possibilities that come with a graduate level of education, there is evidence of an implied attitude which contradicts his expressed attitude. If, on the other hand, the father regularly gives priority to outings and athletics in his activities with the youngster and shows little concern about the child's grades, there would be evidence that his expressed attitude is consistent with the attitude inferred from his behavior.

E. Other Data

An evaluation of the home environment of each family has been made, including type of dwelling, degree of crowding, type and amount of help in the care of the child, affluence of the family, and degree of financial stress, if any.

Special environmental circumstances, such as the birth of a younger child, the mother's return to work, divorce, death in the family, illnesses, accidents, and hospitalization of parent or child, have been identified in each case and the sequence of the child's behavioral responses before, during, and after each such event tabulated. A similar tabulation of each child's responses to weaning and toilet training has also been undertaken.

The presence of any significant handicaps or deviations, such as bowel sphincter dysfunction, neurological damage, intellectual subnormality, or deficient neuromuscular coordination, has been identified and the extent and severity defined. On the positive side, special talents, skills, or abilities have been recorded.

With the occurrence of each special environmental circumstance, handicap, or special talent in the child, the parental attitudes and behavior, as well as those of the child, have been identified.

REFERENCES

1. B. Spock, *Baby and Child Care,* rev. ed. (New York: Pocket Books, Inc., 1957).
2. A. Thomas and Others, *Behavioral Individuality in Early Childhood* (New York: New York University Press, 1963).
3. *Ibid.*
4. *Ibid.*
5. M. E. Hertzig and Others, *Behavioral Style of Preschool Children in Response to Cognitive Demands,* in preparation.
6. W. C. Becker and R. S. Krug, "The Parent Attitude Research Instrument: A Research Review," *Child Development,* 36:329 (1965).

IGNORED

3 | THE CLINICAL SAMPLE

The clinical sample of children with behavioral disturbances which we shall consider consisted of 42 of the 136 children in the longitudinal study. Children were included as members of the clinical sample not merely because of the presence of a symptom about which the parent or school expressed concern, but only when careful clinical diagnostic procedures confirmed the presence of the symptoms and resulted in a clinical psychiatric judgment that a significant degree of behavioral disturbance was present.

The identification of this clinical sample requires some comment. At the time that each infant was admitted to the longitudinal study, each parent was told that the research staff included a child psychiatrist who would be ready to provide psychiatric consultation and advice if behavioral difficulties of any kind occurred at any point in the child's development. The parents knew, therefore, that if the child became a source of concern, psychiatric consultation would be available and that the staff also included several psychologists who could, as required, participate in the evaluation of the problem.

Continuous contact was maintained with each set of parents through the staff interviewer who conducted the periodic interviews. During these interviews, questions were raised by parents regarding the evaluation of any behaviors which appeared deviant or troublesome to them. Between interviews the parents were encouraged to contact the staff interviewer by telephone whenever they felt it necessary. In this way, any behavior of the child which became a matter of concern to the parent was readily brought to attention.

Parental concerns derived either from their own observations of the child's behavior or from reports by the nursery or elementary school teacher. When the parent reported a concern to the staff interviewer, the latter consulted the child psychiatrist. Not every child whose behavior was brought to notice in this way was clinically studied. In many instances, the reported problems represented age-specific behaviors that, though troublesome, were not deviant. In still other cases, it appeared clear that the issue was a simple one involving inappropriateness in the routines which the parent had adopted to manage the given child. A total of thirty-one children fell into these two groups. In these cases, parental action based on simple suggestions made by the psychiatrist through the interviewer for modifying aspects of child care practice resulted in the disappearance of both the "problem" and the parental concerns. In other instances, however, such simple changes of routine did not result in desired alterations of the child's behavior, and the undesired patterns of functioning persisted or became more extensive. In such cases, a psychiatric evaluation was advised. In the cases of other children, the symptom patterns reported by the interviewer were of such a nature as to arouse immediate psychiatric concern. In these cases a psychiatric evaluation was advised instead of attempting to remedy the disturbances through indirect transmission of parental guidance.

With a single exception, all psychiatric evaluations derived from the parents' expression of concern. This exception was a girl whose mother had a strong tendency to minimize or deny the existence of problems, but whose behavior was noted by us to be grossly deviant during the course of the psychological evaluation and play observation session when she was three years old. In this case, it was felt that the problem was sufficiently important to require psychiatric evaluation, and the parents were so advised. In no other instance was the attention of the parents directed by the interviewer or by other members of the research staff to presumably deviant behavior.

Three criteria were used as the basis for accepting a child for psychiatric evaluation. These were: 1] the relation of the complaint to the age of the child; 2] the degree to which the symptom was an isolated phenomenon or part of a more general pattern of maladaptation; and 3] the degree to which the presenting symptom was an alerting signal of potential psychopathology.

It was especially important to distinguish between age-specific behaviors that were merely annoying, and those that had psychiatric importance. The existence of normative information made it possible to identify frequently occurring age-specific behaviors having no special significance for psychopathology. Thus, the presence of occasional tantrums in a preschool child whose behavior pattern was otherwise undisturbed was not, in itself, considered a sufficient basis for recommending psychiatric evaluation. The same judgment applied to the crying of a preschool child left in a strange place, or to continued soiling in a two- or three-year-old. However, if any of these behaviors were still present at significantly older age ranges than the ones at which they most frequently occur, the symptom was given more serious consideration. Thus, frequent episodes of kicking and screaming in a ten-year-old, or encopresis, in the absence of an anatomic causation, in a school-age child were considered to warrant more detailed evaluation. Similarly, expressions of distress at separation from the mother in the preschool years were not considered a basis for clinical concern, but their persistence into the school years was so considered.

The presence of an isolated symptom in a child's behavior usually did not in itself constitute an adequate basis for accepting the child for psychiatric evaluation or for including him as a clinical case. However, if the presenting problem was only one of a number of other disturbing behaviors, acceptance was more likely. Thus, if a preschool child not only had frequent temper tantrums but also manifested head-banging and sleep disturbance, and was clinging and dependent, the set of associated symptoms would provide sufficient basis for psychiatric evaluation. Not only the number of symptoms, but also their severity contributed to the decision to evaluate the child. If in a set of four or five presenting problems, each occurred to a mild degree, the child would not necessarily be accepted for evaluation. However, if any single symptom were severe, or if all symptoms were present in moderate degree, psychiatric concern and evaluation would be highly likely.

Certain syndromes were viewed as danger signals and were always responded to by psychiatric evaluation. These included: 1] a report that development was significantly below the norm in various areas of functioning; 2] repeated self-destructive or self-endangering behaviors in a child at an age when danger could be comprehended; 3] inadequacy of contact with the environment or significant unresponsiveness in relation to age-specific expectations; 4] flagrant flouting of social conventions, such as unconcealed masturbation in a school-age child; 5] significant and continued disturbance in language development and speech; 6] indications of perceptual or perceptual-motor inadequacies; 7] isolation from peers or persistent annoying or aggressive behavior toward them that progressively isolated the child; 8] school failure in the absence of any evidence of intellectual deficit.

The symptoms described above were viewed as sufficient grounds for making a psychiatric evaluation, but their presence did not in themselves constitute a sufficient basis for including the child in the clinical sample. Such a conclusion could be arrived at only after the clinical psychiatric evaluation had been conducted. Therefore, the designation of a behavior problem in a child involved both 1] *the presence of symptoms;* and 2] *the psychiatric judgment following a clinical evaluation that a significant behavioral disturbance existed.*

THE PSYCHIATRIC EVALUATION

All the psychiatric evaluations were done by the project child psychiatrist (S.C.) with one exception. In this one case, a full report on the child's psychiatric evaluation was obtained from the psychiatrist who had examined her. In addition, the project child psychiatrist made a home visit at which this child's interactions with mother, father, and younger sister were observed.

Each psychiatric evaluation was conducted in a manner identical with a standard consultation carried out either with a private patient or with a case presenting at a child guidance clinic. The parents were interviewed first. In 75 per cent of the cases, both parents participated in the interview, but in the remainder only the mother was seen, either because of the father's unavailability or refusal to attend. The parents were asked to describe in detail the specific behaviors of the child, the features of his functioning, and the aspects of the parent-child relationship that were of concern. A full clinical history was then taken, including the details of the child's developmental course and a description of the factors that could have had pertinence for the development of the maladaptation.

The child was then seen by the psychiatrist for a play session interview carried out in a fully equipped playroom. Any additional play sessions required for evaluation were held in the same playroom. During the play session, the child's use of materials in individual and joint play with the examiner was observed. As with other data collection in the longitudinal study, care was taken to record the details of the child's behavior in the play session in factual descriptive terms. Play materials available included aggressive toys, drawing materials, household objects, blocks, and a variety of human figures. The examiner also involved the child in discussions during the course of his play. A judgment was made of the age appropriateness of the child's use of materials and style of functioning, his spontaneity, degree of personal isolation, dependency, independence, and cooperativeness. His expressed mood, degree of warmth, relatedness to the examiner, and appropriateness of affect to the content of his activities and verbalizations were assessed. The child was given the opportunity both to play and talk out his problem areas. His awareness of his problems and his attitudes toward them were explored. Information was obtained as to his attitudes toward family and friends. His responsiveness to demands was assessed in the course of requesting him to do specific things in play and to terminate the play session when time ran out.

Two extended opportunities in which to make assessments of parental attitudes and practices were provided by the psychiatric evaluation schedule. The first was during the interview of the parents conducted to identify the presenting complaint. The second occurred during the discussion following the clinical evaluation of the child, in which the findings and recommendations for treatment were communicated to the parents.

In the initial clinical interview the parents were asked to state, in their own words, the problems with which they were concerned, as well as their own judgments as to the possible causes of the child's disturbing behaviors. As they presented their impressions, questions were interjected as to the measures the parents had used in coping with the problem behaviors. At all points, the parents were questioned regarding their attitudes toward the child, as well as toward each other, both generally and in relation to child rearing. The parents were encouraged to discuss nonproblem behaviors of the child. In this phase of the discussion, opportunities existed for them to express positive attitudes toward the child, as well as patience or impatience with specific aspects of his functioning. In addition, the parent's ability both to formulate a program of child-rearing practices and to carry it through was evaluated.

In the final discussion, the parents were advised of the diagnosis and presented with recommendations for management. They were also encouraged to raise questions and to react to the recommendations. Their reactions and queries provided a rich source of information on their liking for the child, their reactions to his qualities as a person, and the styles with which they approached their responsibilities for helping with his difficulties.

Special sensory, neurological, or psychological studies were undertaken when a child's history and the psychiatric findings suggested the need. If the presenting complaint involved aspects of his school or nursery school functioning, the teachers were interviewed and additional observations on the child were carried out in the school setting.

On the basis of the clinical evaluation and supporting data, a judgment as to the presence or absence of a significant behavior problem was made. In some cases, the functioning of the child and the issues with which the parent or school or both were concerned were judged to be within the normal range of functioning. In these instances, parents and schools were advised of the findings, and no treatment was proposed beyond offering suggestions for the most effective management of the child in terms of his type of functioning. There were five children in whom the initial psychiatric evaluation resulted in the judgment that a significant behavior problem did not exist. Three of these children thereafter pursued an essentially normal developmental course. The other two later developed increased and additional symptoms and on a second clinical study, clear-cut evidence of behavioral disturbance was found. These latter two children were included in the clinical sample.

Where clinical evaluation indicated the presence of a significant behavior problem, a diagnosis was made.* The diagnostic categories

* The criteria utilized were those included in the project child psychiatrist's text: S. Chess, *An Introduction to Child Psychiatry* (New York: Grune and Stratton, 1959).

included acute and chronic brain injury, developmental lag, reactive behavior disorder, neurotic behavior disorder, childhood psychosis, and mental retardation. In the cases thus far followed, there has been no instance of character neurosis or psychopathic personality. One child with psychotic behavior was judged to have perinatal brain injury.

A further differentiation with respect to severity was made within each diagnostic category. Such judgments were based on a four-point scale—mild, moderate, moderately severe, and severe. The extent of functional disability occasioned by the disorder formed the basis for assigning the degree of severity. For example, the behavior problem was judged *mild* in a youngster who, although anxious about separating from his mother, was comfortable when left at the homes of several specific friends, developed constructive interpersonal relationships with peers, and attended school regularly. In contrast, the problem was classified as *moderately severe* in a child who had somatic symptoms in school that brought him home several times a week and who isolated himself from peers because of inability to join them in activities away from his own home. Psychological difficulties which produced a learning problem and which left a child of superior intelligence doing merely average work, were considered *moderate*. A child with equally superior intelligence whose difficulty prevented him from learning at all in a structured group situation and who showed increasing functional deficit, was judged as *moderately severe*. A youngster with a piling up of problems, the aggregate of which was total isolation, poor learning, constant anxiety, clinging, and sleep disturbances was judged as *severe*.

Further differentiation has been made in the clinical cases between "active" and "passive" symptoms. The children included in the passive group were largely nonparticipators. They stood on the sidelines watching, taking no part in the activity. Where the nonparticipation was simply that and nothing more, it was considered to be passive rather than active. To be included in the passive group, it was essential that the youngster show neither evidence of anxiety nor defenses against anxiety. Thus, the nonparticipator who stood aside crying was considered to have active symptoms. The nonparticipator who developed nausea, stomachaches, or dizziness at the invitation to participate, was regarded as a child with active disturbance. This was also true of the nonparticipator who came running in to his mother complaining that nobody liked him.

Following the diagnostic evaluation, there was a review of the anterospective information available on the child by virtue of his participation in the longitudinal study. No diagnosis was changed because of this review but, in each case, the formulation of the dynamics of the child-environment interaction and the ontogenesis of the behavior problem was derived from a composite of clinical and research information. A decision was then made as to the advisability of direct treatment of the child, parental guidance, or other patterns of therapeutic intervention. The child psychiatrist then communicated the treatment plan in detail to the parents.

Detailed follow-up of the children with behavior problems was carried out in the course of the longitudinal study's regularly scheduled interview with parents and teachers and through direct observations of the child in school and in test situations. Where direct treatment of the child was instituted, regular follow-up reports were obtained from the therapist. When the follow-up information indicated the need for additional data, special inquiries were carried out, such as psychometric testing, perceptual and perceptual-motor evaluation, neurological examination or a reexamination by the staff child psychiatrist.

The 42 clinical cases comprise 31 per cent of the total study population, a figure which approximates those found in other prevalence studies.[1,2] These data are cumulative, and the actual prevalence of behavior problems at any point of time in our population was, of course, lower than the cumulated figure of 31 per cent. The latest of the clinical cases was identified in June, 1966, ten years after the beginning of the longitudinal study. Clearly, it is possible that new cases will be identified as the younger children grow older.

CHARACTERISTICS OF THE CLINICAL SAMPLE

Table 1 (p. 36) summarizes the source of referral, sex, age of onset of the behavioral disturbance, age at time of psychiatric evaluation and diagnosis, time span between onset and evaluation, presenting complaints, diagnosis and severity, and recommendations of the child psychiatrist for the clinical cases. Age of onset was defined as the first date at which specific parental concerns or complaints over the child's behavior were expressed, or at which problem behavior was reported to the parent by the school. This date was determined by a scrutiny of the anterospective records.

The cases have been numbered from 1 to 42, with the numerical order determined by age at onset. The child who was youngest at time of onset was designated as Case 1; the next youngest at time of onset was designated as Case 2; and so on. Each case is also designated as M (male) or F (female). Though the sex distribution in the longitudinal study sample was almost equal, the clinical cases show a clear preponderance of boys over girls, twenty-six to sixteen.

Table 2 indicates the number of children at different age-periods at the time of psychiatric evaluation and clinical diagnosis.

TABLE 1 / CLINICAL CASE CHARACTERISTICS AT TIME OF INITIAL CLINICAL DIAGNOSIS

Referral Initiated By	Case #	Sex	Onset of Symptoms	Psychiatric Evaluation and Diagnosis	Time between Onset and Evaluation	Presenting Complaints[1]	Diagnosis and Severity	Recommendations
Parents	1	F	24 mos.	49 mos.	25 mos.	Tantrums with denial of request, change in routines; sleep problem (delays going to sleep, has bad dreams); motoric problem (hyperactivity, poor coordination); difficulty in following directions; very strong tendency to set up rituals.	Brain Damage With Severe Secondary Behavior Disorder	Parent Guidance
Parents	2	F	24 mos.	28 mos.	4 mos.	Sleep problem (night awakening with demanding behavior and tantrums when not given what she wishes).	Mild RBD[2]	Parent Guidance
Parents	3	M	30 mos.	56 mos.	26 mos.	Sleep problem (delays getting to bed, has brief and irregular sleep pattern); nocturnal enuresis; poor eating habits, likes limited foods, eats "on the run" and intermittently; never relaxed (usually runs, never walks, won't let anyone else relax); nail tearing, nose picking; lisp.	Mild RBD	Parent Guidance
School and Parents	4	F	34 mos.	43 mos.	9 mos.	Bowel problem (constipation, withholding, pain, refusal to use toilet).	Moderate RBD	Parent Guidance
Parents	5	M	36 mos.	44 mos.	8 mos.	Sleep problem (resists going to sleep, tantrums at bedtime, night awakening and screaming).	Mild RBD	Parent Guidance
School	6	F	36 mos.	76 mos.	40 mos.	School problem (uncooperative, misbehaves, learning is being impeded); challenges authority at home; provokes older brother; fusses at meals; peer relations hindered by her aggressiveness.	Moderately Severe RBD	Parent Guidance and Periodic Review
Parents	7	M	36 mos.	39 mos.	3 mos.	Excessively wild behavior (throws things, won't take orders); won't play alone, nags; stutters; period of preoccupation with diapers (talked	Moderately Severe RBD	Parent Guidance

						of diapers incessantly, examined babies' diapers and hit the babies, draped diapers on himself, urinated in inappropriate places); fears going into a room alone; allows older children to take his toys and hits younger children; refuses to wear certain clothing; aggressive toward other children at nursery school; masturbates.		
Parents and School	8	M	36 mos.	46 mos.	10 mos.	Does not participate at nursery school, stands aside and watches; insists on specific kinds of relationships and routines with specific people; delays going to sleep.	Mild RBD	Parent Guidance
Parents	9	M	37 mos.	50 mos.[3]	13 mos.	Poor peer relations (unassertive, has deviant interests from peers); hypersensitive to loud noises; fears moving apparatus; pedantic use of language, overly polite and formal; overmeticulous and unable to deviate in following directions; lacks persistence in new tasks if he does not meet with immediate success; does not participate in nursery school activities.	Mild RBD	Parent Guidance
Parents	10	M	39 mos.	49 mos.	10 mos.	Tantrums when request is denied, when reprimanded; avoids climbing apparatus in playground.	Mild RBD	Parent Guidance
School	11	M	41 mos.	54 mos.	13 mos.	Will not conform at school; aggressive toward other children; disturbed sleep with night awakening; stutters.	Mild RBD	Parent Guidance[4]
Parents and School	12	F	42 mos.	48 mos.	6 mos.	Sleep problem (resists going to sleep, night awakening); shows resistance to new situations (period of fussing on arrival at nursery school and refusal to join other children, shy with strangers, initially negative to anything new); tantrums and vomiting when pressured; stutters.	Moderate RBD	Parent Guidance

TABLE 1 / CONTINUED

Referral Initiated By	Case #	Sex	Onset of Symptoms	Psychiatric Evaluation and Diagnosis	Time between Onset and Evaluation	Presenting Complaints [1]	Diagnosis and Severity	Recommendations
Parents	13	M	42 mos.	85 mos.	43 mos.	Stealing; protective lying; under-achieving academically; easily frustrated; attaches great importance to certain things that represent status to him.	Mild RBD	Parent Guidance
Study	14	F	42 mos.	43 mos.	1 mo.	Disregards the need to listen to or to follow directions in situations demanding problem solving; treats all situations as social.	Moderate RBD	Parent Guidance
School advised therapy	15	M	42 mos.	45 mos.	3 mos.	Problem in adjusting to nursery school; resists separation from mother, cries and clings to her.	Moderate RBD	Parent Guidance
Parents and School	16	F	46 mos.	61 mos.	15 mos.	Fear of cars; does not participate at school.	Mild RBD	Parent Guidance
Parents	17	M	48 mos.	76 mos.	28 mos.	Refuses to carry out parental requests; hesitates to try new things, gives up easily.	Moderate RBD	Parent Guidance
Parents	18	F	48 mos.	53 mos.	5 mos.	Tantrums (with parental request to which she objects or with failure to succeed in self-initiated endeavor); sensitivity to tight or rough clothing; demands unnecessary servicing; insists on being center of attention.	Moderate RBD	Parent Guidance
Parents	19	F	48 mos.	51 mos.	3 mos.	Aggressive toward baby brother; resists discipline, is bossy, defiant; insatiably demanding.	Mild RBD	Parent Guidance
School and Parents	20	M	48 mos.	61 mos.	13 mos.	Expresses fear of growing up, which he equates with growing old and dying; refuses milk (which parents said would make him "big and strong"); has fears at bedtime; awakens very early and insists on going into parents' bed; school problem (resists going and separation from mother, very slow in-	Moderate RBD	Parent Guidance

38

Source	No.	Sex	Age	Age	Duration	Description	Diagnosis	Recommendation
Parents (for advice about operation)	21	M	48 mos.	71 mos.	23 mos.	volvement with group); provokes older brother. Upset at separation from mother (since infancy); fearful and shy with new people, reluctant in new situations; appears withdrawn at nursery school; apprehensive at bedtime.	Mild RBD	Parent Guidance
School	22	M	53 mos.	63 mos.	10 mos.	Aggressive in nursery school; strong willed in demanding his desires with tantrums when request is denied; unwilling to shift from ongoing activity; rejects many foods.	Mild RBD	Parent Guidance
Parents and School	23	M	53 mos.	54 mos.	1 mo.	At home, disregards discipline and teases; at school, jumps on children and teases them; masturbates; sleep disturbance with night awakening and crying; clings to mother and housekeeper.	Mild RBD	Parent Guidance
Parents and School	24	F	53 mos.	61 mos.	8 mos.	Tantrums when she does not wish to comply with a demand; eats little, avoids certain foods; sucks fingers.	Mild RBD	Parent Guidance
Parents	25	F	53 mos.	54 mos.	1 mo.	"Truculent and negativistic"; less alert than younger sisters; less verbal than sisters (late speech development); narrow range of expressiveness.	Mild RBD	Parent Guidance
School	26	M	54 mos.	72 mos.	18 mos.	At school is shy, doesn't listen, doesn't follow directions, rarely participates; with peers, does not conform, is not accepted.	Mild RBD	To return for re-evaluation (not followed)
Parents	27	F	60 mos.	63 mos.	3 mos.	Exhibits immature behavior (thumb-sucking, hair pulling); withholds bowel movements; reacts with explosive anger; fears the dark; lies about misdeeds; relates poorly to groups of children; has insatiable desire for attention, for sweets (for a period took money to buy sweets).	Moderately Severe NBD [5]	Psychotherapy

TABLE 1 / CONTINUED

Referral Initiated By	Case #	Sex	Onset of Symptoms	Psychiatric Evaluation and Diagnosis	Time between Onset and Evaluation	Presenting Complaints [1]	Diagnosis and Severity	Recommendations
School	28	M	60 mos.	84 mos.	24 mos.	At school, is inattentive, doesn't check work, avoids work which requires effort and self-discipline; hypersensitive, cries easily; teases and fights with brother.	Moderate RBD	[6]
Parents	29	M	60 mos.	63 mos.	3 mos.	School refusal in kindergarten; now in first grade, resists going; fears new situations; panics at separation from mother; dominated by older brother; self-conscious and very particular about clothing; has periods of overfrequent hand washing; demands unnecessary servicing; exhibits severe autonomic reactions to stress.	Mild RBD	Parent Guidance
Parents	30	M	68 mos.	69 mos.	1 mo.	Stutters; aggressive at school; demanding and argumentative at home; appears disturbed by parental friction.	Mild RBD	Parent Guidance
School	31	M	70 mos.	70 mos.	0 mo.	Frequent, daily tantrums at school (when not permitted to continue an activity, when reprimanded or criticized); resists school authority; appears very unhappy.	Moderately Severe RBD	Parent Guidance
School and Parents	32	F	72 mos.	82 mos.	10 mos.	Learning difficulty at school; a perfectionist; poor peer relations, insists on her own way; oversensitive to teasing.	Moderate RBD	Parent Guidance and Remedial Reading
Mother	33	M	72 mos.	84 mos.	12 mos.	Avoids most endeavors (will master only what catches his interest or what he has been told specifically that he must master); recent test shows drop of 16 points in I.Q.; once he masters an activity he loses	Mild RBD	Parent Guidance

interest and demands service; is not fluent verbally; cries easily and excessively.

Parents	34	F	78 mos.	95 mos.	17 mos.	Poor relations with younger sister; becomes very upset with criticism; excessively disturbed with any change in plans; underachieving academically; a perfectionist; a worrier (in reaction to criticism, change in plans and, recently, even to well-meant comments from parents); chooses younger children as playmates.	Mild RBD	Parent Guidance
School	35	M	80 mos.	92 mos.	12 mos.	Underachieves at school, disruptive in class; speech characterized by unclear diction; poor peer relations, disregards effect of his behavior on others.	Moderate RBD	Parent Guidance
School	36	M	84 mos.	85 mos.	1 mo.	Anxiety about school performance, has crying spells; anxiety about his status in the family, whether he is on a par with other members; general insecurity (apprehensive about such things as God, punishment, injustice, possibility of buildings falling down); confusion in right-left dominance, makes reversals; poor coordination.	Moderate Developmental Language Lag with Secondary Behavior Disorder (Moderate)	Parent Guidance; Parents to Tutor; Advice to School
Mother	37	M	90 mos.	93 mos.	3 mos.	Anxiety at separation from mother; mild attempts to avoid school by claiming illness; sleep disturbance with night awakening, fears, nightmares.	Mild RBD	Parent Guidance and Periodic Review
School advised therapy	38	M	92 mos.	96 mos.	4 mos.	Overreacts, is easily upset by things not going as he wishes; disorganized in approach to activities, dawdles; immature and silly behavior; poor peer relations; unwilling to shift from ongoing activity; tic; minor reversals in writing.	Moderately Severe RBD	Parent Guidance

TABLE 1 / CONTINUED

Referral Initiated By	Case #	Sex	Onset of Symptoms	Psychiatric Evaluation and Diagnosis	Time between Onset and Evaluation	Presenting Complaints [1]	Diagnosis and Severity	Recommendations
Parents	39	F	93 mos.	99 mos.[3]	6 mos.	Whines over many issues; used to cry excessively; parents find it difficult to teach her things because she argues, resists taking direction; a perfectionist; verbally critical of others and self; gets "fresh" when her desires are blocked.	Mild RBD	Parent Guidance
School and Parents	40	M	96 mos.	101 mos.	5 mos.	Poor peer relations, lacks friends, is oblivious to effect of his behavior on other children; very selective in interests and excludes other things which may be expected of him.	Mild RBD	Parent Guidance and Periodic Review
School	41	F	101 mos.	102 mos.	1 mo.	Behavior problem at school; avoids studies; is rude to parents.	Mild RBD	Parent Guidance and Advice to School
Parents	42	M	104 mos.[7]	105 mos.	1 mo.	Academic problem, takes excessive time to do assignments and avoids them by fussing and crying; enunciation unclear when excited; slow language development; makes reversals in letters and numbers.	Mild Behavior Disorder Secondary to Brain Damage	Parent Guidance; Tutoring; Advice to School

[1] Presenting Complaints are listed in order of priority as stated by the parents at the time of consultation.
[2] RBD = Reactive Behavior Disorder.
[3] At previous consultation was not considered clinical case.
[4] No final parent discussion. Mother was called; "forgot there was a problem."
[5] NBD = Neurotic Behavior Disorder.
[6] Consultation incomplete; child seen only informally. No final parent discussion; they deny problem.
[7] Periodic advice about language lag since 12 months; not clinical problem previously.

TABLE 2 / AGE, IN YEARS, AT TIME OF CLINICAL DIAGNOSIS

	2–3	3–4	4–5	5–6	6–7	7–8	8–9	9–10	Total
Male	0	4	5	7	3	5	2	0	26
Female	1	3	4	3	2	1	2	0	16
Total	1	7	9	10	5	6	4	0	42

As can be seen from Table 2, only one case was diagnosed before three years of age, following which there was a sharp rise in incidence to a peak at four to six years of age, with a progressive drop in new cases in the subsequent years. This finding is similar to that reported in the Berkeley Study.[3]

The short interval between onset of symptoms and psychiatric referral and diagnosis in the present study is indicated in Table 3.

TABLE 3 / TIME, IN MONTHS, BETWEEN ONSET OF SYMPTOMS AND DIAGNOSIS

Sex	0–3	4–6	7–12	13–18	19–24	25–30	31–36	37–42	43–48	Total
Male	9	2	6	4	2	2	0	0	1	26
Female	5	4	3	2	0	1	0	1	0	16
Total	14	6	9	6	2	3	0	1	1	42

As can be seen from these data, the largest group of cases, fourteen out of forty-two, came to psychiatric attention within three months after the onset of the symptoms. The great majority, 65 per cent of the boys and 75 per cent of the girls, came to attention within one year after the onset of symptoms.

Table 4 indicates the frequency of the cases in relation to severity of disturbance and diagnosis. Most of the cases in the clinical sample were mild or moderate reactive behavior disorders. Four cases were judged to reflect severe reactive disorders; one was a case of moderately severe neurotic behavior disorder. One child (Case 1) was psychotic

TABLE 4 / SEVERITY OF DISTURBANCE AND DIAGNOSIS

	Mild RBD *	Moderate RBD *	Moderately Severe RBD *	Moderately Severe NBD †	Brain Damage With Severe 2 ° Beh. Disorder
Male	17 ‡	6	3	0	0
Female	8	5	1	1	1
Total	25	11	4	1	1

* RBD—Reactive Behavior Disorder.
† NBD—Neurotic Behavior Disorder.
‡ In one case the RBD was secondary to brain damage.

and, upon full evaluation, exhibited clear evidence of central nervous system abnormality. She was classified as a case of organic brain damage with secondary and elaborated behavior disorder.

Table 5 details the relation of severity of behavior disorder to the duration of symptoms in months before psychiatric evaluation and diagnosis.

As may be seen from this table, 32 per cent of the mild cases came to psychiatric attention within three months of the time of symptom onset, as compared with 27 per cent of the moderate cases, a difference which is not significant. The comparison for the percentage of cases coming to attention within one year of onset showed a similar lack of significance for the two groups—68 per cent for the mild cases and 73 per cent for the moderate cases. There were too few cases diagnosed as moderately severe (five) and severe (one) to make meaningful comparisons with these groups.

Of greater interest are the relationships between the ages of the children at the time of psychiatric diagnosis and the frequency of symptom occurrence, as detailed in Table 6. In this table the different symptoms exhibited by the children are grouped into twelve symptom areas. For each symptom area, the number of male and female cases exhibiting the symptom are tabulated. In each tabulation the ages of the children at the time of psychiatric diagnosis and the number of children for each of the age periods are indicated.

The data of Table 6 are of interest in that they reflect a relationship between the kinds of issues and values that the parents considered to be important and the nature of the child's behaviors about which they complained. There were only two cases with symptoms referable to feeding difficulties. Moreover, in these two instances, the feeding problems were not the major source of parental concern over the child's behavior. Elimination difficulties were also an infrequent basis for complaint, with two cases of bowel problems and only one of enuresis. Masturbation, though frequently reported, was rarely an expressed

TABLE 5 / RELATION OF SEVERITY TO DURATION OF SYMPTOMS IN MONTHS BEFORE DIAGNOSIS

Duration		0–3	4–6	7–12	13–18	19–24	25–30	31–36	37–42	43–48	Total
Mild	Male	5	1	5	3	1	1			1	17
	Female	3	2	1	2						8
Moderate	Male	2		1	1	1	1				6
	Female	1	2	2							5
Moderately Severe	Male	2	1								3
	Female	1							1		2
Severe	Male										0
	Female						1				1
Total	Male	9	2	6	4	2	2	0	0	1	26
	Female	5	4	3	2	0	1	0	1	0	16

TABLE 6 / AGE DISTRIBUTION, IN YEARS, AND FREQUENCY OF SYMPTOMS AT TIME OF DIAGNOSIS

Symptom Area *		2–3	3–4	4–5	5–6	6–7	7–8	8–9	Total Children in Each Symptom Area †
Sleep	M		2	3	2		1		8
	F	1	1	1					3
Feeding	M			1					1
	F				1				1
Elimination	M			1					1
	F		1		1				2
Mood	M		1	1	2	2	2	1	9
	F	1	1	3	2		1	1	9
Discipline	M		1	1	4	2	2		10
	F			3	1	1		2	7
Habits	M		1	2					3
	F				2				2
Motor Activity	M		1	3					4
	F			1					1
Somatic	M		1		2		1		4
	F		1	1					2
Speech	M		1	2	1	1	1	1	7
	F		1	2					3
Peer Relationships	M		3	4	6	1	3	1	18
	F		1	2	2	2	1	2	10
Learning	M			1	2	4	1		8
	F		1			2	1	2	6
Other	M			1	2		1		4
	F			1	1				2

* The symptoms included under each symptom area are listed in Appendix A.
† The total number of children in the various symptom areas exceeds the number in the clinical sample (42), because of the existence of multiple symptoms in almost every case.

concern. In the two cases in which a concern over masturbation was expressed, the source of complaint was the school, not the parents. By contrast, symptoms in the areas of sleep, discipline, and mood disturbances were much more frequent and of greater parental concern. Greatest concern was generally exhibited over speech difficulties and over problem behavior in peer relationships and learning. Requests for evaluation and guidance were usually made as soon as the parents were aware of any deviant functioning in these areas.

The variations in frequency of symptoms referable to different aspects of the child's functioning parallel very closely the child-care practices and expressed standards and attitudes of the total parent group, including those with, as well as those without, problem children. Irregularity of feeding was frequently reported by the parents in the routine interviews but with the statements that they realized this was "not important," the child's "health was not suffering," it was "so easy and inexpensive" to prepare the child's meal that it did not matter if he was "picky and choosy" with his food, etc. A similarly permissive attitude was expressed toward toilet training; if anything, early training was considered less desirable. Masturbation was observed and reported by many parents in their infants and preschool children, but again with the statement that since they knew it was "harmless and normal," they did not interfere with it. It was the impression of the staff interviewers that some parents were not fully at ease with this stated attitude toward their child's masturbation and that they might have intervened were it not for the weight of authority.[4]

The parents as a group were not as ready to be tolerant of deviant functioning in the areas of sleep and discipline. A child who intruded repeatedly on his parent's evenings instead of going to bed quickly and quietly, or who awakened his parents frequently during the night, did realistically inconvenience them or even impair their functioning. A child who learned the rules of safety or of social living in the family slowly and incompletely could also objectively be a problem to the family. These facts were stated clearly by many of the parents, were implied by others, and were reflected in substantially greater levels of demand on the child in these areas than in feeding and toilet training.

The relatively large number of cases with symptoms of mood disturbance, difficulties in peer relationships, speech problems, and learning deficiencies closely paralleled the parents' hierarchies of goals and values for their children's optimal developmental course. As a group the parents were actively aware of and sometimes even preoccupied with their children's emotional and social functioning. Educational aspirations for the children were uniformly high, and most of the parents showed active interest in and paid attention to all phases of their children's learning.

The patterns of presenting complaints, therefore, reflected parental values and attitudes as much as they did problems of functioning intrinsic to the child. Moreover, the nature of what was complained about and what was of concern, but unexpressed, suggest a significant shift in recent decades in what middle-class parents believe it is permissible to be concerned about. This phenomenon, though of significant interest for all students of parental ideology, is too complex for full treatment in this volume. However, such ideological considerations do appear to affect the nature of interactions between the parent and the child, and to represent an important dimension defining the nature and focus of the parents' concerns with aspects of their children's behavioral development.

REFERENCES

1. R. Lapouse and M. A. Monk, "An Epidemiologic Study of Behavior Characteristics in Children," *Amer. J. Public Health,* 48:1134 (1958).

2. J. C. Glidewell, H. R. Domke, and M. B. Kantor, "Screening in Schools for Behavior Disorders: Use of Mother's Report of Symptoms," *J. Educ. Research*, LVI (1963).
3. J. W. McFarlane, L. Allen, and H. P. Honzik, *A Developmental Study of the Behavior Problems of Normal Children between 24 Months and 14 Years* (Berkeley: University of California Press, 1962).
4. B. Spock, *Baby and Child Care,* rev. ed. (New York: Pocket Books, Inc., 1957).

4 STRATEGY OF DATA ANALYSIS

Having defined a clinical sample within the longitudinal study, it became possible to carry out two types of analysis. The first of these compared the children with behavior disorders and those without disturbance to determine whether differences in temperamental attributes and constellations obtained between the two groups. The same comparisons for differences in temperament were made between the clinical cases with active symptoms and those with passive symptoms, and between each of these two clinical subgroups and the nonclinical cases.*

The second analysis first identified children with certain similar temperamental patterns, and for each pattern compared those who developed behavioral disturbances with those who did not. A major goal of this analysis was the determination of the reasons for difference in outcome when the temperamental type was similar. In this analysis it was also possible to consider the reasons for differences in kinds of symptoms in the children who developed behavior problems.

Clearly, these two types of analysis complement each other. The first is concerned with the identification of differences in temperamental patterns for different groups of children; the second is concerned with the identification of the reasons for different outcomes for children with the same temperamental pattern. The findings of the first analysis are presented in Chapter 5, and those of the second analysis in Chapters 7 through 15.

Through these two sets of analyses a number of specific questions could be examined. These questions included:

1] Is the occurrence of behavioral disturbance associated with any typicality in the antecedent and concurrent patterns of temperamental organization? 2] Are differences in types of symptomatology of children with behavior disorders associated with differences in temperamental organization? 3] Why do some children with given temperamental characteristics develop behavior disorders, while other children with the same temperamental patterns develop normally? 4] How do specific symptoms evolve and become elaborated in the course of the development of behavioral disturbance? 5] Does an analysis of temperament

---

* See Chapter 3 for criteria for active and passive symptoms.

suggest modes of therapeutic intervention in children with behavior disorders?

Attempts to answer these questions required a complex series of both quantitative and qualitative analyses of the various bodies of data available to us. Although in the life of the child none of the different factors which influence his development acts as an isolated entity, for purposes of analysis it is necessary to consider the data in a stepwise fashion. Unless this is done, one cannot identify the contribution made by different elements present in a pattern.

The steps in our analysis are sixfold and range from an initial consideration of temperament per se to an examination of techniques for the management of behavior problems and their effectiveness. These six steps can be enumerated as follows:

1] The quantitative comparison of each temperamental trait in the defined clinical and nonclinical groups. 2] The identification of trait clusters and factors since we recognize that temperamental traits are intercorrelated, not unitary. These findings may then be applied to the defined clinical and nonclinical groups. 3] The qualitative analysis of temperament-environment interaction through a review and selective extraction and utilization of the anterospective records of the clinical and nonclinical groups. The object of this qualitative analysis is to define a number of patterns of temperament and then trace the interaction of children with such patterns with parents, peers, teachers, and other significant individuals and features of the environment. 4] The consideration of stress from the standpoint of dissonance between the child's characteristics and specific environmental demands and expectations. 5] The study of the formation and evolution of symptoms through an analysis of the data on behavioral development. 6] The evaluation of the effectiveness for treatment of management methods that take into account the child's temperamental style.

In carrying through this stepwise analysis, both quantitative and qualitative methods have been utilized. The application of quantitative analytic techniques has made possible the systematic comparison of specific temperamental characteristics in the defined clinical and nonclinical groups. A year-by-year comparison of consistency and variability among the characteristics of temperament for the clinical and nonclinical groups has also been feasible through the use of quantitative methods. These methods have also permitted the delineation of patterns of intercorrelations among temperamental traits and the identification of clusters of categories by factor analysis.

The qualitative analytic methods have made it possible to explore many items in the data that could not be adequately evaluated by the available quantitative methods. As an example, in the parent interview protocols at different age periods the item-scoring for the characteristic of *persistence* in one youngster had shown a small number of scorable items. Though most of the scores were high for persistence, the final weighted score did not indicate that this child differed substantially from a number of other children with high persistence scores. However, an inspection of the individual behavioral items indicated an extraordinary level of persistence, even in infancy. For instance, at eighteen months, he began to learn to tie shoelaces. For several days he spent most of his waking hours tying and retying his brother's and father's shoelaces, as well as his own. One evening, when his mother forcibly interrupted this activity in order to put him to bed, he responded with a prolonged tantrum. The identification in the longitudinal behavioral records of similar incidents of intense prolonged involvement with selective activities, combined with severe frustration reactions when interrupted, led to the judgment that persistence was an outstanding temperamental characteristic for this boy.

Qualitative analysis has also been useful for the identification of specific constellations or syndromes of temperamental traits which show themselves in certain children and appear to characterize many significant aspects of the child's behavioral functioning. Finally, the qualitative analysis of the data has been found especially valuable in tracing the course of behavioral development over time in individual children, both in those who developed behavior disorders and those who did not.

To engage in such a series of qualitative analyses required the development of a technique whereby the pertinent data scattered throughout the huge bulk of longitudinal records accumulated for each child could be identified and extracted. Without such selective extraction, any attempt to deal *in toto* with the vast amount of information in each child's records would, at best, have had to be impressionistic and unsystematic. Such a technique for selective extraction and utilization of the anterospective records was developed and applied to each of the forty-two clinical cases. In this procedure, the child psychiatrist, soon after she completed her clinical evaluation of each child, drew up a list of symptoms and significant clinical features of the child's functioning and of parental and other environmental influences. This list contained the items for which the anterospective records were to be searched. The records were not searched systematically for temperamental characteristics, but for index behaviors and interactions. However, in the search of the anterospective records, any items describing unusual or extreme temperamental responses were extracted and recorded.

All the records available on the parental interviews, psychological tests and behavioral observations in the test situation, teacher interviews and direct observations in the school, were searched for the list of items by a staff member who had not participated in any of the data-gathering procedures or in the psychiatric evaluation. Supplementary information on parental characteristics was obtained from the special interview on parental practices and attitudes conducted when the child was three years old. The staff member was instructed to extract and record verbatim all pertinent statements and to identify the date and data source of each item. She was also told to record any data which appeared strikingly unusual, even if it was not included in the list of items to be extracted. She was not briefed regarding the specific content, but only regarding the general category. Thus, one child who reacted to new situations with quiet withdrawal and another child who reacted with a loud tantrum, would both have the same item for extraction, "reaction to new situations." Similarly, two mothers, one of whom was inconsistent in her functioning with the child and the other highly consistent to the point of inflexibility, would both have the same item for extraction, "consistency of child-care practices." For each item the extraction of verbatim statements started with its first mention in the longitudinal records. Note was taken in all subsequent records at later age-periods of the presence or absence of any mention of that item. All statements were extracted verbatim, and the absence of a statement regarding the item was also recorded.

In a number of cases the search of the anterospective records revealed significant items not included in the original list. Thus, for example, in one child the extraction of data regarding "fears" indicated their occurrence primarily in relation to strangers. This indicated the desirability of a search for "reactions to strangers." In another case, the search for "consistency of child-care practices" revealed opposition and conflict between the parents in their approach to the child, and "conflict between parents" was added to the list of items for searching.

The nature of the data recorded by this process of selective extraction of the anterospective data is illustrated by the samples in Appendix B.

The selectively extracted data in each case were utilized for a number of qualitative analyses. They were used, first, to supplement the original clinical formulations made by the child psychiatrist. Second, the extracted data made possible a systematic study of the origins and subsequent course of the behavioral disturbance, as well as of the specific symptomatology, in each individual case. Finally, the data were utilized for both theoretical considerations and for purposes of parent guidance to delineate a number of constellations of temperamental attributes and to identify the environmental demands and expectations which appeared to be excessively stressful and potentially pathogenic for each constellation.

Detailed qualitative analyses of the anterospective records of a number of the children without behavior problems were also done in order to compare the developmental courses of these children with those of the clinical cases. These children without disturbances were

selected on the basis of having constellations of temperamental characteristics similar to the children with behavior disorders. These analyses
have made possible a number of comparisons between the course in
development of the clinical and the nonclinical cases.

The findings of our sixfold step-by-step series of quantitative and
qualitative analyses will be presented in sequence in the following
chapters.

5 THE RELATION OF TEMPERAMENT TO DISTURBANCE: A QUANTITATIVE ANALYSIS

The first step in our analysis of the antecedent characteristics that distinguished children who came to clinical notice from those who did not develop behavior disorders was a quantitative consideration of temperamental characteristics at specific ages. In making this comparison the children were divided into four groups defined as follows: 1] clinical cases with active symptoms who came to notice before the age of five years, comprising fourteen children; 2] the total group of clinical cases with active symptoms irrespective of the time they came to notice, comprising thirty-four children; 3] clinical cases with passive symptoms, comprising eight children; and 4] nonclinical cases, comprising sixty-six children over five years of age (see Chapter 3 for criteria by which symptoms were classified as either active or passive). These groups are treated separately or in combination in accordance with the specific question under scrutiny. Since detailed information on behavioral style was available for each of the subjects from the first months of life onward, it was possible to compare and contrast the features of temperament which characterized the clinical subgroups both before and after the onset of behavioral disturbance and to relate these findings to the developmental courses of the nonclinical cases.

In order to make quantitative comparisons of temperamental characteristics, it was necessary to decide upon a standard method for scaling these attributes in the children studied. A weighted score model, which takes into account the item scores in all of the three scale positions used for scoring each temperamental category, was adopted.* In this method, one of the extreme scale positions was represented by "0," the middle position by "1," and the other extreme position by "2." The number of items scored at each position was multiplied by the scale value (0, 1, or 2), and the products were summed. The sum of the three products was then divided by the total number of scored items in the category. Thus, a child's weighted score in any category can range from 0 to 2. This scoring method takes into account the distribution of

* Previous analyses of these data [1] have utilized preponderant ratings and percentile rank scores. In a monograph now in preparation (S. Korn, H. G. Birch, A. Thomas, and Others, "Stability and Change in Temperament over the First Five Years of Life") the usefulness and limitations of these two methods are enumerated and the advantages of the weighted score method are discussed.

53

scored items in all three scale positions, decreases the likelihood of tied scores, and is both efficient and relatively simple to apply to the data.

The weights, 0–1–2, assigned to each of the ratings in the categories are, of course, arbitrary, and the question of the appropriateness of such values cannot be unequivocally resolved. This problem, however, is shared by other scoring methods, such as the per cent rank method, which also makes arbitrary assumptions as to the value of distances between rank positions. Although the issues regarding the conversion of ordinal scales to interval scales and the relative merits of parametric and nonparametric statistical analyses have received considerable attention,[2] there is as yet no general agreement as to an acceptable solution. We have, therefore, in the interests of simplicity and parsimony, assigned equidistant weights to the ratings in each category as the most straightforward way in which to identify polar extremes and a middle rating (the latter is defined by an intermediate term or by the occurrence in a behavioral description of equal elements of both polar extremes). To assign other than equal intervals between the ratings would in such circumstances be no less arbitrary and far more cumbersome.

The average number of items for each age and scale position for

TABLE 1 / AVERAGE NUMBER OF SCORED ITEMS PER CHILD FOR EACH SCALE-POSITION IN THE POOLED-YEAR INTERVIEWS

Category	Rating	Year 1	2	3	4	5
Activity	High	12.0	16.7	16.4	8.5	7.5
	Mod.	17.4	19.4	17.9	9.4	8.3
	Low	6.2	5.5	6.8	4.0	3.6
Rhythmicity	Reg.	17.0	9.0	7.2	5.1	4.1
	Var.	3.3	1.5	1.5	1.9	1.4
	Irreg.	7.8	3.6	3.2	1.7	1.0
Adaptability	Adapt.	36.0	27.5	28.9	19.3	16.9
	Var.	13.6	5.0	4.5	3.6	3.0
	Non A.	14.9	13.8	11.4	7.9	6.5
App./With.	Appr.	12.0	6.3	6.5	8.1	7.2
	Var.	0.8	0.9	0.9	1.2	0.8
	With.	4.7	2.3	2.1	2.3	1.8
Threshold	High	9.8	5.3	3.6	5.3	4.4
	Mod.	5.3	3.0	2.4	10.4	8.5
	Low	21.8	13.6	10.9	14.1	12.0
Intensity	Intense	30.3	24.3	20.2	15.6	14.7
	Var.	3.7	2.4	1.7	2.1	2.4
	Mild	29.8	18.4	20.0	23.1	21.4
Mood	Posit.	25.7	23.7	25.0	28.6	23.9
	Var.	4.3	2.8	2.4	3.6	4.1
	Neg.	33.0	26.2	24.6	24.1	15.9
Distract.	Distr.	7.3	5.4	4.6	3.1	2.0
	Var.	0.6	0.4	0.4	0.3	0.2
	Non D.	1.5	1.0	0.9	0.9	0.3
Persistence	Persist.	11.3	12.2	12.4	9.3	8.3
	Var.	0.6	1.2	1.3	1.3	1.2
	Non P.	1.4	3.2	4.9	3.7	3.2

years one to five are presented in Table 1, and the distribution of weighted scores in each category for the sample as a whole in Figure A.

It may be seen from these data that for six of the temperamental categories the scores are symmetrically distributed, and that for two, approach/withdrawal and persistence, although such symmetry is not

FIGURE A

Frequency distribution of weighted scores for the total sample in each of the nine categories pooled for years 1–5.

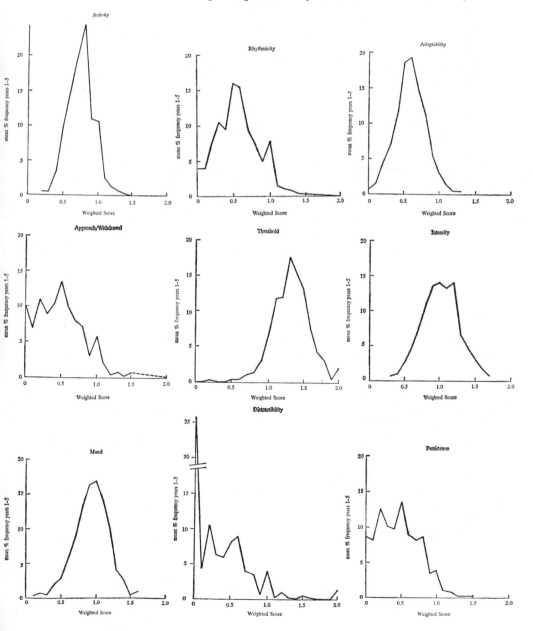

achieved, the values are widely distributed. In only one category, distractibility, is the distribution markedly of a "J" type. The method of scaling, therefore, has provided distributions with sufficient spread to permit the characterization of the temperamental attributes of the chil-

FIGURE B

Mean scores of three subgroups for the nine categories for years 1–5.

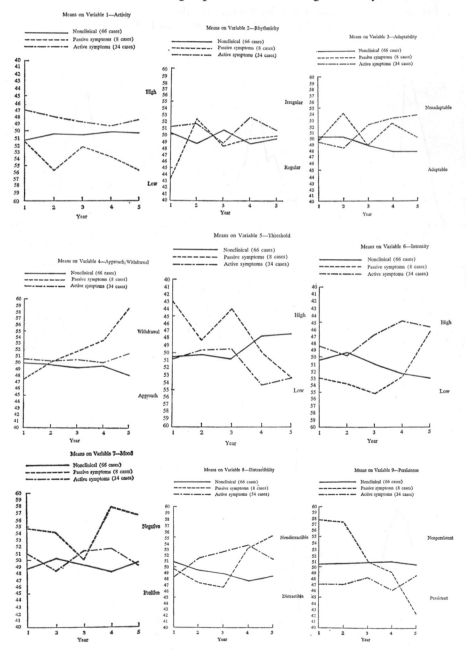

dren with good differentiation in at least eight of the nine categories of temperament being considered.

When the subgroups of children are compared with respect to their scale-scored temperamental characteristics over the first five years of life, it is found that they differ from one another in significant ways. The general depiction of subgroup patterns of temperament over the first five years of life for the total active symptom group, the passive symptom group, and the nonclinical group are reflected in the graphs comprising Figure B. These patternings for each of the nine characteristics of temperament can be considered in turn.

1] *Activity*

It will be noted from the data in Figure B that the active clinical cases considered as a whole were initially characterized by a higher level of activity than were the other groups. Moreover, they persisted in being so characterized in each of the succeeding years. In contrast, the passive clinical cases did not differ initially from the nonclinical group. However, by the second year of life and for each year thereafter, they were less active than the nonclinical cases.

2] *Rhythmicity*

A more complex picture was noted when rhythmicity was analyzed. The active clinical cases were initially more irregular than were the normal children in the nonclinical group. This continued to obtain in all succeeding years except year three. In contrast, the group of cases with passive symptoms, who were originally the most regular of the three groups, in successive years varied widely in their rhythmicity and exhibited no definitely expressed relative position for this temperamental attribute. At best, their position from year to year could be described as inconsistent, with no year functioning as a good predictor of relative position for any subsequent year.

3] *Adaptability*

The three groups were markedly similar in their ratings for adaptability during the first year of life. Thereafter, the clinical groups came to be increasingly less adaptable than the nonclinical cases. The pattern of change was linear and at two points, age two for the passive group and age three for the active group, a weak reversal of trend was exhibited. However, in an overall sense, both types of clinical cases came to be less adaptable than the nonclinical group over the age span considered.

4] *Approach/Withdrawal*

In the first year and for all succeeding years except year five, the active cases were relatively indistinguishable from the nonclinical cases. Both these groups exhibited a preponderant tendency to maintain consistent score positions from year to year, with a secular course that paralleled the abscissa. In contrast, the clinical cases of a passive type at first tended to make approach reactions to new experiences to a greater degree than did the other two groups. By age two they were indistinguishable from either the nonclinical or active clinical cases. In each succeeding year, however, their behavior came to be increasingly marked by a tendency to withdraw from rather than to approach new stimuli.

5] *Threshold*

In the first year of life and for the succeeding two years, the active cases and the nonclinical cases exhibited markedly similar threshold characteristics. In contrast, the passive cases during this three-year period were defined as having higher thresholds. However, in the fourth and fifth years, a change was noted with both clinical groups characterized by lowered thresholds of responsiveness.

6] *Intensity*

The age-specific characteristics of the three defined groups with respect to the intensity of reactions is of considerable interest. In the first year of life, the active clinical group was slightly higher and the passive clinical group significantly lower in intensity of reaction than was the nonclinical group. The active clinical group remained with the nonclinical group through the second year of life; thereafter it came to be increasingly characterized by behaviors having a high intensity component. The nonclinical group, during the same period, exhibited a gradual diminution in the intensity of reaction from year to year. In contrast to the other two groups, the intensity course of the passive clinical group appeared to be bidirectional. From years one to three, its course paralleled that of the nonclinical group and gradually exhibited a reduction in intensity level. From the third year onward this course was reversed so that by the fifth year of life the passive clinical group was behaving at as high an intensity level as was the active clinical group.

7] *Mood*

In the first year of life both clinical groups tended to exhibit more negative mood than did the nonclinical group. This tendency was more apparent in the children who comprised the passive clinical group than in the active clinical type. Through each of the successive years this passive group remained, despite variations, consistently more negative in its expression of mood than the nonclinical cases and, in four of the five annual periods, more negative than the active clinical cases. The active cases exhibited a variable course for this characteristic. At three ages they were more negative than the nonclinical group, but at the other two ages, indistinguishable from it.

8] *Distractibility*

In the first year of life, the three groups of children differed very little with regard to distractibility. By the second year, clear differentiation came to exist for the groups and was continued in the third year. The active clinical cases began to exhibit less, and the passive clinical cases more easy distractibility than did the nonclinical group. This trend was sustained for the active cases through the fifth year. However, after the third year, in a manner markedly reminiscent of the findings for intensity, the passive clinical cases reversed their previous course and became, by the fifth year, less distractible than either of the other two groups.

9] *Persistence*

Clear differences among the groups in the distribution of persistence were noted during the first year of life. The passive cases were markedly less persistent and the active cases significantly more persistent than were the nonclinical cases. Greater persistence characterized the behavior of the active clinical group for each of the five years. In contrast, the passive clinical group, which started out by being clearly nonpersistent, pursued a steady course toward increased persistence. After the third year, this group was more persistent than the nonclinical group and, by the fifth year, the most persistent of the three groups.

NUMERICAL ANALYSIS OF THE VARIABLES OVER THE FIVE-YEAR PERIOD

Cases with Active Symptoms versus Nonclinical Cases

Parametric analysis serves to confirm the impressions derived from a consideration of the distributions of temperamental characteristics with age and their graphic representation. As a first step, the weighted scores for each of the temperamental characteristics at each year for

TABLE 2 / SIGNIFICANT t TESTS—TOTAL ACTIVE (N = 34) VERSUS NONCLINICAL (N = 66)

Activity	Year 1	$t = 2.60$	$p < .01$
Rhythmicity	Year 4	$t = 2.09$	$p < .05$
Adaptability	Year 4	$t = 2.67$	$p < .01$
	Year 5	$t = 2.53$	$p < .05$
Approach/withdrawal		None	
Threshold	Year 4	$t = 3.19$	$p < .01$
	Year 5	$t = 2.26$	$p < .05$
Intensity	Year 3	$t = 2.08$	$p < .05$
	Year 4	$t = 3.82$	$p < .01$
	Year 5	$t = 3.72$	$p < .01$
Mood		None	
Distractibility	Year 4	$t = 3.02$	$p < .01$
Persistence	Year 4	$t = 3.08$	$p < .01$

the total group with active symptoms and the nonclinical cases were compared. The years at which differences in weighted scores between the active clinical and nonclinical cases were sufficiently large to reach acceptable levels of significance are summarized in Table 2.

In the first year of life, activity level in the two groups was markedly different, with the children who later exhibited active symptoms of behavioral disturbance being significantly more active ($t = 2.60$, $p < .01$). Other temperamental variables were significantly different at later ages. Intensity was significantly different in the expected direction in the third through the fifth years of age, adaptability and threshold in the fourth and fifth years, and rhythmicity, distractibility, and persistence in the fourth year.

Cases with Passive Symptoms versus Nonclinical Cases

When the cases with passive symptoms were similarly considered, they differed significantly in the magnitude of their weighted scores from the nonclinical group only in the fourth and fifth years of life. The distribution of the years at which such significant differences were obtained is summarized in Table 3.

TABLE 3 / SIGNIFICANT t TESTS—PASSIVE (N = 8) VERSUS NONCLINICAL (N = 66)

Activity	Year 5	$t = 1.97$	$p < .05$
Rhythmicity	None		
Adaptability	None		
Approach/withdrawal	Year 5	$t = 3.27$	$p < .01$
Threshold	None		
Intensity	None		
Mood	Year 4	$t = 2.55$	$p < .05$
	Year 5	$t = 2.12$	$p < .05$
Distractibility	None		
Persistence	Year 5	$t = 2.47$	$p < .05$

As may be seen from the table, the four temperamental variables for which the weighted scores of the two groups differed significantly were activity, approach/withdrawal, mood, and persistence. Mood was significantly different in years four and five, and the other variables only in the fifth year. The low frequency with which significant differences occurred derived wholly from the small size of the sample considered. The small N made it possible for significant values to be achieved only when differences in weighted scores were very great indeed. The findings, therefore, must be considered as highly capable of reflecting a Type two error, in which important existing differences are obscured by the limitations of the sample size and the statistical technique used.

An analysis of variance was done on all the temperamental variables for the total active and the passive clinical groups and the nonclinical group across the first five years of life. Distractibility and persistence were included in the analysis even though the small number of responses that could be scored for these variables made it less likely that significant differences would be obtained. The summary of the analysis of variance is presented in Table 4.

TABLE 4 / SUMMARY OF ANALYSIS OF VARIANCE

Variable	Groups Main Effect		Groups by Years Interaction	
	2/92 Degrees of Freedom Difference between Groups Across Years 1–5		8/368 Degrees of Freedom Difference in Group Trends or Profiles Over Years 1–5	
	F	P	F	P
Activity	4.22	<.05	1.12	N.S.
Rhythmicity	<1.00	N.S.	1.01	N.S.
Adaptability	1.88	N.S.	1.69	N.S.
Approach/withdrawal	1.45	N.S.	1.60	N.S.
Threshold	1.04	N.S.	2.71	<.01
Intensity	5.50	<.01	2.24	<.01
Mood	3.10	<.05	1.01	N.S.
Distractibility	1.74	N.S.	1.05	N.S.
Persistence	3.26	<.05	1.52	N.S.

The findings of this analysis with respect to each of the temperamental variables may be summarized as follows:

Activity: The main effect for groups was significant ($F = 4.22$, 2/92 degrees of freedom, $p < .05$). This finding reflects the consistently high score of the group with active symptoms and the tendency of the passive group to exhibit low levels of activity.

Rhythmicity: Not significant.

Adaptability: Not significant.

Approach/Withdrawal: Not significant.

The lack of significance for these three variables is based upon similarities in the character of the deviances of the two clinical groups from the comparison sample of children without behavior disorders, and not upon similarities between the nonclinical and clinical groups.

Threshold: Although the main effect for groups was not significant, the interaction between groups and years was significant ($F = 2.71$, 8/368 df, $p < .01$). This finding reflects the tendency for the threshold of the group with passive symptoms to increase across the five years, during which period this feature of temperament remains relatively constant in the other two groups.

Intensity: The main effect for groups was significant ($F = 5.50$, 2/92 df, $p < .01$). This finding reflects the tendency for the group with active symptoms to be high in intensity and the group with passive symptoms to be low in intensity relative to the nonclinical group. The interaction between years is also significant for this variable ($F = 2.24$, 8/368 df, $p < .01$), and is probably due to the tendency of the passive group to increase the intensity of its responsiveness with age, while the active symptom group remains consistently intense across the age period.

Mood: The main effect for mood is significant ($F = 3.10$, 2/92 df, $p < .05$), and appears to derive from the consistent tendency of the group with passive symptoms to be negative in mood relative to the other groups.

Distractibility: Not significant.

Persistence: The main effect for persistence is significant ($F = 3.26$, 2/92 df, $p < .05$), which reflects the consistent tendency of the group with active symptoms to be more persistent than the nonclinical group.

In summary, then, the results of the comparisons of mean differences and of the analysis of variance support the general conclusions of the distributive graphic analyses. The groups differed with respect to defined features of temperament, with particular differences expressed in activity, rhythmicity, threshold, intensity, mood, and persistence. Clearly, these group differences in temperament give us only an incomplete picture of individual trends. To enter into a detailed consideration of individual stability and change in temperamental organization is a complex technical problem is beyond the scope of the present volume. It is, however, one of the principal burdens of the monograph "Stability and Change in Temperament over the First Five Years of Life." [3]

INTERRELATIONS AMONG THE
TEMPERAMENTAL TRAITS

Thus far we have been treating each of the nine characteristics of temperament we have analyzed as an independent variable in terms of which the defined clinical and nonclinical groups may be compared. However, from any theoretical standpoint it is most unlikely that such characteristics are fully independent and highly probable that they are correlated with each other to some degree. Clearly, if such intercorrelation were excessively high, certain of the reported findings would be redundant. To determine whether this danger was real, the data on each of the variables for each annual period were subjected to correlational analysis, and the correlations found among the nine categories of temperament for the total population of children for each of the five years are presented in Table 5.

The range of intercorrelations is from $-.49$ to $+.48$ for the 360 correlation coefficients. It was of interest to note that three of the temperamental variables, intensity, adaptability, and mood, contained the largest number of significant correlations with the other categories. Interrelations among the other variables were of a lower order and only infrequently were at an acceptable level of statistical significance.

Intensity was the characteristic most significantly correlated with other categories and had thirty-one positive and significant correlations

TABLE 5 / CORRELATIONS BETWEEN CATEGORIES FOR YEARS 1–5 (N = 112)

Category	Year	Activ.	Rhythm.	Adapt.	App./W.	Thresh.	Intens.	Mood	Distr.
Rhythmicity	1	−.11							
	2	−.09							
	3	−.07							
	4	−.21 *							
	5	.00							
Adaptability	1	−.05	.27 *						
	2	−.21 *	.18						
	3	−.30 *	.24 *						
	4	−.12	.37 *						
	5	−.05	.30 *						
Approach/W.	1	.05	.01	.38 *					
	2	.02	.03	.26 *					
	3	.08	.18	.14					
	4	.26 *	.12	.17					
	5	.18	.05	.41 *					
Threshold	1	−.17	.13	.32 *	.13				
	2	−.13	.33 *	.18	.20 *				
	3	.10	.16	.14	.13				
	4	−.06	.09	.30 *	.00				
	5	−.12	.14	.14	.16				
Intensity	1	.15	−.20 *	−.35 *	−.26 *	−.28 *			
	2	.29 *	−.21 *	−.40 *	−.19 *	−.18			
	3	.22 *	−.03	−.28 *	−.12	−.04			
	4	.48 *	−.19 *	−.46 *	.01	−.49 *			
	5	.36 *	−.09	−.33 *	−.27 *	−.36 *			
Mood	1	.06	.08	.29 *	.40 *	−.03	−.25 *		
	2	.06	−.04	.43 *	.33 *	−.03	−.29 *		
	3	−.13	.08	.36 *	.46 *	.01	−.30 *		
	4	.07	−.05	.36 *	.28 *	.17	−.33 *		
	5	.00	.12	.41 *	.38 *	.09	−.30 *		
Distractibility	1	−.05	.13	.17	−.10	−.07	−.22 *	.06	
	2	.02	.07	.22 *	.18	.02	−.19 *	.09	
	3	−.33 *	−.09	.14	.03	−.08	−.25 *	.14	
	4	−.08	.01	.31 *	.08	.31 *	−.41 *	.21 *	
	5	−.05	.01	.16	.25 *	.06	−.16	.21 *	
Persistence	1	.13	−.17	.14	.08	.00	.04	.04	−.07
	2	−.22 *	−.04	−.03	−.25 *	−.06	.23 *	−.03	−.17
	3	.01	−.02	−.20	−.07	−.06	.25 *	−.18	.00
	4	.03	.00	−.25 *	.00	−.26 *	.28 *	−.07	−.36 *
	5	.17	−.09	−.17	−.08	−.22 *	.39 *	−.13	.10

* Significant at .05 level of confidence for respective N.

of the forty computed. Moreover, every one of the other categories was significantly correlated with intensity in at least three of the five years. These correlations varied in sign, and it will be noted that intensity was positively correlated with activity and persistence and negatively correlated with rhythmicity, adaptability, approach, threshold, and mood. High intensity, therefore, tended to be associated with high levels of activity and persistence, irregularity, low adaptability, negative responses in new situations, low threshold, and negative expressions of mood.

Adaptability had the second highest number of significant correlations with the other eight attributes of temperament, twenty-four of forty. For only four of the categories, rhythmicity, approach, intensity, and mood, were these significant correlations with adaptability present in three or more years. These correlations were positive with regard to mood, rhythmicity, and approach; and negative with regard to intensity. Thus, the adaptable child tended to be one who was regular, approached new situations positively, was generally positive in his expression of mood, and did not frequently exhibit behaviors of high intensity.

Mood was significantly correlated with the other variables on seventeen of forty occasions. With two of the categories, adaptability and intensity, these correlations were significant for three of the five years. The correlation was positive with adaptability and negative with intensity. Thus positive mood could be expected to be accompanied by high adaptability and infrequency of high intensity reactions.

FACTOR ANALYSIS

The overall level of correlation among all the variables was low, and even the highest and most significant correlation coefficients accounted for only small portions of shared variance. However, the presence of clusters of significant correlations, as well as their directional patterns, led us to believe that a factor analysis might be useful for delineating dimensions of function which would contribute to our better understanding both of temperamental organization and of its relation to behavior disturbance. To this end the body of data, comprising nine variables for each of five years, was factor analyzed to ascertain whether meaningful groupings of the categories could be derived statistically.

In a first analysis, Varimax and Oblimax rotations were employed. The Varimax solutions proved to be most useful because they yielded factors that were most consistent from year to year, and were also the most behaviorally meaningful in terms of the attributes which clustered. Three- and four-factor solutions were developed, but the fourth factor was rejected on the latent root criterion. The data in Table 6 are a summary of the principal components rotation of three factors to a Varimax solution in each of the five years. Only loadings of ±.20 or greater are posted in this table.

TABLE 6 / SUMMARY OF FACTOR ANALYSIS—PRINCIPAL
COMPONENTS ROTATION OF THREE FACTORS
TO VARIMAX SOLUTION

Category	Year	Factor A	Factor B	Factor C
Approach/Withdrawal	1	.67	——	−.20
	2	.42	——	−.19
	3	.59	——	——
	4	——	.25	.44
	5	.71	——	——
Mood	1	.61	——	——
	2	.77	——	——
	3	.74	——	——
	4	.46	.29	.27
	5	.62	.22	——
Adaptability	1	.57	.33	−.32
	2	.62	.29	——
	3	.34	.32	−.42
	4	.52	.56	——
	5	.54	.21	.34
Intensity	1	−.41	−.32	——
	2	−.45	−.28	.33
	3	−.35	——	.37
	4	−.71	−.23	.40
	5	−.35	−.77	——
Rhythmicity	1	——	.22	.33
	2	——	.64	——
	3	——	.71	——
	4	——	.71	——
	5	——	——	.75
Threshold	1	——	.76	——
	2	——	.49	——
	3	——	.27	——
	4	.59	.06	——
	5	——	.37	——
Activity	1	——	−.27	——
	2	——	−.22	.38
	3	——	——	.73
	4	——	−.24	.76
	5	——	−.51	——
Distractibility	1	——	——	.61
	2	.22	——	——
	3	——	——	.46
	4	.58	——	——
	5	.33	——	——
Persistence	1	——	——	−.21
	2	——	——	.64
	3	−.25	——	——
	4	−.45	——	——
	5	——	−.46	——

Factor A, which included heaviest weightings for mood, intensity,
approach/withdrawal and adaptability, was selected for further utilization because it met criteria of relative consistency over the five-year
period. The weights of the four categories comprising Factor A are +6,
−4, +5, and +5 respectively. These weights were computed for each
category by summing the squares of the correlations for each of the five
years with Factor A, dividing by 5, and then taking the square root of

FIGURE C

Distribution of cases on Factor A
for years 1–5 (N = 112).

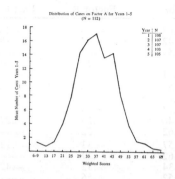

FIGURE D

Mean scores of three subgroups for
Factor A for years 1–5.

the result. Based on these computations, proportional unit weights were
then assigned to each of the four temperamental categories. Thus, a child
who is "Low" in Factor A would be generally positive in mood, mild
in intensity, approaching, and adaptive.

The distribution of Factor A for years one to five for the total
longitudinal sample is depicted in Figure C. The normal character of
the distribution curve is evident.

The mean values for Factor A in the clinical groups with active
and passive symptoms and in the nonclinical group are compared in
Figure D. It will be noted that over the five-year period, despite some
initial overlapping, both clinical groups came to be markedly deviant
toward the side of the scales reflecting negativity of mood, marked
intensity, and tendency to withdraw and to be nonadaptive.

Parametric analysis serves to confirm this impression derived from
the graphic comparison of the two clinical groups and the nonclinical
group. The years at which differences in weighted scores for Factor A
were sufficiently large to reach acceptable levels of significance are
summarized in Table 7.

As may be seen from the table, significant differences for Factor
A between the nonclinical group and the total clinical group with active
symptoms obtained at years three, four, and five, and between the non-

TABLE 7 / SIGNIFICANT t TESTS—FACTOR A

a) Total active (N = 34) versus nonclinical (N = 66)

Year 3	$t = 1.96$	$p < .05$
Year 4	$t = 3.10$	$p < .01$
Year 5	$t = 2.63$	$p < .01$

b) Passive (N = 8) versus nonclinical (N = 66)

Year 4	$t = 2.43$	$p < .05$
Year 5	$t = 2.62$	$p < .01$

clinical group and the clinical group with passive symptoms at years four and five. In both clinical groups the size of the differences tended to increase as the children grew older.

CASES OF EARLY ONSET

Up to this point we have been considering the clinical groups as though they were internally homogeneous. This, however, is clearly not the case. Reference to Table 2 in Chapter 3 indicates that one important feature that differentiated the children in the clinical case group was the age at onset of the behavioral disturbance. A considerable body of data [4, 5] suggests that disorders of early onset are more clearly associated with organismic variables than are those which emerge later in the life course. For this reason it was anticipated that temperamental relations to the development of behavioral disturbance would be most dramatically notable in the children with early onset of behavior disorders. Because of the number of available cases, such an analysis had to be restricted to a consideration of the children with active symptoms of behavioral disturbance.

As may be seen from the data presented in Figure E, in which the children who developed active symptoms of disturbance before the fifth year of age are compared with the nonclinical sample, the previously noted differences in temperamental traits are sustained and magnified. For each of the nine characteristics of temperament and for Factor A, this group of children deviated in temperament in the direction characteristic of greater adaptational difficulty in at least four of the five years. These children with early onset of behavioral disorder were more active than the nonclinical cases in each year. They were markedly more irregular in four of the five years. Adaptability to demands for change in previously established patterns or to new demands and experiences was strikingly less manifest in all five years. The group tended more frequently to withdraw than to approach new opportunities for experience in four of the five years. Threshold was in general lower and intensity of response higher than in the nonclinical cases. In four of the five years, mood deviated to the negative side. Distractibility was more manifest in four of the five years, and persistence was higher than in the nonclinical cases in each year. Perhaps the clearest distinction between the children who developed active symptoms of behavioral disturbance before the fifth year of life and the nonclinical group may be seen through a consideration of Factor A. This factor, as will be recalled, is most heavily weighted for the variables of mood, intensity, approach/withdrawal, and adaptability. In every one of the five years, the children with active clinical disturbances who had come to notice early in life were deviant from the nonclinical group for this factor in a nonadaptive direction. Starting with a small amount of deviance in the first two years, the group

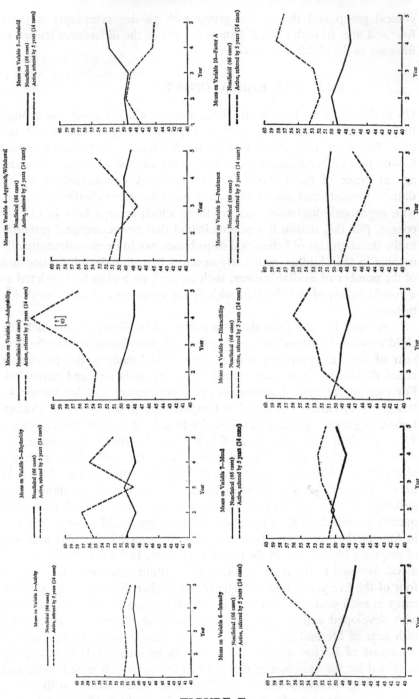

FIGURE E

Mean scores of two subgroups (nonclinical and clinical with active symptoms referred by 5 years) for the nine categories and Factor A for years 1–5.

became increasingly deviant from the nonclinical cases at successive ages. *in a non adaptive direction*

In addition, when the cases with active symptoms who came to notice before the age of five years are compared with the nonclinical sample by parametric analysis, the results are highly similar to those obtained in the comparison of the whole active group with the nonclinical sample. These data are summarized for each of the temperamental traits in Table 8.

TABLE 8 / SIGNIFICANT t TESTS—ACTIVE BEFORE 5 YEARS (N = 14) VERSUS NONCLINICAL (N = 66)

Activity		None	
Rhythmicity	Year 2	$t = 3.35$	$p < .01$
	Year 4	$t = 2.52$	$p < .05$
Adaptability	Year 3	$t = 2.74$	$p < .01$
	Year 4	$t = 5.48$	$p < .01$
	Year 5	$t = 2.92$	$p < .01$
Approach/withdrawal	Year 5	$t = 2.18$	$p < .05$
Threshold	Year 4	$t = 2.05$	$p < .05$
	Year 5	$t = 2.23$	$p < .05$
Intensity	Year 4	$t = 3.42$	$p < .01$
	Year 5	$t = 5.03$	$p < .01$
Mood		None	
Distractibility	Year 4	$t = 3.08$	$p < .01$
Persistence	Year 5	$t = 2.84$	$p < .01$
Factor A	Year 4	$t = 3.56$	$p < .01$
	Year 5	$t = 3.54$	$p < .01$

It will be noted in this table that the temperamental characteristics of rhythmicity, adaptability, approach/withdrawal, threshold, intensity, distractibility, and persistence, as well as Factor A, are discrepant between the two groups. The discrepancies and the variables involved closely resemble those previously found in the consideration of the total group with active symptoms, but express them more sharply.

SUMMARY

The data thus far presented demonstrate that both before and after the development of symptoms of behavioral disturbance, the clinical groups differ from the nonclinical group in the organization of temperament. They are characterized by an excessive frequency of both high and low activity, irregularity, nonadaptability, intensity, persistence, and distractibility. The clustering of certain of these traits, as reflected factorially, also differs from that of the nonclinical group. However, it must be remembered that these findings only reflect general conditions of increased risk of the development of behavioral disturbance and in no way support the view that a given organization of temperament is in itself directly pathognomonic or pathogenetic. Individual case analyses show clearly that there are children in the nonclinical group who had organizations of temperament highly similar to those of children in the clinical groups. Conversely, certain children in the clinical groups had characteristics of temperament that were identical with those typifying the nonclinical group as a whole. Therefore, to understand the etiology of behavior disorders it is insufficient to refer to temperamental organization alone. Such organization clearly modifies the degree of risk, but does not directly convert risk to reality. To understand this conversion it is necessary to consider the interaction between children with given organizations of temperament and the environment, both broad and intimate, to which they are relating. It is to this task that we shall now direct our attention.

REFERENCES

1. A. Thomas and Others, *Behavioral Individuality in Early Childhood* (New York: New York Univ. Press, 1963).
2. J. Cohen, "Some Statistical Issues in Psychological Research," *Handbook of Clinical Psychology,* ed. B. B. Wolman (New York: McGraw-Hill, Inc., 1965).
3. S. Korn, H. G. Birch, A. Thomas, and Others, "Stability and Change in Temperament over the First Five Years of Life." (A monograph in preparation.)
4. I. Belmont, D. F. Klein, and M. Pollack, "Perceptual Evidence of Central Nervous System Dysfunction in Schizophrenia," *Archives of Gen'l Psychiat.,* 10:395 (1964).
5. H. G. Birch, ed., *Brain Damage in Children: Biological and Social Aspects* (New York: Williams and Wilkins Co., 1964).

6 THE INTERACTION OF TEMPERAMENT AND ENVIRONMENT IN THE DEVELOPMENT OF BEHAVIORAL DISTURBANCE

The next group of six chapters deals with the principal constellations of temperament which have been identified in the children with behavior problems. To assume that the temperamental patterning per se produces the behavioral disturbance would be to repeat the frequent error of identifying a single etiological influence and labeling it as *the cause* of a clinical syndrome. Behavior disorders have multiple causes, and temperament, as such, is a style of functioning, not a behavioral disturbance. For a given temperamental pattern to contribute to the development of a behavioral disturbance, it requires particular kinds of interaction between the child with the temperamental pattern and his effective environment. We shall try to make this clear in the following chapters by considering the development of children with the temperamental features excessively represented in the clinical cases. Some of these children, of course, developed behavior problems. Others, however, characterized by similar temperamental organization, did not do so. In these latter instances, idiosyncracies of temperament merely contributed to define individuality of behavioral style.

A comparative analysis of children with common temperamental constellations, some of whom do and some of whom do not develop behavioral disturbance, provides a basis for the definition of styles of care and rearing and other environmental influences which, when interacting with a given temperamental pattern, serve as pathogenic or positive influences on growth and development.

The temperamental traits and constellations identified by the frequency of their association with the behavior disorders included: 1] a combination of irregularity, nonadaptability, withdrawal responses, and predominantly negative mood of high intensity; 2] a combination of withdrawal and negative responses of low intensity to new situations, followed by slow adaptability; 3] excessive persistence; 4] excessive distractibility; and 5] markedly high or low activity level. Another group of children also found among the clinical cases, though with less frequency than in the total longitudinal sample, showed the characteristics of regularity, adaptability, approach responses, and preponderantly positive mood, all expressed with mild or moderate intensity. They, too, will be considered in this analysis.

While each of the following chapters concerned with the findings of

71

the qualitative analysis will focus on specific issues of temperament, environment, and the interaction of temperament with environment, it is important that a number of general cautions be kept in mind throughout.

TEMPERAMENT

Systematic analysis of the role of temperament in the ontogenesis and evolution of behavioral disturbances requires that these characteristics be dissected and isolated from other attributes of the child's personality. In reality, however, no individual trait exists or manifests itself in isolation from other characteristics of the child. Thus, on the one hand it is necessary to speak of a "highly active child," a "persistent child," a "distractible child," and so on, in order to examine the manifestations of the temperamental traits subsumed under each label and to assess their influence on the developmental process; on the other hand, it is clear that high activity, persistence, distractibility, and every other temperamental attribute may in given children be found in many different combinations with other characteristics. A persistent child may have a high or low activity level, be regular or irregular, mild or intense in his reactions, intelligent or dull. The same possibilities hold true for other temperamental attributes or constellations. Furthermore, an attribute is rarely, if ever, global in its manifestations. To call a child distractible indicates that his responses are *predominantly* but not *universally* of this type. In other words, different children with the same temperamental pattern may show different admixtures both of degree and of kind in the behavioral manifestations of the trait. Finally, temperament represents just one facet of personality and is not a term equivalent with personality. Individual personality structure is composed of a number of components including motivations, goals, and ideals (the *why* of behavior), cognitive competences, skills, and talents (the *what* and *how well* of behavior), in addition to temperament or the stylistic aspect (the *how* of behavior). Thus, the examination of the influence of any given temperamental attribute or constellation on a child's development must also consider the simultaneous operative influences of other temperamental traits, of the degree and selectivity with which the particular attribute manifests itself in different areas of the child's functioning, and of nontemperamental (e.g., motivational and cognitive) components of the child's total personality structure.

ENVIRONMENT

Obviously, the objective surroundings and circumstances with which a child interacts depend, among other things, upon the age of the child and the social class to which he belongs. In our group of young middle-class children, objective conditions of stress such as deprivation, overcrowding, familial disorganization, educational disadvantage, and other conditions of potential stress deriving from want are either extremely rare or totally absent. As a consequence, in the present study sources for stress, influence, and variation in the effective environment derive primarily from intrafamilial factors and from the child's experiences with schools and with peers.

In the period of infancy, the analysis of the environmental factors affecting the children in our study focused on parental attitudes and practices. In the preschool period and early school years, the consideration of parental functioning continued but was supplemented by an examination of other intrafamilial factors and of the influence of peer groups and of the school.

Extra- and intrafamilial factors, of course, do not operate in isolation from each other. Thus, in some cases extrafamilial factors tend to intensify the influence of the parents, whereas in other cases they may modify or attenuate it. In still other instances they produce consequences for a child's development which are different from but harmonious with those influenced by parental functioning. For example, a parent may be fostering negativistic tendencies in a slowly adaptive child by insisting on quick adaptations to various new situations that are either very difficult or impossible for that youngster to make. If the nursery school teacher makes similar demands, the influences encouraging negativistic trends will be intensified. If, on the contrary, she allows the child to adapt at his own pace, the negativistic tendencies may at least in part be modified or attenuated. Thus, in no case can it be assumed that the direction and intensity of a child's reaction to parental influence occurs in isolation or necessarily continues unchanged as the child grows older.

Similarly, the influence of the school, peer groups, or other environmental factors may themselves change over time. Analysis of the anterospective records is required in each case to delineate the nature and consequence of any interaction of the child with environmental factors and to trace the vicissitudes of these interactions and consequences over time.

INTERACTION OF TEMPERAMENT
AND ENVIRONMENT

As a first step, the delineation of the interaction between a child with a given pattern of temperament and his environment has required the consideration of significant temperamental and environmental factors as though they were separate independent entities. In fact and in theory, however, environment and temperament are not completely independent entities. Environment and temperament not only interact, but they also can modify each other. A parent's attitudes toward and practices with a specific child may reflect preexisting, long-standing aspects of the parent's personality structure. But, these attitudes and practices may also be reactive and reflect a response to the temperamental characteristics of the given child. The ease or difficulty of caring for the child, the degree of congeniality of the child's temperament for the parent, the congruence of parental expectations with the behavior of the child, all may influence not only the parent's behavior with the child, but also the form of expression of parental attitudes.

Similarly, environmental influences may profoundly modify the expression of temperament. A child with an initial pattern characterized by frequent negative reactions may shift to a more frequent expression of positive mood if his life experiences are benign and favorable. A very adaptable child who is repeatedly faced with impossible demands and expectations may, after a time, become increasingly less adaptable in his behavior. An older child may learn to modify or control certain temperamental reactions at times when their expression would be undesirable. Thus, a child is not an inert and malleable mass to be shaped at will by the environment. Nor is he a rigid structure whose characteristics are fixed and unchangeable over time.

With these cautions in mind, we can turn our attention to the consideration of the different kinds of interactive processes which occur when children with specific temperamental patterns are exposed to different environmental influences.

7 | DIFFICULT CHILDREN

When the children in the longitudinal study population were still under two years of age, and far in advance of the appearance of any behavioral disturbances among them, one subgroup came to particular attention. These children were variously characterized by their mothers, the interviewers, and all other members of the research team in terms of a series of pejorative labels, ranging from the expression "difficult children" by the more sedate and formal of our colleagues to "mother killers" by the more graphic and less inhibited.

When the behaviors of these children were analyzed, they were found to be characteristically deviant from the overall sample of children with respect to certain attributes of temperament. These attributes included irregularity in biological functions, a predominance of negative (withdrawal) responses to new stimuli, slowness in adapting to changes in environment, a high frequency of expression of negative mood, and a predominance of intense reactions.

It is of great interest that the organization of temperament in this early identified group of so-called difficult children corresponded closely to the temperamental cluster found from later data to characterize a disproportionally high number of the children who developed behavioral disturbances with active symptoms. The temperamental cluster reflects a high weighting on Factor A and is made up of the temperamental attributes of nonadaptability, tendency to withdraw from new stimuli, and predominantly intense reactions of negative quality.

The irregularity in biological functioning of the difficult children may show itself in a variety of ways and is particularly evident in the early months and years of life. These infants sleep irregularly and, in many cases, seem to need less sleep in a twenty-four-hour period than does the average infant of the same age. The child may awaken two or three times a night at unpredictable intervals, and at other times may sleep for as long as five or six hours at a stretch. Such babies do not quickly develop lengthened periods of sleep. It is not at all unusual to find that during the first two or more years of the child's life the parents have been awakened by his crying several times during the night and have not succeeded in getting him to sleep through, no matter what training procedures they have used.

Hunger, too, is expressed irregularly. In early infancy, the baby

75

may take only half an ounce of one feeding and then refuse more, or on another day may take a number of ounces. He may be hungry again within half an hour, or not accept food for five or six hours. Irregularity is characteristic of the child both in the periodicity of feedings and in the quantity of food consumed at each. In most cases, attempts to feed such infants by a self-demand schedule do not result in the emergence of a regular pattern. In addition, the child may develop fads and exhibit a strong preference for a specific food and not accept anything else for a period of time. He may then abruptly shift and refuse the previously preferred food and either exhibit another exclusive food preference or come to accept a wider variety of foods. Hunger frequently continues to occur at irregular intervals, and as the child grows older, he does not conform easily to the family schedule of meals.

Patterns of elimination are also typically irregular. There is considerable variability in the timing, frequency, and size of bowel movements. Often, the only thing that is predictable is irregularity itself. As a result, toilet training procedures which are predicated on a child's regularity and predictability in elimination often do not work.

Frequently, difficult children exhibit withdrawal responses when exposed to every new aspect of the environment. However, there are some children who react negatively only to selected stimuli or sense modalities such as tactile or taste experiences, and not to new people, while others do the opposite. In any event, withdrawal from new demands is especially obvious in early infancy when a constant stream of new experiences impinges on the child. Infants are bathed for the first time, given a succession of new foods which vary in taste and consistency, dressed in different clothing appropriate to age and weather changes, exposed to new people and caretakers, and taken to new places. Thus, the difficult child's predominantly negative responses to new stimuli will be brought into high relief again and again during the first year of his life. He cries when immersed in the bath for the first time; he cries and spits with each new food; he cries at each new visitor to the home; and almost every excursion brings an initial response of withdrawal, clinging, loud protest, or crying.

Slow adaptability to change may manifest itself in different ways at different age periods. In infancy, the baby typically withdraws from the new experience as described above. Eventually he adapts, but only after habituation by frequent and repeated exposure to the stimulus. For example, the difficult infant may kick and scream his first time in the bath, and he may continue to behave this way each time he is placed in the tub for an extended period of time. However, if the child is bathed daily for several weeks, there will be a gradual but noticeable diminution in his negative behavior, and eventually he will show either a quiet acceptance of the bath or a vigorous positive reaction to it with laughing, splashing, and playing. But, he may now frequently protest and cry when he is taken out of the tub. Generally, it is impossible to know at the start whether such a child will eventually develop a liking for any introduced food, since his first response is usually negative. Only after he has been offered a food on a number of occasions and has become familiar with its taste and texture can such a determination be made. Some of these children ultimately come to like most offered foods and develop a wide range of diet.

The difficult child typically follows this pattern of very slow adaptability in most new situations and reveals a need for many familiarizing exposures to new experiences before he can make a positive adaptation. If given an opportunity to experience the new without pressure for an immediate positive response, such children will in time adapt. The stranger becomes a familiar person, liked or not as the case may be; the new bed is taken for granted; riding in an automobile and going to public places all become an accepted part of the daily routine. However, if the child is not given regular and repeated exposures, and the given novel experience is repeated only intermittently, often after a long gap of time, the child will tend to display his original withdrawal response on each new exposure.

These difficult children are not truly nonadaptive, they are slowly adaptive. Once they have made their adjustment, their responsiveness to a situation may often be indistinguishable from that of children who had adapted quickly. Thus, during periods in life when few new exposures occur, the child's routine behavior and temperament may seem to have changed. This may happen first during the second or third years of life. However, the change is more apparent than real. Once a new set of demands occurs, such as attendance at nursery school or birthday parties or exposure to a wider range of travel experiences than before, the child's typically slow adaptability again becomes manifest. After the child has learned to adapt to the school experience in general, he may display his typical negative response only for a short time at the beginning of the new school year or when there is a change in schools or in teaching personnel. However, when he is confronted by the next new set of social demands, the child once again may well demonstrate his initial avoidance tendency. He hesitates to engage in organized recreational activities or has difficulty each time a new demand for learning is made. This latter reaction can be so marked that a very bright child may be initially misjudged by the teacher as slow to learn and academically misplaced, although he will in most cases eventually come to demonstrate his high learning capacity after repeated exposures to the new learning demand have permitted it to become familiar.

The predominance of negative mood means that the difficult infants cry more than they laugh and that as toddlers they fuss more easily than they express pleasure. Naturally, the frequency of negative mood is more evident at times when the child is experiencing new situations and new demands. At such times, the negative mood is often the most striking aspect of the difficult child's withdrawal response to the new.

The final characteristic included in the cluster of temperamental traits that typifies the difficult child is the predominance of intense reactions. These are the children who shriek more frequently than they whine, who give belly laughs more often than they gently smile. Such a three-year-old will express his disappointment not with a whimper, but a bang. Frustration characteristically produces a violent tantrum. If, for example, such an infant has adapted positively to the bath, he may cry, scream, and kick if he is removed from the tub before he has had an opportunity to play in the water. Or, when he is two years old and is pressed to go outdoors at a time when he is engaged in a favorite indoor activity, he may react with a tantrum. Moreover, when he is started back to the house from his outdoor excursion, an equally violent tantrum may ensue. Pleasure is also expressed loudly, often with jumping, clapping, and running about.

The intense reactions of these children are not necessarily an accurate index of the importance to them of the activity which evokes them or toward which they are expressed. Their reactions tend to have an "all or nothing" quality, with little modulation, so that most negative responses are intensely negative, and most positive responses are expressed with great enthusiasm; difficult children seldom express merely mild enthusiasm. As a result, indices other than intensity of response must be used to determine the importance of an experience. For example, such a child will tend to cry loudly when he is hurt whether he has a minor scratch or a deep and painful gash; the number of decibels in his cry do not differentiate one wound from another. He may fuss as intensely when he makes a spelling mistake in a minor bit of homework as he may when he makes an error in an extremely important project in which he is engaged. When frustrated, such children may destroy whatever they are working on whether it be a minor construction with tinker toys or a complicated model which has been worked on for several weeks.

Children with the cluster of temperamental characteristics typifying difficult children comprised approximately 4 per cent (four children) of the nonclinical sample, but made up 23 per cent (ten cases) of the behavior problem group. It should be noted that the difficult children were identified as behavior problem cases not on the basis of their temperamental attributes, but only when clear-cut behavioral symptomatology had developed. It is of interest that approximately 70 per cent of the temperamentally difficult children developed behavior problems, and only 30 per cent did not. The children in this latter group were able to adapt, albeit slowly, to successive demands for normal socialization as they grew older, and learned to behave in ways that were consonant with those of their families, their schools, and their peer groups. Once they had learned the rules, so to speak, they functioned well and consistently. The fact that they also functioned energetically because of their tendencies to exhibit high intensity levels often became an asset in their positive interactions with the environment.

It is necessary at this point to consider the characteristics of the parents of these difficult infants. Since in many of our families there were two-, three-, or four-child sibships, it was possible for us to examine the interaction of such parents with the difficult child under study as well as their interaction with their other offspring. The difficult child occupied no set ordinal position, and the number of times he was the first, second, third, or fourth child in the family was no greater than would have been expected by chance. In addition, the siblings showed a wide variety of temperamental characteristics, and no clear-cut correlation of temperament between the difficult children and their siblings was evident.

Examination of the characteristics of the parents who had a difficult child revealed that they did not differ from those of the parent group as a whole with regard to their approach to child care. Also, there appeared to be no special attitude with which these parents had greeted the conception or the birth of the difficult child that differed significantly from that which they manifested toward their other children. Nor did the attitudes with which these parents approached the early care of their several infants suggest any systematic difference. However, as the difficult infant grew older, parental attitudes that were unfavorable for the child's healthy development did arise in a number of cases, and these appeared to be reactive to the special problems in coping with and caring for the child.

Nurturing a difficult child placed very special demands on parents and acted as a stress for them. In each case, the parental reaction depended on a number of factors, but as difficulties multiplied, parents generally sought explanations that would give them some rational understanding of the problems and provide a basis for modified practices that they hoped would bring better results. A frequent tendency in this parent group was to seek explanations based on psychodynamic theories that try to account for a baby's behavior in terms of the mother's attitudes. In these theories, a loving and accepting mother should have a happy and contented child,[1] from which it follows that an unconscious maternal attitude of rejection could be the only explanation for a difficult screaming child. As a result of reliance on these theories it was not unusual for the mother of a difficult infant who screamed frequently and who made all routines a crisis, to develop self-doubts and feelings of guilt, anxiety, and helplessness unless she was unusually confident in her adequacy as a woman and a mother.

In attempting to eliminate her infant's frequent periods of loud crying, one mother with such feelings of guilt and helplessness redoubled her efforts to help him—walked him at night, spent long periods of time with him, and responded to his needs as soon as they were expressed. The father reinforced her feelings of ineptitude and guilt by articulating the thesis of her sole responsibility for the child's behavior. The mother's attempts to quiet the child whenever he cried appeared at first to make the youngster happy and serene. However, such "happiness" lasted only as long as the mother continued to respond immediately to the child's demands. Once she failed to do so, the child's loud protests and slowness to adapt to demands made upon him made it clear that the mother's previous efforts had not served any constructive purpose. Rather, they had reinforced and perpetuated the child's negative and intense reactions by rewarding them each time they occurred.

Another mother, who always knew she "could never do anything right," became convinced that her first easy baby was an accident and that the second one, a difficult child, really reflected her ineptness. By contrast, competitive parents became determined that no child was going to rule the roost entirely and converted the facts of the child's behavior into a motivational issue. They responded to the child's irregularity, negative mood, and intensity as if this were a deliberate effort on the part of the infant to make life difficult for them. His failure to fall asleep promptly when tucked into bed was seen as calculated defiance. His shifts in food preference and his screaming when dressed to be taken outdoors were regarded not as negative behavior, but as negativistic behavior specifically directed against the plans and desires of the parents. When the parents responded by insisting on compliance with all their demands, the child's intense negative responses were heightened. A chain reaction then began in which the parents' responses to the difficulties of daily handling intensified the behavioral characteristics of the child that had initially made his care difficult. And, as the child grew older, the parents' demands for swift compliance and quick adaptation to new situations and new endeavors led the child to develop the very defiance and negativism that he was incorrectly assumed to show in early childhood. In other instances, parental inconsistency in handling a difficult child resulted in patience with some aspects of his behavior, coercion with others, and a failure to reexpose the child to new stimuli so that he could become familiar with them and adapt.

No parent was homogeneous in either his attitudes or practices. In other words, in different situations and with different children, varying parental functioning was evident. Thus, the attitudes and practices of each parent described above did not represent his expression of parenthood to all his children, but had come to be the specific manner in which he related to the difficult child in the family. For another thing, parents frequently showed differential attitudes toward the difficult child with regard to varied aspects of interaction and would handle different aspects of the child's daily care in quite different manners. For example, one set of parents tangled with their daughter over her going to bed, her choice of clothing, and her putting dirty clothes in the hamper. These demands on the child were made loudly, angrily, and inconsistently. On the other hand, the parents had no difficulty in getting the child to follow safety rules. To explain their calm, firm, and consistent approach in this area they said, "You can't let her pick up sharp knives. There's nothing to do about it except make sure each time it happened that she was held back or the object was taken away. There was no need to make a fuss about it. After all, how can she know how dangerous it was?"

Another parent turned a child's hesitation to attend social functions into a power struggle but, on the other hand, was quite patient and accepting of the youngster's reluctance to try a new food. As a result, the child gradually learned the rule that he must taste, but need not finish, new foods, and that he could eat as much or as little as he wished. This allowed for pleasant family mealtimes. By contrast, the suboptimal parental handling of social experiences led to a period of intense parental rage and wild weeping by the child before every outing.

Thus, the parent of a difficult child can show combinations of attitudes and practices including calm strictness, permissiveness, punitiveness, peremptoriness, dislike of some of the child's behavior and admiration of others, in addition to admixtures of guilt and resentment. No global categorization does full justice to the wide range of feelings and handling that may be present.

Not all parents of difficult children developed methods of handling that were inappropriate for this type of child. Some parents were able to maintain consistent approaches based on objectivity toward the child's pattern of reactivity. Thus, one set of parents spelled each other at wearying times with the mother going off to visit friends while the father stayed home to take care of the youngster and listen to his screaming. Similarly, the parents frequently alternated in taking their son on excursions and expeditions in which tantrum behavior could be anticipated. Some of these parents who handled their children effectively had their moments of self-doubt when they were almost sure the child's behavior was really all their own fault, or when fatigue became overwhelming and they wondered how long their situation was to go on. But as time passed, the rewards of their firm and consistent approach became apparent. Adaptation often did occur and, even though it had been slow in coming, the final product was clearly positive. The family became a smoothly functioning unit in which the basic routine behaviors were taken for granted. Then, when the next set of new demands confronted the youngster, these parents were able once more to set about the task of seeing to it that the child moved gradually and repeatedly into his new experiences and was given the opportunity to make, in his own stormy and slow way, a new set of adaptations.

When a difficult child became a behavior problem, there was a wide range of specific presenting disorders. The areas of malfunctioning involved eating, sleeping, elimination, peer relationships, school, or problems in relation to siblings and parents. One child developed excessive fears or phobias, and another showed learning difficulties. Still others showed symptoms of stealing, lying, or rituals of speech and action. There was also a great variety in the types of symptoms relating to general attitudes. One child was defiant, another ignored demands and requests, and others appeared excessively concerned with pleasing or displeasing adults or peers. The actual areas in which symptoms developed, in general, depended upon the specific features of the parent-child interaction. Thus, for example, when the parents succeeded in introducing a child gradually to new social groups and situations, the youngster began to withdraw and hesitate less and less intensely when beginning each school year, when entering a new social group, or when taking on new subject matter or new methods of work. In contrast, the child who did not have the benefit of such appropriate opportunities for gradual adaptation became very tense at the beginning of each school year, avoided most social situations, and perhaps showed such inhibition that learning difficulties and social isolation resulted.

The differences in the developmental courses of difficult children which result from differences in parent-child interactions are illustrated by the contrasting behavioral courses of two of the study children. Both youngsters, one a girl and the other a boy, showed similar characteristics of behavioral functioning in the early years of life, with irregular sleep patterns, constipation and painful evacuations at times, slow acceptance of new foods, prolonged adjustment periods to new routines, and frequent and loud periods of crying. Adaptation to nursery school in the fourth year was also a problem for both children. Parental attitudes and practices, however, differed greatly. The girl's father was usually angry with her. In speaking of her, he gave the impression of disliking the youngster and was punitive and spent little or no recreational time with her. The mother was more concerned for the child, more understanding, and more permissive, but quite inconsistent. There was only one area in which there was firm but quiet parental consistency, namely, with regard to safety rules. The boy's parents, on the other hand, were unusually tolerant and consistent. The child's lengthy adjustment periods were accepted calmly; his strident altercations with his younger siblings were dealt with good-humoredly. The parents waited out his negative moods without getting angry. They tended to be very permissive, but set safety limits and consistently pointed out the needs and rights of his peers at play.

By the age of five and a half years, these two children, whose
initial characteristics had been so similar, showed marked differences
in behavior. The boy's initial difficulties in nursery school had disappeared, he was a constructive member of his class, had a group of
friends with whom he exchanged visits, and functioned smoothly in
most areas of daily living. The girl, on the other hand, had developed
a number of symptoms of increasing severity. These included explosive
anger, negativism, fear of the dark, encopresis, thumb-sucking, insatiable
demands for toys and sweets, poor peer relationships, and protective
lying. It is of interest that there was no symptomatology or negativism
in the one area where parental practice had been firmly consistent,
i.e., safety rules.

The boy, though his early handling had been difficult for his
parents, was never considered by them to have a behavioral disturbance.
They understood that the youngster's troublesome behavior was the
expression of his own characteristics. With this constructive parental
approach, these troublesome items of behavior did not become trans-
formed into symptoms of a behavior disorder. The girl, in contrast,
suffered the consequences of parental functioning which was excessively
stressful for a child with her temperamental attributes and developed a
neurotic behavior disorder (Case 27).

Jimmy is another example of a difficult child who has not become
a behavior problem. At six months he was not different from the other
difficult children we have described. He lustily rejected most new foods
he was given with kicking, screaming, and the flinging of dishes. He
frequently screamed when he was dressed for an outing and continued
raging until he was finally outdoors. Then, when the carriage was
turned around for the return trip, the screaming would start again.
Most new visitors were greeted with a screaming tantrum. It usually
took at least several weeks for a change in feeding or other routine to
be accomplished. Nevertheless, ten-year-old Jimmy was a delightful
child. He had many friends and was a good athlete and a good student.
He was thoughtful and considerate, and exuberant in his enthusiasms
and his humor. Despite these facts, each new experience was difficult
for Jimmy. He almost always attempted to avoid anything new, but
each time was either persuaded or firmly urged by his parents to try
it out, given the promise that after he had been in the situation half
a dozen times he might then give it up if he wished. Yet, once he
had participated to this extent in a new recreation group, in a music
lesson, or in learning to ice-skate, his initial withdrawal gave way to
vigorous enjoyment. His companions and mentors tended to forget the
first difficult period because it became overshadowed in an overall
sense by the lengthier periods of positive adaptation. Routines at home
went smoothly. The parents remembered, but Jimmy did not, the fact
that each routine had been established only after considerable parental

persistence and quiet insistence on what must be done. Homework had been done haphazardly in the earlier grades. The parents then established a firm and unvarying rule of no television during the week and gave him a specific time, place, and set of conditions for doing his homework. The initial tantrums when these rules were applied gradually gave way to compliance, and the youngster gave his full attention to mastering the work. There was still periodic distress when new subject material was introduced, and Jimmy would become absolutely certain that he would never learn it. During these periods the child would slam his way in and out of rooms and assure his family that he was the dumbest boy in the class. The parents laughed through such sessions, knowing that these would soon be displaced, as they were but a minor aspect in the child's eventual good adaptation. In other families, these beginning manifestations of self-doubt and self-depreciation by a difficult child were not handled in a manner appropriate for this type of youngster and led to the development of a behavior disorder. Jimmy, on the other hand, is finally learning that he dreads the new, but that the sooner he gets started, dread and all, the sooner it will become the familiar, the old, the comfortable, and the enjoyable. Jimmy started out as much a difficult child as others who developed moderate or severe behavior problems. The difference in the final outcome lay in the use Jimmy's parents made of the child's ability to adapt once he was shown the route to achieve the desired final outcome.

It is true that of all the temperamental patterns it is usually the one characterizing the difficult children that makes the greatest demands on the parents for effective functioning. At the same time, it is also true that, given an optimally appropriate style of parental care, the difficult child will have the chance to develop along a healthy course.

REFERENCE

1. L. J. Saul and S. E. Pulver, "The Concept of Emotional Maturity," *Int'l. Jour. Psychiat.*, 2:446 (1966).

8 | EASY CHILDREN

In our analysis of the relation of temperament to the development of behavior disorders, we were struck by the presence of a group of children among the clinical cases whose temperamental organization was such that it usually made their early care remarkably easy. These children were preponderantly positive in mood, highly regular, low or mild in the intensity of their reactions, rapidly adaptable, and unusually positive in their approaches to new situations. Indeed, they were children who, not infrequently, contributed to the mother's sense of well-being and to her conviction that she was an effective, skillful, and "good" parent. The more objective and experienced mothers sighed gratefully and recognized that they were fortunate to have an "easy" baby.

Most of these easy children did not develop behavior problems. In contrast to the difficult children described in the previous chapter, they contributed only a small number of cases to the clinical sample, in relation to their total number in our longitudinal study sample. Before considering the factors involved in the development of behavioral disturbance in the easy children, it is pertinent to outline their characteristic patterns of behavior.

During infancy, the child's biological rhythmicity shows up in the regular timing of his naps and his periods of wakefulness, hunger, eating, and elimination. It is possible for caretakers to plan the day's schedule with full confidence that the baby, unless ill, will do the same things at about the same time every day. Such infants tend to have regularity of appetite, and one knows the time of day at which they will take large feedings and the time at which they will take small feedings. Such a child is a perfect candidate for self-demand feeding since he will settle spontaneously into a schedule of crying with hunger at regular times. As he grows older and is shifted to a pattern of three meals a day, regularity continues to characterize his appetite. One can predict from the start how many bowel movements an easy child will have each day and just when they will occur, and toilet training generally tends to occur smoothly. Knowledge of the time when a bowel movement is likely makes it possible to place the youngster on the toilet seat at the time of regular elimination and thus helps him to develop an association between bowel movement and the toilet quickly.

Positive approaching responses to new stimuli are the rule with the easy child. Most new foods are accepted from the beginning, and changes in foods, the place of the feeding, or the person feeding the child make little or no difference. His first tub bath is usually a source of evident pleasure. The child can be left with new people, dressed in different clothing, taken to new places, and these events will go smoothly and pleasantly for all concerned. This is the kind of baby who, when wheeled in the carriage, smiles and babbles to the strangers who look in at him. At three or four, he can be counted upon to smile and bring his own greeting such as "See my new shoes" when he goes visiting. The first day in nursery school goes like a dream with the child ready to start new activities and eager to move into the new situation.

The rapid adaptability of such youngsters means that family plans can proceed without concern lest the child behave badly. He will adapt easily to a new home, a change in feeding and sleep routines, a new way of life. It requires only a few exposures before this youngster is behaving as if there had been no changes and his current activities had been going on since birth.

The predominance of positive mood means that the child smiles and laughs considerably more than he cries. Indeed, it frequently is said of such a child that he never cries unless he is hungry or sleepy. Nevertheless, the intensity of these children's moods may vary. Pleasure may be shown by a smile or a belly laugh. One can be sure, however, that if this type of child cries, there is indeed something amiss. Understandably, these children generally evoke pleasant responses in others and, as a result of the gentle handling and genuine affection they often inspire, they experience the world as a very warm, accepting, and happy place. As they grow older, these youngsters tend always to find something good, even in disappointing situations. The postponement of a plan may not only be taken good-naturedly, but the child may even be a Dr. Pangloss, who finds some reason why it may be better in the end that things worked out the way they did. This is a child who comforts another youngster who is sobbing with disappointment.

Why then should behavior problems ever appear in any of the children in this group? In the first place, traumatic events of a fortuitous nature may occur which cause fears, anxieties, and subsequent problem development. Thus, a succession of deaths of people who are of importance in the child's life or a series of family illnesses and dislocations may occur. In addition, even the easy child's adaptive capacity may be overtaxed by extreme and persistent inconsistency and vacillation in care and in the inappropriateness of the demands or expectations made of him by some important and influential adult figure in his life.

Secondly, and interestingly, a cause of behavioral difficulties in easy children can derive from their very virtues, particularly their high degree of adaptability. The children easily develop the behavioral patterns that are taught them at home. They mirror the rules, regulations, mores, and manners of their parents, sometimes exaggerated to the point of caricature. At times, however, the expectations of the peer, educational, or recreational group in which the child spends his time outside of the home may conflict with the parental mores, standards, and behavior patterns that the child has assimilated. If the conflict is not too severe, the easy child can usually develop flexible adaptive responses so that his functioning in different environments and with different people is appropriate to each. However, if the contradiction between parental and extrafamilial standards of acceptable behavior is extreme and acute, and if the parents insist upon their style, it may be impossible for the child, no matter how adaptable he is, to develop separate behavior patterns that will obviate the negative effects of the conflicting expectations of his family and the outside world. Once unresolvable dissonance between the standards of behavior within and without the home arises, the subsequent features of the child-environment interaction may intensify the child's difficulties.

Commonly, the child who has learned a pattern of functioning at home which meets with disapproval from peers, teachers, or both, finds himself the object of unexpected and bewildering criticism, punishment, teasing, or ridicule. To protect himself, he may engage in various defensive maneuvers. He may remain his old self within his home or in specialized environments which permit his accustomed way of acting to be honored and welcome, but outside these areas he may withdraw or become aggressive. His predominantly positive mood may give way to unhappiness, fussiness, and tantrums. With increasing experience that new situations and new settings end in unhappiness, he may now begin to avoid such situations or other new demands or endeavors. Thus, despite good intelligence, he may become an educational problem, and despite good coordination become a spectator rather than an active participant in sports.

Identification of the parental demands and expectations that lead to socially inappropriate behavior in the child is the key to understanding the origin of such behavior problems in these easily adaptable children. The child's initial behavior pattern, before defenses arise, gives clear clues to the type of behavioral organization that was considered appropriate by the parent. To understand the child's behavior one must then understand the values of the parents and the ways in which these parents approach child training, remembering that in this type of case it is not conflict between the parent and child that underlies problem development, but rather conflict between the parent-child unit on the one hand and the expectations of the wider environment on the other hand.

In many cases, the parent's awareness of the behavior problem may not give a very clear indication of its origin. For example, the parents of four-year-old Hal (Case 9) worried because he let the other children take his toys, did not defend himself but, instead, came home crying. This behavior represented qualities in their son of which his parents did not approve and never had approved. The basic issue, however, was that the other children as a group ganged up on Hal because of his inappropriately formal manners and his habit of asking with meticulous politeness to share their toys; they saw him as a strange creature. Hal's formalistic manners actually were the direct reflection of the standards and approaches imposed by his parents, who were not aware that his politeness would cause him to become the target of teasing. They considered the other children badly brought up but, even so, they wanted their son to be manly and capable of standing up for his rights.

Another child, Isobel (Case 32), who presented with a learning difficulty in second grade, was of concern to her parents because they honored education highly and knew the youngster to be above average in intelligence. On the surface it appeared that the child had not adapted, despite her intellectual ability, to their academic standards. However, Isobel's learning difficulty stemmed from her unwillingness to take instruction, and this, in turn, derived from the parental focus on uniqueness, the right of each person to be individual. They encouraged self-expression in the child, and simultaneously she developed a disregard for rules in play with peer groups and in learning situations in school. When engaged in dramatic play, Isobel was outstanding in her creative imagination and no problems arose. When in the classroom, however, she did not consider the group directions to be her concern and expected individual instruction. The net result was failure to build an educational base because the environment simply had no provision for the child who refused to avail herself of group instruction and required, no matter how pleasantly, the teacher's entire attention.

A sample history of such a child further clarifies these issues. Eight-year-old Stuart (Case 35) was in the first quarter of third grade when his mother was called to school for an interview with his teacher. Stuart was showing behavior that his second grade teacher previously had found annoying. By this time he had become a disruptive influence in the class. The youngster was in the habit of making loud personal remarks during class sessions or recreational periods. These remarks were either very perceptive and frequently exposed an individual's weak spot, or were simply personal and inappropriate when directed to an adult, though they might have been acceptable if addressed to a child. In general, Stuart's remarks precipitated merriment and laughter, but commonly this was in the middle of a lesson and often it was directed toward the classroom teacher, making it difficult for her to maintain class discipline. Both in school and at home it was noted that his friendships were usually short-lived, and both teacher and mother ascribed this to his habit of making remarks which discomforted his playmates. A second problem was the child's failure to learn at a level commensurate with his intellectual capacity. He did shine in learning situations which involved discussion. Here he had many good ideas that showed evidence of logical thinking, retentive memory, and good conceptualization. However, once left on his own to deal with subject matter in the absence of a social situation, Stuart began to take shortcuts and skim through his lessons. This resulted in gaps in his knowledge and failure to master the subject material fully. In a sense, one might say that Stuart had to scintillate or bust.

Scrutiny of parental attitudes and behavior revealed that the father and mother both had looked upon Stuart as a delight from the time of his precocious speech development during his second year of life. His comments and questions in his penetrating little boy voice were so often incisive that parents and even strangers would stop to express their amusement. Indeed, even the target of his remarks was often greatly entertained. However, as he grew older, these critical personal remarks lost their "cuteness" and became more and more embarrassing to the recipients. His parents occasionally scolded him for provoking such embarrassment, but at the same time made it clear that it was only the specific remark that was objectionable and not the general habit of making such comments. Indeed, Stuart's tendency to be the *enfant terrible* was encouraged by the parents and made for pleasant table conversation at home when guests were present. Thus, despite the fact that Stuart's parents did not themselves commit social gaucheries, they were quite inadvertently reinforcing the tendencies in behavior which made their son socially objectionable. Furthermore, his positive responses to this parental reinforcement led the child to make cleverness, instead of genuine sensitivity to other people, a way of life. He also began to use this behavior as a poor substitute for realistic dealing with the content of learning material.

The three children, Hal, Stuart, and Isobel, were not able to make the double adaptation, one style for the home and one for outside the home, which many other easy children in the study did. They could not do so because the parental standards were in such sharp conflict with those of the school and peer groups, because parental behavior reinforced the child's behavior so readily, and because the children's behavior outside the home produced such unfavorable consequences for them.

In Hal's case, his parents actively continued to train the child to be formal and polite and reproved him when he failed to act this way, even when his difficulties in nursery school had already begun. Simultaneously, the neighborhood children made a game of mocking and excluding Hal. Once his peer group had established this response pattern, they no longer presented Hal with the easy give and take of child society as a model to which he could relate his own behavior. Aware that his learned responses brought ridicule, Hal was left with the alternatives of fighting or fleeing and chose the latter.

The creative girl who had a learning problem was confronted by the twin factors of continued and reinforced parental disdain for ordinariness and consequent changes in the outside situation (increasing retardation in formal learning) that interfered with its usefulness as a model for new adaptation. By the time the teacher and parents were aware that there was a problem with regard to Isobel's educational foundation, she had fallen so far behind in school work that she no longer could be included in class instruction. The third grade curriculum was now too advanced for the child and she truly required individualized assistance. In order for her to attain an extrafamilial adaptation, it was necessary to plan individual remedial work which would bring her up to the academic level of the group and, simultaneously, for her parents to instruct her that social and educational situations required a degree of conformity.

With Stuart, too, there was continued and active parental reinforcement of the cute remarks and a failure of the outside world to present a clear model for alternative adaptation. Stuart shone sufficiently often in an interpersonal learning situation for this to be quite satisfying. The loss of old friends was offset by the gain of new ones. It was when his teacher and parents finally foresaw that the cumulative effects of his gaps in learning and his shallow friendships would in the future lead to significant and possibly demoralizing results that more appropriate behavior models were established and Stuart was able to adapt successfully.

Another type of undesirable interaction between easy children and their parents involves those situations in which the parent has taught the child a type of behavior which the parent himself later finds annoying or far from ideal. In these cases the problem is not so much that the parent-child unit moves into conflict with the outside environment, but that the parent-child unit appropriate to one age is in conflict with the parent's expectations of the child when he has become several years older.

Nicholas, for example, had no behavioral aberrations, but his mother found it very annoying to be awakened by him early in the morning to start the day. Nicky as an infant quickly developed a regular sleep rhythm and was sleeping through the night by three months of age, but his biological clock for morning awakening remained firmly fixed at 6 A.M. At this hour, he either cried to be fed or, by two years of age, when he had learned to climb out of his crib, came to his mother's bedside, pried open her eyelids and said cheerfully, "Mommy, play with me." Nicky's mother, less than cheerful at that hour, discovered that if she gave her son a bottle of milk and turned on the television set, she would be able to go back to sleep for at least another hour. This became the routine to which Nicky adapted. He also made a firm association between bottle and television set, so that he began to insist on a bottle whenever he watched television. One day, when the child was five years of age, his mother looked at the tableau of Nicky and his two younger siblings stretched out in front of the television set, each with a bottle, and blew up, scolding her oldest child roundly for being such a baby. But, although the mother now tried to discourage the youngster from bottles during the day, she still expressed only the feeblest of protests when Nicky would quietly go to the refrigerator each morning, deftly pour milk from the container into a baby bottle, and keep himself amused without troubling her. Thus, the problem which the mother defined as immaturity and excessive dependence on the bottle, was actually a well-fixated behavior pattern which she herself had taught to the child.

The issue, of course, is not whether the parents initially raised their child properly or improperly. In Nicky's case, his mother could have continued to tolerate the bottle-television scene, or she could have undertaken a quiet and consistent campaign to retrain the youngster. The problem behavior arose when the mother was inconsistent and yelled and punished the child at one time for the same behavior she condoned at other times. From this point on, Nicky's mother was training her son to ignore her admonitions and to push steadily forward with his own preferences. The result was that the child no longer had a clear basis upon which to judge the acceptability and nonacceptability of a behavior since the frequency of his mother's fussing was determined more by the stresses of her daily life than by what he did. His pattern of easy adaptability was still operative, but the adaptation was to inconsistent and unpredictable maternal demands.

These different examples make it clear that no temperamental pattern as such guarantees a child against the possibility of developing a behavior disorder. Even the easy children, who generally did well in the widest variety of life situations and demands, could, under special circumstances, find themselves vulnerable to adverse influences because of their quick adaptability. In these instances, then, a temperamental asset may be converted into a functional liability.

9

CHILDREN WHO ARE
SLOW TO WARM UP

It will be recalled from Chapter 5 that the clinical cases with passive symptoms tended as a group in infancy and the preschool years to show low activity level, initial withdrawal responses, slow adaptability, low intensity of reactions, and a relatively higher frequency of negative mood responses than did the nonclinical cases. Nevertheless, a number of children in our longitudinal study who did not develop behavior problems also exhibited this constellation of temperamental attributes. Taken as a whole, children with this temperamental pattern respond to a new food offered in early infancy by letting it remain in an open mouth and gradually dribble out. A first contact with strangers usually evokes a turning away or clinging to the mother, sometimes accompanied by mild fussing. Their first few weeks in nursery school are typically spent on the sidelines, quietly watching the activity of the group. In elementary school, a new academic subject may evoke the announcement, "I don't like it," or, more typically, initial silent nonparticipation. In each circumstance and at each age, if allowed to adapt at their own tempo, many of these children gradually overcome the initial negative response. They then become positively involved and finally are indistinguishable in their responses to former strangers, nursery school, or previously new academic subjects from the children whose responses had been positive from the beginning.

Temperamentally, these children have initial withdrawal reactions to new situations and adapt slowly. Their moods are characteristically of mild intensity so that their initial negative reaction is quiet. If and when behavior problems develop, however, there may be a shift to more intense negative expressions. Activity level is usually low or moderate. The appellation "slow to warm up" appears to be an apt if inelegant designation for these children.

These youngsters may vary in other attributes of temperament. They may be easily distracted or not. They may or may not have long attention spans or be particularly persistent. Although these other temperamental characteristics may color their experiences and influence the reactions of those around them, the significant core of their pattern is usually quiet withdrawal from and slow adaptation to the new. The following illustrations are typical of behaviors found with high frequency in children of this temperamental type.

Four-year-old Stanley and his two older sisters were taken on a weekend trip to a seashore area where the family stayed at a motel. The three children were put to bed in the same room, and when the parents opened the adjoining door a half hour later to check on them, the two older children were asleep in their respective beds while Stanley was sitting in the middle of the floor, solemn but not crying. Their attempts to induce him to get back into bed were fruitless. He simply repeated "I don't like that bed." The parents, prepared for this response by similar incidents in other new places, picked him up, tucked him into bed, made soothing noises, sat with him for a bit, and then left. As his mother was on her way out of the room, she heard the child climbing out of bed again. When she asked him his intentions, he said, "Sit on the floor," and was apparently prepared to sit out the night. When he was brought into the parents' bedroom and provided with a bed more closely resembling his crib, he promptly fell asleep.

Harriet, age five, was another child who was slow to warm up. She had attended nursery school for two years, and at the beginning of each year had started off as a silent, wide-eyed watcher. It took several weeks of persistent attention to bring her from the sidelines to her first use of the materials. It was not until the winter that she exhibited in nursery school the carefree, gregarious behavior the parents considered characteristic of her when she played in the playground familiar to her since her baby-carriage days. By the spring of each of her two nursery school years, the teachers reported that she had finally come out of her shell. Once again, in her third year of school, in a kindergarten class, Harriet went through the same progression but, this time, much more quickly. The teacher, therefore, was chagrined and puzzled to find on a day given over to visits from the parents and a performance by the children that Harriet refused to join in the group singing. She spent the entire time sitting next to her mother with her head on her mother's lap. The confrontation with a new situation, albeit within a familiar context, once again made her display her characteristic initial withdrawal reaction.

Stanley and Harriet characteristically moved into new activities slowly, gradually, and steadily, unless they were rushed. If the adults about them tried to push them too quickly, the youngsters retreated, ran out of the room, or ducked behind their mothers' skirts. These children did not have tantrums. Rather, they clung, moved away, or stood by, silently watching. However, it was clear from their later behavior that this initial period of standing by and watching did not constitute unresponsive detachment. On the contrary, they were responsive and alert and gradually incorporated the new into their accustomed environment. In infancy this gradual positive adaptation involved habituation to the new; at older ages it also involved selective decisions and judgments as to long-range involvement with each new situation and person.

The optimum approach of parents and school to the children who are slow to warm up is one which combines patience with a willingness to wait. It assumes that eventually a positive interest in the new activity, new place, or new food will emerge and consequently gives the child an opportunity to reexperience the new situation repeatedly, without pressuring him to act at an early stage. Whether or not this ideal handling is carried out may depend on a number of factors. The parental attitudes and behavior will depend a great deal on the parent's temperament and concepts of what makes for a happy child. A mother who is herself impatient and easily moves rapidly to meet new events may find her youngster quite bewildering. It is easy for such a parent to become impatient with a child who is slow to warm up. She may often feel that the youngster's hesitancy reflects badly on herself as a parent and thus make repeated efforts to change his behavior by urging, coaxing, ordering, or propelling. A battle between mother and child can thus develop. The more the parent pushes the child, the more the child's behavior tends to reflect his discomfort with the new demand. This may appear as a shift from quiet stubbornness to negativism. At other times, he may become truly insecure and develop innumerable tactics for avoiding any or all circumstances that could conceivably put him in the position of having to involve himself in an activity with which he does not yet feel comfortable.

For example, nine-year-old Harry permitted friendships to develop only to a certain point of intimacy and then would unaccountably draw away and isolate himself. He finally explained this behavior when he was invited to stay overnight at a friend's house and remarked that the invitation was his fault because he shouldn't have invited the boy previously for a weekend at his own family's summer place. A host of previous social behaviors of a similar kind suddenly were clarified for the parents. They now remembered the disturbance when Harry was five years of age and, after having begged for and received permission to sleep at a friend's house, had to be brought home at midnight after having apparently developed a stomach upset accompanied by vomiting and crying. Once home, he had quieted down and gone to sleep, and by the next morning was completely recovered. The cause of the illness was unclear. What was clear, however, was that Harry later said that he felt strange sleeping away from home and had successfully avoided all such invitations until age nine. The parents also remembered that Harry always had difficulty falling asleep during the first weeks that they were in their summer quarters, but that after a while he became used to the changed house and was very comfortable. The child apparently was generalizing his specific difficulty in adjusting to sleeping away from home to the point where he began to avoid all friendships that might lead to an exchange of invitations and thus the creation of a condition of risk. Because the parents were themselves highly sociable people, they had opposed Harry's withdrawal by trying to arrange social occasions over the child's protests. These efforts met with little success, because on each occasion a stomachache or episode of vomiting and diarrhea occurred which made it impossible to implement the arrangement.

Some parents become helpless with a youngster who avoids new experiences. Although they do not pressure the child with repeated insistence on participation, they may on the other hand not provide the youngster with the repeated exposures that are necessary if he is to adapt and become comfortable. Thus, when Bobby at age six months let his carrots dribble out of his mouth, his parents immediately decided that he didn't care for them and eliminated this vegetable from his diet. His similar reactions to many new foods were handled likewise, and by the time Bobby was ten years old he ate hamburgers, applesauce, medium-boiled eggs, and very little else. When Bobby, age two, backed away from other children in the playground, the parents felt that there was no reason to expose him to such a noisy place and limited his recreational activities to play with his older brother and his cousin in his own home. When he attended his first birthday party, at age four, he backed into a corner and gazed wide-eyed at all that was going on. Although he showed no active sign of distress, his mother quickly presented his gift to the birthday boy and took Bobby home. The list of such occurrences could go on endlessly, but fortunately certain other experiences happened to be more suitable to the child's temperamental pattern. Thus, despite the fact that his first venture on the tricycle at age four was unsuccessful, the tricycle remained in his bedroom, and several weeks later his parents discovered, much to their surprise, that Bobby had been quietly practicing on it when he was alone. When they brought the tricycle onto the street, they and he discovered that he was an accomplished cyclist who could negotiate curves and sudden stops with great skill and enjoyment. Activities which Bobby found interesting and which he could practice by himself at his own speed did become accomplishments and sources of pleasure. On the other hand, the mastery of those new activities which required his parents to reexpose him a number of times in as nonstressful a way as possible, or those in which the tempo was set by other children, remained outside his ken. Thus, by age ten, he was an excellent swimmer, ice skater, and roller skater, but avoided baseball and other team games. He was an excellent model maker and had collections of rocks and stamps, but would not join the Scouts. Underlying Bobby's avoidance of group participation and his concentration on solo activities was a slow to warm up temperamental pattern supported or reinforced by his parents' helpless response to these temperamental qualities and their failure to intercede appropriately and provide him with the kind of repetitive opportunities he needed to familiarize himself with new endeavors.

On the other hand, in many cases where the parent's handling of such a child has been constructive and enhances the youngster's capacity to make a socially successful adaptation, the exigencies of the larger environment may be such as to put undue pressure on the child. An example of this is seen in the case of Grace.

Ten-year-old Grace developed a phobic reaction to school for which there seemed little reason. Grace was pretty, had many friends, and was one of the top students in her class. The factor which precipitated her reaction seemed to be a shift from the small and individualized setting of her original grade school where every child was known by the principal, to the more impersonal, departmentalized setup of a new school she entered at the fifth-grade level. Children from several other schools were also fed into the new school. Grace thus moved simultaneously to a new school building, a new scholastic setup, a new aggregation of fellow students, and a new level of academic demand.

In going over the history of her earlier development, it turned out that Grace had the typical pattern of a child who was slow to warm up, including an initial withdrawal when started in kindergarten. The parents had forgotten this, since by third grade her initial hesitancy at the beginning of a new term was very minor and was limited to worrying a bit in the week preceding school about what her next teacher would be like.

Neither Grace nor the parents were prepared for the impact of the new school setting in the fifth grade. Here was a situation in which the environmental demands were such that the child, with her temperamental attributes, could not master them. It was only by reassigning her to classes in which there were a number of her former schoolmates, arranging for individualized contacts with her guidance counselor, and bolstering up her academic work with a period of tutoring, which primarily involved giving her a chance to rehearse her recitations ahead of time, that she was able to make a successful adaptation.

A typical sequence of behavior problem development in a child who is slow to warm up can be illustrated by Michael (Case 15). Michael was referred for clinical evaluation at three years nine months of age. His nursery school teacher had recommended psychiatric consultation because of evidence of poor adjustment in the school situation. He showed a lack of participation in group activities which was marked and did not improve as the months went by. In addition, each morning when his mother brought him to school he clung to her and cried when she left.

His mother reported that Michael resisted going for his appointment with the child psychiatrist because he wished to go to nursery school; he had suggested that she keep the appointment for him. On the way to the office he asked her to go into the playroom with him.

He was a pleasant-looking youngster who appeared his stated age. When the examiner first approached him, he put his head in his mother's lap, but then, holding a paper bag of toys he had brought from home, he trailed her as she followed the examiner into the playroom. At the invitation to play with the examiner's toys, he leaned closer to his mother and half buried his head in her lap. As the examiner continued to talk to him, inquiring about his own toys, he took them out of the bag one by one. Approximately five minutes after the interview began, when the examiner attempted to snap the pieces of his manipulative game together, apparently not quite correctly, the child went over to correct her. Through the remaining forty minutes, the child's involvement with the examiner became gradually more active, including some verbal exchanges. As he explained some of the special features of a toy, he moved from his mother's side to the examiner's side, although he intermittently returned to his mother. He then began to answer questions with some elaboration concerning the play equipment at school, school activities, his relations with his friends, and his peer activities with his brother and sister. His verbalization was clear, connected, to the point, and superior in quality.

There was no evidence from the psychiatric evaluation that Michael was basically an insecure child. His behavior in the clinical interview illustrated the temperamental quality of initial withdrawal in new situations with gradual warm-up. In nursery school, however, his behavior had become sufficiently deviant and nonadaptive for him to be considered a behavior problem. Diagnosis was a reactive behavior disorder of moderate degree.

The clinical judgment that his response to a new situation was based on temperamental qualities and not on anxiety was confirmed by an analysis of the anterospective longitudinal data. At age three months, and again at six months, it had been noted that the child initially rejected new foods, especially when the consistency was other than loose or fluid. Gradually he accepted thicker purées and, by age one, table foods, although at first presentation any new food was rejected. At his first bath at age three weeks, he screamed. After that he gradually cried less until by two months he smiled and relaxed in the tub. However, when he was changed from one kind of tub to another at nine months, he resumed screaming before he gradually developed a positive reaction to the new bath.

Similarly, he required many exposures to every new baby-sitter or mother surrogate before he would accept being put to bed or having other routine features of care carried out by someone other than his mother or father. And, the first few times that new procedures such as medication or temperature taking were required, the child responded by crying and fussing.

The first day at nursery school was traumatic. Michael's mother had promised to stay with him, but when they arrived they found that the school policy had been changed, and she was not permitted to remain. He had a kicking, screaming tantrum when his mother left, and during the entire unhappy first week, he clung to her, cried when she left him, and did not participate in any activity. In addition, he returned to dependence at home and demanded servicing that had long since been given up.

After a week, Michael was enrolled in a second nursery school. On the first day he allowed his mother to leave after she had stayed with him for an hour. In the next few weeks, the time his mother was required to stay gradually shortened. During this first period of school, Michael was an onlooker in the classroom, standing quietly apart and watching the other children play. Gradually he moved into the games, welcomed by his classmates, and began participating in their activities. Even while he stood on the sidelines in school, Michael spoke with pleasure of school activities and spent much time duplicating school craftwork at home. In the morning he was dressed and ready for school at least fifteen minutes before it was time to leave, and even requested to go to school in the station wagon.

Then, in November, Michael developed an upper respiratory infection which kept him out of school for a week. On his return to school, his nonparticipating behavior was again in evidence. He began to rejoin the group as the days went by, but then suffered another acute illness which again kept him from school. For the next half year this pattern of brief periods at school interrupted by upper respiratory illnesses continued. There was a setback in independence each time he returned to school, and his lack of participation became more extreme. He began to cling to his mother in the morning and to express unhappiness about having to go to school.

In contrast, during the same period Michael was a regular visitor at the neighborhood playground, with which he had been familiar since babyhood. Here, his parents observed, he joined in play with children of his own age and even approached new children who came to the playground. There was a familiar basic group of children there, and a familiar set of activities in which all participated.

To summarize, the temperamental characteristic of initial withdrawal from new experiences with subsequent slow adaptation, apparent from early infancy, was a major factor in the child's development. The nursery school teacher, who was alarmed at the child's seeming inability to adjust to school, was not aware of this, nor did she consider another and contributing factor, the child's frequent and extended illnesses. Whenever a characteristic behavior pattern of eventual adaptation and participation in school activities was just beginning to assert itself, he unfortunately became ill and suffered a setback in his nursery school adjustment. As long as his initial negative and withdrawal reactions were dominant, eventual good adjustment could make little headway. His mother was sympathetic, but somewhat worried; on the whole her treatment of the child's difficulties was appropriate.

On the basis of the above evaluation of the nature and origins of his behavior problem, both school and parents were advised to take Michael's temperamental quality of initial withdrawal and slow warming up to new situations into account in handling him, but not to assume that the trouble was caused by fearfulness or insecurity. Patience, not psychotherapy, appeared to be in order. The parents and teacher were effective in acting on this recommendation, and the result was good.

During the following year at nursery school, and then in kindergarten and first grade, the same initial withdrawal pattern was manifest. He clung to his mother for the first two and one-half weeks before he left in the morning for his four-year-old nursery group. At first she remained in school throughout the morning with fifteen- to thirty-minute intervals out of the room. Gradually Michael involved himself more in activities and began to visit children in their homes after school without his mother. He began spontaneously and insistently to dress himself, except for shoelaces. By the end of the second month he began to go to school by bus, and the rest of the school year went well.

In kindergarten and first grade there was initial resistance, shyness, and nonparticipation, moving gradually into enthusiasm, relatedness with other children, and good participation. The report on follow-up confirmed the original analysis, that the slow to warm up temperamental constellation was sufficient to account for his difficulties and his recovery from them. It had not been necessary to invoke some other dynamic factor producing anxiety or insecurity to account for his behavioral disturbance.

These cases indicate that successful management of initial withdrawal and nonparticipation responses is dependent, in the first place, upon determining whether the behavior is a direct expression of temperament in a child who is slow to warm up, a reflection of deepseated insecurity, or some combination of these two possibilities. The presumption on a priori theoretical grounds that one or another of these mechanisms is the sole etiological possibility cannot be considered valid and is to be avoided in the interest of responsible diagnosis and management.

10 | PERSISTENCE

In themselves, temperamental attributes are neither good nor bad. Whether a given temperamental trait of a child meets with approval or disapproval, results in praise or criticism, or proves convenient or inconvenient to adults or peers can depend upon its appropriateness to the situations in which it is expressed and upon the degree to which its manifestations correspond to the value judgments of others.

The temperamental quality of persistence is one which illustrates this point well. Few parents are critical if their infant tries persistently to turn over at four months, to sit at six months, to stand at nine months, or to walk at twelve months. On the contrary, they will view this behavior as an asset for the child. But when the same infant fusses persistently to be picked up in the middle of the night or, at two years of age, pokes continuously at electric outlets, the parental estimation of the same temperamental trait is likely to be very different. Instead of praise and approval, there is now annoyance and disapproval. In other words, the response of others to a child's persistence is strongly influenced by the specific activities in which he is persistent, i.e., the selectivity of the attribute.

Even the most persistent of children is not likely to be equally persistent in all situations and activities. One child may be especially persistent in gross motor activities, such as games and acrobatics; another in fine motor-perceptual tasks, such as intricate puzzles; another in social relations, such as imitation of adults, conversation, or social play. Whether persistence contributes positively or negatively to a child's interaction with others will be affected by whether or not the acts selectively persisted in have common positive value for parent and child, teacher and child, peer and child, etc.

As the persistent child grows older, the selectivity in his interests and activities becomes increasingly influential in his development and in the reactions of others to him. On the one hand, a persistent interest in learning to master the printed word and to write his name can be a delight to observe and the basis of great gratification for the child himself. If, on the other hand, the child were to decide that what he needed to make him happy in life was a new bicycle, contrary to his parents' plans or budget, the equivalent persistence now is called

100

nagging, and daily contact with the youngster who never forgets his campaign of persuasion can become a source of parental annoyance. The persevering boy who is learning to read is called studious and declared to have depth of intellect, while the boy persistently campaigning to get his bicycle is considered selfish and inconsiderate—yet both may merely be exhibiting the same temperamental characteristic of persistence.

At still an older age, the selectivity of his interests may play yet a larger part in determining how one evaluates the development of the child. To the extent that he persists in working at athletic endeavors which also interest his friends, carries through to the end any task he undertakes, is responsible and thorough about all his homework, and maintains consistent contact with desirable companions, parents and teachers have every reason to be content. However, when the youngster pursues only special recreational activities and usually refuses to shift to other games at his friends' requests, when he studies only those subjects in which he is interested and with equal persistence ignores the others, and when the friendships about which he is tenacious are with youngsters disapproved of by his parents, then there will indeed be many complaints about his behavior from parents, teachers, and peers.

Whether persistence results in positive or negative interaction with others is determined not only by the selectivity of the child's interests and activities, but often also by his other temperamental characteristics. Of particular importance is the association of persistence with high or mild intensity of reactions, high or low activity level, and distractibility or nondistractibility. The persistent child who is mild in intensity will be quiet in his pursuits, lengthy though they may be. When five years old he can be left quietly in one spot attempting to duplicate a complicated three-dimensional model with an erector set, and when one returns several hours later, the child will have scarcely moved. He has been completely unaware of the passage of time and has cheerfully worked out the problems of construction and built an almost completed model. The highly intense persistent child also may remain in the same spot for five hours working at a project, but each problem that arises will have aroused storms, protests, or even tantrums. If parents and others are tolerant of the stormy expressions of the child as he struggles with the difficulty, he, as well as the mildly expressive persistent youngster, is likely to derive feelings of competence and pleasure from attempting difficult endeavors. However, if the uproar creates annoyance in parent, teacher, or older sibling, the resulting child-environment interaction may become unpleasant on both sides during the course of the activity. When the environment responds to him with such impatience and annoyance, the highly intense and persistent child may experience a host of situations which tell him that difficult endeavors end in unpleasantness; that most people are either uninterested in or even opposed to his activities; and that life is indeed a stormy series of traumatic events. If such a negative child-environment interaction persists and gathers momentum, the predominant tone of the child's behavior may become one of disagreeableness, in which he is as persistent as he is in other things he does. If parents and others in his environment reinforce the negative behavior by their irritation and impatience, this then may become the dominant style and oppositional behavior may even develop as the child persists in doing that which is interdicted and in refusing to do that which is requested.

Nancy is such a child whose temperamental pattern includes both persistence and intensity. When engaged in play that is convenient to those about her and that she has herself selected, her gay and lengthy involvement arouses much pleasure in the onlooker. On the other hand, Nancy is equally persistent about desires that her parents consider inappropriate, and most of the intense commotions at home stem from her insistence on prolonging pleasurable activities that are inconvenient to them. At such times she gives no heed to their statements that the time is wrong, that she has already had several extensions of play, that her father is late for an appointment, and so forth. Unfortunately, the child's storms often bring a reversal of the original parental request for the cessation of an activity, and they consent to give her one more time extension. In so doing, the parents reinforce still further the inappropriate and maladaptive expression of the child's persistence and intensity.

Another temperamental component that can influence the persistent child's functioning is his activity level. The low or moderately active persistent child will sit quietly or move about only slightly when involved in whatever job he has set for himself. Not so the persistent child whose behavior has a high motor component. For him, the appropriateness of time, place, and person is brought into sharp relief and may influence the constructive nature of his persistence. The toddler who explores the children's zoo with great persistence may be a source of enjoyment to those who took him on the outing; an equally persistent exploration of the relative's home to which he has been taken visiting, with insistence on opening all drawers and peeking behind all doors, may be predominantly a source of embarrassment and discomfort to the adults concerned. If such a child begins to romp around in an open field or in an uncrowded playground, it will be harmless fun even though he keeps it up endlessly. However, though his intentions are equally good, should he become involved in active horseplay with an inappropriate person, in a public bus, or during the dinner hour, the effect of his persistent high activity can be of extreme concern since it may produce parental remonstrance, threat, and even reprisal. Yet the very same child at the age of twelve, mowing the lawn or practicing his baseball pitching, may be the most desirable and reliable youngster in the world for that particular occupation.

Donald (Case 28) was a child who showed both persistence and high activity level. He was first observed informally by one of the authors at age four when he, together with a large group of parents and children, was waiting below on the sidewalk for the door of a school auditorium to be opened. Donald was running cheerfully about on the outskirts of the crowd bothering no one. When the door was opened, he ignored his parents' request that he stay with them and dived into the multitude. His progress could be followed up the flight of stairs by the eddy in the wave of people as one after another moved aside, looked down in a puzzled manner, then smiled. When his parents arrived in the auditorium, Donald was in happy and active possession of choice seats for all, announcing their reservation loudly and continuously. Cute and convenient as this had been at age four, by age seven his behavior was virtually the same and was described by his second-grade teacher less happily. It was stated that he failed to follow directions and persistently pursued his own desires instead, getting up and moving about the classroom, disregarding the disruption of teaching that this might occasion.

Incompatible as it may at first seem, the child who is persistent may also be distractible. He may be the kind of child who insists that he can do his homework best while listening to the radio—and he may be right. He may interrupt his work to comment on a conversation going on in the next room, then suddenly remember something that he has forgotten to do, and finally, displaying his usual persistence, return to the unfinished task. One knows that no matter how many distractions occur, such a child will keep returning to the endeavor until he has brought it to completion.

The easily distractible persistent youngster will cheerfully engage in a diversion that interrupts his activity and then happily return to his task. On the other hand, the persistent child who is not so easily distractible becomes very angry at interruptions and finds it literally painful to have his activity interfered with. A demand that he stop what he is doing for a few moments and give a helping hand may be met with screams of outrage. Yet the same youngster may actually be very helpful when his attention is available.

In certain circumstances, each of the styles of functioning described above can become the nucleus of a behavior disorder. For example, if a persistent child's reluctance or refusal to follow orders when he engages in an unswerving pursuit of his own interests is interpreted by the parent as a specific and planned defiance, the parent's demand on the child may become peremptory and insistent. The youngster may then respond by becoming stubborn; the behavior which had been originally identified inaccurately by the parent as motivated defiance may indeed become so as the child tries to prevent himself from being coerced. A parent-child battle of this kind may start over relatively trivial events, such as whether or not the youngster will wear rubbers and raincoat or wash his hands before dinner, or over a host of other minutiae. In such a case the child's persistence becomes focused on carrying through a negativistic response to parental demands rather than on a positive achievement.

Still another youngster may thoroughly bewilder his parents as to which issues are of consequence and which are not since his degree of persistence may be the same in all of them. Helpless parents will respond to the child's requests either immediately, to avoid a siege, or when the child's campaign is well under way. In these cases the child fails to develop a sense of discrimination; he does not learn which desires are worthy of his full efforts because they are of unique importance to him and which ones are passing fancies. If the parents respond primarily to the amount of fussing the child exhibits rather than to the objective value of his requests, the duration and the intensity of the fussing may finally become the basis on which they decide either to accede to or refuse a specific desire. Impatient parents, on the other hand, may assume that all of the child's stated requests are unimportant. Their consistent ignoring of the child's long appeals may cause the youngster to feel rejected. He may easily develop a strong and persistent feeling that his brothers and sisters obtain everything they want as soon as they ask for it, while even if he fusses, his requests are not taken seriously.

Responses to a persistent child will differ in accordance with the parent's temperament and personality organization. While there will be no global parental attitude, it is possible nevertheless to give some guidelines for assessing the contribution the parent makes to the interaction and relationship with the child. Whatever the dominant characteristic of parental handling, one must keep in mind that there will be variations determined by the age of the child, whether the problem interaction is the first or the fiftieth of the day, and whether the parent has strong or mild feelings about the actual behavior in which the child is engaged. One may schematically categorize parental reactions to and functioning with a persistent child as follows:

1] *Parental and School Handling That Is Unlikely to Result in Problem Formation*

These parents have made clear to the child (and themselves) which behaviors are looked upon with favor, which with disfavor, and which will vary in accordance with other circumstances. Such a parent, when dealing with persistent behavior of which she disapproves, for example, a three-year-old persistently throwing sand in the eyes of another child, will quietly and consistently state and repeat the demand for cessation of the activity and eventually, but firmly, remove the child from the scene, disregarding his protests. Another example of appropriate parental handling may occur if the child's persistent behavior is disapproved of only mildly, for example, an eight-year-old youngster talking endlessly to an adult passenger on the train who, while appearing to wish the child would go away, protests to the mother that the child isn't bothering him. The parent merely asks the child to end his conversation soon and tells the passenger that whenever he would like to be relieved of his fellow conversationalist she will be glad to make an issue of it. Such an appropriately reacting parent also learns to anticipate circumstances that will require the child, although engaged in an activity, to withdraw. Thus, a mother will warn a twelve-year-old, "I would suggest you don't start that television program because you must leave in twenty minutes if you are to get to your clarinet lesson on time, and you won't want to stop watching in the middle." Such parental techniques that keep the child from becoming involved in an activity that may have to be terminated abruptly will not stop the persistent child from being persistent, nor will they obviate immediate distress at the time the child is dissuaded from initiating the activity. However, they will prevent the formation of a maladaptive interaction, which can occur when a demand is made that the child immediately stop something in which he is deeply engrossed.

The teacher is also in a key position to preserve and encourage the constructive aspects of persistence in a pupil and to minimize its less convenient manifestations. To do so, it is necessary that she recognize this quality in the child as part of his temperamental organization. Otherwise, she may interpret his difficulty in shifting from one activity to another at her request as uncooperativeness, disobedience, or inattention. In such a case, her resulting impatience with the child may initiate a sequence of interaction that does finally lead to the child's becoming rebellious, negativistic, or anxious. If, on the contrary, the teacher does recognize the child's persistent behavior for what it really is, she can make herself his ally and sympathize with his distress at being asked to terminate an incomplete task. The understanding teacher can then make the necessary explanations to the child and arrange whatever minor changes in scheduling are possible so as to avoid significant disturbance in the persistent child's school functioning.

2] *The Helpless Parent*

One parental reaction to the child whose behavior is characterized by a seemingly endless pursuit of his desires is that of helplessness and abdication of authority. Such a parent may make a feeble and token effort to impose restrictions on the child's behavior. She says to the three-year-old who is throwing sand, "Please stop it. Johnny doesn't like sand in his eyes." Of the youngster making a general nuisance of himself on the train she thinks, "I do wish that child would leave people alone," and about the twelve-year-old television enthusiast she sighs, "I just know he's going to be late for his clarinet lesson again." The parent, for whatever reason, is unable to carry through the established rules and regulations with a persistent child although such a mother might very well be able to deal quite adequately with a nonpersistent, adaptable youngster. The net result of the helpless approach is that the persistent child ignores parental desires or heeds them only insofar as they permit him to mobilize a better organized attack on the attempted restrictions. The child then fails to learn which behaviors are appropriate and which are inappropriate, and may come to find himself in situations in which his persistence is very unwelcome. As a result of subsequent extrusions, scoldings, and comments of opprobrium, the persistent youngster may become a truly pesty child whose motivation is to annoy and inflict his presence in a negative fashion on those who appear to be his enemies.

3] *The Competitive Parent*

This parent regards the child's persistent expression of his desires as a defiance of himself and moves into competition with the youngster, determined to show him who will be the boss. Using the prerogatives of parenthood to establish the structure of behavior that is acceptable, the competitive parent feels it necessary to break the child's will, to force him to recognize who is boss in each unwelcome, lengthy involvement. Although such a child-parent pair will have many areas of positive involvement when the child's persistence is exhibited in an activity of which the parent does approve, it is likely that clashes will be frequent and vigorous when the parents do not approve. Unfortunately, it is also likely that the child will fail to gain any clear understanding of the parent's standards for behavior and may indeed begin to assume that the parent's main motivation is to spoil his (the child's) pleasure. The child's persistence then may deteriorate into whining, lengthy tantrums, demoralization, and a self-concept of unworthiness. In such a case, one may again find the youngster developing into a negativistic or a sullen and uncommunicative child. Of such offspring parents often say, "If I say it's black, he'll say it's white. If I explain a fact, he will contradict me and go on and on trying to prove he's right. Every conversation turns into an argument, and every argument lasts an hour."

4] *The Inconsistent Parent*

The inconsistent parent may have particular difficulties with the persistent child. This kind of youngster requires very clear guidelines for his behavior since he may be carried away by the extent of his capacity to remain involved with any task or activity he undertakes. With consistency of parental approach and the creation of definite rules, it still may be difficult for him to learn to modify his spontaneous behavior, but with inconsistency in handling, the child may be completely bewildered because his actions are sometimes highly approved of, while at other times they are condemned.

Eighteen-month-old Gary, playing with the pots and pans, is one day given great approval since his activity keeps him busy for two hours while his mother completes a task, while three days later he is scolded and spanked for the very same behavior because his mother had just finished arranging the pots and pans and did not wish them disturbed. Six-year-old Gary is encouraged to eat his dinner while watching television because it is so difficult to drag him away and, besides, if his attention is engaged he eats more since he is not mindful of the food. The same Gary, two weeks later, is scolded roundly for sitting himself down in front of the television set at dinner time because mother has suddenly decided that it is not proper to eat in front of the television. Two weeks later she may have gone back to her first approach.

Because of these inconsistencies, Gary has difficulty learning exactly what is approved or disapproved of and thus has no standard models of behavior against which he can balance the difficulty or ease of tearing himself away from an ongoing activity. Lacking such opportunity, he may simply use his own preference as the sole determinant of what is appropriate and what is not, and lose all capacity for objectivity.

5] *The Explosive Parent*

The explosive parent, whether consistent or inconsistent, is characterized by intense outbursts whenever he disapproves of the activity or behavior of his persistent youngster. To the child who is either quietly going about his business oblivious to the passage of time or noisily and actively keeping himself busy and assuming that everyone else is enjoying things as much as he is, these are inexplicable experiences of intense parental disapproval that he can understand only in terms of being disapproved of and disliked. Depending on the child's other temperamental qualities, his reaction then may be fearfulness, aggressiveness, negativism, or obsequiousness. He may start making persistent and eternal demands for parental expressions of approval and affection, begin having nightmares, or indulge in a variety of antisocial acts, knowing only that he can expect parental explosions of rage, though he is not able to understand why. As a result, he very well may develop reactive behaviors which might be ill-adapted to meet the underlying expectation the parent has of him.

In each of the above situations, once the unhealthy parent-child interaction has extended and become extreme and chronic it will appear at first glance as if the specific pathological behavior and attitude constitutes a dominant and fixed feature of the parent's personality structure. The father or mother is easily labeled, with apparent justification, as hostile, competitive, helpless, etc., and reasons are developed to explain the characteristic on the basis of one or another presumed intra-psychic drive and conflict. In some cases it is certainly true that the particular unhealthy attribute will be strongly in evidence in the parent's behavior with all his children. What is impressive in our study population, however, is how frequently the attribute appears specifically in the interaction with one child with a particular temperamental pattern and how differently the same parent will function with a child of another temperamental type. The same parent who is intensely competitive with a persistent nondistractible child may be ready to acquiesce cheerfully to the occasional insistent desire of a less persistent and more generally distractible youngster. The parent who is helpless and overwhelmed by a persistent or difficult child may be constructively assertive and self-confident with an easy child. By contrast, another parent who can empathize with and encourage the dogged efforts of a persistent child may be impatient with and very critical of a highly active distractible youngster, who finds it difficult to sit still with any endeavor for more than a brief period of time. It would be just as much of an erroneous oversimplification to label the parent in the second instance as globally noncompetitive or competent as it would have been to attach labels in the first instance of competitive, helpless, etc. Parents, like other individuals, have personality structures composed of many different attributes, some of which may be contradictory and in conflict. Unless they are neurotically dominated in all situations by a single fixed and compulsively expressed psychological constellation, different relationships, situations, and demands will accentuate different attributes and minimize others. This is seen very clearly in a parent's relationship to a child since the intensity, continuity, and importance of the involvement to each creates especially powerful possibilities for the intensification and magnification of specific attitudes and behaviors of both parent and child.

11 DISTRACTIBILITY

The child who is distractible is one whose attention is easily drawn away from his ongoing activity by peripheral and chance stimuli. Thus, a distractible infant who is sucking his bottle will pause if another person enters the room, if there is a noise, if the light is turned on, or if his position is shifted. Within a remarkably short period of time, the distractible toddler who is playing with one toy may, if his attention is caught by another object, shift his activity, only to shift it again to trot into another room where he hears a noise, leaving a path strewn with forgotten objects behind him. The highly distractible three- or four-year-old will start some task requested of him but, if it requires prolonged and continuous attention, there is little probability of his completing it, since he typically becomes sidetracked by ambient stimuli. The school-age child comes home with books, starts to take them to his room, catches sight of one of his playthings, and drops the books on the first chair or table he sees. He leaves his jacket in one place, his shoes in another, and rarely can find his homework when it is needed, having in each instance been pulled away by a new interest before he completed his original activity.

It would, however, be wrong to consider the trait of distractibility only in terms of its negative consequences for the child. The same distractibility that interferes with task completion also makes the child responsive to a wide range of ongoing environmental stimuli. This may facilitate a high level of general alertness and an awareness of the nuances of other people's behavior and feelings that may be more difficult for the nondistractible child to achieve.

The consequences of marked distractibility on the child's functioning and the degree of annoyance this trait produces in others are significantly influenced by whether the youngster is also persistent or nonpersistent. As indicated in the previous chapter, distractibility and persistence are not necessarily antithetical. The persistent child will tend to return repeatedly to complete an interrupted activity, whether the interruption is due to the intervention of an outsider or to his own distractible response to a fortuitous stimulus. When present in the same child, persistence and distractibility will tend to cancel each other out as far as the eventual extent of task completion is concerned. The distractibility will frequently cause the child to abandon an activity before

109

it is completed; the persistence will tend to make him return to the activity, several times if necessary, until it is completed. Where the nature of a task requires immediate completion, however, the combination of these two temperamental qualities does not guarantee a positive result. When the child turns his attention back, he will find that the cake he was baking is burned, that the task he began has been completed by the person he was supposed to be helping, and that the bath water he was running has flooded the floor.

The distractible child who is also nonpersistent is likely, by contrast, to have his problems with task completion compounded. The nonpersistent child typically tends to have difficulty in returning to an activity once it has been interrupted. If the frequency of such interruptions is increased by his own distractible responses to extraneous stimuli, he may indeed have a significant problem because of the number of tasks he leaves only partially finished. It is, therefore, no surprise that in our longitudinal study population, the distractible children who developed behavioral disturbances were those who were also nonpersistent in their temperamental patterning.

The age of the child can also influence the degree to which his distractibility creates difficulties in handling for his caretakers. During infancy a distractible child is not likely to present management problems. It is quite easy for his caretakers to minimize interruptions when he is eating. Most other nurturing procedures, such as bathing and diapering, are not interfered with by the baby's distractibility. In other instances, the ease with which his attention can be deflected may even be an asset. Thus, if the child resists being held still during dressing or diapering, he can usually be quieted by interesting him in a toy. In the area of safety precautions, the removal of the crawling infant from a potentially dangerous activity, such as poking at an electrical socket, may be greatly facilitated if his attention can be quickly diverted.

This temperamental quality, however, may not be as convenient when the child grows older and it becomes desirable to rely upon him to carry out directions fully. The degree to which distractibility becomes a nuisance will depend upon the importance of task completion to the parents and the degree to which the tasks require the child's constant and consistent attention. Thus, if a child is asked to clear the table and it makes little difference to the mother whether he does all or only part of the job, his failure to finish will not result in scolding or parental annoyance. However, if a parent places a very high value on the trait of a "sense of responsibility" and equates the child's failure to complete clearing the table with deficiency in this attribute, intense scolding and perhaps punishment may ensue.

The educational expectations within the environment also tend to determine the frequency with which a distractible child receives approval or disapproval. In the middle-class family in which academic achievement is highly prized and conscientious completion of all homework assignments demanded, the distractible child frequently will be scolded for his inability to concentrate on his homework. As a result, he may then come to the conclusion, even if he is superior in intelligence, that he is actually stupid.

As previously indicated, the trait of distractibility does interfere with the attainment of the goal of task completion. The effect of this interference on the child's development, however, depends on the response of parents and teachers. The parent or teacher who understands that the child's distractibility is not motivated by a desire to avoid completion of a task is less likely to become antagonistic or punitive. Such a person is more likely to respond in a way that will help the child be productive in his functioning. In the overall longitudinal study, a number of the parents have been capable of this positive approach to their distractible children. These parents were able to accept with good humor the child who, after cheerfully starting off to bed and only half undressing, became sidetracked to play with his little sister. Such parents knew to check quietly on the youngster after short intervals and, without scolding, complete his bedtime routine. Where the level of lesson preparation was lowered by the typical way in which these children approached their homework, the parents were able to be helpful with similar friendly reminders. Eventually some of these children themselves learned to use techniques such as setting a kitchen timer or an alarm clock so that the ringing would remind them to return to the task from which they had taken a break.

In these cases, the distractibility did not prove a significant deterrent to healthy development. Even when their concentration on a task or learning procedure was interrupted one or more times by extraneous stimuli, their overall positive involvement enabled the children to achieve satisfactory levels of task mastery and academic achievement. As they grew older, these normally developing distractible youngsters learned to take responsibility themselves for returning to interrupted activities and tasks that required completion. In other words, they grew to recognize when they were being distracted by an extraneous stimulus and gained the ability to turn their attention back to the interrupted task instead of forgetting it completely.

In other families in the study, however, parental reactions to the child's distractibility were in a negative direction, leading to an excessively stressful parent-child interaction.

Roy (Case 17) was a highly distractible little boy. This quality had been noted in his behavioral histories from early infancy when his parents reported how immediately reactive he was to people, to objects, and to sounds. During his infancy they were not at all upset by this, and in fact found his social responsiveness quite delightful. But, as he grew older, his mother began to get more and more annoyed with his behavior when, as a three-year-old, he rarely finished putting his blocks away after he stopped playing with them; when, as a five-year-old, he strewed articles of clothing about the house; when, as a six-year-old, he dawdled over getting dressed in the morning; and when, as an eight-year-old, he could not remember to come directly home from school to keep a dental appointment or to purchase new shoes. Homework increasingly became a problem as the academic demands became greater. The child would interrupt his homework to watch television and have to be pulled back to do his work. With increasing frequency his teacher complained that his work was careless, cursorily done, or incomplete. Nevertheless, Roy made steady academic progress and his scores on achievement tests were consistently above grade. In the brief periods of attention he did give to his school work, he apparently comprehended what was being taught.

Roy was a cheerful and sociable boy. After school he would often go home with a classmate; the fact that he had forgotten a plan to stop off at a hobby store with another classmate was actually of little consequence to either child. At home, however, the mother-son relationship deteriorated steadily. The mother correctly designated herself as a "nag." She described herself as perpetually reminding Roy about something: "Get up"; "Put your right shoe on"; "Put your left shoe on"; "Wash your face"; "Did you remember your homework?"; "Don't forget to come straight home from school"; "You lost your gloves again"; and so forth. Throughout the haranguing, Roy remained cheerful, but he began increasingly to tune out his mother's voice until it was clear that he not only failed to carry through her instructions but, in addition, he no longer tried to record what she wished him to do. His mother used such phrases as, "He does everything he can to make my life miserable," and "All he has to know is that I want him to do something for him to do the opposite." However, a detailed scrutiny of the child's behavior records revealed, according to other of the mother's statements, that the child was quite capable of forgetting a date he himself had made with a friend for some pleasurable activity if some other enticing proposal arose. While she was quick to say that she could not understand why Roy's friends tolerated such incidents, or why he kept on being such a popular child, it was very hard for his mother to realize, from these circumstances, that his distractibility was a general quality and not one aimed specifically and deliberately at her.

Attempts were made to discuss this negative interaction through an extended series of parent guidance sessions with the mother. The father was not involved since his handling of the boy did not present a significant problem. He would occasionally become aggravated with the child but, basically, he was unperturbed by the youngster's forgetfulness. He kept after Roy to complete a task if it was important; less important things he let ride. When mother and son were engaged in an altercation, the father faded into the background and refused to be drawn in, much to his wife's displeasure.

The guidance discussions attempted to make the mother aware that:

1] Roy's behavior was not directed against her, but was rather the expression of his temperamental pattern.

2] Her categorical demands should be restricted to really important issues, with minimum involvement in Roy's routine activities.

The guidance attempt was, in all respects, a failure. For example, an effort was made to deal with Roy's routine of getting dressed in the morning, so that he and his mother might begin the day without a quarrel. Since Roy liked school and was proud of his good attendance record, it seemed possible to give the child the responsibility for getting up and out to school. Both mother and child agreed to the following procedure: Roy was to have his own alarm clock, which he would set. If he was not out of bed within ten minutes after the alarm rang, his mother would wake him up once. He was to be called to breakfast at an agreed upon time. If Roy failed to come to breakfast, there were to be no reminders. If he was dawdling and it appeared that he might be late, his mother was to do nothing. Should the youngster be late for school, he would have to answer to the teacher for the consequences.

In a discussion a week later, the mother reported, "It was a failure." She said the trial procedure failed because, although Roy dawdled, he had rushed at the last moment and consequently had not been late for school. Since there had been no negative consequences, he had not "learned the lesson." Patient restatement of the purpose of the recommended morning procedure failed to convince her that she should continue to play no part in the routine. She finally explained that she couldn't tolerate this way of functioning because she herself always arrived at appointments exceptionally early. In similar fashion, all other attempts to alter the mother's handling of the boy failed.

Unfortunately, Roy's inattention to his mother's instructions not only intensified, but also finally came to characterize his reaction to his teachers. As a result, his teachers became increasingly annoyed with the boy and his overall school adjustment and academic achievement gradually deteriorated.

Norman (Case 3) was another highly distractible child whose interaction with a parent, in this case his father, became increasingly unhealthy as he grew older. In the early years, it was the mother who, in a manner very similar to Roy's mother, was more impatient and critical of the boy. During these preschool years, his father was the boy's champion, even though at times he would also become inconsistently and explosively annoyed with the youngster. As Norman moved into grade school, his father's high regard for "character" came into play. Character to him meant assuming and completing responsibilities, no matter what might interfere. He could not tolerate seeing his son interrupt a homework exercise, even though the boy was most cheerful about returning to it when quietly reminded to do so by his mother. From occasional paternal scoldings, there gradually developed a situation in which Norman saw himself "disliked" by his father, who actually used this word in describing his attitude to the boy. Increasingly, his mother could see the unfairness and destructiveness of her husband's approach, and she now became the boy's champion. Neither the child's acceleration in first grade, which placed him in a class for gifted children, nor his high level of academic accomplishment convinced the father that the youngster's behavior was acceptable. He felt that Norman had an irresponsible character and was heading for future failure. This child was more sensitive than Roy to parental attitudes. When Norman's father expressed disapproval of his son's inability to complete his homework or other tasks without interruption, the youngster tried to comply by sitting still for long periods of time. This he found impossible to do, and the attempt at motor restraint resulted in shifting tics, as well as general tension.

In discussion with the study child psychiatrist, Norman's father expressed agreement with the view that distractibility is a temperamental characteristic, but stated that he could not change the value he attached to the uninterrupted completion of tasks and commitments. He expressed serious doubt that he would ever change his approach to the boy. His solution was to devote his major attention to his other son with whom he was temperamentally compatible. Ignoring Norman was the only way he could refrain from criticizing him. In fact, his behavior with the boy fluctuated between scoldings and avoidance, but with a consistent attitude of disapproval. As a result, Norman's relationship with his father continued to deteriorate, though his school functioning remained unimpaired.

In his eleventh year, Norman developed an intense desire to be admitted to the private school that his older brother attended. Knowing that this school's academic requirements for admission were very high, Norman began to concentrate intensively on his school work. He demanded of himself that he sit and complete all his homework every evening without yielding to any distraction. During the first few weeks of this program, his tics recurred. Whenever he rose from his chair after finishing his homework, he jumped up and down and ran about frantically. However, a gradual adaptation occurred, so that after three weeks the enforced concentration became progressively less irksome. He was able to relax, his tics disappeared, and he became enormously proud of himself. His temperamental characteristic of distractibility remained, but he had become able to modify and even inhibit its expression in a specific type of activity.

The failure of parent guidance in the cases of Roy and Norman illustrates a finding that is considered in relation to treatment and follow-up (Chapter 16). Distractibility has proved to be the temperamental trait most difficult for parents in the study population to accept; even the constellation which characterizes the difficult child has been less bothersome. In the task achievement oriented middle-class society, distractibility is not an asset. At best, it is a potential hindrance whose ill-effects can be minimized if the child learns quickly and performs rapidly during his short periods of task involvement, and if the youngster can be trained to return to his original commitment after diversion by other stimuli. It is our impression that the quality of distractibility may in some cases facilitate a child's social functioning by making him quickly responsive to verbal and nonverbal communication from other individuals. However, as much as middle-class parents may prize a child's talent for social sensitivity and gregariousness, they treasure even more the ability to master tasks and learn effectively, perhaps reflecting the hierarchy of values in a highly complex industrial society.

12 ACTIVITY LEVEL

HIGH ACTIVITY LEVEL

Although elevation of activity level characterized our clinical group with active symptoms in each of the first five years of life, no child was brought to notice with the specific complaint of hyperactivity except for one girl with brain damage (see case description of Barbara in Chapter 13). This finding contrasts with the more usual clinical experience [1] in which hyperactivity in a child is not infrequent as a presenting symptom. The absence of such complaints in our longitudinal study may stem, firstly, from limited sampling opportunities which necessarily restrict the frequency and type of disorder observed. In addition, the parents in our study population, with very few exceptions, had both the desire and the financial resources to provide ample living and play space for their children. As a result, almost all the children were provided with playrooms in their homes, were taken to playgrounds if the family lived in the city, or had their own backyard available if the family lived in a suburb. It was, therefore, usually possible for the children with high activity levels to engage freely in active motoric play without endangering their own safety or clashing seriously with the needs and desires of other members of the family.

Despite these limited opportunities to study the developmental consequences of hyperactivity, the attribute of high activity level occurred with sufficient frequency in both the clinical and nonclinical groups to permit a consideration of its role both in the development of problems of management and of symptom formation. The findings in these children are illustrative, in modest form, of the phenomena found in much more extreme form in cases of hyperactivity.

In general, it can be said that the child with a high activity level presents more problems of management in an urban environment than does the youngster with the attribute of moderate or low activity. The child who moves quickly and frequently is more likely to break things, to get burned or bruised, and to dart out into the street in front of an oncoming car. As a consequence, he requires more vigilant attention than does the slowly moving youngster. The highly active child is also more apt to collide with others, to interfere unintentionally with the activities and comfort of others, and to present problems of restlessness

116

in situations such as bus or auto rides in which sitting quietly for long periods is necessary. Unless the parents have the understanding and patience to deal cheerfully with such consequences of the child's rapid and almost continual movement, their response to this type of youngster can easily become one of annoyance and irritation. If such negative reactions from parents, teachers, or others to his motoric functioning become frequent, the highly active child will again and again experience situations in which his normal style of behavior is considered undesirable. Such environmental intolerance of his rapid and frequent movement may finally create a dilemma in that he will be scolded and considered "bad" unless he sits still or moves slowly, a difficult and sometimes even impossible task for him.

A parent who repeatedly makes demands on the highly active child for unrealistic restraint of motor activity not infrequently interprets the child's lack of compliance as deliberate disobedience. It is very easy for the mother, who finds herself repeating endlessly the same admonitions which her other children obey easily, to begin to suspect that the youngster is disregarding her requests on purpose. If this leads the parent to scold or punish the highly active child for each infraction of the rules, the youngster may indeed decide that there is no point in trying to please his mother and that he might just as well ignore or resist her wishes altogether. He may then, in fact, become disobedient.

The character and extent of the management problems presented by a highly active child depend in part on his other temperamental attributes. A combination of high activity level and easy distractibility may create frequent and rapidly executed shifts in attention. The resulting behavior may be so unpredictable that even routine situations will require diligent adult supervision.

The highly active child who is also intense in his reactions typically shows very different behavior from the highly active child of mild intensity. The intense child does everything with vigor. If he rushes to greet a playmate, he not only moves quickly but he gives him a bear hug and may knock him over in his exuberance. If he is displeased, he not only may rush around expressing his annoyance with loud shrieks, but he may knock things off tables and shelves, kick and hit and fling objects. Under the best of circumstances, a quickly moving youngster is likely at times to run full tilt into the sharp edge of a piece of furniture or into a companion. The active child whose reactions are also expressed intensely is usually prone to a greater frequency of such mishaps.

By contrast, the highly active child who is predominantly mild in his responses usually makes less severe management demands on parents and teachers. Such a child moves at a fast pace, but his expressions of interest and disinterest, of pleasure and displeasure, are gentle and good natured. If he sees his grandfather, he may run to greet him and smile shyly while holding his face to be kissed. He may wiggle and squirm at dinner, and if offered a food he dislikes, may say quietly, "I don't like it." He plays actively with his friends, running swiftly about in a game of tag and making a face of mild chagrin when he is tagged. If plans for a day's outing are changed, he fusses mildly, and if he can be involved in a substitute program allowing a high degree of motor activity, he is usually quickly content. If appropriate accommodations to such a child's needs for motor outlets are made, other aspects of his handling are likely to present little problem.

If the highly active child also shows predominantly positive mood, he, too, is more likely to evoke patient and accommodating responses from a caretaker. A fast-moving or restless youngster who is simultaneously friendly and cheerful will be tolerated and even encouraged in his lively, gay activities, while the same degree of motor expression in a fussy or whining child can be expected to stimulate a high degree of annoyance and irritation in most parents and teachers.

Though only one child (Case 1) in the clinical group had hyperactivity as a presenting complaint, there were two clinical cases who showed the temperamental attribute of high activity level. In one child, the temperamental trait primarily involved in the development of a behavior disorder was persistence; in the other, it was distractibility. In both, high activity level served to accentuate the difficulties of management and, in the second case, to influence the specific pattern of symptomatology that developed.

The first child, Donald (Case 28), has been described in Chapter 10 (Persistence). His high activity level created difficulties for his parents primarily in his preschool years when the family lived in a small apartment. During this period his almost constant movement kept interfering with his parents' attempts to relax evenings in their small living room. His mother was chronically annoyed with and critical of the youngster; his father was more tolerant. Donald was also a boy with predominantly positive mood of mild to moderate intensity, which gave him a cheerful pleasant demeanor in almost all situations. With the exception of his mother, others responded so positively to his cheerfulness and good humor that he experienced few of the scoldings or punishments that his almost continual motor activity might otherwise have occasioned. When the family moved to a larger apartment when Donald was five, the added space for free movement diminished his intrusions on his parents' comfort, and even his mother's negative responses to him dwindled markedly.

As indicated in Chapter 10, Donald's behavior problem developed primarily in the school situation when his marked persistence in those activities that selectively interested him brought him into conflict with classroom routines and teacher demands. His disregard of the teacher's instructions and his nonconformity with the class activities were especially disruptive because they entailed frequent and rapid movement about the classroom. In this situation, therefore, his high activity level served to exacerbate the problem created by his persistent involvement in inappropriate selective interests.

In the second child, Norman (Case 3), the key temperamental issue was marked distractibility, and the most significant unfavorable environmental influence was the father's critical and disapproving judgments of the behaviors resulting from this distractibility. The parent-child interaction in this case is presented in some detail in Chapter 11 (Distractibility). The attribute of high activity increased the problem in two ways. First, Norman's frequent distractions from assigned tasks were more obvious and irritating to his father because they were so often manifested by conspicuous movements and lively conversation. Secondly, his interruptions of the activities of others, when these caught his attention and distracted him, were made more annoying by the speed with which these intrusions were accomplished. It is also of interest that during stressful periods when Norman's motor activities were restrained, his symptoms were expressed largely in the form of aberrant motor activity, namely, multiple tics.

As indicated at the beginning of this chapter, most of the parents in our longitudinal study were able to tolerate the noise, turmoil, and breakage so often created by a high activity child in his early years. Their tolerance and patience were uniformly rewarded when they saw the youngster gain increasing mastery and direction over his physical movements and so turn this temperamental quality into an asset instead of a liability as he grew older.

LOW ACTIVITY LEVEL

The temperamental trait of low activity was also excessively evident in the clinical sample. In sharp contrast to high activity level, however, an attribute that characterized the clinical group with active symptoms, low activity level appeared specifically for each of the first five years of life among the clinical cases with passive symptoms (see Chapter 5).

The child with the temperamental attribute of low activity level is slow moving and content to remain quietly in one place for long periods of time. Such an infant will lie still in the crib and, at the end of several hours, may be in exactly the same spot as he was originally placed. The tasks of dressing and diapering the baby are made quite easy because the infant rarely squirms, twists, or turns. Thus, the quality of low activity may indeed make caring for such an infant very easy.

With increasing age, the child may for a time continue to be a convenient member of the household. He can be seated with toys and, even if he loses interest in them, he can generally be counted upon either to stay put or to move infrequently and at slow speeds, interfering very little with the mother as she performs her household chores.

Parental displeasure arises when the slowness of the child's responses interferes with the family's schedule. Impatient hurrying of such a youngster only slows him up more. Typically, the family has finished dinner, but such a child is still slowly chewing the main dish. The rest of the family has dressed, and all are waiting impatiently to leave the house on a family expedition while the slowly moving child is still putting on his clothes. Repeatedly, such a youngster finds himself scolded or harassed, or else the task is taken over by someone else. Slow movements can then give way to inertia. It becomes easier for the mother to dress the slowly moving child than to wait for him to get dressed, and if this is how he is handled, he may eventually respond by standing inert while clothing is deposited upon him, rather than by trying to do it himself.

Two low activity level children in our clinical sample were girls. Kate (Case 16), one of fraternal twins, was slow moving in contrast to her sister, a child with average activity level. In early infancy, this temperamental characteristic only evoked mild annoyance because of the length of time it took her to finish a bottle. The mother easily dealt with this, however, by propping up the bottle and letting the infant proceed at her own speed. With four young children in the family, there were many occasions when a family excursion necessitated close timing. More and more Kate was told, "Hurry up. Must you always keep us waiting?" At mealtimes her mother or her older sister would frequently speed things up by spoon-feeding her even when she was as old as five years of age.

In addition to her low activity level, Kate was slow to warm up, with initial negative responses of mild intensity to new situations followed by slow adaptation. The long time she usually required for adaptation to the new, when combined with her low general activity level, tended to make her appear sluggish and even apathetic in coping with new demands. Accentuating these temperamental characteristics was the fact that she also had marked bulging and ptosis of one eye about which she was sensitive, especially in her relations with peers.

In school Kate's pattern of functioning resulted in initial misjudgments of her intellectual potential by her teachers. Thus, her kindergarten teacher, having had the repeated experience that Kate took a long time to involve herself in new procedures and did so "sluggishly," hesitated about advancing the child to first grade. She considered the youngster slightly slow intellectually, and felt that she would not be ready to deal with first grade immediately. By the end of the kindergarten year, when the final recommendation had to be given, the teacher reviewed Kate's work and realized that although the child was still extremely slow in motoric movements and in her responsiveness when called on, the fact was that she had in actuality mastered the cognitive demands as well as most of the children in the class. As a consequence, she recommended that Kate be promoted to first grade on a trial basis. At the beginning of the next school year, her first-grade teacher felt that a mistake had been made because Kate was so slow and plodding in her work. By the end of the year, however, the teacher reversed herself. She had discovered that Kate never gave up and, in the end, mastered the work and was one of the better pupils. This awareness that her slowness did not indicate intellectual retardation was communicated by each teacher to the next one. As a result, her low activity level was respected as normal for her, and her plodding style of learning was respected. Kate, now in the third grade, has a level of academic achievement commensurate with her intellectual capacity and shows a satisfactory level of social integration with her classmates.

The mother-child relationship has been aided by the fact that the older sister spontaneously assumed the primary responsibility for Kate. Previously, there regularly had been an early morning hassle because Kate did not move quickly enough to suit her mother. By contrast, the sister starts her in plenty of time and lets her move at her own pace, confident that Kate eventually will get her clothes on by herself without being prodded.

Dorothy (Case 25), another child in the clinical sample with a low activity level, first began to have difficulties because of her slow movements when she was three and one-half. At this time, her younger sister, age two, with a much higher activity level, began to move faster than Dorothy. The sister would jump to carry out a request made by the mother, while Dorothy was only just beginning to mobilize herself to move ahead.

The younger sister was also of superior intelligence, while Dorothy had an I.Q. score in the average range. This difference in intellectual potential put Dorothy at an additional disadvantage with regard to quickness of comprehension and language development.

The mother, in making the initial complaint, stated that Dorothy used to be obliging but now had become less so. However, scrutiny of the data revealed that Dorothy still was as obliging as she had ever been as long as her sister, who was both more verbal and more active, was not present and that she was unaccommodating only when her sister would do what was requested of Dorothy. At these times, Dorothy, a child with low intensity of expressiveness, would whine and fuss about not having been permitted to do the task. Since she was also a persistent child, her fussing would be prolonged, much to her parent's annoyance. When her mother would say, "You had your chance," the child continued to whine. The fact was, of course, that Dorothy had not had her chance since her own pace of activity did not permit successful completion of the task in the allotted time. Unfortunately, her motoric slowness was compounded by a developmental lag in language development, which added to her verbal slowness. To make matters even worse, the youngest child in the family also grew into a quick-moving, vivacious, and very verbal girl of superior intelligence. In the bustle of a household in which two younger, quick-moving, and brighter sisters competed with her, Dorothy's opportunities to be successful at her own leisurely pace became less frequent. And, while trying to care for three youngsters, the parents became less able to meet Dorothy's need for sufficient time to complete any activity.

Dorothy also was slow in her application to scholastic work. In this area her parents were quite objective and wished only to know whether she was below average intellectually, which she was not. Once they were made aware of the slow pace at which Dorothy assimilated knowledge, the parents were quite responsive to the need to give her sufficient time and did not rush her in the area of learning.

The parents understood the temperamental issues once these were discussed with them in detail and applied to Dorothy area by area. At home, they were able to put into practice the recommendation to protect Dorothy from being overshadowed by her sisters and to keep them from taking over her assigned tasks. They themselves were rather fast-moving people, but they made conscious efforts to reorganize their attitudes. When periodical tensions would mount, they would return for renewed discussions to review their handling of the child. From time to time, they also would phone to report a briefly deteriorating situation in which they realized they once again, unfortunately, had put undue pressure on the child to move more quickly, or had expressed for a sustained period of time dissatisfaction with her temperamental characteristics.

In one situation, in fact, they became aware of the child's high level of common sense and her understanding of herself. Dorothy was transferred from one school to another between second and third grades. At the preentrance interview, the school director stated that Dorothy was just barely able to begin the third-grade curriculum and, in view of the mother's report of her slowness in functioning, they wondered whether it would not be more favorable for the child to go into a second-grade class where she could feel immediately competent. The parents discussed this issue with Dorothy who said matter-of-factly, "If I go into second grade I'll never find out if I can do third grade. If I go into third grade and I can't do it, then I can go back to second grade. I promise you I won't feel badly." This was done, and the child worked responsively, consistently, and slowly. She made adequate progress and was able to maintain a third-grade status.

For both the high activity and low activity child, there is a danger that lack of understanding of the temperamental pattern by parents, teachers, or peers will lead to derogatory misinterpretations of the youngster's behavior. Most typically the high activity child is considered wilfully disobedient, and the low activity child dull and inept. If such a judgment shapes the approach to the child, the consequence may very well be a self-fulfilling prophecy in which the child does finally become disobedient or inept.

REFERENCE

1. S. Chess, "Diagnosis and Treatment of the Hyperactive Child," *N. Y. State Jour. Med.*, 60:2379 (1960).

IGNORE

13 | THREE CHILDREN WITH BRAIN DAMAGE

Even when the primary basis for the development of a behavior disorder is a damaged nervous system, our findings indicate that the nature of the behavioral response is not a direct manifestation of cerebral dysfunction, but the result of the interaction of a child with a damaged nervous system and his environment. These children, as is the case for normal children, develop specific types of behavioral disturbance in accordance with their temperamental patterns and the interaction of these with other characteristics of the child and with aspects of the environment, particularly the style of parental handling.

The identification of three children with brain damage in our longitudinal sample has provided the opportunity for at least a limited study of the influences of the child's temperament and the characteristics of the environment as sources for individual differences in behavioral development and symptom formation exhibited by brain-damaged children. Our data do not permit us to consider the influence of physiological factors, namely the type, size, and locus of the brain lesion, the time of life at which the nervous system was damaged, and the character of the neuropathological process.

CASE 1

The first of the three children is Bert (Case 42), who was born prematurely with delivery one month prior to term and with a birth weight of 4 lb., 12 oz. (1.8 kg.). Neonatal course was stormy, with acute respiratory distress accompanied by periods of apnea and dyspnea appearing shortly after birth. Respiration improved by the third day of life, and supplemental oxygen was discontinued. As a neonate, his sucking and swallowing were noted to be poor. However, growth was adequate, and the infant was discharged from the premature nursery at twenty days of age.

Development during the first two years of life was significantly retarded. Sitting without support did not occur until eleven months, and the onset of walking was delayed until the age of twenty-two months. Swallowing, particularly of a spontaneous and nonnutritive type, was inefficient, and from fifteen months onward, drooling was markedly excessive and of considerable concern both to the parents and the pediatrician. Adaptive motor functioning, such as reaching and grasping and object manipulation, was grossly clumsy and uncoordinated. Transfer of objects from hand to hand was poor even at eighteen months of age.

On neurological evaluation at age five years four months, he was noted to be grossly awkward, with poor gross motor coordination and inability to climb and to skip. Fine coordination, such as finger opposition, was, however, at an age appropriate level. Reexamination at age six years confirmed the findings.

Although Bert's comprehension of language, as indicated by appropriate responsiveness to speech, appeared to be good, his own expressive language development lagged significantly behind age expectation. Consistent single-word usage did not appear until the child was thirty-nine months of age, and expressive language improved very slowly over the next nine months. At four years, however, the range of his expressive language was almost age appropriate, but speech itself was grossly dysarthric, contained much slurring and cluttering, and was largely incomprehensible, even to his parents. In the ensuing year, some improvement in enunciation occurred. However, his speech continued to be characterized by poor rhythmicity, excessive rate, slurring, and a high-pitched tone containing little or no variation. On independent formal speech evaluation at age five years two months by a speech therapist, his "articulation was noted to be poor, speech markedly slurred, rate excessive, marked by multiple consonantal substitutions, and exhibiting the retention of infantile pronunciations for earlier learned words." Speech therapy was recommended and initiated. The youngster cooperated actively in this endeavor and practiced correct pronunciation spontaneously. As a result, his speech improved, though even at age ten years his enunciation remained a bit slurred, and he spoke rapidly in a high-pitched tone.

School progress was excellent except for a tendency to reverse letters and numbers, which interfered with correct writing and correct written arithmetic. His oral arithmetic was at a superior level.

Psychometric testing at four years one month resulted in a Stanford-Binet I.Q. of 110. The score was considered minimal because of the difficulty experienced by the examiner in understanding the child's speech. A repetition of intelligence testing at six years two months resulted in an I.Q. of 122, with a ceiling performance at ten years and wide scatter among age levels. Again the I.Q. was estimated to be minimal because of the child's distractibility and slowness in working. Unevenness of performance within the testing session was manifested by the passing of items at the ten-year level that had been failed at the eight-year level. The Wechsler Intelligence Scale for Children (WISC) evaluation at the age of six years also showed a wide scatter of subtest performances, with best performance on information and memory tests, and worst performance on comprehension and vocabulary. The overall I.Q. obtained was equivalent to the one reported for the Stanford-Binet, and no verbal-performance discrepancy was noted.

From early infancy onward, Bert's temperamental characteristics were those of an easily functioning child. Although an active boy, he showed no evidence of hyperkinesis. He was rhythmic in his functioning and tended to express his needs regularly and clearly. He was adaptable, and in new situations tended to approach rather than to withdraw. He had a moderately high sensory threshold, and thus was not excessively responsive either to auditory or to visual stimuli. When he did respond, his responses were of mild to moderate intensity, and his mood was preponderantly positive. Although he was somewhat distractible, he was also persistent, and could, from infancy, sustain his orientation in goal-directed activities.

At a later age Bert retained these characteristics of temperament, and when misunderstood in his efforts at verbal communication, he would patiently and persistently repeat his statements until they were comprehended. If he was not successful, he would continue his repetition and quietly proceed to demonstrate in pantomime what it was that he wished to communicate. In nursery school and in the early school years, the other children teased him about his peculiar speech. His response to this teasing was to work conscientiously to improve his enunciation.

Bert's parents combined a generally permissive approach to child care with demands for and expectations of high intellectual achievement. As a consequence, they were most attentive to the details of his developmental course, constantly comparing it with that of the children of their friends and acquaintances. Each developmental lag was the occasion for active concern and a request for developmental and psychiatric consultation from the study team. In particular, Bert's delayed language development and cluttered speech aroused profound parental anxiety because of the possibility of intellectual subnormality. It was not until after psychometric evaluation had demonstrated his general intellectual intactness, and his receptive language function had been found to be at a superior level, that they were reassured as to his intellectual competence, despite the continued disturbance of expressive language and motor functioning.

In contrast to their demands for intellectual competence, both parents were markedly permissive and underdemanding in connection with the immediate requirements of daily living. When the child failed to comply with a request, their tendency was to permit the situation to stretch out in terms of innumerable time extensions. In addition, they frequently failed to establish clearly defined limits. In a few areas, however, the father in particular made extremely clear-cut demands that were peremptory and in part unreasonable. These included his insistence upon instantaneous and invariable compliance with certain rules for safety and for the inviolability of parental possessions.

When management problems deriving from lack of clear parental structuring developed during Bert's preschool years to a point where they became genuinely irksome to the parents, advice from the study psychiatrist was requested. Parental guidance was given and in general fell into two categories: 1] the suggestion that the requirements for expected behavior be more clearly defined, and that no modification in the demand be made until it was certain that the child had understood what was expected of him; and 2] reassurance, by the indication that to a considerable degree the types of management problems encountered were normal for the age and that it was incorrect to view these problems as additional evidences of neurological or psychological pathology.

The parents were able to modify their practices in accordance with these suggestions and, while maintaining a generally permissive atmosphere, provided the child with a clearer definition of the requirements for social behavior. In accord with his general temperamental pattern, Bert responded positively and quickly to the setting of limits. As a result, he became a pleasant companion and functioned well with his parents in his early school years. His predominant attitude of approach to other children, and his predominantly positive mood coupled with his persistence, also resulted in his being accepted by his peers and in his having no significant problems in relating to children of his own age during the same period of his life. Several psychiatric evaluations during this period, through the age of eight, consistently failed to reveal any evidence of significant behavioral disturbance.

However, during the ninth year of life, Bert developed impairment of school functioning associated with difficulty in reading and arithmetic, which included letter and number reversals. Avoidance reactions to reading occurred, and there was frequent fussing and crying over homework. In addition, social difficulties with other children appeared for the first time. He became the scapegoat of his class, and his friends began to avoid him. On clinical interview at eight years nine months, he showed some residual speech difficulty. Marked right-left confusion was present. He frequently did not listen to what the examiner was saying. No other pathological findings were noted. The diagnosis was brain damage with primary perceptual difficulties and mild reactive behavior disorder. The major new source of stress appeared to derive from the father's relationship to Bert. Great pressure of work had kept the father quite busy during most evenings and weekends, as well as daytimes, during the preceding year, and he became very annoyed when Bert interrupted him at his work. At the same time, the father also became increasingly critical of Bert's speech, correcting him in a loud voice and, at times, shouting until the boy was reduced to tears.

This new stress, superimposed upon Bert's already existing difficulties with his speech and with reading and written arithmetic, was sufficient to significantly impair his social functioning with his peer group. However, even in this situation of multiple stresses his temperamental characteristic of marked adaptability was still in evidence, and the behavior problem that did develop was only of mild degree.

CASE 2

The second neurologically impaired child is a boy, Kevin, who was the result of his mother's first complete pregnancy following thirteen years of marriage. Problems of infertility and spontaneous abortion had existed previously, but the current pregnancy was uneventful, the delivery uncomplicated, and the child had a birth weight of 8 lb., 1 oz. (3.6 kg.).

His neonatal course was difficult, with poor feeding and frequent vomiting. During the first two months of life, he sweated excessively and had pylorospasm with propulsive vomiting after each feeding. There were repeated respiratory infections during the first months of life; one episode at four months of age was sufficiently severe to require brief hospitalization.

The development of both motor functioning and language was significantly delayed. Kevin did not sit without support until eleven months of age, and did not stand without support until the age of twenty-one months. The parents and pediatrician were concerned with his slow development by the time the child was six months of age. A Gesell evaluation at that time indicated that he had motor and adaptive backwardness and atonic musculature. On examination at age twenty-one months, he was found to have marked pronation of the feet, significantly reduced muscle tone, and behavioral organization appropriate for a child fifteen months of age. Language and speech developed slowly. Single syllables were not repeated until the child was over two years of age; single words were not used until after he was three years of age, and short phrases only appeared between the fourth and fifth years. Drooling and poor swallowing patterns were noted by the parents and pediatrician throughout the first five years of life.

Neurological examination at three years eight months indicated a marked disturbance of gait, a wide base, short-stepping and waddling, and pronation of both feet. Deep tendon reflexes were excessively brisk in the lower extremities, and unsustained clonus was elicited bilaterally. Language was estimated to be at least nine months behind age expectation, with poor pronunciation and infantile substitutions and distortions. Swallowing, too, was noted to be poor and drooling excessive. Neurological reexamination one year later confirmed the earlier findings.

Speech evaluation at five years four months resulted in the finding of dysarthric speech characterized by abnormal sound substitutions and distortions together with elements of echolalia and perseveration. Speech therapy, which was started but discontinued after nineteen sessions, had resulted in no gain.

The first formal psychometric evaluation was carried out when Kevin was four years three months of age. At testing, he was found to be friendly, cheerful, cooperative within limits, but readily distractible and restless. His speech was sparse and frequently incomprehensible. Testing was incomplete because he tired quickly. However, a basal age on the Stanford-Binet of two years six months was established, with some successes occurring at the four-year level. Intelligence testing was repeated at five years one month, at which time the Stanford-Binet was administered over two sessions because of the child's easy fatigability, restlessness, and distractibility. A mental age of three years eight months, with an I.Q. score of 72, was recorded. He was noted by the testing psychologist to have poor manual coordination, to drool excessively, and to have his mouth "full of saliva most of the time." Verbalizations relevant as answers to questions asked could be understood only with difficulty. Test performance was uneven, with the child hyperactive and readily distracted by all stimuli, including minimal ones. He also tended to be imitative and perseverative, to turn tasks into games, and to show a high degree of randomly associative behavior, such as responding to small test automobiles by beginning a game of auto racing and crashing.

Perceptual testing at age seven years three months showed impaired form discrimination, inadequate recognition of shapes when spatial orientation was changed, and poor right-left awareness. The overall perceptual defect was categorized as mild.

Kevin, despite his mildly subnormal intelligence, occasional hyperactivity, and prominent motor and speech disorders, was not an excessively difficult child to manage. Although he was moderately active and irregular as an infant, he characteristically tended to approach new situations and to express a positive mood. His thresholds of arousal were fairly high, and he was moderately nonadaptive. An early easy distractibility, coupled with a high level of persistence in the first year, came to be replaced after the second year by moderate distractibility but continued high levels of persistence. Perhaps most significantly, from the early months of life onward he was a child whose responses were characterized by a low level of intensity. Thus, even abnormal behaviors were mildly expressed.

From the sixth month of life onward, when they first became convinced of abnormality in his development, his parents accepted the fact that his difficulties in learning and his developmental delays derived from primary neurologic damage. Within this framework they have been highly accepting and very fond of the boy. Demands have usually been appropriate to the level of his intellectual and physical capacities, and efforts at training have been both consistent and patient. Social contact with other children was encouraged and planned for, and the child was placed in a normal nursery school for children one year his junior. Since the age of six he has been in a special school for brain-injured children. Within his limitations, his course in school has shown good social functioning with peers and teachers. Learning has been slow, but progresses. His overall behavior has not presented major problems other than those involving the modifications of management necessary because of his intellectual and physical limitations. At no time has he been considered to present any significant degree of behavioral disturbance.

CASE 3

The third child is a girl, Barbara (Case 1), who was the product of a full-term pregnancy and normal spontaneous delivery, with a birth weight of 7 lb., 15 oz. (3.6 kg.). Neonatal course was uneventful and discharge from the nursery occurred at the expected time.

At seven weeks of age, hemangioma of the chest wall and inversion of the feet were noted by the pediatrician; the latter condition was treated by the application of Denis Browne splints. The achievement of motor and language landmarks was well within normal age ranges. However, as language developed during the second year, she showed a marked tendency to be querulous, repetitious, and echolalic. Behavior at this age, too, tended to be echopraxic.

Play was generally age and sex appropriate in its initiation, but never became fully elaborated, and tended to remain both disjointed and ill-directed. Misuse of language was common, with a tendency to concretism and confusions of relatedness. Adjective usage, particularly when relating to amount and degree, was frequently confused, with words such as "large" and "small" distributed randomly in her speech. Adjectival reception was similarly confused, and adjectives designating amount were poorly interpreted, resulting in frequent failures in following simple directions.

Although motor landmarks were achieved at normal age expectations, coordinated motor functioning was markedly inadequate. Clumsiness and gross incoordination, accompanied by much tripping and falling, were noted throughout the first four years of life. At thirty-nine months of age, the parents complained of the child's frequent tripping, excessive falling, repeated running into obstacles, and serious misjudgments of distance. Repeated neurologic examinations from age four years on resulted in findings of alternating hyperphoria of the adducting eye in lateral gaze, jerky movements of the trunk on sitting, choreiform movements of the arms and body when the arms were maintained in extension, clumsiness of gait with some rigidity of the lower extremities, generally diminished muscular tone, and brisk deep-tendon reflexes. The general diagnostic impression was that of mild dyskinesia accompanied by hyperactivity.

Intellectual testing was conducted at age four years one month with the Stanford-Binet, and at six years nine months with WISC. The I.Q. score at the first testing was 92, and at the older age was 106. Wide scatter was shown in both verbal and performance scales, with poorest achievement on comprehension, and best on picture completion. During testing she was both distractible and perseverative, and frequently developed irrelevant associations and extensions of her responses to test items. Perceptual and perceptual-motor testing at six years of age resulted in performances that were significantly below her intellectual level and age expectancy.

In her temperamental characteristics, Barbara was highly active, persistently irregular and arrhythmic, very slowly adaptive, and had a tendency to withdraw from, rather than to approach, new stimuli and social situations. Her threshold of responsiveness was relatively low, and she tended to respond intensely even to weak stimuli. Her mood tended to be negative, and her distractibility and persistence high. The pattern of high levels of activity, arrhythmicity, nonadaptability, negative mood, and intense reactivity has persisted and increased as the child grew older, until, at the ages of four and five years, she was always in the upper quartile of children in the longitudinal study sample with these characteristics.

As the youngster grew older, she gradually elaborated a pattern of hyperkinesis, restlessness, arrhythmicity, deviance in language usage, ritualistic behavior, tendency toward tantrums, destructiveness in play, ready distractibility, and poor motor coordination manifested in clumsiness, tripping, and frequent falling. She was the only one of the three children with brain damage we have followed from infancy whose behavior, developmental course, and current style of functioning fit the stereotype of "the brain-damaged child."

Perhaps the most disturbing of her behavioral aberrations was the tendency to develop ritualistic behaviors. Such tendencies expanded and eventually developed into rituals for most routines. These consisted of specific whisperings of nonsense words, of requiring individuals to sit in specific positions when holding her hand, of taking only certain specified objects to the playground, and many others.

Both in her play and in her goal-directed activities she tended to be markedly perseverative. Such perseveration and nonadaptiveness were of a pathologic degree. At age thirty-one months, she repeatedly put her hand into a frying pan of hot oil to get food despite being burned upon previous occasions when she had engaged in similar activity. Even after she was burned upon a specific occasion, she would continue to reach into the hot pan for a desired object.

Both the practices and attitudes of the parents toward the child involved complexities and features of evolution over time that are of considerable interest. During the child's infancy, they attempted to be permissive and to organize their relations to her in terms of the consistent application of a child-centered, self-demand viewpoint. Such practices had disastrous consequences, readily illustrated by the course of events surrounding bedtime behavior. At the beginning, the parents attempted to follow the child's own sleep rhythm as a basis for scheduling. However, her arrhythmicity, manifested both in the irregular timing of sleep-wake cycles, and the unpredictable duration of either the sleeping or waking phase, resulted in a complete disruption of the family's pattern of rest. The parents then attempted to impose a reasonable schedule, to which the child responded by crying. Since the parents believed that if she cried when put to bed it was their responsibility to remain with her and comfort her, they lengthened the contact. As the child became capable of making more specific demands at bedtime, the mother responded by trying to satisfy them. She sat in places prescribed by the child and performed such acts as whispering nonsense words or tucking her into bed to a repeatedly respecified degree of tightness. The child demanded that all routine acts be carried out in a precise sequential order. Such interactions gradually expanded until they were of unwieldy proportions. The mother's efforts to minimize the routines resulted in persistent crying by the child. This, in turn, increased the degree of parental irritation, and a pattern evolved in which going to bed extended over the entire evening and culminated in a parental outburst. Following this, the terror-stricken youngster would run around the house shrieking, "I'll be good. I won't cry anymore."

The ritualistic tendencies present in bedtime behavior also came to characterize other features of routine, including dressing, feeding, play, bathing, and toileting. When the parents would attempt to reduce such tendencies by the introduction of structure, the child tended to respond by disorganization. The parents responded to this initial reaction of the child to their efforts at change by quickly reverting to the old routines. The inconsistency was accompanied by affective fluctuation. Their behaviors toward the child ranged from tenderness to highly punitive beating and incarceration, despite her extreme panic when she was locked up or hit. Such punitive practices were carried out primarily by the father, with the mother continuing to remain relatively consistent in her display of positive feelings.

Despite these real and continuing difficulties in management during the preschool years, the parents persisted in denying excessive difficulty and in minimizing the pathologic character and inappropriateness of the child's behavior. Under most circumstances, they tended to interpret her impulsiveness as spontaneity, and her hyperactivity and compulsive intrusion into other people's affairs as desirable curiosity and interest. Only when such behaviors began to result in the disruption of normal social functioning did they acknowledge them as signs of abnormality.

By age six, Barbara's social relations with her peers were markedly negative. She was friendless, incapable of remaining in a normal school situation, dangerous to herself and to other members of the household, destructive, perseverative, and impulse ridden. These behaviors resulted in her being placed in a residential institution for training and care at six years eleven months of age.

The case materials presented have summarized our findings on three children who have been followed continuously from birth into the early school years. Each of the children has been representative of a different type of developmental course that may attend neurologic damage acquired in early life. They have differed in their intellectual functioning, ranging from mild mental subnormality to a superior level of intelligence. Motor dysfunction, grossly present in the most intellectually damaged child, was manifested either as developmental lag, mild dyskinesia, or articulatory disturbance in the other two cases. Most striking from the point of view of the prognosis of later behavioral functioning have been characteristics of temperamental organization already manifest during the early months of life.

The central question to which the findings of these longitudinal case studies can most appropriately be related is the problem of why one child with brain damage follows a path of development that leads to positive social adaptation and environmental mastery, whereas another follows a developmental course characterized by increasing diminution in the effectiveness of environmental control, maladaptation, and eventually severe psychopathology. Clearly the degree of intellectual deficit attendant upon brain damage cannot in itself account for the divergences in developmental course. In the three children we have followed, effective adjustment was made by one child who was mentally subnormal; mild disturbances developed in one with a superior level of I.Q.; and severe maladaptation occurred in the child exhibiting a level of general intellectual functioning at the population average.

Methods of parental management and parental attitudes were not markedly different among the sets of parents during the early infancy period. In fact, the basic attitudes and practices of the parents of the child, Bert, who made relatively good progress, were virtually indistinguishable from those that were present in the parents of the child, Barbara, who made by far the worst adjustment. Further, an older sibling of Barbara's, who at another center had been diagnosed in early childhood as having primary neurologic dysfunction, interacted positively and effectively with the parents and has made good school and social progress.

Temperamental organization was the feature of behavior that appeared to be most useful as a predictor of subsequent developmental course in the cases considered. The two children who were primarily positive in mood, rhythmic in functioning, readily adaptive, moderate in activity level, mild in intensity, and who had no significant lowering of response threshold, had a relatively good behavioral outcome. The child who was negative in mood, arrhythmic, nonadaptive, high in activity level, intensely reactive, and who had a low threshold, pursued an increasingly disturbed behavioral course. It would be wrong to assume that the behavioral consequence was the simple and direct product of the unfolding of temperament, since in other children in our longitudinal study sample having equally difficult temperamental characteristics, behavioral outcome has in some cases been good, probably as a result of a favorable combination of parental and environmental circumstances.[1] The findings lead one to the view that the course of behavioral development in brain-damaged children is the complex product of the interaction of a child having a given set of response tendencies with parental attitudes and practices and more general features of environmental demand. The child's response tendencies appear to be determined largely by the combination of temperamental attributes and the pathological reaction to environmental stimuli resulting from the brain damage. Flexible parents having highly similar attitudes and practices can modify these attitudes and change their procedures in accordance with the manner in which the child to whom they are applied responds. It is most likely that the response will be in the parentally desired direction if the child possesses temperamental characteristics including easy adaptability, ready modifiability, predominantly positive mood, and predictable rhythmicity. Under these circumstances, the prognosis for a positive parent-child interaction is likely to be good. In contrast, when the brain-damaged child is also temperamentally arrhythmic, negative in mood, markedly nonadaptive, and has a low response threshold and short attention span, the likelihood of a parental procedure resulting in a desired modification of behavior is reduced. In some children with such characteristics, extraordinary patience and consistency on the part of the parents, coupled with a stable and well-structured environment, may eventually result in progress in the desired developmental direction. However, in most instances in which a brain-damaged child also has the temperamental pattern of the difficult child, the parents who are confronted with daily evidence of the ineffectiveness of their efforts in directing the child's behavior react with feelings of helplessness, frustration, anger, and guilt. These understandable reactions still further diminish the parent's effectiveness, and the result of the parent-child interaction appears to be the progressive worsening of behavior in both parent and child, increasing degrees of familial disorganization and conflict, and the eventual inability to retain the child within the family setting.

The three cases considered in this chapter suggest the need to reassess prevalent notions of the nature of behavioral disturbances in brain-damaged children. Since the reports of Bradley,[2] Goldstein,[3] and Strauss and Werner,[4] describing a syndrome of behavioral dysfunction in children with central nervous system damage, there has been a growing tendency to convert these descriptions into a stereotype of the "brain-damaged" child. The consequences of brain damage in childhood have tended to be discussed as though there regularly appears a single syndrome characterized by hyperkinesis, distractibility, perseveration, perceptual disturbance, emotional lability, atypical cognitive functioning, and disturbances in impulse control. As a result, the label "brain damage" has come to be synonymous with the hyperkinetic syndrome of behavioral disturbance.

We, of course, recognize,[5] as do Laufer and Denhoff,[6] and Eisenberg,[7] that there can be little doubt that the hyperkinetic syndrome does occur in some children as a direct consequence of central nervous system damage. At the same time, the behavioral sequelae of brain damage in childhood can be most diverse, and may range from no apparent behavioral disturbance, through absence of behavioral disturbance but presence of mental subnormality, to serious disorganizations of social, intellectual, and interpersonal functioning, which are phenomenologically indistinguishable from the major psychoses of childhood. Despite this manifest diversity of consequence, there has continued to be preoccupation with the youngster who fits the behavioral stereotype commonly referred to as the "hyperkinetic child."

It is, therefore, pertinent to emphasize that of the three children with brain damage in our longitudinal study, only one showed the hyperkinetic syndrome of behavioral disturbance. This finding emphasizes that no one pattern of behavioral dysfunction can be considered to fit all brain-damaged children. Our findings further suggest the importance of the brain-damaged child's temperamental characteristics, and of the reactions of parents to them in influencing his developmental course. It appears, therefore, that in the evaluation of such children and in the recommendations that are made for fostering their development as socially functioning individuals, more attention than is usual should be paid to an analysis of temperament and to the inclusion of the findings of such an analysis in the recommendations for management.

REFERENCES

1. S. Chess and Others, "Interaction of Temperament and Environment in the Production of Behavioral Disturbance in Children," *Amer. J. Psychiat.*, 120:144 (1963).

2. C. Bradley, "Characteristics and Management of Children with Behavior Problems Associated with Brain Damage," *Ped. Clin. N. Amer.*, Nov. 1957:1049.
3. K. Goldstein, "Modification of Behavior Consequent to Cerebral Lesions," *Psychiat. Quart.*, 10:586 (1936).
4. A. A. Strauss and H. Werner, "Comparative Psychopathology of Brain-Injured Child and Traumatic Brain-Injured Adult," *Amer. J. Psychiat.*, 99:835 (1943).
5. H. G. Birch, ed., *Brain Damage in Children: Biological and Social Aspects* (Baltimore: The Williams and Wilkins Co., 1964).
6. M. W. Laufer and E. Denhoff, "Hyperkinetic Behavior Syndrome in Children," *J. Pediat.*, 50:463 (1957).
7. L. Eisenberg, "Behavioral Manifestations of Cerebral Damage in Childhood," *Brain Damage in Children*, H. G. Birch ed. (Baltimore: The Williams and Wilkins Co., 1964), pp. 61–77.

14 STRESS: CONSONANCE AND DISSONANCE

In previous chapters, the factors involved in the ontogenesis of behavioral disturbances have been considered from several vantage points. The quantitative comparison of temperamental scores of the clinical groups with the nonclinical children, as detailed in Chapter 5, served to identify those temperamental characteristics that tended to make children more vulnerable to the development of a behavior problem. In the succeeding chapters, the factors in the child-environment interaction that contributed to favorable and unfavorable developmental courses were examined for a number of specific temperamental constellations. In the present chapter, the types of pathogenic stress and dissonance that have been identified in the clinical sample will be reported. This consideration is related to, but is more general than, and therefore distinct from, the identification of factors responsible for specific symptom choice and evolution, an issue which will be dealt with in the next chapter.

We have found it useful to consider specific types of stressful interactions and dissonances within the framework provided by the evolutionary concept of "goodness of fit." [1] This concept implies that the adequacy of an organism's functioning is dependent upon the degree to which the properties of its environment are in accord with the organism's own characteristics and style of behaving. According to this view, optimal development in a progressive manner derives from the interaction of the individual with environmental opportunities and demands that are consonant with his capacities and behavioral style. Conversely, disorders of functioning may be viewed as deriving in the first place from dissonances or discrepancies between the respective characteristics of the individual and his environment. This approach does not imply that an optimal developmental environment is a restricted one, making no "upsetting" demands on the individual. Nor does goodness of fit mean a static condition of minimized demands for functioning. Rather, it suggests that a "good fit" is one in which reorganizations of functioning resulting from environmental requirements proceed in an orderly and progressive manner, and "poor fit" is one in which there is distorted or retrogressive direction of development.

To avoid confusion, it is necessary not merely to have a conception

137

of the child's characteristics of functioning and the nature of his developmental environment, but also a concept of what constitutes progress in development. The concept of progress is always a social value which, in most cultures, includes the anticipation that with increases in age the child will achieve expanded environmental mastery and productive social involvement. Thus, goodness of fit is never an abstraction, but is always goodness of fit for certain end results. For example, behavioral distress resulting from the introduction of a child to a new social situation demanding functioning of a new kind is not necessarily a signal to the parent to withdraw the child in the interests of his immediate comfort. Rather, his ability to master these new demands at the given time must be evaluated. If the child can cope with the new demands, his efforts should be encouraged and, if necessary, assisted. If, however, an evaluation suggests that mastery cannot readily be achieved at the given time, other more effective tactics, including delay in such experiences, may have to be elaborated for the development of his expanded social competencies. Thus, the concept of goodness of fit is not used as a homeostatic principle in the area of behavioral functioning, but as a homeodynamic one, which has as its end result change and expanded competence rather than stability. Obviously, under certain circumstances stasis would represent an optimal interaction between the child and his surroundings, where, for the consolidation of gains, stability, consistency, and the restriction of new demands represent essential conditions for functioning. However, in other circumstances, change and the expansion of competence represent the necessary pattern for reorganization and growth.

Within this framework, stress can be distinguished from an easily accomplished demand by considering it to represent a demand upon the child either for an alteration in a habitual pattern of functioning, or for the mastery of a new activity or task that is difficult for him to achieve. This formulation parallels the definition of physiological stressful stimuli as forces "which tend to drastically alter some phase of body homeostasis and to which the body is [sic] not or cannot readily adapt." [2] However, if the demand, even if it is very difficult, is consonant with the child's characteristics and capacities, expanded environmental mastery and developmental progress will occur, and the demand will have constituted a healthy stimulus for the child. If, however, the demand is so dissonant with the child's behavioral style and ability that mastery is not possible, its persistence will not contribute to a healthy outcome. In this situation, the stress can be excessive and, if continued, may lead to the development of a behavioral disturbance.

Thus, demands and stresses, when consonant with developmental potentials, may be constructive in their consequences and should not be considered as an inevitable cause of behavioral disturbance. The same is true of conflict, which can be considered as one contributor to stress, and which may be resolved either in a healthy or in an unhealthy direction. The issue is one of *excessive* stress. The causes of excessive stress leading to disturbed behavioral functioning can perhaps be best subsumed under the rubric of *dissonances*. The term dissonance, connoting disharmony and poorness of fit, appears appropriate to designate those child-environment interactions in which a demand is made on the child that he is not capable of mastering or that leads to maladaptive functioning.

The term cognitive dissonance has been used by Festinger to designate "items of information that psychologically do not fit together." [3] Our concept of dissonance similarly emphasizes a poorness of fit, namely, between an environmental demand and the child's capacities or characteristics. Such dissonance may create stress that the child cannot master constructively and that, if the dissonance persists, can lead to maladaptive functioning and behavioral disturbance.

In considering the types of dissonance operative in the development of disturbed functioning in the clinical cases, the following categorization has been useful:

1] Dissonance between the parental practices or demands and the child's temperament or capacities. 2] Dissonance between values and behaviors developed in the home and behavioral expectancies at school and in peer groups. 3] Inconsistencies in the patterning of parental practices and attitudes resulting in excessive stress for the child. 4] Interparental dissonance and the use of the child's characteristics as a weapon in interparental conflict. 5] Dissonance between the child's expectations of acceptance and affection and parental feelings and behavior. 6] Dissonance between the mode of functioning of the teacher or other person *in loco parentis* and the characteristics of the child.

A brief example of each of these types will illustrate the use of the concept of dissonance in defining the characteristics of the child-environment interaction patterns that lead to excessive stress and so contribute to behavioral disturbance.

1] *Dissonance Between the Parental Practices or Demands and the Child's Temperament or Capacities*

A] Ned (Case 5) was referred at three years eight months of age because of a sleep problem that was exhibited in two ways: 1] He resisted falling asleep and then, after finally dozing off, would awaken once or twice during the night. At these times he might stay quietly awake in bed, or he might scream wildly. 2] He had tantrums at bedtime when he refused to go to sleep as his parents ordered.

A pattern of brief and irregular periods of sleep was noted from birth. By the time of the consultation, Ned had never slept through one night. At eight months of age he was allowed to cry himself out when he awoke, and after eight to ten weeks of this handling, there were many nights when he awakened without crying. However, when he had any minor illness, he would again cry at night when he awoke, and this pattern would persist for a number of weeks, then disappear until it recurred with his next illness. There were no reports of significant disturbances in other areas of functioning.

When seen for psychiatric evaluation at three years eight months, Ned appeared to be a pleasant and alert youngster. When greeted by the examiner, he responded silently by nodding his head. He at first seemed determined to have nothing to do with the playroom and refused the invitation to come into it by leaning firmly against his mother. She entered the playroom, but he remained in the waiting room by himself for about ten minutes until his mother went to get him. Then he returned with her with no apparent hesitation. In the playroom, invitations to use the play equipment were ignored. Only when his mother began to build with the blocks did he appear interested. After a few moments, he joined her and then slowly took over direction of the activity. Five minutes later, when his mother moved to the side of the room, he ignored her withdrawal and continued playing with seemingly no further concern about her. The examiner then joined him, and he played with the blocks with her and answered her questions.

Gradually he began to wander about the room more and more, generally behaving at ease and as if he were enjoying himself. When asked to put the blocks away, he continued to play. When his mother began to help the examiner put the blocks away, Ned joined in and spontaneously grouped the blocks by size and shape, duplicating the arrangement that he had found when he had entered the playroom.

It took a push to get Ned started and, when it was time to go, it required an additional effort to get him to terminate his activity. This appeared to be inertia, not negativism. Once involved he was cooperative and responsive to suggestions. Rather, both at the beginning and at the end of the session, he was slow to adapt to demands for change. On the basis of the limited but definite symptoms and the essentially normal findings on clinical examination, a diagnosis of mild reactive behavior disorder was made.

The anterospective material revealed that through his first fifteen months of life, Ned displayed a definite pattern of withdrawal reactions to new situations but, after a period of exposure, his reactions often became intensely positive. After fifteen months, he also began to show a strong tendency to imitate others and to insist on the maintenance of routines. Scrutiny of the data concerning intensity of reactions revealed that many of his responses, both positive and negative, tended to be extreme: he would shriek and scream when pleased, just as he would shriek and scream when displeased. His sleep, feeding, and elimination patterns were highly irregular. His sleep needs, as measured by the amount of time he spent sleeping, were relatively small from early infancy onwards.

The parents had attempted to deal with the sleep problem in a variety of ways without great success. A self-demand permissive approach to feeding and sleeping in Ned's first year of life did not alter the irregularity of sleep and night awakening evident from the time he was brought home from the hospital. A shift to a punitive approach was no more successful. Generally, if they spanked him when he awoke crying, he would scream more than ever. If they were less punitive, he would cry less at each awakening and have fewer tantrums before going back to sleep. Nevertheless, the father periodically became angry at the child's nightly awakening and screaming and would shout at and spank his son. The mother occasionally, but less frequently, reacted in the same way. The family pediatrician, when consulted by the parents, interpreted the sleep difficulty as a manifestation of anxiety and insecurity. He advised the parents to stay home at night until the problem passed, and to respond lovingly and patiently whenever the child cried at night. This approach also did not work. Ned appeared pleased with his parents' affectionate responses, but the manifestations of the sleep problem did not change.

The review of the anterospective data and the findings on psychiatric evaluation indicated no basis for a diagnosis of anxiety and insecurity. Rather, the disturbance appeared to be the result of dissonant parental handling of a child with an irregular sleep pattern and relatively small sleep needs. The parents, on one hand, demanded that he not call them at night and that he go to sleep at a regular time; on the other hand, they were inconsistent in dealing with his resistances to their demands. Ned's characteristic reaction to the demand that he adapt more quickly than he was able to involved failure to respond to the stimulus or intense physical and verbal protest in the form of a tantrum. Thus, in the negative interplay at bedtime, the parents demanded something the child could not achieve, going to sleep, and as a result, stress developed and Ned's general tendency to react strongly was increasingly evident.

The parents were advised that the child's irregular sleep did not appear to be due to insecurity or anxiety. It was suggested that they insist that Ned stay in his room when he awakened and take care of his toileting and other needs himself without calling them. They were told to make this demand in a persistent and quiet but nonpunitive manner. They were further advised to demand not that he go back to sleep, since this was something impossible for the child to do, but that he stay in bed quietly, a demand he could meet. They were also told to give the child the period of acclimatization he needed before he could move positively into new situations.

Follow-up revealed that the tantrums which had accompanied

bedtime and the screaming during the night had diminished in the space of three to four months. Ned still showed his characteristic irregularity of sleep and still reacted to illnesses and new situations by having difficulty falling asleep or by awakening during the night, but this was now being handled more consistently by the parents. Because of this successful modification of parental handling and the clarification of what was important—that Ned not disturb anyone at bedtime if he couldn't fall asleep or woke up—and what was not important— immediate compliance with the order to go to sleep—the child was able to respond to what was demanded of him, and the stress-producing dissonance was diminished.

B] Dorothy (Case 25) was referred for consultation at age four and a half because of truculent and negativistic behavior. Although she was older than her two sisters, her speech development was inferior to that of her three-year-old sibling, and not much more advanced than that of her other sister who was one and a half years old. She persisted in the use of babyish pronunciations and extremely simple sentence structure. She also had difficulty in following directions. In addition, either because she did not listen or had so much inertia in starting, her sisters would move in ahead of her. However, when she was truly interested in a task, she could carry it out, even if it was more difficult than a task she could not or would not perform.

When invited into the playroom at the start of the diagnostic interview, Dorothy shrank toward her mother. When the mother was invited in, Dorothy followed her and remained close to her side during the first fifteen minutes. Eventually the child began to direct her attention to the examiner and to participate in play activities without requesting aid or attention from her mother. Nevertheless, each time the latter left the room or changed her seat, Dorothy suspended all activity until her mother was resettled.

The child herself chose what she wanted to do and tended to struggle with difficult tasks before asking for help or accepting proffered aid. Her enunciation was indistinct and her phrasing babyish. She resorted to pantomime when she could not name an object. However, she listened to oral directions and was able to carry them out correctly the first time.

In general, Dorothy's demeanor in the playroom was that of a quiet and grave child whose narrow range of facial expressiveness made it difficult to use this latter as a guide to her moods. Rather, the direction and persistence of her activity indicated her enjoyment or lack of it. A developmental language lag appeared to be present, but her symptoms of impaired behavioral functioning could not fully be accounted for by this lag. A diagnosis of mild reactive behavior disorder was made.

The reports on Dorothy's development revealed that from age two months onward, she had shown great selectivity in her responsiveness, and she was very persistent and not easily distracted from certain issues and desires, and nonpersistent and easily distracted from others. Whether positive or negative, her responses were typically mild in the intensity of their expression. In general, she indicated her positive desires by persistence and smiling rather than by intensity of verbal expression or behavior, and indicated negative reactions by persistent whining.

Dorothy also tended to be a slowly moving child in most activities, and she was temperamentally characterized by a low activity level.

The developmental lag in speech was an important factor in understanding Dorothy. Throughout the history, there was mention of her small vocabulary and poor pronunciation. By two and one-half years of age, Dorothy began to have tantrums whenever she was unable to explain herself. This happened especially when her sister, fifteen months younger than she, would intrude to gain the parents' attention or to carry out the task being asked of Dorothy. By thirty-nine months, Dorothy was using language concretely, although her vocabulary was small. At four years, she often could not find words for her thoughts and could not pronounce some words so as to be understood. Her intellectual capacities, as measured by psychometric testing, were low average, which also contributed to her difficulties in keeping up with her younger sisters, both of whom functioned at superior intellectual levels.

Both parents were quick-moving and highly verbal people who valued these characteristics greatly. Therefore, they were particularly concerned about Dorothy's slow movements and difficulty in communicating her desires, and attributed her unexpressiveness to feelings of little depth. They were overtly less concerned with her lack of intellectual precocity as such, but were critical of her difficulties in language use. Both parents frequently became impatient with the child's whining and lack of enthusiasm for activities planned for her, as well as with the length of time it took her to complete an activity. The mother would often explode in frustration, shout at the child, and frequently shake her. The father was less intense in his reactions. Both found the two younger girls more congenial to be with because these youngsters moved quickly and expressed their feelings and desires clearly and sharply.

The crucial element in the interactive process was the parent's discomfort with a "deadpan," slowly moving child with poor speech and moderate intellect who did not or could not express feelings clearly. This contrasted sharply with their own style of functioning and with their expectations that their children should be "lively," bright, and clearly expressive of their desires. They found her slow pace maddening, and her persistent quiet fussing frustrating, and demanded the impossible from her, namely, that she be a lively articulate girl who would participate in activities with overt expressions of joy.

Although the parents realized that Dorothy's delay in language usage was due to slowness in development, they were not aware that this could cause poor comprehension of family conversations and difficulty in verbal expressiveness. As a result, they responded unfavorably to her in comparison to the two younger children, who had more advanced verbal capacities for their age levels. Their demand for a level of verbal expression that was impossible for Dorothy led her to rely on crying and whining, rather than language, to gain her ends.

The parents were advised to give more conscious consideration to Dorothy's poor language development and low activity level by making sure she had opportunities to express herself at her own pace without causing her to worry that her time for expression was limited. It was explained that if she were not rushed or placed in competition with her sisters, Dorothy would be able to formulate her ideas more clearly and have more time to understand what was expected of her before her siblings interfered. The parents were also counseled to revise their attitudes toward the child's lack of overt responsiveness and to understand that her enjoyment could be as great as that of her sisters, even if it were not so clearly or intensely expressed.

The parents quickly understood the issues and the need for them to accept the differences between their style of functioning and Dorothy's. They were able to modify their approach, became more patient with the child, and learned to understand her slow and mild form of expressing her feelings and desires. Also, as her language capacity developed, her level of communication and comprehension expanded progressively. These changes were followed by marked and sustained improvement in her symptoms of negativism and whining.

2] *Dissonance Between Values and Behaviors Developed in the Home and Behavioral Expectancies at School and in Peer Groups*

A] Hal (Case 9), age four, was referred for consultation primarily because the children at nursery school considered him a curiosity. He talked in pedantic language, and the other children neither understood him, nor liked his tone. As a result, some children would hit him and he would cry.

His parents also had noticed that Hal would cry and run to his mother if another child took something of his. He was described as being poised and polite and as deliberately practicing good manners in exaggerated imitation of his father. He practiced these manners with both children and adults.

Hal greeted the examiner with formal politeness at the interview. He said, "Hello, my name is Hal. How do you do, Dr. C.?" and held out his hand to be shaken. Such formalities occurred at other truly inappropriate but formally appropriate moments throughout the interview. During the session, the outstanding characteristics of the child's activity were his verbosity and his tendency to take over direction by stating an intention to act and, if not challenged, proceeding to act on it. When an oral self-direction contradicted a previous direction given by the examiner, and the latter repeated her request, the child would reiterate his own statement of intention. This could go on for three to six exchanges after which the child would do as asked with the same affective quality he displayed when his counter statement of desire was not challenged and he was permitted to do what he had suggested.

The child's use of language was at a uniformly high level, and there was a running commentary throughout his activity, much of which demanded a reply. His play interests were appropriate to the age of six, though there was a ponderous quality about his physical movements and his verbalization. His affective behavior was appropriate, but of a narrow range. Very striking was the apparent contradiction between the child's meticulous politeness and his actual disregard of the effect of his behavior on the examiner when he sought to direct and control her activity. A diagnosis of mild reactive behavior disorder was made.

Review of the anterospective data revealed that Hal had been a very adaptable child who easily accepted routines at home and made them into formal and moderately ritualistic activities. He had also been particularly meticulous in following directions. His formalistic manners and pedantic use of language were the direct reflection of the standards and approaches imposed by his parents.

Both parents were satisfied with Hal's behavior except: 1] when his insistence on overpoliteness was inconvenient to them; and 2] when it became clear that he was teased and baited by other children who thought him peculiar. Both admitted that his language was pedantic, but the father, while ostensibly deploring this, recounted with apparent relish and pride several extreme examples of the child's use of language. They believed that he should be encouraged to modify his manner, not because it was inappropriate, but because it brought ridicule from other children.

Hal was a highly adaptable child and had been trained at home to develop a formal pattern. This, though approved of by his parents, was dissonant with the behavior expected of a child his age by his peer group and by families of neighborhood friends. Having no guidelines to deal with the unexpected dissonance, Hal's main reactions were: 1] to advance more firmly and assertively his repertoire of formal behavior, which had been acceptable at home; and 2] to retreat in disorganized apprehension when his best efforts only increased the ridicule and rejection.

On the basis of this interpretation, the need to establish a formula that would enable Hal to deal with both the home and outside environments and reduce the dissonance between them was emphasized. The parents accepted the need for them to direct him to be aware of and to consider the wishes of other children rather than always to insist on his own. They were told to encourage him to hit back and to refrain from crying when he was hit or when his possessions were taken. They were also to try to restrain his tendency to use pedantic language.

The parents were able to modify their handling as directed. This was followed by marked diminution in the deviant behavior pattern and the beginning of positive involvement with peer groups, which was made easier by a fortuitous move to a new community. However, the gains were not permanent and different problems, which will be considered in the next chapter, did develop at an older age.

B] Isobel (Case 32) was brought to clinical attention two months before her seventh birthday because of learning difficulties. In second grade, she was reading at first grade level, and had experienced reading difficulties from the beginning of the first grade when she complained that the teacher did not give her enough time and that she felt rushed. In addition, her relationships with other children were poor. She tended to avoid the playground at recess and made little effort to play with other children. She was sharply critical of her peers and seemed to prefer to be by herself.

The final problem was described as perfectionism. If she did not immediately accomplish something, she would withdraw quickly or attack the problem furiously and insist upon doing it herself. If corrected, she felt hurt.

On the first contact with the examining psychiatrist, Isobel made a striking impression because of her extremely attractive appearance and her charming, poised manner. She could have posed as a model for a storybook, with her pretty round face and two ponytails. She had a mobile face, and a lovely voice with charming tones of enthusiasm. She turned her full attention to the examiner, chatted continuously, and gave great praise to the toys. As she expressed each interest, she was invited to make use of the toy she had just admired—immediately she praised something else. After several such incidents, Isobel finally did begin to use the shell jewelry, handling it very deftly. Once thus engaged, the child began to request that materials be handed to her; as the examiner complied, other demands for servicing were made, all in a charming manner. However, when the examiner did not comply with her request that she place a soiled tissue in the wastebasket, Isobel cheerfully carried out the task herself.

Isobel answered questions about activities and friends and quickly moved into fantasy. Affect was appropriate to words and acts, but expressed with a somewhat exaggerated tone of voice and a slightly artificial manner. Her use of language was superior, and her expressed interests were appropriate to age and sex.

The diagnostic impression was that this was a highly adaptable child with a moderate reactive behavior disorder.

Isobel was superior in intelligence (I.Q. at age three was 139, at age six, 146). Language had always been a strong area of functioning, but by six years of age, she showed the first evidence of a reading problem and was slow in getting started, missed directions, then asked for help in a demanding way, and refused to start until she was given individual instruction. Combined with this was a low level of frustration tolerance.

The longitudinal data revealed that she had been a highly adaptable child from early infancy onward. Her mood was predominantly positive; she approached most new situations, and her reactions were generally of mild or moderate intensity. Temperamentally, she exhibited a pattern characteristic of the easy child. She had always fitted into routines easily, was sensitive to people, and had always tried to make individual and special relationships with others. In nursery school, she had many friends despite her tendency to demand the best role in imaginative play. In kindergarten and first grade, however, her social relationships decreased to the point where she was practically without companions.

The influence of her parents is especially important for a full understanding of Isobel. Both were very creative and successful people who made high demands on themselves and on their children. Their esteem for individuality and creativity led them to encourage self-expression and disapprove of commonplace or unimaginative behavior by their children.

Isobel was a highly adaptable child who learned to follow the family prescription to be self-expressive and spontaneous. However, in so doing she developed a disregard for rules and procedures in play with peer groups and in learning situations in school. The one-sided emphasis on self-expression did not permit her to become sufficiently responsive to the needs and desires of others. As a result, there was a gradual loss of friends and poor classroom achievement. The dissonance between what her parents expected of her and what was necessary for success in school led to superficiality in social relationships, evasion of her peer group, and unsatisfactory school progress as she persisted in following the individualized course of behavior to which she had adapted.

Once the parents were able to see the relationship between Isobel's insistence on her uniqueness and her lack of graciousness and failure to follow directions, they were able to formulate a new set of standards for the child's behavior. She was to accept incorporation into the group and to modify her attempts to stand out. Although creativity was still to be encouraged, the parents were shown the necessity of giving the child a set of rules that would permit her to function in outside situations and reduce the dissonance between intra- and extrafamilial standards. Remedial tutoring was also recommended to bring her up to grade level.

The parents applied the recommendations given, and Isobel's high adaptability made it possible for her to shift her behavior into forms that permitted her to make scholastic advances and maintain a group of friends. She continued to initiate ideas for joint activities, but became able to accept and follow the suggestions of others. When she was assigned to an individual remedial teacher she began to make use of her superior intellectual capacity and her reading progress leaped forward. At the same time, she learned to take directions from her teacher in the group, something which she could not do before the dissonance was resolved.

3] *Inconsistencies in the Patterning of Parental Practices and Attitudes Resulting in Excessive Stress for the Child*

Ronald (Case 11) was brought to clinical attention when he was four years six months of age with a variety of problems, the details of which were not clear because the mother's concerns were diffuse and reported with many qualifying statements: 1] Sleep. The child would periodically awaken at night and go into his mother's bed. 2] School. His nursery school teacher reported that Ronald was aggressive to the extent that other children stayed out of his way. The child complained that other children didn't like him. 3] Speech. Stuttering was reported to occur when he was excited or hurried and when something was expected of him.

Ronald was a handsome boy who immediately engaged in friendly conversation with the examiner. He went into the playroom eagerly and left his mother without hesitation for his interview. However, he did request that the door to the room in which his mother was sitting be left open.

The child gave a running commentary on his choice of toys and freely answered questions about his play. He talked about his own ideas steadily, smiled throughout the session, and appeared happy. However, he parried questions about nursery school and friends. There were no actual refusals to reply, but rather vague responses followed by a cheerful return to his interests. When pressed to answer more specifically, he became annoyed and peremptory. As soon as the subject of nursery school or friends was dropped, his positive mood returned.

His activities in the playroom were well organized, and his motor functioning was appropriate for age and well coordinated. His speech was superior. At the end of the interview, he attempted to prolong the interpersonal contact by stating that he wasn't finished playing. Then, when given the opportunity to play by himself while the examiner spoke to his mother, he kept repeating that he wanted the examiner to play with him. He finally gave verbal acceptance to the idea of playing by himself, but came into the next room several times with a request for aid or for admiration or to state that he wished to go home. Ronald's final farewell speeches were also prolonged and repetitive.

Following the interview, a diagnosis of mild reactive behavior disorder was made.

The parents had separated when Ronald was an infant. Though he lived primarily with his mother, responsibility for handling him had been divided between the mother, father, grandparents, and a housekeeper, but the extent to which each had a role was not clear. When the mother was in charge, the timing of daily events depended on the hour she awoke and the activities she had planned for that day. Her handling of the child was unstructured, highly variable, and disorganized. The mother had reported that the child generally responded well to firm, calm directions, but added that unfortunately she did not often speak to him this way. Increasingly, Ronald had developed the pattern of demanding adult attention by fussing, crying, or persistently returning to the adult and demanding to be played with. The father, who saw him at frequent intervals, tended to be consistent and firm about rules. He reported that the child had insisted upon his full-time attention during his first visits, but that he had succeeded in training the child to play by himself or with other children when he was otherwise occupied.

Sleep difficulties were found to date from the time Ronald first learned to climb out of his crib. He would do this as often as ten to fifteen times a night by thirty-three months of age. His mother sometimes sat with him and at other times permitted him to climb into her bed. When his grandmother sat with him, he would stay in the crib and fall asleep. His father, during Ronald's visits with him, had firmly and consistently refused to sit with his son when he was put to bed, and the child had eventually stopped asking and went right to sleep.

From infancy onward, Ronald was a regular and very adaptable child. His mother was often impatient, upset, and inconsistent in her approach to him and, in addition, frequently took out her irritability on the child. The inconsistencies in her expectations and demands and unpredictable annoyances, combined with dissonance between her method of handling Ronald and that of his father, led to severe stress for the child. Even for a youngster with Ronald's marked capacity to adapt, the environmental disorganization was so extreme that he could not cope with it successfully, and symptoms of a behavior disorder developed.

It was not possible to influence the mother to modify her functioning to make it less stressful for the youngster. The inconsistencies and dissonances in demands and expectations continued, and Ronald's symptoms increased. Three years later follow-up interviews with the mother and Ronald's second-grade teacher revealed his main problem now to be his poor relationship with peers. Whereas this problem had been minimal in kindergarten and first grade, he was now reported to tease and hit other children and call them names. Other symptoms had also appeared, including academic underachievement, difficulty in communicating his ideas to others, apprehension over physical activities, and fear of germs.

Another clinical interview was arranged and in the one-to-one circumstances of the office visit Ronald was constructive and organized. He was partially aware that the complaints about his school behavior were legitimate, but tended to minimize them and project blame onto others.

The parents also were seen individually at this time, and though they both were aware that Ronald needed a highly structured scholastic environment and consistent home handling, it seemed unlikely that either requirement would be met. The mother, because of her own poor organization, was unable to give the child the handling he required. At this time, the diagnosis was changed to neurotic behavior disorder.

4] *Interparental Dissonance and the Use of the Child's Characteristics as a Weapon in Interparental Conflict.*

Nora (Case 27) was brought for clinical evaluation at the age of five years seven months. Her presenting problems included the following:

1] Explosive anger, begun between ages two and three, which had developed from what her parents called her uncompromising behavior when she disliked something. She would burst into tears and become uncontrolled in trivial circumstances, and her reactions to most parental directions were negative. She was also considered a disobedient child. 2] Withholding of bowel movements and false reporting of bowel evacuation. There had been a history of irregularity and constipation from birth. 3] Insatiable desire for attention and sweets, since the age of two and one-half. 4] Lying about misdeeds and taking small sums of money to buy sweets, which had begun at approximately age five. 5] Poor relationships to other children, first noted at age three and one-half. 6] Babyish behavior, such as persistence in thumb-sucking, a tendency to whine, and excessive requests to be cuddled by her mother. 7] Fear of the dark, present since age one and one-half.

Nora was a very pretty girl, daintily dressed, gravely polite. She parted easily from her parents to go into the playroom with the examiner. She was pleasant in her statement of preference for drawing materials rather than the toys that had been provided. In the play interview, she was a quiet, cooperative, reserved, and slightly shy child who spoke little unless questioned, and who tended to avoid detailed replies. None of the "babyish" behavior was in evidence, and she did not suck her thumb or whine. Also, her high intensity of reactivity was not displayed. For the duration of the visit, Nora was a perfect "lady." She was cooperative and her verbalizations were logical, relevant, and coherent. However, when asked about her behavior in the problem areas, she was evasive and gave "I don't know" answers.

Because of the character, multiplicity, and severity of the symptoms, a diagnosis of moderately severe neurotic behavior disorder was made.

The anterospective data revealed that Nora had a consistent pattern of reactions of great intensity as early as five months of age. These responses were equally sharp in a positive or negative direction. Adaptability to most new situations was slow. There were also repeated reports of persistent behavior, especially when a demand was not fulfilled. Many negative reactions occurred when Nora was stopped from doing what she wished or when she was not successful in attempts at a task begun on her own initiative. From five months on, there were repeated reports that Nora was markedly persistent in her responses. As she grew older, she became insistent upon personal attention. This behavior continued and reached increasingly annoying proportions.

Her mother had a positive, warm relationship with Nora in early infancy. The child's clear and definite reactions made her easy to handle. As the child grew older and some of her demands either could not be met appropriately or became annoying, such as her insistence on constant attention, the mother showed increasing inconsistency in her handling. At times she was permissive, and she and the child would strike bargains. At other times, she showed a growing tendency to be annoyed at the child and to push her away. Then, in response to the youngster's fearfulness, she would cuddle and reassure her. However, in contrast, when safety was involved, the mother tended to stick to her rules quietly and persistently. After several tantrums in response to the invoking of such rules, the child began to accept prohibitions, first with a token tantrum, and then with good grace.

The father was less inconsistent in his behavior. He, too, had been proud of his infant daughter's refusal to compromise. But, as she grew older, he became critical of both child and mother. His firm rules became overdemanding and punitive, and he began to dislike the child from age two and one-half on. He made a series of stringent rules for both mother and child to follow with regard to Nora's difficult bowel movements, and shouted at Nora when success was not achieved and she did not produce a bowel movement. At the time of consultation, it was clear that he disliked the child.

Nora was a persistent, slowly adaptive and intense child who, for optimal development, required firm and consistent handling. When she received this treatment, she could eventually adapt and learn to follow rules, as she did in the area of safety. However, in most other areas, her parents did not provide her with the structure she needed. They made demands and had expectations that were dissonant with her temperamental characteristics. This was one reason for the excessive stress and behavior problem development. An additional special source of dissonance stemmed from the general marital discord and conflict which existed between the parents.

A major aspect of this marital friction involved the father's attempt to dominate the family and especially his wife. In this context he seized upon the mother's difficulties in dealing with Nora as an excuse to label her inadequate and incompetent as a mother, and thus to justify his assertion of overall dominance of the family. He gave the mother peremptory orders and set arbitrary rules by which she was to handle Nora. The mother, already insecure because of the problems of managing Nora, was easily intimidated and submitted, though with resentment and anxiety. However, when she tried to carry out her husband's dictates, the unreasonableness of the demands on Nora resulted in storms and panic in the child, which caused the mother to vacillate and back down. This seesawing between being influenced by her husband's orders and by her child's explosions only intensified her feelings of inadequacy as a mother, and led to increased inconsistency in dealing with Nora.

Individual psychotherapy was recommended for Nora, and she attended weekly sessions for two and one-half years. Concurrently, the parents made a great effort to modify their behavior with their child. The father attempted to be less strict and arbitrary with small issues, and the mother tried to be more consistent.

Although the basic pattern of the marital relationship remained unchanged, the father did respond to the guidance discussions by substantially reducing his exploitation of Nora's difficulties in his power struggle with his wife. This in turn made it possible for the mother to handle Nora with less anxiety and conflict. The combination of improved parental functioning and the help given the child through psychotherapy resulted in gradual improvement in Nora's behavior to the point where the child functioned satisfactorily in school and with her peers. Thus, though her tendency toward constipation, her intense reactions, her persistence in her desires, and her demand for attention all continued to be present, she no longer withheld her bowel movements, stole, lied, or was isolated from her peers.

5] *Dissonance Between the Child's Expectations of Acceptance and Affection and Parental Feelings and Behavior*

Bert (Case 42) was brought for clinical evaluation when he was eight and one-half years of age. The precipitating problems included the following: 1] He had become the scapegoat of the class. 2] He had been tattling on other children in school. 3] His habits of nose picking and finger-sucking were so pronounced as to be considered offensive by his classmates. 4] His friends recently had become quite reluctant to spend time with him, whereas formerly he had had many friends and a very full social life.

Bert was born after an eight month one week pregnancy, and developed pneumonitis shortly after birth. Although his later health was good, there was some delay in the achievement of motor milestones. Accompanying this was poor gross motor coordination and, by age four, his speech was still slurred and incomprehensible. His school progress had been excellent except for a tendency to reverse letters and numbers, which interfered with correct writing and correct written arithmetic. The child's oral arithmetic was superior.

During the interview, Bert was a pleasant, friendly boy who wanted to spend most of the time socializing or playing. He was consciously aware of his disappearing friends and of his difficulty with letter and number reversals, and wished to know what to do to improve his peer relationships and his writing. His speech at this time was good, but his enunciation was a bit slurred and he spoke rapidly in a high-pitched, unvaried tone. In the heat of discussion, he frequently did not listen to what was said to him, although the examiner's reply might be in response to his request for information. When finally he would listen, he was most friendly, but often would become distracted once again.

Diagnosis was mild behavior disorder secondary to brain damage.

A review of the anterospective data revealed that Bert had shown interest in other children and in cooperative play at an early age although he was not well able to make himself understood verbally. With peers and adults, he patiently indicated his desires through pantomime. He was basically a child of mild intensity and positive mood.

In order to overcome his poor speech, speech therapy had been begun when he was five years old. The child gave his conscious cooperation to this endeavor and frequently practiced correct pronunciation spontaneously.

Examination of the parent's relationships with the child showed increasing paternal criticism of Bert. The father would correct the child's speech in a loud tone of voice or flick Bert's hand away from his mouth. At times he would shout at the child until the boy was reduced to tears. Great pressure of work had kept the father quite busy most weekends and evenings during the preceding year or so, and he would become very annoyed when the child walked into the study and interrupted him at an inopportune time. The mother agreed that his criticisms of the child were legitimate, but felt that they were overdone. The father tended to agree with her.

The issue in this case appeared to be one of a parent who, while aware of the child's concrete problem, a neurological deficit with a lag in development, was nevertheless intensely annoyed at the child's deviation from the behavior he expected of him. Moreover, because of the father's busy schedule, almost all of the child's relations with him were characterized by a negative interaction. This treatment was dissonant with what the child expected from his father. It seemed, therefore, that the frustration and demoralization the child developed in his dealings with his father were carried over into his outside relationships where he again felt helpless to defend himself against any negative attitudes.

Modification in paternal attitudes and behavior was recommended, with the emphasis placed on planning activities in which father and child could have a positive affectionate interchange. Follow-up indicated some change in paternal functioning in the recommended direction, with intermittent but unsustained improvement in the child's symptoms.

6] *Dissonance Between the Mode of Functioning of the Teacher and the Characteristics of the Child*

When he was referred at five years ten months of age, Richard (Case 31) was having many tantrums in first grade. These had begun shortly after the beginning of the school term and then became increasingly frequent (up to five tantrums per school day) and disruptive in succeeding weeks. Finally, the school announced that unless the parents and child undertook psychiatric treatment, it would be necessary to have the child withdrawn from school.

Initially, the tantrums were precipitated whenever Richard objected to stopping what he was doing and moving on to a new activity. As time passed, the number of incidents that would evoke a tantrum increased, especially since the other children had begun to laugh at his crying. Concurrently, he had begun, with much persistence, to ask his teacher that he be taught formal reading. This was not possible inasmuch as the school's educational philosophy emphasized reading readiness procedures in the first grade, and the postponement of instruction in formal reading itself to the second or third grade.

Richard separated from his mother for the clinical interview without hesitation and appeared to be at home in the playroom immediately. He explored the various play possibilities, and his choice of activities was appropriate for age and sex. He was well coordinated. Although he made no unusual use of language, his verbalizations were of superior quality. He spontaneously limited the discussion to the ongoing activity and he answered the examiner's questions about school, although he did not mention his tantrums or any negative interchanges. When faced with a mechanical difficulty in one of the games, he handled it with patience, persistence, and good humor.

On the basis of the history, the teacher's description, and the absence of any pathological behavior in the clinical interview with the child, a diagnosis of moderately severe reactive behavior disorder was made.

Richard, a second child, was born fourteen years after his brother. From earliest childhood, he had characteristically displayed a long attention span and great persistence. The child also had selective interests and tended to be even more than usually persistent in returning to these activities when he was interrupted. In addition, he actively resisted being separated from one of these activities and might have a tantrum if such separation was enforced. By contrast, his reactions in other situations were usually of only mild intensity, even when a demand of his was ignored because of parental preoccupation elsewhere. It appeared that a major reason for the small number of tantrums at home after the age of three was that his parents and older brother had learned not to let him start an activity that did not permit completion. If an interruption was necessary, they expected a fuss on his part, followed by cheerful compliance. The family considered this behavior merely an individual characteristic of the child, not a problem. There was, however, a tendency on his parents' part to ignore some of Richard's legitimate demands when they were inconvenient to them and to respond only if he had a tantrum. This reinforced his tantrum behavior as a technique for gaining attention when frustrated.

Richard's nursery school teachers had also considered his long attention span and the fact that he did not like shifting from an activity before he had finished it as a characteristic, not as a problem. The tantrums, which occurred when it was necessary to insist that he terminate an activity, were aborted easily by comforting from the teacher.

Just before Richard began first grade, his father had a second coronary occlusion, and his brother, with whom he had been close and who had taught him to read, had gone back to college for his sophomore year. Because of their understanding of Richard, his parents had been able to minimize the effect of these crises on his home life.

However, once he entered the scholastic environment, stress did develop. Three issues were involved: 1] Because of the curriculum, Richard was denied an activity that he had anticipated would be part of school and to which he had expected to give an extended amount of attention; namely, reading and writing. 2] The activities of the classroom were scheduled in such a manner that when the program changed at intervals appropriate for the attention span of most youngsters in the group, Richard was often still deeply absorbed in the activity and very reluctant to shift. As a consequence, there were many demands on him to shift when he was not ready to do so and, therefore, many circumstances which typically elicited a tantrum response from him. 3] As soon as the other children began to bait him by calling him baby, a new interaction developed, and Richard constantly anticipated being teased.

It was suggested to the parents that his present school was inappropriate to Richard's temperament, goals, and patterns of interest, and that his difficulties derived from this dissonance. It was therefore recommended that he change schools and enter one appropriate for him in which he would be able to undertake formal reading, writing, and arithmetic training. It was also recommended that he be permitted to spend a longer time than the average first-grader at one learning activity before he was shifted to another. The parents were also advised to train themselves to listen to the child's mildly expressed desires. They should respond to his legitimate requests so that Richard would not need to resort to tantrums; to requests which were not appropriate, they should explain their refusal and not simply ignore the youngster's expressed desire.

After his transfer to a more appropriate school in which more intensive reading, writing, and number work were part of his curriculum, Richard was reported to have had two tantrums on the first day and none thereafter for a period of several months. The teacher, aware of Richard's characteristic of persistence, permitted him to continue reading and writing, even when she changed her schedule. In this way, the program he followed and his basic interests were parallel and consonant to his temperamental adaptation and his scholastic success. (Subsequent problems, which developed at an older age because of new situations of dissonance between environmental demands and expectations and his temperamental characteristics, will be considered in the next chapter.)

The cases presented illustrate several varieties of dissonant stress that contributed to the development of behavior disorders. The object in presenting these illustrations was to indicate that dissonant stress is by no means a homogeneous entity, but one which varies in accordance with temperament, capacity, developmental level, environment, and the nature and structuring of demands. Such dissonance produces disturbance rather than progress. The form that the disturbance will take is not explicitly dictated by the fact or type of dissonance, but is dependent upon opportunities for symptom selection and elaboration that need now to be considered.

REFERENCES

1. L. J. Henderson, *The Fitness of the Environment* (New York: Macmillan Co., 1913).
2. M. R. Nocenti, "Adrenal Cortex," *Medical Physiology,* ed. P. Bard (St. Louis: C. V. Mosby Co., 1961), p. 842.
3. L. Festinger, "Cognitive Dissonance," *Scientific American,* 207:93 (1962).

15 | THE DEVELOPMENTAL DYNAMICS OF SYMPTOM FORMATION AND ELABORATION

Despite the fact that it is the symptom that the patient or the parent presents to the psychiatrist (indeed, the symptom may even constitute the principal reason for the seeking of help), little agreement exists in the fields of either child or adult psychiatry as to the mechanisms of symptom selection and the processes involved in symptom elaboration. The range of positions that have been advanced to account for the origin, selection, and development of symptoms varies widely, and includes constitutionalist, motivational-psychodynamic, learning theory, and sociocultural concepts.

The method of treatment selected is clearly related to the therapist's view of symptoms. If the symptom is considered as an adaptive maneuver having stabilizing properties, attempts at its removal will be avoided because of the concern that disruption of functioning will occur, or that an even more disabling symptom will be adopted in an effort to maintain equilibrium. If the symptom is viewed as being merely adventitious, it may be ignored entirely. When it is considered as a symbol, it may serve as a signpost indicating the appropriate direction for therapeutic inquiry. If the symptom is considered as equivalent to the disorder, symptom removal as such becomes the basic goal of the therapeutic strategy.

A study of symptom formation, therefore, is clearly relevant to an understanding of the origins of psychological disturbance, to the management of psychiatric illness, and to theories of psychological development. The data of our longitudinal study have made it possible to explore the dynamics of the symptom because they permit an analysis both of the general features of child-environment interaction that tend to result in behavioral disturbances and of the developmental dynamics of symptom selection and elaboration. Because the data were acquired anterospectively, they have provided a special opportunity to pursue a developmental approach in tracing the origins, elaboration, and course of different symptoms manifested by the children with behavior problems.

In tracing the emergence and evolution of behavior developmentally, it is not enough to recognize that it has antecedents in the life course of the individual. To do this is merely to argue that behaviors are caused. What is needed, if we are to understand symptom formation

157

and evolution, is a consideration of its course in terms of the developmental stages and transitions from action to ideation that characterize development from the infant to the adult. Symptoms in the young child are primarily abnormalities of overt behavior and reflect the character of the young organism in whom action and ideation, as has been suggested by Gesell,[1] Werner,[2] and Piaget,[3] are as yet relatively undifferentiated as systems of psychological organization. As the child grows older, he develops more complex mechanisms of behavioral mediation. These include an increasingly expanded subjective life characterized by ideation, abstraction, and symbolic representation. These changes with age are reflected in the nature of the child's emotional and social functioning, which become increasingly ideational and less dominated by immediate stimulation and direct expression in action. These developmental changes have two major consequences for symptom evolution. One of these is an alteration in the expression of disturbance, and the other is an increasing effect of ideas and attitudes on behavior, so that disturbance comes to be expressed more indirectly and to involve a variety of substitutes for action in the form of verbalizations, feeling-states, and attitudes. Further, the child becomes increasingly responsive to the attitudes, values, and concepts communicated by significant adults and peers as he grows older. His reactions, thus, come increasingly to be influenced by what others think and say, as well as by what they do.

These changes in the child's psychological organization as he grows older result in a developmental progression of symptoms. Failure to recognize such a developmental course may result either in the erroneous attribution of complex psychological mechanisms to the young child, or in the assumption that simple mechanisms of symptom formation and expression characteristic of the young child also obtain in older individuals in whom newer and more complex modes of adaptation are operative. The first of these tendencies is most readily perceived in a number of psychoanalytic and other psychodynamic presentations, and is well described by Anna Freud who noted that "Some psychoanalysts credit the newborn already with complex mental processes, with a variety of affects which accompany the action of the various drives and, moreover, with complex reactions to these drives and affects, such as for instance guilt feelings." [4] The second tendency can be frequently found in behaviorist theories.[5]

With the above considerations in mind, the longitudinal data relevant to symptom formation and evolution for each clinical case were scrutinized for answers to the following questions:

1] Given a child-environment interaction that is excessively stressful, what factors determine the specific symptoms that appear?

2] Once a symptom appears, how do its consequences affect the development and evolution of the symptom?

3] What consequences for symptom characteristics occur as the result of increase in age and the development of a new age-stage level of functioning?

SYMPTOM FORMATION

The functional areas in which a symptom developed appeared, in the main, to be the result of environmental influences. The standards and values of the parents, peer group, or school teachers determined the areas in which persistent demands were most likely to be made on the child. Such persistent demands, when inappropriate to the child's capacities, temperamental qualities, or previously developed behavioral patterns were productive of dissonance and excessive stress. Thus, the infrequency of complaints in the areas of feeding, elimination, and masturbation, and the greater frequency in the areas of sleep, discipline, mood disturbance, speech, peer relationships, and learning, paralleled closely the level of parental concern and demand in these areas of functioning. The expectation of certain teachers that all normal children should quickly be able to become active members of the group resulted in excessive demands and stresses on children who were slow to warm up, with the consequent development of maladaptive patterns in the school setting. The behavioral patterns learned without stress in the home environment by certain easy children (see Cases 9 and 32 in Chapter 8) became maladaptive in school because of their dissonance with peer group standards or with the demands of formal learning, and led to symptom development in these areas of functioning.

For the slowly adaptive child, inconsistency in parental functioning was also influential in determining symptom choice. These children usually required patient consistency in parental practices in any specific area of functioning to give them the opportunity finally to adapt. In those areas in which this type of consistency existed, symptoms usually did not develop. On the contrary, where inconsistency in parental functioning was evident, symptoms frequently materialized in slowly adapting children. This was typified by Nora (Case 27, see Chapter 7), in whom symptoms developed in a number of areas in which the parents had been impatient, inconsistent, and punitive. On the other hand, in the area of safety, in which parental practice had been firm and consistent, symptoms of behavioral disturbance were not manifested.

In contrast to the predominance of environmental influences evident in the choice of functional area in which a symptom developed, the behavioral form taken by the symptom appeared to be related to the individual child's temperamental pattern. This can be illustrated by considering the different behavioral responses to frustration or to excessive environmental demands made by children with differing patterns of temperamental traits.

Frustration, whether it resulted from a youngster's unsuccessful struggle for task mastery, his removal from a pleasurable ongoing activity, or the refusal of a desire, typically produced behavioral manifestations that reflected his temperamental characteristics. The intense, highly active, and persistent child commonly developed tantrum behavior, with screaming, kicking, throwing himself around, and throwing objects, in various combinations and for varying lengths of time. The persistent child with mild intensity whined and fussed. The mild child with a low activity level typically showed quiet withdrawal, such as standing apart sucking his finger and gazing into the distance. The easy child, who adapted quickly to a new situation or demand, usually tolerated frustration easily unless it was prolonged and repeated. The easily distractible child tended to show only brief reactions to frustration and was readily diverted from the frustrating situation.

A child's behavioral response to an excessive environmental demand also tended to reflect his temperamental characteristics. Thus, the child who was slow to warm up usually responded to the pressure for immediate involvement in a new situation with withdrawal reactions of mild intensity. One such child ducked quietly behind his mother on entering nursery school after an absence due to illness; another came to a dead stop when urged to participate in a new group game; and a third refused to budge when his father tried to take him into a strange store. The difficult child, whose negative reaction to the new was intense, usually protested loudly and sometimes developed negativistic oppositional behavior. The easy child, on the other hand, who tended to adapt quickly and without tension to environmental demands, did not customarily exhibit withdrawal or oppositional behavioral responses to pressure. He tended, rather, in his deviant behavior, to reflect the inappropriate demands to which he had been subjected and to which he had adapted. Thus, for example, Hal (Case 9), one such easy child, obediently parroted the formalities and manners taught him at home. At lunch he insisted that his mother greet him with the words with which she greeted his father at dinner. He sat in father's seat and mimicked his mannerisms. He carried this behavior outside the home, even though it made him the object of the ridicule of other children. Isobel (Case 32) not only refused to play the "ordinary" games of her peers, but also gave her parents new knowledge of themselves when they heard her imperious little voice in an accurate replication of impatient parental disdain say, "That's not a creative game, it's stupid." In Diana (Case 4), the presence of a tight anal sphincter in infancy, combined with inconsistent parental handling of the resulting mechanical problems in evacuation, led to the habitual withholding of bowel movements and refusal to use the toilet.

CONSEQUENCES OF SYMPTOM EXPRESSION

As the children in the clinical sample were followed over time, it became abundantly clear that the course of the behavior disorder and the pattern of symptom evolution were in most cases profoundly influenced by the consequences the symptom had for the child. In other words, the child-environment interactional process was responsible not only for the origin of the problem behavior, but also for shaping the dynamics of its subsequent course. Some specific consequences of symptom expression on the subsequent course of the behavior problem in the different clinical cases have been classified under the following headings:

1] *Amelioration*

In some cases the parents reacted to the appearance of a symptom with genuine concern for the child's welfare. They recognized that the symptom was a danger signal warning that an unhealthy developmental trend, which required correction, might be operating. They were eager to obtain help and advice, and addressed themselves objectively and effectively to carrying through the psychiatrist's recommendations once the problem was defined and a treatment plan outlined. Examples are Isobel (Case 32), with her poor peer relationships, unsatisfactory school performance, and consequent defensive withdrawal reactions; Dorothy (Case 25), with her slowness, whining, and fussing; and Elaine (Case 34), with her tantrums, fears, and perfectionist trends. In each case, the parents had been unaware that their handling of the child was contributing to excessive stress until symptoms appeared and the course of the disturbance was defined in the psychiatric evaluation. Once the problem was identified and defined, these parents were able to institute changes in their own behavior, which quickly led to marked improvement in the child's symptoms and overall functioning.

2] *Intensification of the Original Symptoms*

A frequent consequence of a symptom was an initial worsening of the child-environment interaction from which it had derived. Thus, the inconsistent, pressuring, and punitive parental approach to Nora (Case 27), a difficult child, led to an exacerbation of her negativistic and non-adaptive responses, and this in turn led to an intensification of the parental responses. The annoyed impatience of Roy's (Case 17) mother with his lack of task completion resulting from his easy distractibility, led him increasingly to ignore her requests and demands, with lessened task fulfillment and greater maternal annoyance.

3] *Inadequacy of Functioning Leading to Defensive Behavior*

This well-known clinical phenomenon was evident in a number of the cases. Inadequacy of functioning in peer relations with children or retardation in formal learning caused the youngster to fall behind his class and frequently led to isolation from the group. Such isolation, combined with overt or implied derogation, stimulated defensive responses. The defensiveness took the form of withdrawal, of provocative behavior, or of behaviors aimed at gaining recognition or at camouflaging deficient achievement, all resulting in increased academic retardation, further social isolation or both.

4] *Deficient Self-Image*

In several cases where the symptoms provoked disapproval and condemnation by influential figures in the child's environment, the negative value judgments began significantly to affect the nature of the child's developing image of himself. An example is Richard (Case 31, see case report later in this chapter), whose explosive tantrums led to recurrent disturbances in which he was branded the culprit by teachers, classmates, and playmates, until finally he began to speak of himself as "bad" and as always bound to get into trouble no matter what he did. Another example was Laura (Case 39), a girl who developed increasing disturbance in social functioning with her peers. As her difficulty in making friends increased, she began to speak of herself in a derogatory fashion as the kind of person who didn't make friends. Simultaneously, she also developed an "I'm too good for them" defense, saying such things as, "I have different kinds of interests"; "I'm not catty the way they are."

5] *Secondary Gain*

This phenomenon, frequently described in many case reports in the literature, was only occasionally noted in our case material. It is true that a number of parents or teachers interpreted the child's symptom as deliberately motivated to achieve some purpose such as the fulfillment of a desire to which the parent was opposed, the avoidance of a difficult task in school, or the intent to "annoy" or "upset" the parent. In almost all such instances, however, it was possible to understand the origin and development of the symptom in terms of interactional processes and without the need to invoke such hypothetical intrapsychic purposes or goals. There were a few instances in which the child's verbalizations made it clear that he did use his symptom, *once it had developed,* to achieve some specific purpose. This was evident in Linda (Case 12), a girl whose temperament fitted the difficult child constellation, and one in whom intense negative withdrawal reactions in infancy were frequently accompanied by vomiting. At three and one-half years of age, she was scheduled for psychometric testing, but refused to come. Her parents coaxed her into coming, and as she entered the office, she announced to her parents, "If you make me go into the room to play with the lady,

I'll vomit." Her parents insisted, whereupon she vomited vigorously, turned, and left the room crying triumphantly, "See, I told you that if you make me go in, I'll vomit." The clear use of the symptom for control of others by this child was in contrast to almost all the other cases in the sample, where evidence of purposive manipulation of others by means of a symptom was either absent or at best capable of being only very indirectly inferred.

SYMPTOM EXPRESSION AT DIFFERENT AGE-STAGE DEVELOPMENTAL LEVELS

The sequential analysis of the characteristics of symptom expression and evolution as the children in the sample grew older has shown a significant relationship between symptom change and developmental level. Of greatest interest in these instances has been the shift from symptoms expressed primarily on an overt behavioral level in the preschool years to those reflecting complex subjective states, attitudes, distorted self-images, and psychodynamic patterns of defense by school age. These shifts appeared to reflect the normal transition from action to ideation that characterizes the course of development from infancy to adulthood and may be illustrated by three case histories.

1] Diana (Case 4) was first referred for psychiatric evaluation at the age of forty-three months because of constipation, painful bowel movements, withholding of bowel movements, and refusal to use the toilet. Her problem had originated as a physiological difficulty deriving from a defect in anal structure. Infrequent and constipated bowel movements were evident in the first few months of life, and her pediatrician determined the cause to be a tight anal sphincter. At four months of age, manual dilatation of the sphincter was carried out, but with only temporary relief, and her problem of evacuation remained chronic. There were periodic recurrences of constipation coupled with large and painful evacuations. Medications were shifted frequently, but none was found to be entirely satisfactory.

Development was otherwise normal. Temperamentally, Diana showed the characteristics of any easy child; she was adaptable, friendly, and approached new situations with eagerness. The bowel difficulty, however, did not improve as she grew older. Rather, the persistent organic problem was aggravated by marked inconsistency in the mother's handling of the issue. She repeatedly shifted her approaches and ran the gamut from permissiveness to pressure, from reassurance to anger. Over time, the bowel difficulty began increasingly to be a source of tension and antagonism between mother and child. At age three years, the developing psychological disturbance was further intensified by the refusal of the nursery school in which she had been enrolled to allow her to continue with the group. The school stated that she was a delightful and lovely child, but they could not tolerate the problem of cleaning up her intermittently huge and odorous evacuations.

Following her expulsion from nursery school, Diana developed the habit of hiding in corners, behind the drapery, or behind the furniture when she moved her bowels. At other times, her parents could tell from her facial expressions and by the way she held her body that she was withholding a bowel movement, but even at such times could not persuade her to go to the toilet.

When seen for psychiatric evaluation at forty-three months of age, Diana was a charming, spontaneous, and gay youngster. She was friendly and self-assured. Her functioning in the clinical play session showed no abnormalities. She used the toys with enjoyment and imagination. Her verbalizations were at a high level, affect was appropriate, and she appeared quite relaxed. She answered questions about her bowel problem in a matter-of-fact fashion and gave correct factual information, but without elaboration or spontaneous discussion.

The diagnosis was a reactive behavior disorder, mild. Parent guidance was attempted. It was emphasized to the mother that an organic problem did exist and that a patient, quiet, and consistent approach was necessary. The harmful psychological consequences resulting from attempts to pressure or punish the child for her difficulties with toileting were outlined. However, the advice did not result in any significant change in the mother's functioning.

Diana finally began to use the toilet when she was four years old, though recurrent episodes of severe constipation, withholding of bowel movements, and overflow incontinence and soiling continued to occur intermittently. The mother continued to be inconsistent in handling the issue and, in addition, now began to exhibit an overall tendency to minimize the extent of the problem as Diana grew older.

Diana herself cooperated with her mother's denial and avoided acknowledging the existence of a problem and, by eight and one-half years of age, had developed a neurotic denial mechanism in which she insisted that she had not soiled herself, even when it was olfactorily evident that she had. If her parents noticed her wiggling in an obvious attempt to hold back a bowel movement, she denied that she had such a need. When she went to the toilet, she came out as quickly as she could, frequently failing to flush the toilet. The diagnosis was changed to neurotic behavior disorder, moderately severe. No attempt at direct treatment was at first possible because of the child's persistent denial that any problem existed. Of interest was the remarkably normal and equable social and academic development Diana showed despite the chronicity of the bowel problem and the elaboration of a neurotic defense mechanism of denial to deal with it. There were also no overt or indirect manifestations of anxiety extending to other areas of functioning.

Finally, at age nine, the denial pattern was abruptly discarded and Diana requested help for her bowel difficulties. Her determination to deal directly with these problems at long last developed as the result of two events. First, she had been sent home from camp during the previous summer because her counselor and bunkmates simply could not tolerate the constant presence of a fecal odor, even though they assumed the matter was beyond Diana's control, sympathized with her, and otherwise liked her very much. Diana accepted this with apparent good grace, stated her agreement with their decision, but later said, "I used to think that nobody really noticed. When I got sent home from camp, I learned that I can't really hide it so I better get over it."

The other incident was a discussion with a friend. She and her friend were in Diana's room "talking about secret things." They were conversing about their dolls when the friend commented, according to Diana, "Sometimes you have a look on your face that looks as if you're afraid you have to make a B.M. and you're trying to hold it in." Diana quickly returned the conversation to the dolls. "Lucky for me she forgot about it." But this reaffirmed her awareness that her disguise was not perfect, and her attempts to solve her problem by denial were not succeeding.

On her first visit to the study psychiatrist, when she was nine years old, her changed attitude was expressed by the following exchange after a few minutes of chitchat. "I would like to discuss my problem." The psychiatrist responded, "I'll be very happy to do so. The reason I didn't ask you about it today is because the last time you were here you didn't want to talk about it." She replied, "Yes, but unless I talk about it with you and solve it, I'll still have it and I don't want to have it."

A series of discussions was initiated in which all aspects of her bowel difficulties and her neurotic mechanisms of dealing with the problem were freely discussed. In each of the first two sessions, there was a period in which Diana was observed wiggling in her chair. On each occasion, after this had gone on for some ten to fifteen minutes without Diana acting on it, the psychiatrist inquired, "Do you have to go to the bathroom?" Diana denied that this was the case. It was pointed out, "You were wiggling just like somebody who needs to go. Maybe you should make sure—maybe you need to have a bowel movement now or to urinate." On the first of the occasions, Diana obediently went and urinated. On the second, she said, "No, it's just that I like to wiggle in my seat," and refrained from wiggling for five minutes. She then said, "I think I need to go now," went to the lavatory, and urinated. On neither occasion did she flush the toilet. On the first, the psychiatrist did so, but on the second, she said, "I think you forgot to flush the toilet." Diana promptly returned and flushed it. Thus, even when the issue was first being actively discussed with her, the pattern of automatic denial was still very much in evidence, accompanied by conscious rationalization of her avoidance of toileting functions. On subsequent visits, this sequence did not occur. Diana went to the bathroom several times on her own volition and flushed the toilet each time.

Parallel to the regime of psychotherapy, a schedule of nightly suppositories was initiated to help the child develop a regular routine of bowel evacuation. She cooperated in this readily, in contrast to previous abortive attempts in this direction, and a regular pattern of daily bowel movements was quickly established. The psychiatric treatment was discontinued after six weekly sessions as no longer necessary. After four to five months, the suppositories were decreased to one every other night and shortly thereafter discontinued altogether. At follow-up, several months later, there appeared to be normal bowel functioning and, as before, no other evidence of psychological disturbance.

In summary, this was a child who started with organic bowel symptoms in early infancy that then became a source of tension and stress because of unfavorable maternal responses and disapproval in nursery school. An avoidance mechanism developed which, in the three- to four-year age period, was expressed primarily in behavioral terms— withholding of bowel movements, hiding in corners when she evacuated, and refusal to use the toilet. As she grew older the avoidance mechanism became increasingly ideational and symbolic, taking the form of denial and rationalization. Finally, at age nine years, the reactions of disapproval by others in her environment became so sharp and frequent that her denial mechanism became ineffective. She then consciously and successfully addressed herself, with the psychiatrist's help, to dealing directly with the problem.

2] Richard (Case 31), an extremely persistent child, had severe tantrums in nursery school and first grade when ongoing activities in which he was absorbed were abruptly interrupted by his teachers. His early development and the temperament-environment interaction leading to this symptom are detailed in Chapter 14. The tantrums, which brought him to psychiatric attention at age six years when he was in the first grade, were alleviated by transfer to another school in which his persistent intensive interest in academic work was not only permitted, but encouraged. Two mild tantrums occurred during the first week in the new school and none for the rest of the year, or during the following two years. In the remainder of the first grade, as well as in the second and third grades, his teachers were fond of him and approved of the persistence with which he applied himself to assignments.

Problems began again at the start of fourth grade. Very early in the year situations arose in which the teacher scolded Richard for not complying quickly with her orders. Richard argued with her about the rationality of her demands. This only led to punishment, to which he reacted by first arguing and then bursting into tears. On other occasions, he told the teacher to shut up and was wildly out of control, sobbing, and flinging himself about. Several discussions with the study child psychiatrist were held in which Richard gradually identified his inappropriate behaviors and tried to make his peace with the idea that he must follow the directions his teachers gave, even if he felt them to be unnecessary and inappropriate. He also gave recognition to his great persistence and to the difficulty he had in shifting activities, and discussed the need to take responsibility himself for making such changes instead of resisting the attempts of others to get him to stop. Over a period of several weeks, the uncooperative and tantrum behavior in school diminished markedly.

Then a poster contest for public school children was announced. The teacher had obtained a specified number of poster papers, selected the children from the class who were to be permitted to enter the contest, and gave them paper. Richard did not get any and, quite innocently, assumed that it would be all right to get his own poster paper. He proceeded to do so and then brought in his finished poster. The teacher interpreted this as insubordination, scolded him for being disobedient, and tore up his poster. The other children laughed, and Richard erupted by flinging his notebook, which hit the teacher on the nose. The teacher reported this to the principal, which made the episode automatically an assault charge with mandatory dismissal of the child.

Richard was enrolled in another school in which his adjustment was at first quite satisfactory. After a few months, however, several explosive reactions to frustration again developed. The most severe episode occurred one day when the baseball team of which Richard was the captain lost a game to another team whose captain was a girl. The other children teased him about losing the game and about losing to girls. He became upset, they teased further, and by the time he returned to the classroom, he was crying wildly, screaming to the teacher that it was all her fault, that she had made him lose. In the station wagon on the way home, a classmate told the others (not classmates) about Richard's tantrum, whereupon Richard punched wildly and was punched in return. He arrived home with a nosebleed and met his parent's inquiry about the cause of the nosebleed with a sulky, "It's none of your business."

After this last episode, when Richard was almost ten, he was seen for psychiatric reevaluation. Although previous contacts with the study child psychiatrist had been positive, with free discussion by him of ongoing activities and problems, on this occasion he said, "I don't like to talk about it. It makes me feel bad. That's the way I am and I can't do anything about it. I guess those things are just going to happen to me the rest of my life." He then busied himself determinedly with play activities in the playroom and would not discuss his problem. Other than the avoidance of his problem behavior, Richard was very free in his discussion of his play activity. His range of affect was normal and appropriate to the content of play, and his verbalization and use of language were superior for age and showed no peculiarities or idiosyncratic usages.

Thus, at this point, Richard had accepted the repeated expressions of disapproval and condemnation by teachers and parents of his explosive tantrums as valid and had begun to think of himself as a "bad boy," doomed to repeat his irrational explosions and to suffer the consequences. Helplessness and hopelessness were evident as soon as he was pressed to face the problem, and his only defense was to refuse to discuss the issue.

The diagnosis was neurotic behavior disorder, and a program of individual psychotherapy was arranged. Richard at first persisted in his use of avoidance, stating repeatedly that he did not wish to talk about his problems and that nothing could change him. When in a number of sessions he was permitted to engage in activities of his own choosing, interrupted only by the anticipated end of the session, two trends developed: a] a growing curve of positive interaction with the examiner, with mutual engagement in pleasurable activities, such as perceptual puzzles of increasing difficulty; and b] the child's growing insistence on discussing issues of his behavior. He would say, "Aren't you going to ask me anything about school?" and, under the guise of being coerced by the examiner, he brought up interactions that involved his having to stop something he wished to do and becoming upset and crying.

After three months of such discussions, he began to state he had nothing new to report. It was ascertained that there had been a growing trend of positive functioning at school and at home, with increasing communicativeness on his part, ability to ask for appropriate aid, and fewer occasions of despair, self-derogation, or babyish behavior. On inquiry to Richard, "Do you still think that bad things will happen every once in a while because you are that kind of person?" he stated clearly that he no longer held this opinion, although he could not put into words what had changed about his self-perception. He simply said that he did not know why, but it was no longer hard for him to stop doing something he wished to do when he knew that it was important to stop. Treatment was terminated after sixteen sessions.

In summary, this is a child whose symptoms of explosive tantrum-type behavior led repeatedly to disapproval, condemnation, and punishment. As he grew older, he began to conceptualize the meaning of his behavior in terms of a derogatory self-image that was fated to endure forever and then developed the defense mechanism of avoidance.

3] Hal (Case 9) had shown pedantic language and formalistically polite mannerisms in the preschool years, which made him the butt of the other children in nursery school. This behavior was an exaggerated imitation of his father, and had been encouraged by both parents, who valued politeness and manners highly. Hal, with the temperamental characteristics of the easy child, had no difficulty in meeting these parental demands. His early development and psychiatric evaluation were presented in Chapter 14. As reported there, parent guidance was successful, and the child's deviant behavior pattern gradually disappeared over the following year, and he was able to develop positive involvements with groups.

Hal was referred for a second psychiatric evaluation at the age of eight and one-half years, with the symptoms of very low frustration tolerance both to criticism in school and to failure to meet his own high standards for academic achievement. These symptoms had begun in the first grade and had now grown more serious. He became annoyed with himself at any careless mistake, and if a test performance was not perfect, he frequently became very angry and berated himself: "I'm the worst in the class, I stink." Criticism by a teacher evoked similar anger and self-derogation. His teachers and mother agreed that at the same time he no longer had a social problem. He had friends who sought his company, was not a show-off, and his language was no longer pedantic. He was not teased by the other boys.

In the clinical interview, he showed none of the over-formalistic manners and speech that had been so striking when he was four years of age. He communicated easily, and his affect and thinking were appropriate. He said he had "a terrible temper" and disparaged himself: "There's nothing to like about me." He reported that "my father has an even worse temper than I do," and described incidents in which his father discovered minor errors in some figures he was working with and began chastising himself at length to the tune of "My God, how could I have been so stupid?" The mother confirmed this picture of the father's extreme perfectionism and self-beratement. In addition, a high school student who lived with the family and was much admired by Hal also showed a similar intensely self-critical attitude.

It appeared that once again Hal was using his father as a model and, with his high adaptability, had easily learned to imitate the latter's melodramatic behavioral characteristics. Selective identification was reinforced by the expression of attitudes similar to the father's by Hal's secondary model, an older boy living in the house.

Parent guidance was initiated again. The factors responsible for the development of the symptoms were outlined, and recommendations were made to the father that he modify his expressions of self-derogation and self-criticism over minor errors. At the time of the present report, too short a period has elapsed to evaluate the effectiveness of the guidance procedure.

In summary, this is a child with quick adaptability who showed two periods of disturbance, at four and eight years, with markedly different symptoms at each age. In both instances the disturbance resulted primarily from imitation of selected aspects of his father's behavior and attitudes. At age four, the symptoms were basically behavioral, and at age eight, ideational in content.

These three cases illustrate several ways in which the shift in psychological organization from action to ideation as the child grows older may influence the nature of symptomatology. In the first child, Diana, the mechanism of avoidance was expressed at an early age predominantly by physical withdrawal and hiding, and at an older age, by denial and rationalization. In the second child, Richard, conceptualization of the consequences of his explosive tantrums was not present at age six, but did develop in the following years. In the third child, Hal, identification with the father resulted in imitation at a behavioral level at age three, and at an ideational level at age eight.

Clearly, other developmental pathways may exist for symptom formation, elaboration, and transformation than those illustrated in the above cases. However, a sufficient variety of both intraorganismic and environmental factors have been identified in the present study as influential in the dynamics of symptom development to make it clear that no single formula can hope to explain the origin and significance of any specific symptom as it manifests itself in different cases. In other words, when symptoms arise at the same age and presumed level of psychological functioning, they may reflect many different antecedent pathways of development. The form taken by the symptom in any individual case appears to be the result of a continuously evolving process of interaction between temperament and other organismic characteristics with specific environmental influences, at all times reflecting the child's level of behavioral organization and ideational capacities. Furthermore, the findings indicate that the origin of a symptom may not necessarily go back to early stress. Excessive stress, dissonance, and special vulnerability leading to symptom formation may arise in the child-environment interaction at any time and at any level of development.

REFERENCES

1. A. L. Gesell and S. L. Ilg, *The Child From Five to Ten* (New York: Harper & Bros., 1946).
2. H. Werner, *Comparative Psychology of Mental Development* (Chicago: Follett Pub. Co., 1948).
3. J. H. Flavell, *The Developmental Psychology of Jean Piaget* (Princeton: D. Van Nostrand Co., Inc., 1963).
4. A. Freud, "Some Remarks on Infant Observation," *The Psychoanalytic Study of the Child*, VIII:12 (New York: Int'l. Universities Press, Inc., 1953).
5. H. J. Eysenck, "Behavior Therapy, Spontaneous Remission and Transference in Neurotics," *Am. J. Psychiat.*, 119:867 (1963).

16 | TREATMENT AND FOLLOW-UP

As described in Chapter 3, both the clinical evaluation of the child's behavior problem and the initial recommendations for management were formulated by the study child psychiatrist. In both the evaluation and the suggestions for management, the temperamental characteristics of the child were utilized for understanding the origins of the disorder and for developing a plan of treatment.

In all but one of the forty-two cases, the therapeutic recommendation after initial evaluation was for parent guidance. By parent guidance, we mean the formulation of a program of altered functioning in the parents that could ameliorate excessive and harmful stress acting upon the child. Whenever indicated, guidance of the parents also included recommendations for other appropriate environmental changes, such as change in school or alteration of living arrangements for the child.

The cause of the excessive stress in each case was formulated in terms of the poorness of fit or dissonance between environmental demands and the child's capacities or characteristics. For each child, the anterospective longitudinal data and the findings of the clinical evaluation were utilized to identify the type of dissonance that was operative in the development of the behavior disorder. A program of altered parental functioning could then be formulated that was calculated to eliminate this dissonance by presenting the child with environmental opportunities and demands that were consonant with his capacities and temperamental characteristics. Whenever appropriate, the program of action recommended to the parents included other ameliorative measures, such as advice to the school, a change to another school, or remedial educational tutoring.

In one case (Nora, Case 27, described in Chapter 14), fixed neurotic patterns found on the initial clinical evaluation at sixty-three months led to the diagnosis of moderately severe neurotic behavior disorder. It was also evident from the longitudinal data and the clinical evaluation that parental practices and attitudes markedly unfavorable for a child with her temperamental pattern existed, and that these would not be easily amenable to change. These findings in the child and the parents suggested a poor prognosis for treatment by parent guidance alone. Direct psychotherapy for the child was therefore recommended.

The basic emphasis in the therapeutic procedure of parent guidance was on change in the parent's *behavior* and *overtly expressed* attitudes, as well as on the alteration of other unfavorable environmental influences, and not on the definition or change of underlying conflicts, defenses, or anxieties in the parent. The goal of parent guidance, in other words, was to change specific aspects of the parents' actual functioning with their child, but not to delineate or attempt to change directly covert attitudes or defense mechanisms that, presumably, might be related to overt behavior and attitudes.

The systematic utilization of parent guidance as the initial therapeutic procedure made it possible to study the effectiveness of this procedure, to determine the frequency with which it proved adequate without recourse to time-consuming and expensive direct psychotherapy with parents, child, or both, and to estimate the reasons for failure in those cases where parent guidance proved unsuccessful.

Psychotherapy was eventually instituted in six children in addition to the one case where it was advised on initial evaluation. In four of these cases, the recommendation for psychotherapy was made because of the failure of parent guidance; in one case, the parents themselves decided to arrange for psychotherapy, despite the recommendation that they give the guidance procedure further time; and in another case, the consequences of the child's temperamental reactions in school and with peers were so unfavorable as to make it necessary for him to gain an understanding of his own maladaptive functioning before change could occur.

In eight other instances where parent guidance has thus far proven unsuccessful, direct psychotherapy for the children or parents has not as yet been advised. In several of these cases, the follow-up period has as yet been too short to determine whether improvement without psychotherapy is unlikely. In the others, parental inability to take an objective and serious view of the child's problems has led not only to the failure of parent guidance, but also to a resistance to consider other therapeutic procedures. The relation of temperamental pattern to the outcome of parent guidance and to the institution of psychotherapy is reported below in this chapter. (See Tables 4 and 7 and accompanying discussions.)

Recommendations for residential treatment were made in two cases. Barbara (Case 1) was hospitalized because of the progression of the illness in spite of parent guidance and psychotherapy. In another child (Case 12) with the difficult child temperamental pattern, failure in psychotherapy, combined with increasing stress and discord in the home, led to the recommendation for residential treatment, which was refused by the parents.

TABLE 1 / LENGTH OF PERIOD OF FOLLOW-UP

3–6	months—	3 cases
7–12	months—	0 cases
13–18	months—	3 cases
19–24	months—	2 cases
2–3	years—	7 cases
3–4	years—	9 cases
4–5	years—	10 cases
5–6	years—	5 cases
6–7	years—	3 cases

Medication was an incidental part of the treatment of several children, but in no case did drug treatment appear to be indicated as a major therapeutic procedure.

FOLLOW-UP *

In this presentation the follow-up period is defined as the time subsequent to the psychiatric evaluation at which the initial clinical diagnosis was established and treatment procedures instituted. In the two cases in which a diagnosis of behavioral disturbance was made not at the first psychiatric evaluation, but on a subsequent clinical examination, the follow-up period is dated from the time of this latter evaluation.

Ratings of degree of improvement or increased impairment were made on the basis of the follow-up data. The category "recovered" was used to designate complete disappearance of symptoms extending over a minimum of six consecutive months.

The length of the follow-up periods as of March, 1966, varied, of course, with the length of time that had elapsed since the psychiatric evaluation at which the initial clinical diagnosis had been established. The periods ranged from three to eighty-four months, and were distributed as shown in Table 1.

As may be seen from this tabulation, in thirty-nine of the forty-two cases, at least one year; and in thirty-four of the forty-two cases, at least two years of follow-up has already been obtained.

The frequency with which different degrees of improvement and worsening occurred are tabulated in Table 2. The evaluation of the direction and degree of change in each case was made by the study child psychiatrist on the basis of an analysis of all the follow-up data. Changes in the severity and nature of the symptomatology were utilized in determining the criteria for the categories of recovered, marked

* See Chapter 3 for details of follow-up procedures.

TABLE 2 / OUTCOME ON FOLLOW-UP

Improved	Boys	Girls	Total	Worse	Boys	Girls	Total
Recovery	3	4	7	Slight	1	1	2
Marked	7	3	10	Moderate	2	1	3
Moderate	8	2	10	Marked	3	1	4
Slight	1	4	5	Unchanged	1	0	1
Total Improved	19	13	32	Total Unimproved	7	3	10

improvement, moderate improvement, slight improvement, unchanged, slightly worse, moderately worse, and markedly worse.

The distribution of boys versus girls in the "Improved" and "Worse" categories is not significantly different from their distribution in the clinical sample as a whole (twenty-six boys and sixteen girls).

It can be noted from Table 2 that 64 per cent of the clinical sample either recovered or were markedly or moderately improved, while only 17 per cent became moderately or markedly worse. In considering these overall improvement rates, the relationship of outcome to original diagnosis and severity of symptoms is of interest. These findings are presented in Table 3.

As may be seen in Table 3, 68 per cent of the cases with initially mild symptoms were recovered, or markedly or moderately improved on follow-up. An almost equal percentage, 64 per cent of the cases with initially moderate symptoms, and 50 per cent of the cases with moderately severe or severe symptoms also improved. These differences in improvement rate show a slight trend in the direction that might be expected, with a greater improvement rate on follow-up for the initially mild and moderate cases, and a lesser in the moderately severe and severe group. However, the differences are neither striking nor statistically significant.

A tabulation was made of outcome on follow-up for different temperamental types. In this and subsequent tabulations, the temperamental type of each case was determined on the basis of the antero-spective data from the first three years of life. A number of the children had multiple characterizations, such as "easy child and irregular," or "persistent child and low activity level." In order to consolidate the number of categories used in this tabulation, the temperamental pattern which on qualitative analysis appeared most prominent in the child's functioning was chosen. Only one of the forty-two cases could not be categorized in terms of a dominant temperamental pattern and this case is listed as "Other." This tabulation is presented in Table 4.

As can be seen from Table 4, the great majority of the clinical cases are distributed among the difficult, easy, and slow to warm up children, with ten, ten, and nine cases in each of these three groups

TABLE 3 / FOLLOW-UP FINDINGS IN RELATION TO INITIAL STATUS

Initial Status

	Mild Symptoms		Moderate Symptoms		Moderately Severe Symptoms		Moderately Severe Symptoms		Severe Symptoms	
	RBD* Number Cases	Average Number Months of Follow-Up	RBD* Number Cases	Average Number Months of Follow-Up	RBD* Number Cases	Average Number Months of Follow-Up	NBD† Number Cases	Average Number Months of Follow-Up	Brain Damage With Secondary Behavior Disorder	Average Number Months of Follow-Up
Recovery	5	45	2	67	—	—	—	—	—	—
Marked Improv.	5	46	2	54	2	70	1	54	—	—
Moderate Improv.	7	39	3	20	—	—	—	—	1	60
Slight Improv.	2	54	1	48	1	15	—	—	—	—
Unchanged	—	—	—	—	1	3	—	—	—	—
Slightly Worse	2	29	—	—	—	—	—	—	—	—
Moderately Worse	2	38	1	44	—	—	—	—	—	—
Markedly Worse	2	34	2	48	—	—	—	—	—	—

* RBD = Reactive Behavior Disorder. Includes one case where the RBD was secondary to brain damage.

† NBD = Neurotic Behavior Disorder

TABLE 4 / TEMPERAMENTAL PATTERN AND OUTCOME ON FOLLOW-UP

	Difficult Child	Easy Child	Slow to Warm Up Child	Persistent Child	Distractible Nonpersistent Child	Low Activity Child	Other
Recovered	2	2	2	—	—	1	—
Markedly Improved	3	3	2	2	—	—	—
Moderately Improved	1	2	5	—	—	1	1
Slightly Improved	1	1	—	2	1	—	—
Unchanged	1	—	—	—	—	—	—
Slightly Worse	—	1	—	1	—	—	—
Moderately Worse	1	—	—	1	1	—	—
Markedly Worse	1	1	—	—	2	—	—
Total	10	10	9	6	4	2	1

respectively.* The improvement rate, if cases with recovery, marked, or moderate improvement are considered, is approximately the same for the difficult and easy children—60 per cent and 70 per cent respectively. The improvement rate for the slow to warm up children is substantially higher—100 per cent. The outcome for the persistent group is less favorable, with 33 per cent improvement. The distractible, nonpersistent children are of interest because of the striking difference in outcome from the other groups. The number of cases is small, only four, but none showed any substantial improvement; one was slightly improved, and three were either moderately or markedly worse. A possible explanation for this unfavorable outcome for the distractible, nonpersistent children is presented below in connection with a discussion of the results of parent guidance. The number of cases with a low activity level is too small to permit any generalization of the outcome findings.

It is of interest that the findings suggest that difficult children with behavioral disturbances have as good a prognosis as the easy children. The greater vulnerability to stress of these difficult children is, however, shown here in two ways. While 59 per cent of the total clinical sample had mild symptoms on initial psychiatric evaluation, only 20 per cent of the difficult children were in the mild category. This was true in the absence of any significant differences between these children and the total group in age at onset of symptoms or age at psychiatric

* It must be borne in mind that the easy children constitute a much higher proportion of the total longitudinal sample of 136 children than do the difficult or slow to warm up children. The incidence of behavioral disturbance in the easy children, therefore, is lower than in these two other groups, even though the absolute number of cases for each type in the clinical sample is about the same.

referral for evaluation. Also, five of the seven cases for which not only parent guidance but also psychotherapy was required were difficult children. In other words, these youngsters appear to be more vulnerable to the development of behavioral disturbance and to present more severe symptoms when they become disturbed. They are also more likely to require psychotherapy. However, the overall prognosis in treatment need not be less favorable for these than for the other children.

RESULTS OF PARENT GUIDANCE

The results of different treatment procedures can be tabulated first with regard to parent guidance. For each clinical case, an estimate was made of the degree to which the parents modified their functioning with the child in the desired direction following the guidance sessions. In some cases, one parent was responsive to advice while the other was not. In these instances, the rating was based on an estimation of the degree of change in combined father-mother functioning as experienced by the child in the course of daily living. The estimate of parental change was then compared with the direction and degree of change in the behavior disorder in the child on follow-up. This comparison is tabulated in Table 5.

As may be seen from Table 5, there is a marked relationship between the degree of change in the parents and the direction and degree of change in the child. Of the eight cases in which there was marked change in parental functioning, four recovered, and the other four showed either marked or moderate improvement. Of the twelve cases with moderate parental change, one recovered, five were markedly improved, five moderately improved, and one was slightly worse. The outcome in the eight cases in which only a mild degree of parental change in functioning occurred was somewhat less favorable, with two recoveries, one marked improvement, two moderate improvements, two slight improvements, and one child who was slightly worse. Strikingly

TABLE 5 / RESULTS OF PARENT GUIDANCE

Degree of Change in Parents in Desired Direction	Recovery	Marked Imp.	Mod. Imp.	Slight Imp.	Unchanged	Slightly Worse	Mod. Worse	Markedly Worse	Total
Marked	4	2	2						8
Moderate	1	5	5			1			12
Mild	2	1	2	2		1			8
No change			2	3	1		4	4	14

Outcome in Child

unfavorable findings on follow-up were evident in the group of fourteen clinical cases in which parental guidance attempts failed, i.e., in which parental functioning did not change at all in the desired direction. In this group, no child recovered or improved markedly, two were moderately improved, three were slightly improved, one unchanged, and eight cases showed varying degrees of worsening in the severity of their behavioral disturbance over time. Stated differently, in the twenty families where the parents showed marked or moderate changes in the direction suggested by the study child psychiatrist, there was, with one exception, either recovery, marked improvement, or moderate improvement in the children. Even in the eight families where less extensive, but still appreciable, amounts of change in parental behavior occurred, the outcome in the children was predominantly favorable except for two children who only improved slightly and one who worsened. In contrast, in the fourteen families in which parental guidance was a failure, eight (57 per cent) of the children became worse as they grew older.

In four of the five cases in which improvement in the child occurred in spite of the failure of parent guidance, it appeared to be related to an especially benign and constructive influence of the extra-familial environment on the child's development. In other words, quick acceptance of the child by peer groups as he grew older, or successful social and academic school functioning served to attenuate the influence of an unhealthy parent-child interaction in these children. In the fifth child in this group, improvement followed a course of psychotherapy.

RESULTS OF PSYCHOTHERAPY

As indicated above, seven children received a course of psychotherapy. In four of these cases, this followed the failure of parent guidance. One of these children had mild symptoms initially, two had moderate, and one had severe symptoms. In this group the results of psychotherapy were very favorable in one child with the easy child temperamental pattern. In the three others, the results were unfavorable: one child with the combination of the difficult child pattern and brain damage remained basically unchanged, and two were markedly worse after treatment. Of these two latter cases, one had the easy child and the other the difficult child pattern. In the case with the difficult child pattern and brain damage, long-term hospitalization was necessary, with only slight improvement after three years. In the three other cases of the seven receiving psychotherapy, parent guidance was utilized concurrently and was considered moderately successful in two cases and slightly successful in one. All of these cases showed moderately severe symptoms initially, and all showed marked improvement following the combination of psychotherapy and parent guidance. Two of these latter three cases had the difficult child temperamental pattern, and one showed marked persistence as his most striking temperamental attribute.

RECOVERED CASES

The seven cases who recovered were studied in detail in the attempt to identify the factors that were influential in promoting an optimal outcome. This inquiry was especially pertinent because of the long follow-up period of four to five and one-half years since initial evaluation in six of the seven cases. In the one remaining case, the follow-up period was fifteen months.

In five of the seven recovered cases, initial symptoms were of mild severity, and in two cases they were of moderate severity; in all seven, the diagnosis was reactive behavior disorder. There were no significant differences between the recovered and the nonrecovered cases of comparable severity and diagnosis in relation to the age of onset, the interval between onset and psychiatric referral, or types of symptomatology at the time of initial psychiatric evaluation. A significant difference between the recovered group and the other clinical cases, however, was found with regard to the level of success of parent guidance, as may be seen in Table 6.

It is evident from the above table that there was a substantially higher percentage of very successful parent guidance cases, as well as an absence of parent guidance failures, in the recovered group. Of further interest is the fact that the one case in which recovery occurred with only moderately successful parent guidance was that of a slow to warm up child; the two cases which recovered in spite of only mildly successful parent guidance were both easy children. In these three cases, a change in the living arrangements, a spontaneous improvement in the relationship with an older sibling, or increasingly successful functioning outside the home with peer groups and in school seemed fortuitously to ameliorate the parent-child relationship.

The above findings in the recovered cases, while very tentative because of their small number, suggest several conclusions. Recovery from a behavioral disturbance in childhood may be possible for the difficult as well as for the easy child. Such recovery may be significantly

TABLE 6 / RESULTS OF PARENT GUIDANCE

	Total	Markedly Successful	Moderately Successful	Mildly Successful	Failure
		Recovered versus Other Cases			
Recovered Cases	7	4 (57%)	1 (14%)	2 (29%)	0
Other Clinical Cases	35	4 (11½%)	11 (31½%)	6 (17%)	14 (40%)

related to the ability of the parents consciously to alter their functioning with the child. One may speculate that such parental change may perhaps be most necessary in the case of a difficult child and may be less crucial for the easy child, perhaps because of the latter's greater ability to respond quickly and fully to other environmental influences.

The need for the parents to know and respect their child's temperamental pattern was a major element in our approach to parent guidance. In each case, the specific ways in which they were attempting unrealistically to change the child's characteristics of reactivity were delineated for the parents, and they were advised to eliminate such attempts. Guidance was not restricted to this issue, but concerned itself also with any other aspects of parental functioning that were producing or exacerbating stress for the child. Where the child was of school age, the parents were also advised as to how to give the child insight into his own temperamental characteristics. When this insight was achieved, it became possible, in some cases, for the child to learn to recognize the situations in which his spontaneous behavioral reactions would be inconvenient or harmful to himself and to modify or control their expression at such times.

As indicated in Table 6 above, parent guidance was evaluated as very successful in eight cases, moderately successful in twelve, mildly successful in eight, and a failure in fourteen cases. Thus, twenty of the parent-pairs, or almost 50 per cent of the total group, responded to direct advice and guidance, with a marked or moderate modification in the desired direction in their functioning with their behaviorally disturbed child. This was accomplished with an average of only 2.3 guidance sessions. It is possible that the small number of sessions required for successful parent guidance bore some relationship to the awareness of many of the parents through their participation in the longitudinal study of the meaning and significance of the concept of temperamental individuality, although the first time they were actually informed of our categorization of their child's temperament was in the parent guidance session.

The average number of parent guidance sessions for the failure group was 2.7. In these unsuccessful cases, the small number of guidance sessions reflected the resistance of the parents to engaging in this therapeutic procedure.

To summarize, the parents who responded favorably to parent guidance did so quickly, and those who responded unfavorably also manifested their reaction quickly.

Finally, the findings as to the relationship between the child's temperamental type and the results of parent guidance were tabulated and are presented in Table 7.

As may be seen from Table 7, parent guidance was mildly, moderately, or very successful in the majority of cases in each temperamental pattern group, except for the distractible, nonpersistent group

TABLE 7 / PARENT GUIDANCE AND CHILD'S TEMPERAMENTAL PATTERN

Results of Parent Guidance (Change in Parent)

	Markedly Successful	Moderately Successful	Mildly Successful	Failure	Total
Difficult Child	4	1	1	4	10
Easy Child	1	3	4	2	10
Slow To Warm Up Child	2	5	1	1	9
Persistent Child	——	2	2	2	6
Distractible, Non-persistent Child	——	——	——	4	4
Low Activity Child	1	——	——	1	2
Other Types	——	1	——	——	1

who had parents with whom guidance was a failure in four out of the four cases. One factor responsible for the failure of parent guidance when the children were distractible and nonpersistent concerns the overall standards and values of the parents as a group. They attached great importance to educational achievement for both sexes and to success in professional careers or business for the males. For both of these goals, persistence, i.e., "stick-to-it-iveness," is considered desirable and even essential. It is, therefore, harder for these parents to accept the validity and normality of the temperamental qualities of relative nonpersistence and easy distractibility in their children, especially in boys. In a few cases, this attitude was expressed openly in the parent guidance sessions with remarks about the offspring such as, "He lacks character." In this connection, it is of interest that these four cases with nonpersistence and easy distractibility were all boys. Inasmuch as a major demand made on the parents in the guidance procedure was that they truly accept the individuality of their child's temperamental pattern, this group's special difficulty in doing so may very well have contributed very significantly to the failure of parent guidance.

The temperamental characteristic of persistence often won relatively easy acceptance and even approval by the parents once they understood its nature and manifestations. The pattern of the easy child was also accepted without difficulty by most parents, though some were chagrined that they could not take credit for its presence. Most of the parents could also learn to tolerate the initial maladaptive reactions of the difficult or slow to warm up child in new situations, once they were convinced that patience and forbearance on their part would aid the child finally to achieve behavioral levels that were congenial to their own standards. In other words, for the parents of these children, a change in their handling of the child could bring the outcome they desired; for the parents of the distractible, nonpersistent children, a change in their handling of the child could still leave the child functioning in a fashion uncongenial to them.

17 | THEORETICAL IMPLICATIONS OF THE FINDINGS

The findings of our longitudinal study of children who developed behavior disorders clearly indicate that features of temperament, together with their organization and patterning, play significant roles in the genesis and evolution of behavior disorders in childhood. Both before and after they developed symptoms, groups of the children with behavioral disturbances differed in temperament from those who did not develop such disturbances. The clinical cases, as a group, were characterized by an excessive frequency of either high or low activity, irregularity, withdrawal responses to novel stimuli, nonadaptability, high intensity, persistence, and distractibility. No single temperamental trait acted alone in influencing the course of the child's development. Rather, combinations of traits forming patterns and clusters tended to result in an increased risk for developing behavioral disorders. Differences in types of behavior disorders and of symptoms, too, were found to be associated with differences in temperament.

A given pattern of temperament did not, as such, result in a behavioral disturbance. Deviant, as well as normal, development was the result of the interaction between the child with given characteristics of temperament and significant features of his intrafamilial and extra-familial environment. Temperament, representing one aspect of a child's individuality, also interacted with abilities and motives, the other two facets, as well as with the environment, in determining the specific behavior patterns that evolved in the course of development.

Given our findings on the relevance of temperamental factors to the genesis and evolution of behavior disorders, we may explore their implications for general theory in psychiatry and child development. As is the case when any significant influencing variable is identified, there is an understandable temptation to make temperament the heart and body of a general theory. To do so would be to repeat a frequent approach in psychiatry which, over the years, has been beset by general theories of behavior based upon fragments rather than the totality of influencing mechanisms. A one-sided emphasis on temperament would merely repeat and perpetuate such a tendency and would be antithetical to our viewpoint, which insists that we recognize temperament as only one attribute of the organism. In our view, temperament must at all times be considered in its internal relations with abilities and motives and in its external relations with environmental opportunities and

182

stresses. Consequently, the relevance of the concept of temperament to general psychiatric theory lies neither in its sole pertinence for behavior disorders, nor in its displacement of other conceptualizations, but in the fact that it must be incorporated into any general theory of normal and aberrant behavioral development if the theory is to be complete. Existing theories emphasize motives and drive states, tactics of adaptation, environmental patterns of influence, and primary organic determinants. The central requirement that a concept of temperament makes of such generalizations is that they come increasingly to focus on the individual and on his uniqueness. In other words, it requires that we recognize that the same motive, the same adaptive tactic, or the same structure of objective environment will have different functional meaning in accordance with the temperamental style of the given child. Moreover, in such an individualization of the study of functional mechanisms in behavior, temperament must be considered as an independent determining variable in itself, and not as an *ad hoc* modifier used to fill in the gaps left unexplained by other mechanisms.

A formulation of the role of the child's own characteristics that fails to give temperament serious consideration together with other mechanisms is illustrated in a recent discussion of autistic psychosis. The author, herself a longtime student of organismic individual differences in children, asserts an a priori hierarchy assigning prime importance to "mothering" and secondary importance to the child's characteristics: "Children who suffer from this illness have in common the lack or distortion of a mutual relationship with a mother person . . . in some instances this deficiency arises because there was no mother who responded to the baby as normal mothers do—an environmental deficiency. But the illness also occurs in children who were raised by normally responsive mothers who provide all that other children receive. But the child is so constituted that he cannot participate in the usual patterns of interaction, probably due to an inborn deficit yet to be specified. The child deficient in the capacity to respond is just as motherless as is the normally equipped child without a mother." [1]

This formulation assumes that autism is a deficiency disease; and that the essential nutritive element is "mothering." It implies that there is one pattern of mothering that may be classified as adequate for all children and assumes, on hypothetical grounds, that such a universal "adequate" for the mothering process does exist. However, a recognition of temperamental differences and their significance for development makes it impossible to accept such universals, whether for the mothering process or any other environmental influence, and emphasizes the need to clarify and define "adequacy" in terms of the goodness of fit between the organism cared for and the pattern of care, if such care is to result in certain socially defined consequences.

A contrasting illustration, in which temperament is seriously treated as a determining variable rather than as an *ad hoc* consideration, can be cited from the recent literature. In a psychiatric study of children with poor school achievement, Ross [2] defines a syndrome of behavioral disturbance which he calls "the unorganized child." He identifies the specific attributes of the child's individuality and parental functioning as independent but mutually interacting influences, and avoids any hierarchal designation of one as more fundamental than the other. Ross identifies the pertinent factors involved in the development of the unorganized child as the combination of the temperamental characteristics of high distractibility, short attention span, and low persistence in interaction with the parental attributes of overpermissiveness or disorganization of functioning. He further points out that specific manifestations of the syndrome will depend on whether these temperamental qualities are combined with high or low activity level and intense or mild responses. Specifically, Ross suggests that the unorganized child may show restlessness and a tendency to chatter disruptively if he also has a high activity level, daydreaming if he is less active, and tantrums when frustrated if he is also intense in his reactions.

Thus, a truly interactionist approach rejects the attempt to impose a priori hierarchal judgments of relative importance on child and environment in the developmental process. Moreover, it rejects the dichotomy of child versus environment and recognizes that the effective environment is the product of the selective responsiveness of the child to aspects of the objective situation to which he is exposed.[3] An interactionist approach also cannot be satisfied with the application of global characterizations that children have "different constitutional dispositions" or that some mothers are "good" and others "bad" to explain all the vicissitudes of normal and disturbed development. What is required, first of all, is not merely an acceptance of the statement that children differ, but knowledge of *how* they differ and *how* these differences are continuously expressed as significant determinative factors in psychological growth. What is also required is not the categorization of parents as better or worse, more or less hostile, anxious, etc., but the delineation of those *specific* attributes of parental attitudes and practices and of other intra- and extrafamilial environmental factors that are interacting with the *specific* temperamental and other organismic characteristics of the child to produce *specific* consequences for psychological development.

MOTIVATIONAL AND NONMOTIVATIONAL FACTORS

Although a long-term study must have a defined focus if it is to avoid the dangers of diffuseness and tangential pursuits, it is inevitable that such focused inquiry will have certain serendipitous outcomes. Such outcomes derive from the fact that what is being considered in detail is the developmental course of normal and aberrant behavioral styles, an issue which is more broadly encompassing than is temperament. Consequently, the sequential data on behavioral development necessary to assess the role of temperament in development are also entirely pertinent to a consideration of motivational features of functioning. As a result, the findings on symptom selection and evolution provide a substantial basis for considering the interrelations of motivational and nonmotivational factors, intrapsychic maneuvers, anxiety, and psychodynamic defenses in the development of normal and disturbed behavior. The implications of the findings for these issues can now be considered.

A major aspect of most theoretical formulations on the causes and nature of behavioral disturbances is the extent to which conceptualized intrapsychic purposes and aims are invoked as explanatory principles. Classical psychoanalysis and certain forms of contemporary learning theory present opposite and extreme positions with regard to the importance of such motives in the causation of disturbed behavior. For the orthodox psychoanalyst, motives are all-important. As stated by Freud in one of his final systematic formulations, "The symptoms of neuroses are exclusively, it might be said, either a substitutive satisfaction of some sexual impulse or measures to prevent such a satisfaction, and are as a rule compromises between the two." [4] In other words, the primary force is considered as motivational, i.e., the aim to either satisfy or prevent the satisfaction of a basic drive. The motivational preoccupation of psychoanalytic theory has been ubiquitously evident in its search for the sources of psychopathological phenomena in underlying purposes, motives, and conceptualized goals and aims. A typical contemporary expression can be found in a discussion of child psychiatry in the *American Handbook of Psychiatry*. The general assertion is made that "there is evidence of repression and of the 'return of the repressed' in the symptoms of the neurotic child," [5] and various specific symptoms are considered within this motivational framework. As an example, sleeplessness is stated to reflect "a vigilant attempt at protest against a frightening impression of the environment." [6] At the other extreme, are the learning theorists, such as Eysenck, for whom "neurotic behavior consists of maladaptive conditioned responses of the autonomic system and of skeletal responses made to reduce the conditioned sympathetic reactions." [7] With this formulation goes a denial of the existence of underlying motivational states. Thus, Eysenck states further that "there is no underlying complex or other 'dynamic' cause which is responsible for the maladaptive behavior; all we have to deal with in neurosis is conditioned maladaptive behavior." [8]

Our findings that temperament-environment interactions play an important part in the development of behavioral disturbance in the young child suggests that it is frequently unnecessary and unparsimonious to postulate the existence of complex intrapsychic motivational states to account for maladaptation during the period of early development. The concern of such child analysts as Spitz,[9] who have lamented the difficulty of studying intrapsychic states in young children, therefore appears unnecessary, inasmuch as the objective behavioral data obtainable for this age group appear quite sufficient for the study of the course of psychological development.

Furthermore, as detailed in the chapters on "Stress: Consonance and Dissonance" (14), and "The Developmental Dynamics of Symptom Formation and Elaboration" (15), even in the older child it is frequently possible to trace the course of symptom formation and elaboration without recourse to hypotheses concerning complex underlying motivational states. It is certainly more parsimonious to avoid such hypotheses when they are not necessary to explain the phenomena of a behavioral disturbance.

Concepts of learning theory, based on conditioning, offer a nonmotivational explanation for the manner in which specific maladaptive patterns may arise. It does not appear possible, however, to encompass the dynamics of symptom evolution in some of the older children entirely within the framework of a simple conditioned reflex model. Thus, as the growing child's subjective life expands and his psychological organization is increasingly influenced by ideation, abstraction, and symbolic representation, conceptualized motives and aims may, in some cases, begin to play an important part in symptom formation and evolution at older age periods. This is clearly seen in the cases of Diana (Case 4), Richard (Case 31), and Hal (Case 9), reported in Chapter 15.

To summarize, our findings would suggest that it is merely confusing to attribute elaborate psychological motivational mechanisms to the young child if a simpler explanation accounts for all the facts. In the older child, it may be necessary to invoke such motivational states when efforts to explain the behaviors in terms of simple mechanisms appear inadequate.

THE ROLE OF ANXIETY, INTRAPSYCHIC CONFLICT, AND PSYCHODYNAMIC DEFENSES

Common to many influential theories is an emphasis on the primary role of anxiety in the origin and development of behavioral disturbances. Although anxiety may be defined in one theory as subjective distress and in another as autonomic reactions to painful stimuli, both classes of theory view the symptom as a technique for the reduction of anxiety and for the insulation of the individual from it. For example, when Freud spoke of a symptom as representing either the substitute satisfaction, the repression of a drive, or a compromise between opposing drives, implicit in this formulation was the view that the function of such a symptom is the reduction or avoidance of anxiety that would arise as the result either of a conflict between drives or between a drive state and social requirements.

Some learning theorists, too, consider anxiety as causal, and view a symptom as a defensive maneuver designed to protect the individual from the painful consequences of autonomic arousal. Thus, Wolpe, a leading member of this group, gives anxiety "a central role in his theory of neurosis" [10] and says it is "invariably present in the causal situations." [11]

Neo-Freudian psychoanalytic modifications, such as Horney's concept of "basic anxiety," [12] or Sullivan's view that anxiety arises from disordered interpersonal relationships,[13] while they substitute social for biologic sources of anxiety, do not depart from the classic psychoanalytic position as to the prime role of anxiety in disturbed development and symptom formation. Similarly, the bridge-building concepts of Miller and Dollard aimed at linking psychoanalytic and reinforcement learning theories reaffirm the view that "an intense emotional conflict is the necessary basis for the neurotic behavior" [14] and that such a conflict arises primarily from anxiety.

Common to these various theories regarding the central role of anxiety is an emphasis on the concomitant importance and ubiquity of intrapsychic conflict in the ontogenesis of neurosis. The formulations vary as to whether such conflict is considered to be an antecedent or a consequent of anxiety, or both, and whether the conflicting intrapsychic forces consist of innate instinctual drive states, learned patterns, internalized social standards, or some combination of these elements.[15] However, there is general agreement among them that conflict between the child and environment evolves into intrapsychic conflict, which becomes the basic chronic pathogenic force. Thus, the Oedipal situation of Freudian theory, which is presumed to cause a child's fear of punishment by the parent, changes into an intrapsychic conflict as the environmental demands and threats are incorporated into the child's ego and superego. Similarly, the pathogenic influence of the "hostile world" threatening the helpless infant in Horney's concepts becomes internalized into anxiety and conflicting self-images. For the learning theorists, pathogenic environmental experiences perpetuate their influences through the formation of conflicting conditioned reflex patterns.[16]

The different theories also view the basic maneuver that leads to symptom formation as an attempt at the reduction or avoidance of anxiety and intrapsychic conflict. For the learning theorists, this takes place on a simple level in the form of conditioned avoidance responses.

For the psychoanalysts, the avoidance of anxiety and the resolution of conflict is mediated through a variety of psychodynamic defense mechanisms having ideational content, such as repression, displacement, sublimation, rationalization, etc.

Considered formally, the various hypotheses connecting symptom with anxiety have the logical implication that anxiety, however defined, must in temporal sequence antedate the symptom. If there were no antecedent anxiety, there could be no symptoms. Thus, if it can be demonstrated that symptoms antedate anxiety, the keystone of the theoretical structure is removed. Moreover, for those formulations that view the symptom as purposively evolved to reduce anxiety and conflict, the removal of a symptom as such should result either in a rise in anxiety, in increased disorganization of functioning, or in the replacement of old symptoms by new.

Our findings bear directly on these questions. The anterospective longitudinal data have made it possible for us to determine the time relations between anxiety and symptom formation. And the procedure of parent guidance, which in most cases was focused on the direct elimination of symptoms, has given the opportunity to determine the consequences of symptom removal. As has been demonstrated in the case histories presented in the previous chapters, in the young child, anxiety has not been evident as an initial factor preceding and determining symptom development. Where anxiety has evolved in the course of the development of the child's behavior disorder, it has been a secondary phenomenon, a consequence rather than a cause of symptom development and expression. However, when it has arisen, it has affected symptoms and their expression. Similarly, the removal of symptoms by a successful parent-guidance procedure has had positive consequences for the child's functioning, and has not resulted in the appearance of overt anxiety or of new substitutive symptoms.

We have found it unnecessary to invoke concepts regarding presumed states of intrapsychic conflict or the operation of psychodynamic mechanisms of a purposive ideational character to explain the origins of behavioral disturbances in young children. In each case of an excessively stressful and maladaptive interaction between the child and his environment, a parsimonious formulation in terms of objective and overtly evident characteristics of the child, patterns of parental functioning, and other specific environmental influences has been sufficient to account for the genesis of the problem behavior. However, intrapsychic conflict and psychodynamic defenses, as well as anxiety, have been evident in some older children as later developments in the child's response to the unfavorable and sometimes threatening consequences of an initial maladaptation.

It is, of course, true that once anxiety, intrapsychic conflict, and psychodynamic defense mechanisms appear, they add new dimensions to the dynamics of the child's functioning and contribute to his inter-actions. When this happens, they may substantially influence the subsequent course of the behavior problem. The painfulness of severe anxiety when it is overt makes it a striking symptom which may dominate our perceptions of the clinical picture. The elaborate psychological techniques utilized to minimize or to avoid distress may also contribute dramatically to the elaboration of pathological patterns of behavior and thought. It is, therefore, not surprising that in retrospective studies that begin when the child already presents with an elaborated psychological disturbance, the prominent phenomena of anxiety and psychodynamic defenses dominate clinical thinking, and come to be labeled as primary, rather than as secondary, influences in the genesis of behavior disturbance.

When our thinking is dominated by such clinical experience, the misinterpretation of many behavioral phenomena as anxiety or as defenses against anxiety can easily occur. Thus, the initial withdrawal of a child who is slow to warm up from a new group of children may be considered to represent an avoidance of anxiety in social situations when, in fact, it merely reflects his temperamental individuality. The slow movement pattern of the child with low activity may be mislabeled as inhibition by anxiety, the intense negative mood of the difficult child as anxiety or a hostile defense against anxiety, and so forth. If the behavioral expressions of temperament and individuality are not recognized, other more complex explanations may be presumptively advanced. One may say that interpretations of anxiety, psychodynamic defenses, and other intrapsychic motivational states rush in to fill the vacuum created when the fact of temperamental individuality is unappreciated and ignored.

Psychiatry is an eminently practical discipline, and the psychiatrist's theories serve to guide his practice in diagnosis, treatment, and efforts at prevention. Consequently, the clinician's approach to the diagnosis and treatment of behavioral disturbances in children and the mental hygiene worker's approach to the prevention of such disorders will, of necessity, be shaped by their concepts of the etiology of problem behavior and their views as to the mechanism of symptom formation. A theoretical formulation that places prime emphasis on the pathogenic role of the mother or the family constellation will result in focusing the search for noxious elements in the family constellation. The view that a symptom arises out of a need to cope with unconscious anxiety or conflict will lead to the assumption that such presumed anxiety or conflict must exist whenever deviant behavior and symptoms appear. It will also lead to a treatment plan geared to the identification of such anxiety and to its elimination. If, on the other hand, the symptom is considered to reflect a maladaptive conditioned reflex pattern, the clinician's treatment procedures will emphasize extinction, deconditioning, and reconditioning techniques. However, the findings of our longitudinal study make it abundantly clear that no a priori hierarchy of the relative importance of various pathogenic factors is applicable to all children with behavior problems. In any specific case, the significant noxious influences—whether they be the family, the larger social environment, maladaptive learning, psychodynamic defenses, temperamental constellations, or neurological dysfunction—can be identified and their relative importance determined only by an analysis of the specific nature of the child-environment interaction at various age-stage levels of development.

REFERENCES

1. S. K. Escalona, "Patterns of Infantile Experience and the Developmental Process," *Psychoanalytic Study of the Child*, 18:243 (1963).
2. D. C. Ross, "Poor School Achievement: A Psychiatric Study and Classification," *Clinical Pediatrics*, 5:109 (1966).
3. H. G. Birch and Others, "Individuality in the Development of Children," *Developmental Medicine and Child Neurology*, 4:370 (1962).
4. S. Freud, *Outline of Psychoanalysis* (New York: W. W. Norton & Co., Inc., 1949), p. 85.
5. J. B. Cramer, "Common Neuroses of Childhood," *American Handbook of Psychiatry*, 1:806 (New York: Basic Books, 1959).
6. *Ibid.*, p. 805.
7. H. J. Eysenck, "Behavior Therapy, Spontaneous Remission and Transference in Neurotics," *Am. J. Psychiat.*, 119:868 (1963).
8. *Ibid.*, p. 868.
9. R. Spitz, "Relevancy of Direct Infant Observation," *Psychoanalytic Study of the Child*, 5:66 (1950).
10. D. H. Ford and H. B. Urban, *Systems of Psychotherapy* (New York: John Wiley & Sons, Inc., 1963), p. 276.
11. J. Wolpe, *Psychiatry by Reciprocal Inhibition* (Stanford: Stanford University Press, 1958), p. 33.
12. K. Horney, *The Neurotic Personality of Our Time* (New York: W. W. Norton & Co., Inc., 1937).
13. H. S. Sullivan, *The Interpersonal Theory of Psychiatry*, eds. H. S. Perry and M. L. Gawel (New York: W. W. Norton & Co., Inc., 1953).
14. J. Dollard and N. E. Miller, *Personality and Psychotherapy* (New York: McGraw-Hill, 1950), p. 127.
15. Ford and Urban, *op. cit.*, pp. 652–58.
16. Wolpe, *op. cit.*

18 | PRACTICAL IMPLICATIONS OF THE FINDINGS

In the light of our arguments in the last chapter, it is clearly necessary for the clinician systematically to define and evaluate all etiological possibilities before making a diagnosis and formulating a treatment plan. The need to give as much attention to temperamental factors as to environmental and psychodynamic influences in diagnosis requires special emphasis because of the prevalent tendency to ignore the former and attend exclusively to the latter. A child who stands at the periphery of the group in nursery school may be anxious and insecure, but he may also be expressing his normal temperamental tendency to warm up slowly. An infant with irregular sleep cycles who cries loudly at night may possibly be responding to a hostile, rejecting mother, but he may also be expressing temperamental irregularity. A six-year-old who explodes with anger at his teacher's commands may be aggressive and oppositional, but he may also be showing the frustration reactions typical of a very persistent child when he is asked to terminate an activity in which he is deeply absorbed. A mother's guilt and anxiety may be the result of a deep-seated neurosis, but they may also be the result of her problems and confusion in handling an infant with a temperamental pattern that characterizes a very difficult child.

OBTAINING DATA ON TEMPERAMENT IN CLINICAL PRACTICE

As indicated in the above examples, an accurate diagnostic judgment requires that data on the child's temperamental characteristics be gathered with the same care and regard for detail that is considered essential for the evaluation of parental attitudes and practices, family relationships, and sociocultural influences. Naturally, the clinician does not have anterospectively gathered behavioral descriptions of a child's developmental course available to him. But neither does he have available such anterospective data on intra- and extrafamilial environmental influences. With all information gathered retrospectively, whether it be on temperament, the attainment of developmental landmarks, the medical history, the patterns of parental functioning, or special environmental events, the clinician must assess the accuracy, completeness, and pertinence of the data reported to him. In the authors' experience, the collection of behavioral data from which evaluations of temperament can be made has presented no greater difficulties than gathering information on other aspects of the clinical history. Some informants are able to give detailed, factual, and precise descriptions of their children's past and present behavior. Others give vague, general, and subjective reports. In all cases, it is desirable to confirm the accuracy of the data by directly observing the child and, wherever possible, by obtaining information from multiple sources. A number of items in the basic clinical history,[1] such as the course of the child's development and the history of the presenting complaints, will often, in themselves, elicit clues as to significant issues relating to the child's temperament. For example, the parents of a twelve-year-old boy reported that he was unable to study or do homework at an academic level appropriate to his intellectual capacity and his grade placement, and that he started many endeavors, such as music lessons or rock collections, but seemed to lose interest in them rapidly. The parents also complained that routines took an inordinate amount of time to be accomplished although the child was cheerful and apparently well-intentioned. He would start on his way to bed, but might be found fifteen minutes later puttering with some game that attracted his attention, playing with a brother, or involved in a discussion with his grandmother. The composite of presenting problems in this case suggested that the temperamental quality of distractibility might be an important factor in causing the child's difficulties.

As another example, the parents of a nine-year-old girl reported that she found it difficult to undertake new endeavors and to join new groups of children her own age, and she tended to avoid new situations whenever she could. This presenting complaint suggested the possibility that a temperamentally based tendency to make initial withdrawal reactions to new experiences might be relevant to the reported behavioral difficulty.

Following the taking of a basic clinical history, systematic inquiry can be made into the child's temperamental characteristics during infancy, keeping in mind the necessity to investigate similarly other possible causes for the problem behaviors. The inquiry can be started with the general question, "After you brought the baby home from the hospital and in the first few weeks and months of his life, what was he like?"

First answers to such questions are usually very general ones: "He was wonderful"; "He cried day and night"; "He was a bundle of nerves"; "He was a joy."

The next question is still open-ended: "Would you give me some details that will describe what you mean?"

The replies to this second general question often include useful descriptions of behaviors from which judgments of temperament may be made. Further information requires specific inquiry, which is most economically pursued by taking up areas of behavior relevant to defining each of the temperamental attributes one at a time. The questions asked should be directed at obtaining a number of descriptive behavioral items from which the interviewer can then make an estimate of the child's temperamental characteristics. A list of questions appropriate to each of the nine categories can be suggested at this point.

Activity Level

How much did your baby move around? Did he move around a lot; was he very quiet, or somewhere in between? If you put him to bed for a nap and it took him ten or fifteen minutes to fall asleep, would you have to go in to rearrange the covers, or would he be lying so quietly that you knew they would be in their proper place and not disarranged? If you were changing his diaper and discovered that you had left the powder just out of reach, could you safely dash over to get it and come right back without worrying that he would flip over the surface and fall? Did you have trouble changing his diaper, pulling his shirt over his head, or putting on any other of his clothing because he wiggled about, or could you count on his lying quietly to be dressed?

Rhythmicity

How did you arrange the baby's feedings? Could you tell by the time he was six weeks (two months, three months) old about when during the day he would be hungry, sleepy, or wake up? Could you count on this happening about the same time every day, or did the baby vary from day to day? If he varied, how marked was it? About when during the day did he have his bowel movements (time and number), and was this routine variable or predictable?

Parents can generally recall such events. They will say, "He was regular as clockwork"; "I could never figure out when to start a long job because one day he would have a long nap and the next day he wouldn't sleep more than fifteen minutes"; or, "I used to try to take him out for his airing after I cleaned him from his bowel movement, but I never could figure it right because his time changed every day."

Adaptability

How would you describe the way the child responded to changed circumstances? For example, when he was shifted from a bathinette to a bathtub, if he didn't take to the change immediately, could you count on his getting used to it quickly or did it take a long time? (Parents should be asked to define what they mean by "quickly" and what they mean by "a long time" in terms of days or weeks.) If his first reaction to a new person was a negative one, how long did it take the child to become familiar with the person? If he didn't like a new food the first time it was offered, could you count on the child's getting to like it and most other new foods sooner or later? If so, how long would it take if the new food was offered to him daily or several times a week?

Approach-Withdrawal

How did the baby behave with new events, such as when he was given his first tub bath, offered new foods, or taken care of by a new person for the first time? Did he fuss, did he do nothing, or did he seem to like it? Were there any changes during his infancy that you remember, such as a shift to a new bed, a visit to a new place, or a permanent move? Describe the child's initial behavior at these times.

Threshold Level

How would you estimate the baby's sensitivity to noises, to heat and cold, to things he saw and tasted, and to textures of clothing? Did he seem to be very aware of or unresponsive to these things? For example, did you have to tiptoe about when the baby was sleeping lest he be awakened? If he heard a faint noise while awake, would he tend to notice the sound by looking toward it? Did bright lights or bright sunshine make him blink or cry? Did the baby's behavior seem to show that he noticed the difference when a familiar person wore glasses or a new hair style for the first time in his presence? If he didn't like a new food and an old food that he liked very much was put with it on the spoon, would the baby still notice the taste of the new one and reject it? Did you have to be careful about clothing you put on him because some textures were too rough? If so, describe the kinds of things he disliked.

Intensity of Reaction

How did you know when the baby was hungry? Did he squeak, did he roar, or were his sounds somewhere in between? How could you tell that he didn't like a food? Did he just quietly turn his head away from the spoon or did he start crying loudly? If you held his hand to cut his fingernails and he didn't like it, did he fuss a little or a lot? If he liked something, did he usually smile and coo or did he laugh loudly? In general, would you say he let his pleasure or displeasure be known loudly or softly?

Quality of Mood

How could you tell when the baby liked something or disliked something? (After a description of the infant's behavior in these respects is obtained, the parents should be asked if he was more often contented or more often discontented, and on what basis they made this judgment.)

Distractibility

If the child were in the midst of sucking on the bottle or breast, would he stop what he was doing if he heard a sound or if another person came by, or would he continue sucking? If he were hungry and fussing or crying while the bottle was being warmed, could you divert him easily and stop his crying by holding him or giving him a plaything? If he were playing, for example, gazing at his fingers or using a rattle, would other sights and sounds get his attention very quickly or very slowly?

Persistence and Attention Span

Would you say that the baby usually stuck with something he was doing for a long time or only momentarily? For example, describe the longest time he remained engrossed in an activity all by himself. How old was he and what was he doing? (Examples might be playing with the cradle gym or watching a mobile.) If he reached for something, say a toy in the bathtub, and couldn't get it easily, would he keep after it or give up very quickly?

After completing the inventory of the child's temperamental characteristics in infancy, the next step is to identify those attributes that appear extreme in their manifestations and/or those that seem clearly related to the child's current pattern of deviant behavior. This is followed by an inquiry into the characteristics of these temperamental attributes at succeeding age-stage periods of development. Thus, if the history of the infancy period suggests a pattern of marked distractibility, it would be desirable to gather data on behavior related to distractibility at succeeding age periods and in varied life situations, such as play, school, homework, etc. Similarly, if the presenting complaints indicate that the child currently finds it difficult to undertake new endeavors or to join new groups of age-mates, and if the early temperamental history suggests a characteristic pattern of initial withdrawal coupled with slow adaptation, it would be important to obtain descriptions of the child's patterns of initial responses to situations and demands that arose at different points in his developmental course.

The final step in the assessment of the child's temperament is the evaluation of his current temperamental characteristics. The behavioral information obtained for current functioning is usually more valid than that obtained for behavioral patterns in the past, since the problems of forgetting and retrospective distortion are minimized. The inquiry into current behavior will attempt to cover all temperamental categories, but should concentrate on those which appear most pertinent to the presenting symptoms.

Activity level may be estimated from a child's behavior preferences. Would he rather sit quietly for a long time engrossed in some task, or does he prefer to seek out opportunities for active physical play? How well does he fare in routines that require sitting still for extended periods of time? For example, can he sit through an entire meal without seeking an opportunity to move about? Must a long train or automobile ride be broken up by frequent stops because of his restlessness?

Rhythmicity can be explored through questions about the child's habits and their regularity. For instance, does he get sleepy at regular and predictable times? Does he have any characteristic routines relating to hunger, such as taking a snack immediately after school or during the evening? Are his bowel movements regular?

Adaptability can be identified through a consideration of the way the child reacts to changes in environment. Does he adjust easily and fit quickly into changed family patterns? Is he willing to go along with other children's preferences, or does he always insist on pursuing only his own interests?

Approach/withdrawal, or the youngster's pattern of response to new events or new people, can be explored in many ways. Questions can be directed at the nature of his reaction to new clothing, new neighborhood children, a new school, and a new teacher. What is his attitude when a family excursion is being planned? Will he try new foods or new activities easily or not?

Threshold level is more difficult to explore in an older child than in a young one. However, it is sometimes possible to obtain information on unusual features of threshold, such as hypersensitivity to noise, to visual stimuli, or to rough clothing, or remarkable unresponsiveness to such stimuli.

The intensity of reactions can be ascertained by finding out how the child displays disappointment or pleasure. If something pleasant happens does he tend to be mildly enthusiastic, average in his expression of joy, or ecstatic? When he is unhappy, does he fuss quietly or bellow with rage or distress?

Quality of mood can usually be estimated by parental descriptions of their offspring's overall expressions of mood. Is he predominantly happy and contented, or is he a frequent complainer and more often unhappy than not?

Distractibility, even when not a presenting problem, will declare itself in the parent's descriptions of ordinary routines. Does the child start off to do something and then often get sidetracked by something his brother is doing, by his coin collection, or by any number of several circumstances that catch his eye or his ear? Or, on the contrary, once he is engaged in an activity is he impervious to what is going on around him?

Data on persistence and attention span are usually easier to obtain for the older child than for the infant. The degree of persistence in the face of difficulty can be ascertained with regard to games, puzzles, athletic activities, such as learning to ride a bicycle, and school work. Similarly, after the initial difficulty in mastering these activities has been overcome, the length of the child's attention span for and concentration on these same kinds of activities can be ascertained.

The delineation of the child's temperamental characteristics at different age periods may indicate that changes have occurred over time. There are normal variabilities of temperament, and the fate of any temperamental attribute is dependent upon a host of influences. The issue of stability and instability of temperament is too broad an issue to be considered here and is the main burden of a monograph now in preparation.

Temperamental characteristics may also appear to change because of the influence of the process of socialization in blurring the individual behavioral style evident in new situations and experiences. In other words, routine patternings of response, once they are fabricated as an adaptation to a cultural norm, may serve to minimize individual uniqueness. For example, the first attempt at toilet training will cause one child to scream and struggle violently, another to fuss mildly while he sits on the seat for only a few minutes, and a third child to smile and play while sitting on the seat for many minutes. A year later, when all three children are fully trained, their behavior on the toilet seat may be very similar or show only slight differences as compared to the marked individuality of response to the initial toileting demand. Similar blurring of initial differences in behavioral responses as adaptation to the social norm develops may occur with a variety of other experiences, such as entry into nursery school, the beginning of formal learning, changes in the family group, new living quarters, etc. Therefore, when the behavioral history suggests an apparent change in a child's temperament over time, the data should be scrutinized to determine whether the change is evident or disappears when the responses to new situations at the different age periods are compared.

Fragmentary impressions also lead us to speculate that special factors operating at a specific point in time may, in some instances, produce significant alterations of temperamental attributes. Such a factor might be organic, such as an episode of encephalitis, or psychological, such as a series of traumatic environmental events or a succession of exceptionally favorable life experiences. These speculations require further testing before they can be uncritically accepted.

In many instances, additional data on temperamental organization can be obtained by querying teachers or other adults familiar with the child's behavior. For such inquiry, the history-taking protocol for the parents can be utilized if it is appropriately modified to permit a focus on the areas of the child's functioning with which the adult is acquainted.

Observation of the child's behavior during a clinical play interview or in the course of psychological testing can also supply useful information on activity level, approach-withdrawal, intensity of reactions, quality of mood, distractibility, and persistence and attention span. Temperamental characterizations that require information on the child's behavior over time, namely, rhythmicity and adaptability, cannot be made from such single observations over a short time span, and the nature of the clinical observation and testing situations is such that behaviors referable to the sensory threshold characteristic of the child are usually not observable.

PARENT GUIDANCE

Once the child's temperamental characteristics have been defined and other significant organismic and environmental influences have been delineated by appropriate clinical and testing techniques, it becomes possible to formulate the dynamics of the child-environment interaction that have led to the behavioral disturbance.

After a pathogenic interaction has been identified, a treatment plan aimed at modifying this process and reducing maladaptation, dissonance, and stress can be formulated for the individual child. Depending upon the identification of the specific areas requiring change, the appropriate treatment procedures may involve shifts in intra- and extrafamilial environmental influences, amelioration of a handicap, such as by perceptual training or remedial education (speech, reading, arithmetic, etc.), psychotherapy, pharmacotherapy, hospitalization, or some combination of therapeutic modalities.

The therapeutic procedure of environmental change through parent guidance merits special discussion at this point because of its usefulness in clinical practice. Parent guidance, as we have used it, involves first the identification of those elements of parental behavior and overtly expressed attitudes that appear to exert a deleterious influence on the child's development. This is followed by the formulation of a program of altered parental functioning which, by modifying the interactive pattern between parent and child, may lead to an amelioration or disappearance of the child's behavioral disturbance. No attempt is made to define or change any hypothetical underlying conflicts, anxieties, or defenses in the parent that may be presumed to be the cause of the noxious behavior or overtly expressed attitudes. The rationale of the guidance program is explained to the parents, and special attention is given to the description of the child's temperamental attributes and other pertinent characteristics (superior or subnormal intellectual level, special perceptual or cognitive difficulties, etc.) and to the definition of those parental behaviors which are creating excessive stress for the child. Specific suggestions and advice for changing these behaviors are then offered, with each suggestion illustrated by reference to a number of specific incidents in the child's life. Thus, a discussion with the parents of a difficult child might first define the intrinsic nature of the child's intense negative reactions to the new and his subsequent slow adaptability. The discussion would distinguish these reactions from "willful" defiance or anxiety, then identify those parental behaviors that are aggravating and distorting the child's negative responses and slowness of adaptation to the new, and outline a regime of specific changes in these behaviors that should aid, rather than hinder, the child's adaptive course. Similarly, correction would be made of the parental conception that the low activity level of their child indicates inferior intelligence, deliberate dawdling, or "laziness." The parents would then be advised to eliminate their attempts to force the child to perform at an activity level beyond his capacities.

Even with parents who are eager and able to carry through the program of behavioral change suggested to them, several follow-up discussions may be necessary before they can achieve full understanding and application of changed practices. Reviews of the parents' behavior in a number of specific incidents may also be required before they become adept at identifying the situations in the child's daily life in which they must modify their techniques of management. In other instances, parental misconceptions, confusions, defensiveness, anxiety, or guilt may impede their ability to understand the issues involved in the guidance program, and a greater number of discussions may be necessary to overcome these hindrances to their comprehension and implementation of the advice and suggestions offered. Finally, there are the parents whose own psychopathology is so severe that no substantial change in their behavior is possible through these guidance discussions. In these latter cases, other therapeutic approaches will be necessary, such as direct treatment of the child, psychotherapy for one or both parents, or treatment of both parent and child. Direct treatment of the child may in some cases be advisable concurrent with parent guidance, especially if there is a severe degree of psychopathology in the child.

The therapeutic procedure of parent guidance is based on our conviction that parental functioning with a child may be less than optimal for a number of different reasons. Ignorance, poor advice from professional or other sources, unrealistic goals and values, stereotyped concepts of what is normal or pathological behavior for a child, and difficulty in understanding the best approach to a child with a specific temperamental pattern—any of these factors may be responsible for unfavorable parental functioning and may be amenable to amelioration by parent guidance. Even in those cases where psychiatric disturbance in the parent is the prime cause of noxious parental influence on the child, parent guidance may sometimes result in modifying the unhealthy parental functioning significantly even when no basic change in the parent's personality structure is achieved. This approach to the evaluation and modification of the parent's influence on the child argues that the treatment of a child's behavioral disturbance requires the consideration of direct psychiatric treatment of the parent only if simpler measures have failed and there is substantial evidence that significant psychopathology actually exists in the parent. This formulation stands in some contrast to other current approaches in the field of child psychiatry in which the existence of a behavior problem in a child is considered *ipso facto* evidence of substantial psychopathology in the parent or the nuclear family unit. Typical of this view are statements such as those of Howells, that "it is not possible to separate the child's condition from that of his parents or other adult members of the family" [2] because "the parents of disturbed children are usually themselves also disturbed," [3] and of Ackerman, that the primary patient, the child, must be viewed "as a symptomatic expression of family pathology," and not just as an "individual in distress." [4] Implicit in these formulations is the concept that effective treatment of a behaviorally disturbed child requires direct psychotherapy of the parents or family to deal with presumed pathology, direct treatment of the child to insulate him from the harmful influences of the parents, or both. Such a treatment program is usually long and expensive, resulting in severe limitations on the number of cases accepted for treatment by practitioners and clinics. Furthermore, the results of treatment procedures based on the equation of child pathology with parent or family pathology have not been impressive enough to justify the burdensome investment of time and money required of the family or community for each case.[5] Our finding that no one-to-one relationship exists between disturbance in the child and psychopathology in the parents suggests that the disappointing therapeutic results may be due, in part at least, to a faulty theoretical premise, which results in treating the wrong patient.

Parent guidance, by contrast, usually requires markedly fewer treatment sessions than does a regime of psychotherapy. As described in Chapter 16, the average number of guidance sessions per case was 2.3 for the successful cases and 2.7 for the failure group. The guidance procedure was considered markedly or moderately successful in approximately 50 per cent of the clinical cases. It may be argued that the special characteristics of the families participating in the longitudinal study and the influence of their long-term contact with the research staff personnel may have made them more amenable to a guidance program. However, the experience of one of the authors (S.C.) in applying a parent guidance approach to private and clinic child patients with a variety of psychiatric problems has been that an approximately equivalent percentage of success has been possible with parents of diverse sociocultural backgrounds.* The number of sessions required has been

* This experience will be reported in detail in a publication now in preparation (S. Chess and A. Thomas, *Parent Guidance*).

greater than with the longitudinal study group, perhaps two to four times as many, but still markedly less than would have been required for any psychotherapeutic procedures.

We are not alone in suggesting that parental functioning can be modified in many cases without elaborate treatment procedures designed to alter basic personality characteristics. Thus, Anna Freud states that she "refuse(s) to believe that mothers need to change their personalities before they can change the handling of their child." [6] Similar positions are taken by Bibring [7] and Shirley.[8] However, their general assertions of the validity of parent guidance as a therapeutic technique have not been translated into systematic and specific procedures applicable to a wide range of clinical problems. It is perhaps not an unreasonable inference that the development of a useful and comprehensive scheme for parent guidance may require the systematic consideration of the parent's practices and attitudes and the child's temperament within an interactionist framework. If such an approach promises an effective and brief therapeutic modality for perhaps 50 per cent of children with behavior problems, its utilization would appear highly desirable.

DIRECT TREATMENT OF PARENT OR CHILD

In those cases in which parent guidance is unsuccessful or only partially successful, direct psychotherapy of the parent or child, or both, may be advisable or necessary. Even in such instances, a knowledge of the child's temperamental characteristics may prove very useful in the treatment regime. Thus, the therapist's task of delineating and bringing to a mother's awareness a constellation of neurotic attitudes and goals may be expedited by a comparison of the patient's judgments and expectations of her child with the reality of child's temperament. The finding, for example, that a mother is anxious or hostile because her daughter warms up slowly to new social situations may provide the first clue to her neurotic needs for social success. Similarly, a father's refusal to accept the fact that his high-activity and distractible son can sit still and do homework only for short time periods may help to clarify his pathological standards of work achievement. Furthermore, the substitution of healthy for neurotic attitudes and goals may first be possible for the parent in relationship to his child because of clear and strong motivation to be a good parent. Making the same change in other areas of the parent's life may then become easier.

For the older-child patient to know his own temperamental characteristics may be important in several ways. The therapeutic effort to develop a positive self-image in the youngster may sometimes require teaching the youngster to appraise his reactive tendencies correctly. This is especially true when certain of his temperamental patterns are different from the average of the group and therefore tend to be considered as abnormal and inferior by the child and his peers. Thus, it may be very valuable for him to learn that if his activity level is low, this does not mean he cannot with sufficient practice become a good ballplayer; that if he is "shy" in new social situations because of initial withdrawal tendencies, this does not mean he has to be socially inept; or that if he is easily distracted from tasks, this does not mean he cannot become a reliable worker.

The youngster whose temperamental responses have created unfavorable responses in others or precipitated behavior detrimental to his own best interests can also be taught in the psychotherapeutic situation to direct and guide his behavior to eliminate or minimize such unfavorable consequences. For example, the youngster with intense negative reactions to the new can learn to approach such situations gradually and so minimize the negative reactions that may antagonize others. The high activity child can learn to pace himself with activities requiring him to sit still and give himself breaks for active motor play or exercise. The slow to warm up child can learn to wait patiently until his initial negative response disappears and to explain to others that he is shy at first but will get over it in time.

Naturally, the older the child, the more possible it is to give him such insight into his own characteristics and help him work out routines and approaches that will maximize the positive aspects of his temperamental attributes and minimize their unfavorable consequences.

PREVENTION OF BEHAVIORAL DISTURBANCE

The prevention of behavioral disturbances in childhood covers a vast array of issues, including those genetic, biochemical, temperamental, neurological, perceptual, cognitive, and environmental factors that may influence the course of behavioral development. The child's temperament is only one of the many issues to be considered by professional workers concerned with the prevention of pathology in psychological development, though often an important one. As our findings have demonstrated, the degree to which parents, teachers, pediatricians, and others handle a youngster in a manner appropriate to his temperamental characteristics can significantly influence the course of his psychological development. The oft-repeated motto, "Treat your child as an individual," achieves substance to the extent that the individuality of a child is truly recognized and respected. The other frequently offered prescription of "tender loving care" often has great value in promoting a positive parent-child interaction, but does not obviate the importance of the parent's actual child-care practices being consonant with his child's temperamental qualities.

Finally, the recognition that a child's behavioral disturbance is not necessarily the direct result of maternal pathology should do much to prevent the deep feelings of guilt and inadequacy with which innumerable mothers have been unjustly burdened as a result of being held entirely responsible for their children's problems.[9] Mothers who are told authoritatively that child raising is a "task not easily achieved by the average mother in our culture" [10] are not likely to approach this responsibility with the relaxation and confidence that would be beneficial to both their own and their child's mental health. It is our conviction, however, that the difficulties of child raising can be significantly lightened by advocating an approach of which the average mother *is* capable—the recognition of her child's specific qualities of individuality, and the adoption of those child-care practices that are most appropriate to them.

REFERENCES

1. S. Chess, *An Introduction to Child Psychiatry* (New York: Grune and Stratton, 1959).
2. J. G. Howells, *Modern Perspectives in Child Psychiatry* (London: Oliver & Boyd, 1965), p. 270.
3. *Ibid.*, p. 279.
4. N. Ackerman, *The Psychodynamics of Family Life* (New York: Basic Books, 1958), p. 107.
5. L. Eisenberg, discussion of paper "Who Deserves Child Psychiatry" by A. J. Solnit, *Jour. Amer. Acad. Child Psychiat.*, 5:19 (1966).
6. A. Freud, "The Child Guidance Clinic as a Center of Prophylaxis and Enlightenment," *Recent Developments in Psychoanalytic Child Therapy* (New York: International Universities Press, 1960), p. 37.
7. G. L., Bibring, "Work with Physicians," *Recent Developments in Psychoanalytic Child Therapy* (New York: International Universities Press, 1960).
8. H. F. Shirley, *Pediatric Psychiatry* (Cambridge: Harvard University Press, 1963).
9. H. Bruch, "Parent Education, or the Illusion of Omnipotence," *Am. Jour. Orthopsychiat.*, 24:723 (1954).
10. M. Mahler, "Thoughts About Development and Individuation," *Psychoanalytic Study of the Child*, 18:307 (1963).

APPENDIX A

Symptoms included under each area in Table 6, Chapter 3

Sleep: Difficulty with going to sleep; night awakening; fears associated with sleep.

Feeding: Vomiting when pressured; eats little; picky about foods.

Elimination: Enuresis; encopresis; withholding of bowel movements.

Moods: Temper tantrums; easy and/or excessive crying; strong-willed in demanding desires; worrying; excessive fussing; very narrow range of expressiveness; explosive anger.

Discipline: Won't take orders; nags; urinates in odd places; fails to comply; sabotages; no tolerance for school authority; demanding and argumentative; overdemanding, insatiable; negativistic; resists discipline, bossy, defiant; teases, jumps on other children at school; refuses to follow directions at school or to pay attention or do work which requires effort and self-discipline; disruptive in class; protective lying; taking things.

Habits: Thumb-sucking, hair pulling, nail biting, nose picking, masturbation, preoccupation with diapers; tics.

Motor Activity: Runs instead of walks; avoids climbing apparatus.

Somatic: Autonomic reactions; vomiting; marked sensitivities to certain clothing, to noise.

Speech: Stuttering; lisping; sloppy enunciation when excited; unclear diction; lack of verbal fluency; confused use of language; late onset of speech; less verbal than younger siblings.

Peer and Other Social Relationships: Nonparticipation in nursery; problem in nursery adjustment—crying and clinging to mother; anxiety at separation from mother—mild attempts to avoid school by claiming illness; fusses when mother leaves child at school; slow school involvement; resists going and separation from mother; clings to mother and housekeeper; aggression with peers; lack of assertiveness with peers; poor peer relations; oversensitive to teasing; oblivious to others' reactions to his behavior; verbally critical; poor relations with sibs.

Learning: Underachieving (the following behaviors are included when it is known that they definitely impede a particular child's learning); nondirection following; perfectionism; avoids everything that does not catch his interest or that he is not told he must master; hesitates to try new things; gives up easily; disregards need to listen and follow directions—treats all situations as social.

Other: Self-conscious; very particular about clothing; lack of persistence when there is no immediate success (not learning problem);
overly upset with changes; not wanting to grow up—refuses milk for
this reason (connected with fear of death); fear of cars; sensitivity
about eye-appearance and need for eye drops at school (physical
basis).

APPENDIX B

Four illustrative cases with case summaries and selective extraction of data from the longitudinal records

HAL—CASE 9

SUMMARY

AGE AT REFERRAL: Fifty months.

PRESENTING COMPLAINTS:
1] Lack of assertiveness with other children; runs crying to mother if his toys are taken.
2] Fear of moving apparatus and sensitivity to some loud noises.
3] Pedantic use of language; child is overly polite and formal; he does not have interests or participate in activities of peers.
4] Meticulousness and nondeviation in direction following.
5] Lack of persistence in new tasks unless he has immediate success.
6] Nonparticipation in nursery school.

ONSET OF PROBLEM: Thirty-seven months.

CLINICAL INTERVIEW: The child arrived for the interview talking actively in a loud voice to his mother. He responded to the examiner's greeting immediately, then amended his response to a more formal salutation at his mother's direction. His polite formalities continued at technically appropriate moments throughout the session.

The outstanding characteristics of the child's activity were his verbosity and his tendency to take over direction by stating an intention and, if not challenged, acting on it. When his intention contradicted a previous direction from the examiner, which she then repeated, the child reiterated his intention. This sequence might continue through three to six interchanges until finally, if the examiner persisted in her directions, the child would comply, acting as if he had never had any objection. When the examiner did not persist, the child went on with his stated preference and seemed completely comfortable with it.

The child's use of language was uniformly high. He spoke in a loud voice and maintained a running commentary throughout his activity, much of which demanded a reply. In this way he actively maintained contact with the examiner. His play interests were appropriate to sex and to age. He used his hands interchangeably and moved a bit awkwardly, just short of being actually clumsy. There was a ponderous quality about his physical movements and his verbalizations.

There was a significant contradiction between the child's meticulous politeness and his efforts to direct and control the activity, with actual disregard of the effect of his behavior on the other person involved in the relationship. He was totally directed to getting the examiner to allow him to do as he wished, was oblivious to her immediate approval or disapproval, and he determined his success or failure by whether or not he achieved this end.

On this basis, one may assume that the child, in interaction with his peers, would be insensitive to their reactions to a dissonant behavior on his part and that only after a retaliatory act had occurred would he become aware of their disapproval, too late for him to reconstruct events in order that he might correct his behavior in the future. This pattern, while not abnormal, would tend to encourage inimical interplay and the possible development of defensive patterns by the child.

DIAGNOSIS: Reactive Behavior Disorder, mild.

TEMPERAMENT: Hal is an extremely adaptable boy who adopts routines easily and adheres to them with a quality of literalness that often makes his behavior appear inappropriate. His meticulous adherence to a procedure makes it difficult for him to deal with any deviation in a routine for which he is unprepared. Thus, he shows uniformly negative responses to the unexpected, but if the change is announced in advance, he will accept it and actively adapt to it.

The same mechanism of adaptability operates in the way the child incorporates patterns of behavior and clings to them. Imitation of his father from his earliest years has developed into almost a complete identification, and the paternal model has become so integral a part of the child's personality that at times it is difficult to differentiate between the child's own intrinsic temperamental characteristics and those he has taken over from his father.

Also prominent throughout the histories is Hal's lack of persistence in those tasks in which he is not immediately successful. From age two, he would attempt new activities through imitation, but if these were not quickly mastered, he would give them up with disinterest. Also he displays, both through comments and actions, a low threshold of sensitivity, especially to tastes, smells, sounds, and sights.

ADDITIONAL FACTOR: I.Q. 141 at age thirty-nine months.

PARENTAL FUNCTIONING: Parental handling has been consistent but idiosyncratic. The parents are themselves formally polite and pressuring in their constant reiteration of manners and ways of speaking, eating, greeting people, etc. Their emphasis on formality and politeness has been passed on to the child. The father, with all his studied and pompous politeness, is basically a rather rigid and controlling individual who places great emphasis on displays of intelligence. He has been described by the mother as almost completely lacking in awareness of other peoples' feelings so that, in some instances, it is only when she reminds him and he makes a special effort that he avoids giving the impression that he is being rude. He has tried to train himself to be more conscious of this.

Basically, the parents are satisfied with the child's behavior insofar as it conforms to their own standards. They accede to Hal's illogical desires when these involve the child's difficulty in accepting deviations in routines without forewarning, e.g., the father tries to remember to inform Hal if he intends to take the car from its usual parking place, and they merely regard this as a nuisance. In general, his taking over of routines and his insistence on conformity are welcomed by them.

The parents' concern is directed, rather, at the way others in the environment have reacted to Hal's behavior: other children, with teasing and baiting, and other parents, by regarding him as a peculiar child, rather than as a paragon. They would like the child to achieve prestige in the neighborhood without their having to give up their own standards for his behavior.

DYNAMIC FORMULATION: Because of his high degree of adaptability, Hal has incorporated the formalities, politeness, and overt displays of intellectual prowess that his parents have pressed on him. He has become a "carbon copy" of his father. Thus, his effort to direct and control in the clinical session, which, on the surface appears incompatible with the thesis of his basic adaptability, is really an affirmation of this adaptability when we recognize it as yet another reflection of his father's personality.

Problems have arisen because the child's behavior, which is welcomed at home, is in conflict with the standards of the outside environment. Behavior that may be considered merely idiosyncratic in an adult, is ludicrous when duplicated in a young child. Thus, his copying of his father's behavior has made the child an object of ridicule in the neighborhood. Because his peers have reacted to him with teasing and baiting, and because his parents continue to reinforce their model of behavior in the child at home, Hal has not had the opportunity to make a double adaptation to the conflicting demands of the outside and home environments.

RECOMMENDATIONS: The parents must direct the child's behavior so that it will be more appropriate to his age and in better conformity with that of his peer group. He has expressed a strong desire to be included in activities with other children, and this should make him amenable to directions for modifying his language, learning appropriate games, and defending himself when necessary. On the basis of his previously observed pattern of nonpersistence with anything that does not come easily, it may be anticipated that his first reaction to attempting athletic games will be to avoid them. Thus, the parents should first teach him those things at which he can become successful with a minimum of persistent effort so as to minimize his frustration. His motivation for peer acceptance should then be used to encourage his persistence in activities and games that do not come easily to him.

SUBSEQUENT COURSE: By 101 months, the child's original problems, 1., 2., 3., and 6., had disappeared. Symptoms 4. and 5. remained, and he also displayed extreme reactions to criticism in school, gave up angrily if he was not successful the first time he tried something, and refused to work apart from the group at his higher level (I.Q. at 5.11 was 160).

During a second clinical interview, the child, no longer over-formalistic, was able to discuss his problems on a realistic basis and recognized his easy frustration and sensitivity to criticism as traits he must try to control. He compared his reactions to making mistakes with his father's behavior on discovering an error by saying, "My father has an even worse temper than I do."

During the period between consultations, the mother developed a very good understanding of the child, and improvement occurred in his original symptoms as a result of changes in her handling along the lines recommended. In addition, the family moved to a new neighborhood and Hal was able to start fresh with a new peer group. (In his old neighborhood his very presence elicited teasing from his friends, and he had no opportunity to develop an appropriate adaptation to them.) The receptiveness of new children gave him the opportunity to alter his functioning.

The current problem is seen as the combination of this child's basic tendency to become frustrated easily and to react intensely, plus his identification with and imitation of his father, an extremely self-critical person who functions on a high intellectual level. Thus, instead of having learned how to cope with his temperamental difficulty and to accept the inevitability of not being consistently perfect, the child's maladaptive tendencies have been reinforced by the paternal model. The child's desire to remain within the reading framework of his class is seen as a positive factor in his search for social acceptance and does not interfere with his educational advancement as his outside pursuit of reading is more consonant with his interests and capacities.

This formulation was given to the school, and his teacher was told to criticize him when it was appropriate and to wait out his intense reactions, assuring the child that immediate mastery in every area was not to be expected. Recommendations were also given the father for changes in his behavior, but it was unlikely he would be able to follow them through.

Selective Extraction Through First Clinical Evaluation

Politeness, meticulousness, and performance of routines

INTERVIEW I (two months): Feeding by modified demand. Sleeping irregular from 4 P.M. to midnight, otherwise regular. Fairly regular bowel movements.

INTERVIEW II (seven months): Play period before bed. Bowel movements irregular—may have three small movements per day.

INTERVIEW III (twelve months): Father plays games with child before he goes to bed—no protest if he is put to bed early, just plays and talks to himself. Has one bowel movement per day, occasionally two.

INTERVIEW IV (seventeen months): Wakes several times during the night. Routine at bedtime—two particular toys, request for juice or milk. Then ritual language exchange between parent and child.

Meals are regularly scheduled, but are easily delayed. In general, child's likes and dislikes are consistent. Conservative and cautious about new activities. Can usually be diverted if required.

Bowel movements irregular. Always wanting to put on and take off pot cover.

INTERVIEW V (twenty-six months): Has had a routine with father before going to bed for a long time—no set bedtime.

Has food "fetishes," but likes and eats a variety of foods—not one thing to the exclusion of others. Bowel movements never regular.

INTERVIEW VI (thirty-two months): Six-stage bedtime ritual—taken care of by father—takes about three-fourths of an hour. Will only bathe with father—loves ritual of cleaning bath—but accepts it if ritual not followed by mother.

Eats with parents—can wait any amount of time for meals. Bowel movements more consistent. Toilet training difficult until recently.

Puts everyone else's toys away, but not his own. Screams and cries, but cleans up if he is forced. A "purist" with pronunciation—corrects mispronunciations. Corrected observer during direct observation at home.

NURSERY SCHOOL TEACHER INTERVIEW (thirty-seven months): "Easily routinized." "Very polite and well-mannered."

I.Q. OBSERVATION (thirty-nine months): Meticulous and correct speech.

INTERVIEW VII (thirty-nine months): When he woke late one morning mother said he could go to bathroom without slippers. He was half asleep but "automatically" went for slippers, then to bathroom.

Lunchtime service and conversation must be replica of what is done for father at dinner. Breakfast routine—must have things exactly the same—one cup for milk, one cup for juice. Says "Excuse me" before leaving table—"it's automatic." Also says "please," "thank you," "may I have some more." Upset if arrangement of his cars has been changed the least bit. Can't go to bathroom without his book, in imitation of father. No one else is allowed to put his clothes in hamper—"If I did, he would say, 'that's my responsibility.' "

Mother states that school behavior, described by teacher as "subserviant," is replica of general polite atmosphere at home. "But he has been taught such things and we want it that way."

Never uses a word incorrectly. Once heard, a word is incorporated almost immediately and always correctly. Talks like a miniature adult.

Adaptability with regard to the effect of his behavior on other people; contact with other children or adults

INTERVIEW I (two months): No negative responses to strangers—particularly smiles at men.

INTERVIEW II (seven months): Looks strangers up and down, turns to mother, and may then smile. ("Terrifically outgoing—loves everybody" says mother.)

INTERVIEW III (twelve months): Extremely friendly child. Very attached to maternal grandmother.

Attempts to delay being put to bed by father, mother, or sitter, but is no trouble when the routine has started.

Likes dancing and running to and from parents—most play with adults is either reading or talking. If toy taken by another child, Hal pulls it back, but doesn't cry. Pushes other children down if they have what he wants. Prefers adults to children.

INTERVIEW IV (seventeen months): Regular routine at bedtime. Stops crying when picked up at night.

INTERVIEW V (twenty-six months): Doesn't like to ask for help, but will scream instead for an indefinite period until mother can't stand it and comes in.

Shy at first with strangers.

INTERVIEW VI (thirty-two months): Unaggressive—only hits back if told by mother to do so. Friendly and at ease with other children.

NURSERY SCHOOL TEACHER INTERVIEW (thirty-seven months): Left mother easily to go into class. Hardly has any contact with other children. Not unfriendly with other children, but makes no attempt to approach them. Quiet and cooperative with teacher. More exuberant outside.

I.Q. TEST OBSERVATION (thirty-nine months): Left mother easily. Generally followed instructions with occasional attempt to change activity. Refused to follow mother's advice to shake hands with examiner or say good-bye at the end of the session.

INTERVIEW VII (thirty-nine months): Put to bed by housekeeper once a week—adapts to whatever her procedure is.

Neat about eating—"so sensitive to criticism." Has been "barked at" for spills.

In last month scarcely whines at all. Often whined even before he made request. Parents said, "Wouldn't it be better to ask first—if answer is 'no' then you can whine." If mother suggests self-play as alternative to T.V., he "doesn't like it"—gets cranky. Doesn't last long if mother suggests some specific type of play.

Follows—is not a leader. However, doesn't accommodate—if play is not to his liking, will play by himself. No matter what painful experience he has had previously with them, he is always enthusiastic and interested in seeing children and always greets them in the same way. Recently has disregarded strange adults—in contrast to previous very social behavior.

When he was younger, mother had said "don't touch this or that," and he had "assumed" that touching anything was "bad." When observing others touch cloth to feel texture, he asked why others could touch. Mother realized she had gone overboard on touching and thereupon wanted him to touch various objects.

Responds immediately to prohibitions about danger—"I'm almost complacent—I know he won't do those things."

Eager to help set table—does an excellent job. When not enthusiastic about a request, will say "well, right now I'm doing . . ." but will come if he finishes.

Misreports about school. Will say, with great joy, he pushed another child. Mother knows, confirmed by teacher, it is not true.

Persistence in tasks that he is unable to master quickly

INTERVIEW I (two months): No mention.

INTERVIEW II (seven months): Physical accomplishments rapidly achieved with apparently little trying.

INTERVIEW III (twelve months): Plays by himself up to two hours (four and one-half hours on one day). Doesn't cry if not successful with new manipulative toys. Plays longest with his books. Practices saying words in crib.

INTERVIEW IV (seventeen months): Conservative and cautious about new areas and not very active physically. Plays alone up to two hours—especially with books.

Insists on dressing or undressing himself or assisting in same. Will attempt to imitate if shown how to work something, but if not successful, he throws the object away (not in anger, just disinterest).

INTERVIEW V (twenty-six months): Still turns fork upside down, completely inept with spoon (no mention of degree of persistence). Likes to put on clothes he can get on easily—when unable to put on something, he screams or uses jargon—doesn't like to ask for help.

INTERVIEW VI (thirty-two months): Mostly feeds himself—if he wants help, will ask.

Rapid mastery of Play School puzzles. Remarkable memory and rapid learning of new material.

NURSERY SCHOOL TEACHER INTERVIEW (thirty-seven months): Spontaneous play with blocks, puzzles, manipulative toys, and books.

I.Q. OBSERVATION (thirty-nine months): Generally correct responses without difficulty—on one occasion, said he couldn't draw, but when asked again, did so.

INTERVIEW VII (thirty-nine months): Very impatient if he can't do something the first time—he'll cry. If sleeve doesn't come off immediately, he gets furious. Easily frustrated if not able to master immediately an activity involving fine coordination as getting into sleeve, doing buttons. If new task requires physical involvement, he begins to cry if he's not successful right away. With a puzzle, he looked at pieces, knew they had to fit in—put in a few; had no success with others, so left it. Then returned to puzzle requesting that parents show him where pieces belonged; then he was able to put it back. Will carry out requested acts independently without help. Will attempt only things he can do. When he can't master a new situation immediately, he shows frustration or panic, but with repeated exposure he becomes adjusted. (Example cited—trip to zoo—but not described.)

Only time he is not understood is when he talks too fast. After one or two reminders to slow down, if still not clear, he gets angry, cries, says, "listen to me"—persists until understood.

Has been "barked at" for spills—is very alert to them. Used to cry if he spilled, and to this day, if he has accident with milk, he cries—and often needs reassurance.

Overt expression of aggression and other emotions

INTERVIEW I (two months): "Shrieked his lungs out because he wanted to eat every two hours." Refused food on a spoon—turned head away, spat, and cried. Didn't cry at bath, but appeared not to like it. Didn't cry at nail cutting, but pulled away.

Winces at bright light. Startled by noise, but doesn't cry. No objection to being wet or soiled, but cried with every bowel movement—had anal fissure. Smiles at music, but otherwise little smiling.

Screamed so hard when "sleeper" put on that mother had to change him into a nightgown.

INTERVIEW II (seven months): Strong cry when "really hungry." Cries when given food he dislikes. Laughs and is active at pre-bedtime play.

"Not too happy but did not protest" in a big bathtub.

INTERVIEW III (twelve months): "Hates" dressing—won't stay still. Would scream until someone sat him down when he was standing; was unable to seat himself.

"He never cries long for anything."

"Cries every time he sees the doctor."

If another child takes a toy, he pulls it back, but doesn't cry. Pushes other children if they have what he wants. Admonished by father for this.

INTERVIEW IV (seventeen months): Cries intensely when he wakens during night, but soon stops when picked up. Says "no" and pushes away food he dislikes. Laughed, smiled, and clapped hands on starting to walk. "Furious" if not permitted to dress or undress himself—cries and bats arms about. Screamed and cried when hair cut. Fussing mild when face washed. "Screamed hysterically" during visit to pediatrician. Cries when frustrated—short duration only—cries mildly when punished, and briefly before going to bed. Doesn't like to be held or cuddled— occasionally kisses spontaneously.

INTERVIEW V (twenty-six months): Doesn't like to have diaper changed—screams, kicks, and talks in jargon. Screams and pulls head away when washed. Screams at doctor. When he tries but can't put on something, he screams or uses jargon. Timid with other children—incapable of being aggressive or hitting back. Cries or screams if told "no" about something he wants very much. Never cries when he falls.

INTERVIEW VI (thirty-two months): "Cheerful, friendly and outgoing to strangers."

"No fuss" about eating.

"Absolutely unaggressive still." Never spontaneously hits back if he has been hit by another child. "Placid temperament."

Cries when unable to do what he wants—"big fuss."

NURSERY SCHOOL TEACHER INTERVIEW (thirty-seven months): No verbal or physical expression of disagreement or agreement. "Appeared to be the type who would not express any distress."

I.Q. OBSERVATION (thirty-nine months): No physical sign of rebellion.

INTERVIEW VII (thirty-nine months): Told mother he would hold baby's hand because baby was afraid of the dark. Mother said, "Why should baby be afraid of dark? You are not." He indicated he was. With discussion as to why he need not be afraid, he "accepted explanation." Has said, "Thunder makes a loud noise." "It's hard to tell with him if he's apprehensive."

So eager for lunch mother has to forcefully take off his coat and wash his hands—he cries "no"—this always happens.

He starts "the push game" with other children. Then all of a sudden, without being part of the game, will "haul off and push them down." Every night plays football with father.

Cries when child has taken his toy—comes running to parents. This happens constantly no matter how many varying suggestions have been made. Seems at complete loss in the situation.

If ignored, he will say, "I'm very unhappy because you're not listening to me." If put in corner (disciplined for repeated disobeying—this is very rare), he cries violently with tears streaming down his face.

Still negative response to motion games—doesn't like elevator. Mother got him interested in watching the operation—so goes in. Doesn't like the stopping—says he wants to go out at first stop.

Selective Extraction Through Second Clinical Evaluation

Politeness, meticulousness, and performance of routines

INTERVIEW VIII (fifty-three months): Used to eat lunch with particular television program. Now gets up later—mother decided lunch would be later. However, every day when this program goes on he says, "I'm hungry." Mother says it's too early—he complains, grumbles. Mother found that if he is given lunch at this time, he doesn't eat, so she is firm about later time. Now he asks, "Is lunch ready?" is more accepting of delay.

Gives his own order in restaurant—has excellent manners—"it's a pleasure to take him out."

INTERVIEW IX (sixty months): "Happy Hour" with father—an "ingrained institution in our house." Lately it's been information seeking— How do you pitch . . . how does the filament work . . . what makes the light bulb burn out?

Likes to sleep without pajamas—imitative of father.

Teacher reports that other children like him, but he's a curiosity to them. They don't understand him or the words he uses, but he gets along.

"The nicest thing I can say about him is he acts like a little boy, not like a wizened kid." "Acts like a wise guy once in awhile, like other kids in general, seems able to speak their language."

Another mother reports other kids have learned a lot from him. He's always been property conscious and very polite. Would correct other kids when they were careless, climbed all over, or said "Gimme this or that." He said, "We don't do that; my mother doesn't like it." Now visitors are very polite and careful.

KINDERGARTEN TEACHER INTERVIEW (sixty-nine months): Loves to be called on—had an air of superiority earlier in the year. It is still hard for him to contain himself, but he is less offensive, more tolerant than he used to be.

I.Q. OBSERVATION (seventy-one months): No mention.

INTERVIEW X (seventy-one months): Likes things in an orderly way. Very observant if mother serves food in different order, if she wears something new.

Mother says, "He has a very decided way of speaking, gestures as I do when he talks, but I don't consider it a problem." Patterns self after father—walks and talks like his father. "I don't know whether Hal likes the same things as his father or whether he does them because father is interested—like reading history, interest in Scottish ballads, playing baseball and football together. They talk all the time. I saw him watch father do something and shortly after he was trying to do the same thing in the same manner."

Had been so good about asking permission to do everything, mother decided to tell him he could make some decisions on his own. For a while he continued to ask permission, then announced he would not ask—would just tell mother. Mother notices he actually has to stop himself from asking. He starts off in usual manner, catches himself, then "tells," rather than asks.

FIRST-GRADE TEACHER INTERVIEW (eighty-three months): No mention.

INTERVIEW XI (eighty-four months): No mention.

SECOND-GRADE TEACHER INTERVIEW (one hundred months): Always a "little gentleman"—discipline problem with class at first—but not with him.

Adaptability with regard to the effect of his behavior on other people; contact with other children or adults

INTERVIEW VIII (fifty-three months): In play with boys, Hal wanted to be sheriff all the time. They piled up on him and he tripped and fell on rocks. Hurt, he sobbed frantically, "Why do they do this to me? . . . Why only me they hurt? . . . Don't they know I'm their friend?" Upset—had nightmare—persisted in always wanting to be sheriff, and if he could not, would not play.

Had been told not to disturb parents' sleep on weekend mornings. Didn't go into their room, but wakened them by making noise talking. Father told him to play quietly—after two weeks of repeated scolding, he was quiet thereafter. Always praised when he's learned.

When told to undress at bedtime, he argues, dawdles—"I don't want to . . . It's too hard." With threats of spanking, cajoling, he starts, then starts playing again. Twenty minutes later he is still not ready. Says he "can't pull shirt over head," etc. Parents do not service him as he is capable. One evening father told him he would have to be ready at specific time if he wanted to have "Happy Time" (evening routine of play with father). When not ready, father told him there was no time left for play. He "became hysterical," moaned, groaned, cried intensely, wild gesticulation of body. Lasted an hour. Next morning he dressed himself quickly (had been delaying in morning also) and that evening was ready quickly—proudly announced it.

Mother introduced previously disliked foods—"Now that you're four and a half maybe you'll like this." He liked it, ate it all—"Now I'm really getting bigger." Although basically left-handed, he uses right for meals. Parents gave him choice, with explanation that restaurant service was geared to right-handed people—"We'd like him to use right hand for meals, but could use either he prefers."

Had been a thumb-sucker until visit to dentist who told him his nice teeth were beginning to be spoiled, and asked him not to suck thumb. Hal looked very worried, was very quiet. On way home he asked mother if dentist was right—mother confirmed. From that moment on he never put his thumb in his mouth again.

Ready to accept friendly overture following an altercation.

May or may not agree with parental suggestion. When he does act on it, he'll call it to parents' attention and add, "You were right." He generally tries to follow, e.g., mother suggests he speak more quietly. Thus far, if he gets excited he has no control over his voice and will then speak in whining, high-pitched voice. More quickly accepts suggestions from outside authority. With scolding, if mother turns on him and shrieks, he gets "obstinate." Will say, "You always yell at me. You don't respect me." But if mother is really angry, he's cowed—conforms. When told to do what he does not want, he says, "You don't respect me"; When pleased with something mother has done for him, he says, "You respect me—I'm glad."

INTERVIEW IX (sixty months): "He's a routined child. It's the line of least resistance to my demands."

Used to insist his blanket be perfectly even. One night woke mother for second time screaming, "My blanket isn't even." Mother, dead tired, "gave it to him," told him not ever to dare wake her again with such nonsense. Since then has never complained about blanket— or even bothered mother.

Didn't want to wipe self after bowel movement. "I think he thought he wouldn't do a good enough job." Mother told him that however he did it would be fine with her, as long as he did it himself. He has been doing it alone ever since.

Very conscious of growing up—relates it to crying, and has been crying much less often. Takes criticism from father without offense—gives it heed. It is usually a quiet suggestion. He always listens—may offer his own comment. If he likes the suggestion, will get very enthusiastic, often embellish it. If he doesn't like it, will be quiet, offer counter suggestion.

KINDERGARTEN TEACHER INTERVIEW (sixty-nine months): Made friends since first day. His overtures were low-powered but successful. Two girls he's friendly with are not prone to take criticism from anyone. He seems to realize this and does not get into disputes with them—lets them set the pace. Otherwise has tendency to be overbearing, to criticize loudly.

I.Q. OBSERVATION (seventy-one months): Examiner asked if he could read—he answered "no." When she said, "Just a few letters?" he did not answer. Later examiner was informed that observer had seen him read at school. He was given reading and report section of test and read it. Examiner asked him why he had said he could not read (this was during rest period when parents were present) and before Hal could answer, mother said, "That might be our fault—he used to say he could read and some people thought he was bragging, so we thought it better he should not say he could read."

INTERVIEW X (seventy-one months): Occasional complaints of stomachache on going to school. "I told him this would not be tolerated—that he goes to school like father goes to work. Unless he has temperature he goes to school." Physician suggested mother tell him that he does not have to do more than others in class—and they don't get stomachaches, so why should he. Before long, stomachaches were gone.

When something is delayed—as meal—he may balk, whine, fret a bit, but once an explanation is given, he goes along with the change. Complains he can't go to sleep with daylight saving time. However, never mentioned his friends' staying out as reason for his desire to stay up. Allowed into mother's bed when he had nightmare. Happened twice. Then mother said he could come and tell her if he had a nightmare, but she would then escort him back to his bed. Has not had a nightmare since.

Usually tries to get another child to play what he wants to play. If child balks, he would either say he doesn't want to play or accept mother's suggestion that they take turns. When interrupted in pleasurable activity, he gets furious, but ends with doing as mother says.

"Funny you should question me—of course he does as I say" (mother to interviewer).

Can listen for hours to Civil War stories, Scottish ballads. These interests fostered by father.

Will always accept a change if he is just given a reasonable explanation. Generally a threat of punishment is enough to make him stop objectionable behavior.

Masturbation: Mother said to stop—it was not polite and would ruin pants. He stopped—now puts fingers in mouth. Hal was warned he might develop impetigo from picking his nose—never picked his nose again.

FIRST GRADE TEACHER INTERVIEW (eighty-three months): Said very definitely, "I hate to rhyme," but once he started, he couldn't be stopped. Great vocabulary, but adapts it to the age and ability of child or adult with whom he is speaking.

INTERVIEW XI (eighty-four months): May resist having to stop watching ball game when told to take bath—mother gives him leeway, and he adheres to it.

Won't leave what he is doing when another child visits, but will not object to child's joining his activity.

SECOND GRADE TEACHER INTERVIEW (one hundred months): Has conformed to teacher's suggestion of whispering if he must talk when others are working.

Persistence in tasks that he is unable to master quickly

INTERVIEW VIII (fifty-three months): In the realm of physical tasks, his first response is "It's too hard for me," and leaves it. Mother takes him back, explains how it works. "He's content to watch—if he does attempt, it's half-hearted, as if to show me he's trying. Then again he says it's too hard. It's a long, drawn-out struggle. Gradually, after consistent pressure, cajoling, and threats, he'll suddenly master it. I don't know if he would have succeeded without our pressuring."

With puzzle, puts in one or two pieces—as soon as one piece doesn't fit he asks for help. Sits and watches until he's memorized where the pieces go. After he's shown how, goes back to it again and again.

Game called Fascination—tilt board with maze and ball. Initially he was "frantic"—"Why won't it go?" Began to cry—"It's no good." Finally picked up ball and put it in the hole. But he was "fascinated" —worked on it until gradually he "cheated" less and less, and now can beat mother. "We could never have gotten him to work it if he didn't want to." Sometimes, if shown how to do something correctly, will say, "I want to do it my way." For example, about a toy clarinet, he said, "I know more about this thing because it's a toy."

INTERVIEW IX (sixty months): Any new physical endeavor is approached with great caution. First he asks many questions—"What does it do? How does it work?" etc. Then he may leave it alone without any attempt to try it. Parents urge—he refuses. Then at his own pace, he begins to try it.

KINDERGARTEN TEACHER INTERVIEW (sixty-nine months): On first day, when teacher was getting ready to read a story, he went to bathroom. He stayed a long time. When story was over and other children were getting ready to go home, teacher found him crying in bathroom. He couldn't button his pants. He kept sobbing "the button, the button." Teacher helped him, told him the next time he had trouble he should ask for help.

Not able to tie his shoes. Sometimes he tries, sometimes asks for help in complaining voice—"I can't do it." Once he did manage to make a bow. He said, "Oh, I did it, I did it" with great delight. Now more apt to try longer—less apt to say he can't.

Has more self-control now than he did at beginning of year. Would look angry, as if he were boiling inside, if not called on the minute he raised his hand. If he didn't know an answer, his expression was grim and tense. When in a group, he always wanted things to go his way; if they didn't, he would criticize loudly, look angry, and often walk away. Would frequently complain loudly, sometimes to the teacher.

Often looks angry, tense, and close to tears when he is criticized by others, when he is not obeyed by others, when he thinks he's not getting his fair turn, when a child won't stop mishandling material at his instructions—in other words, any time his orders are ignored. If he walks out of an uncomfortable situation, he makes no effort to return. Sometimes mutters loudly to himself—"She shouldn't do that," or "You're not supposed to put it there." Typically, before he mastered skipping, "anger with himself" would show on his face. "He'd get his black-cloud look." Often gets "black-cloud" look when teacher reprimands him for being noisy or for not cleaning up.

Earlier in the year he was hesitant about trying something new that he was uncertain about, that he wasn't sure he could accomplish to his own satisfaction. Teacher feels he has strong perfectionist tendencies. Example: She demonstrated the construction of a paper puppet—asked if everyone knew how to proceed—class said yes. Hal got out all his equipment, and stared at it. He looked angry and upset, didn't ask for help. Accepted teacher's help silently and remained angry-looking. Still doesn't ask for help when he is unable to carry out a project. Teacher has pointed out to him many times that it doesn't matter at all if he colors out of the line or doesn't cut perfectly. (His

manual dexterity is below grade level.) Now he is not so fussy—seems
to have set more realistic goals for himself.

Generally follows instructions. Often needs encouragement to
finish a task, particularly if it is one he doesn't especially care for.

INTERVIEW X (seventy-one months): This year writing bothered him.
He complained and complained—suddenly he stopped complaining
and mother saw that he had mastered it. This is typical. He will
complain or even refuse to do something when he is unable to meet his
standards, then suddenly he will master the activity.

Teacher observed that he was frustrated in his attempts to write.
He did not actually cry, but his eyes would glaze, and he would clench
his teeth.

Complained of stomachaches—didn't want to go to school. "She
(teacher) makes me do too hard things. . . . We have to finish everything."

Very slow warm-up in getting into pool first time. Mother urged
him to ride two-wheeler, held him. He offered much resistance but
tried it. With lack of success, he whined in annoyance and gave up.
Anything physical is difficult for him. If successful, he is so pleased—
full of smiles, and "He's always so amazed at being able to accomplish
anything in this area." If he does not succeed, he will say, "I told you
I couldn't do it."

Sensitive to criticism—often cries quietly.

FIRST-GRADE TEACHER INTERVIEW (eighty-three months): "Temperamental." "Gets upset with self." "To make a mistake is just awful."
In beginning of year had trouble with writing. Would get upset. If
teacher would say gently, "Do you think you can do it better?" he
would say "yes," but would cry, get red in the face, throw pencil on
floor. Anger not with teacher, but with self. He might say, "I know
I can do it but I just hate practicing" or "I hate school" or "Why is
it always me?" If general instructions are given to class, he would still
say, "Why is it always me?" If not called on, will say, "I never get a
chance."

Reading tests indicated he was at fifth-grade level. But he was
reluctant to read fourth-grade book. Actually doing well, but complained
before he came to desk to read. Said he hated it, ranted on. Teacher
returned him to average reading group, and he fit right in, followed
routine, grinned when called on. He is reading with the others in
first-grade reader. Did not want to be separated from his group. Told
this to teacher specifically. Uses third-grade workbook, however, as
teacher did not like to see him waste his ability. Has difficulty with
third-grade workbook—does not have background and teacher does
not have the time to give him special attention. Is pleased to have
the book, bounces up with it when called, grins when he shows his

work to teacher. There were two pages he could not do well—alphabetizing fifty words. He said it was too hard, that he could not do it. He closed the book and put it on teacher's desk. When she tried to go into it he got upset—face got red—he walked around in a circle, pounded fists, fingers always moving. He never did this page. Monotony of detailed work upsets him—if teacher corrects mistakes in his workbook, he says, "Oh, those little things." Said very definitely "I hate to rhyme," but once he got started, he couldn't be stopped.

Tantrums are somewhat quieter now, seems to get mad at himself for getting upset. Things that bring on a tantrum: 1] being asked to walk in a straight line; 2] correction of work or behavior; 3] failure to accomplish a sport or art; 4] most often, his own mistakes. Tantrum is talking out in loud voice, pounding desk, stamping feet, slamming something down, kicking something, talking to self, mumbling. If left alone, he gets over it more quickly. When children said, "You are being a baby," he got worse and it took longer for him to get over it. Used to have two or three per day, now about once a day, and they are milder. Reasoning with him, showing him that everyone makes mistakes, is best way to handle them.

More tantrums during art than any other time. If he can't succeed in making something beautiful the first time, he doesn't want to go over it again. Gives up and goes into a tantrum; then slaps something together and that's it.

He is reluctant to do something that will make him appear less capable than others. Prefers reading; does not like writing or art. His skills in these latter areas have improved. His muscular control was quite poor, but has gotten better—now about average. Afraid of high bars, skipping rope. He was petrified. Had tantrums. Teacher was very patient with him, went slowly, joked. Now he loves parallel bars. Enjoys running. Prefers playing with a couple of boys to participating in a game with rules. Has a tantrum with rules or if he doesn't get a turn.

His hand is always up. Disappointed if not called on. If not called first says, "You never call on me." If he does not have a turn, will have a tantrum.

INTERVIEW XI (eighty-four months): Mother states that he has learned to handle frustration better—helped by teacher's making a joke. Still low threshold. Until midsemester he thought he was going to fail because of poor handwriting. "I don't mind being left back. I'll be the oldest in the class instead of the youngest." Mother told him that was ridiculous—he would not fail.

SECOND-GRADE TEACHER INTERVIEW (one hundred months): Hal is very capable, but cannot accept any correction. Frustration is enormous for even the most minor mistake. Entire class (except Hal) had very poor discipline. When teacher sent everyone back to his seat, even though he was not involved, Hal became furious—stamped his foot, made negative comments, became all tensed up. When teacher finally told class to get in line, he wouldn't move. Said, "As for me—just forget about me." Teacher joked that she could never forget about him—he finally got in line.

Teacher has tried to have him do more advanced work (beyond what group is doing), but he refused. Teacher asked him to use encyclopedia in relation to what group is studying, but he has refused. In math he would not go on to next assignment, and teacher didn't want to push him. Has suggested that he work with another bright boy. They have worked together a few times, but not too often. Doesn't like to do charts or write reports. Teacher hasn't pushed. She felt, for present, it's more important to reach him since he's so easily frustrated.

Physical-education teacher was helping boys with something new and Hal wouldn't even try. P.E. teacher becomes upset with Hal's attitude when she tries to help him—she told teacher he needs psychiatric help.

Hal doesn't feel he's good in art. May sit and do nothing—art teacher hasn't forced him. Very frustrated with animal he was making. A girl helped him. He still said he thought it was terrible, yet seemed pleased to see it hanging on wall with the others. Doesn't like help from teacher—makes him feel inadequate. Not so bad if another child helps him in art. Is so capable in other areas that he seldom needs help. Fairly able in dance, but becomes impatient. Gets extremely upset if he doesn't get special partner he wants. Would always choose same girl.

"Hal is a perfectionist . . . and frustrated (though less so lately). He is not unhappy except when he is frustrated. I wonder if it isn't a pose sometimes. Wanting everything to be perfect is a fetish. Can't admit being interested in anything—almost a pose." (General statement from teacher.)

Behavior is at age level except for reaction to criticism and frustration in physical areas. With something too difficult (as art), he says, "I hate it. I can't do it well." Willingness to recognize that he can make a mistake once in a while has helped his learning tremendously. Gets impatient with others when they answer incorrectly.

If he is conversing with his neighbor and teacher tells him to settle down—even just once—he gets very annoyed—also if teacher makes him do something he's not interested in doing.

Overt expression of aggression and other emotions

INTERVIEW VIII (fifty-three months): When he objects to parental demand, he says, "I don't want to, why must I? I don't like"—uses high-pitched, moderately loud tone, with facial scowling, flailing of arms, and forward or backward motion of body. Intensity of pitch and body movements vary with degree to which he objects. Duration, ten to thirty seconds.

In playing with a group, others piled up on him and he tripped and fell on some rocks. Came in sobbing hysterically, "Why did they do this to me? . . . Why only me they hurt? . . . Don't they know I am their friend?"

One of his friends wanted his guns. Hal refused and when he was pushed, he pushed back and said, "I defended myself." In playing cowboys, insists on being sheriff—if he can't, won't play. True even after others piled up on him and he was hurt on rocks—had nightmare about it. When he can't be sheriff, or win all the time, he cries furiously, says, "I can't stand not doing it right."

When told he had to dress before breakfast (change in routine), he cried, "Why must I?," stamped feet, had mild tantrum. Mother talked, then spanked. Then, when told he would not have time to play game with her, he got dressed in two minutes.

In change from toidy seat to regular toilet—had fear of regular toilet—said, "I'm going to fall in, I'm afraid." Was constipated a few days even with mother's holding and reassuring him. On one occasion, mother called to phone—he remained on toilet and had bowel movement. He was delighted. Third time after this, told mother he didn't need her. Is afraid to flush—mother doesn't make him.

When request is refused, he may throw temper tantrum, scream, flail arms. In play with his younger brother, he often will snatch a toy he wants to use—brother will shriek, he'll offer a substitute, or mother will ask if Hal can use something else. Sometimes he gets a "mean streak"—yells at brother, but never hits him. Sometimes yells because brother blocks view of television. Brother won't move—Hal keeps yelling, yet doesn't touch him.

Visited by a two-and-a-half-year-old girl who frequently kicks and hits Hal. Parents told him in advance to protect brother. Hal put on guns and couldn't wait for her arrival. He was going to be sheriff. There was a fight over a flag he had—she pulled it away, he pulled it back. She pushed—he gave a push that sent her halfway across the room—she screamed. He stood there, very pleased with himself—"I defended myself." He hovered over her making facial grimaces—"I'm gonna see you don't hurt my brother." Girl's mother told Hal he was frightening her, that she didn't know he didn't want to hurt her. Hal said, "I do want to hurt her." Mother told other mother that she was only child Hal doesn't like—bears a grudge from her previous behavior. Mother made no attempt to stop Hal's behavior. Later there was a crash—brother on floor, girl crying. (Hal had pushed girl, and she had fallen on brother.) Mother slapped Hal before letting him explain—then apologized. He cried very hard, said he hadn't meant to push brother, that he had hit girl—was defending himself. She had pushed him first. Later, when girl approached him, he smiled, put his arms around her—played together an hour without altercation. When father put him to bed that night, Hal said proudly, "See, she didn't hurt my brother all day long."

When special book he wanted couldn't be found in library, he refused substitute, spoke intensely in a petulant manner, waving his arms, a scowl on his face. Finally found acceptable book—he smiled, was happy.

INTERVIEW IX (sixty months): Other children astonished that Hal can read—status has gone up. In spite of this, brother treats him viciously. Brother teases—mother has been trying to get Hal to understand this—he takes everything so literally. "We told him he could call his brother names if the latter did. Now Hal is best name-caller on block." Hal still wants to play with brother, in spite of the way he is treated. Whenever Hal acts on mother's suggestion not to play with brother, brother begs him to play with him. Always at each other's throats, with Hal always losing out, although he has learned to "needle" him. Hal has become more self-assertive. Told a kid up at bat, "You hit terribly—come on now—it's my turn."

Was fighting with another child and came whining and crying to mother for third time. Mother told him she is not fighting his battles, that he's acting like a baby, not a five-year-old. He is learning that mother does not intervene unless he's being physically assaulted by more than just fists.

He has found that he is able to cope with another child's aggression by retaliating with verbal threat. This has helped make him sure of himself. Just making a menacing gesture is enough to protect himself.

Is now an integral part of group. Others call for him more often than he does the seeking; they come for lunch more frequently. Recently a six-and-a-half-year-old was teasing him and Hal hit him. When other boy hit him back, Hal didn't cry as he used to—boy commented, "You don't cry and say 'wha, wha, wha' anymore." Hal told mother, "That's because I'm a five-year-old." To be teased is still difficult for him, but he has a greater tolerance for it than six months ago. In dramatic play he shrieks if he doesn't get role of father. Mother thinks other children are so tired of the shrieks that they give in.

Occasional tantrums, but mild—involve nagging, crying, pouting, flailing of arms—also verbal expression. When told to wash face at bedtime he pouts, wrinkles forehead, says, "I don't want to"; argues back and forth with mother—flailing arms, hopping up and down, pouting. When mother gives final demand accompanied by threat, he stamps off and washes face.

KINDERGARTEN TEACHER INTERVIEW (sixty-nine months): Used to look angry, as if boiling inside, if not called on the minute he raised his hand. Has more self-control now. Still has tendency to be excitable, talkative, loud, out of bounds. Mother warned teacher he had tendency to be overbearing, which was quite true. Wanted things his way; would criticize loudly; would look angry and often walk away. Less so now, but still loud voice and critical. Last several weeks, complains of stomachache about once a week.

Except for recent excitability, doesn't get upset easily. Once or twice has cried—in each case because he was unable to do something for himself. However, expression is often angry, tense, close to tears when he is criticized by others, when he is not being obeyed, when he thinks he has not had his fair turn. Sometimes, in rhythms, is apt to get excited, talk loudly instead of listening to music or instructions.

Does not play war or aggressive games. If someone has something he needs and refuses to give it to him, he looks angry but never hits or grabs. He may ask teacher if he may share coveted object—if she says yes, he goes back and reports to child in possession—voice is shrill, loud, gives impression of being excited. Most often abandons the whole deal and makes do with what he has. Never physically demonstrative—does not hold hands, hug; nor does he push or shove.

INTERVIEW X (seventy-one months): With daylight saving time, went to bed later—had to be awakened—was very crabby, easily in tears. Complaints of stomachaches.

Exchanges visits with good friend—girl in his class. One day he came home storming mad—spoke of another girl who had joined them—"I don't like her . . . see no reason why I should play with her."

Boy tackled him in football—he got up, laughed, tackled boy back. Parents relieved and surprised to observe this. Has learned all about football in diagram plays with father. Is the "leader." The other day—bent down to tie his shoe—three boys came along, jumped on him from behind, threw him over, went on their way. He was very upset—ran into house crying, "How could they? Two of them were my friends." Moody rest of day.

Chews on fingers a lot—whenever he is not busy. Started to masturbate again. When told to do it in his own room, he stopped.

Mild and occasional tantrums. No kicking or yelling beyond verbal expostulations and slamming a door—will get ferocious look on face, gnash teeth, make fingers like claws, especially if brother makes him angry, takes his toy. If doing something he is enjoying and is interrupted by a request, he gets furious—frowns, hops, yells, and "mouth is going at same time." Ends with doing as mother says. When scolded, he will cry, whine, protest, hop up and down. When he considers scolding unjust, there is more of this plus verbalization. Accepts criticism if mother is calm; if she is not, he will get very upset, cry, sulk in his room a minute or two.

FIRST-GRADE TEACHER INTERVIEW (eighty-three months): Does poorly with writing. Gets upset, cries, gets red in face, throws pencil on floor.

Tests revealed he was ready for fifth-grade book. Given fourth-grade book—was reluctant to read, complained, got red in face, dragged chair—said he hated this—ranted on. Returned to reading group— became happier, grinned.

Objected to alphabetizing fifty words. Did not get to point of tantrum—teacher joked him out of it. He does have tantrums—some things make him act like "end of the world." Things that bring on tantrums: 1] being asked to walk in a straight line; 2] correction of work or behavior; 3] failure to accomplish in art or sports; 4] most often, his own mistakes.

Can be domineering (his job to get class in straight line), but not obnoxious. Gets upset with rules (of games) or if he doesn't get a turn.

INTERVIEW XI (eighty-four months): A friend had excluded him from play. He came home looking thoughtful but not angry—more surprised. Mother suggested that next time he could exclude other child. "I don't think I'll do that, he's a good friend—I like him anyway."

SECOND-GRADE TEACHER INTERVIEW (one hundred months): Reticent about talking about things that bother him in class—well mannered and little gentleman, therefore won't complain.

Gets very upset when teacher tells *others* they have not been listening.

KATE—CASE 16

SUMMARY

AGE AT REFERRAL: Sixty-one months.

PRESENTING COMPLAINTS:
1] Fear of cars.
2] Nonparticipation at school.

ONSET OF PROBLEM: Forty-six months.

CLINICAL INTERVIEW: Because of her familiarity with the playroom where she had been recently tested and the presence of the psychologist to greet her, Kate quickly appeared right at home and her usual very long warm-up period was not in evidence. Although there was ptosis of her right eye, her features were otherwise not unpleasant and without this defect she might be considered an attractive youngster.

She was seen in joint session with her twin sister, who moved ahead of her into the playroom and immediately became involved with the toys. Kate stood briefly at the doorway, smiling, but within a few moments she followed her sister's lead, joined her at the shelves, and used the precise toys her sister had taken down. She was slow moving in contrast to her twin, and at first her play seemed to duplicate that of her sister. As the session progressed, however, she took an active part in announcing how the use of a toy was to be divided and, after some parallel play, she would return to an activity of her own choice that she had enjoyed.

Although there was no opportunity to observe the period of uninvolvement that had been described as the child's characteristic initial behavior in new situations, there was a distinct rise in her motor and verbal levels of activity and in her interpersonal contact as time went on. During most of the session she was either smiling or otherwise displaying pleasant involvement with her activity.

Her speech was properly used, but of simple construction and often unclearly enunciated. She repeated herself willingly and pleasantly upon request until she was understood.

While the child moved more slowly into an activity than did her sister, there was actually no attempt to imitate and, on the whole, the content level of her play seemed somewhat superior to that of her twin. She produced fewer paintings, but worked more deliberately and with better concepts. Her drawing of a girl was adequate or slightly superior for age. Despite her slower movements, the child reached a level of accomplishment higher than her sister's and, though she initially appeared less bright, she showed a greater degree of independent activity in the end.

The youngster's behavior during this interview was that of a normal but shy child.

DIAGNOSIS: Reactive Behavior Disorder, mild.

TEMPERAMENT: The child's most prominent temperamental characteristics are her low activity level and her initial withdrawal responses to new situations. She requires a long period of warm-up, after which she usually achieves a positive adaptation. She is also persistent and sensitive to the reactions of others toward her and gives little overt expression to her feelings. There is some indication, too, that she has a low threshold to noise.

The low activity level is evidenced in her marked slowness of movement and in her initial lack of participation. These become caricatures of themselves when the child is faced with a new interpersonal situation, when she is getting her bearings, or when she is apprehensive or uncertain.

The history contains repeated instances of timidity and caution with strangers. When a new person ignores her, she remains apart, making no effort to engage herself in the situation. However, when someone "works at" making contact with her, or when she is given proper urging or direction, the child herself will give up a negative reaction and move immediately into a positive interrelationship.

ADDITIONAL FACTORS: Kate has congenital glaucoma and ptosis of one eye. Vision in this eye is poor. Eyedrops are required several times a day.

PARENTAL FUNCTIONING: The mother is generally irritated by the child's slow tempo. As a result, she tends to rush Kate, then becomes angry at the child's ineptness, and finally overservices her by taking over completely; for example, by dressing her rather than letting her dress herself at her own pace. Both parents appear to be oblivious to the child's sensitivity in many areas and seem to assume, because she does not express her feelings directly, that she is not reacting. For example, the mother states that Kate did not resist attending nursery school, yet the child for a while vomited every morning before she left. In addition, they deny that Kate has any sensitivity about her eye condition, in direct contradiction of her teacher's report. Moreover, the eye problem was minimized by the parents from the beginning and medical investigation was delayed. The father minimizes all problems, including those about which the mother expresses concern, and appears uninvolved with his daughter.

DYNAMIC FORMULATION: The child's problems are, in fact, exaggerations of her temperamental characteristics. Her slow involvement in new situations and her tendency to move slowly have been reinforced by the mother's handling, specifically by her tendency to rush the child, to become annoyed at and disapprove of the child's inability to meet expectations, and to overservice her in an irritated manner. The negative interaction which has developed has only increased the child's hesitancy and apprehension. In the mother's own words, "She thinks she will do something wrong and that I will punish her, so she does nothing."

The same pattern of slow involvement in school may have been intensified by her sensitivity to reactions of the peer group to her eye defect, but teachers have been perceptive, firm, and supporting, and gradually the child seems to have responded.

The "fear of cars" described by the parents appears not to be directed to cars per se, as Kate willingly rides in the family car and does not hesitate to get into the school bus once the motor has been turned off and is silent. Rather, the fear reaction seems to be an aspect of the child's particular sensitivity to loud and sudden noises, which became associated with cars and trucks on a specific occasion at eighteen months (from which time the parents date the onset of the problem) when Kate was severely frightened by the sudden approach of a loud and noisy truck. The child was startled, cried, and "bolted." While the parents' handling of this incident is not reported, it is not unlikely that they responded to the child's "bolting" with everything but reassurance, thus reinforcing the child's reaction of fear.

RECOMMENDATIONS: The parents were told that the child's slowness and need for a long warm-up were temperamental qualities that must be accepted as outside of her control, and must be taken into consideration when demands are made of her if they want to handle her appropriately. Attempts to rush her, and the mother's resultant annoyance at Kate's ineptness, only serve to make the child feel more incompetent and discourage her from trying to help herself. It is important for the mother consistently to encourage Kate to take responsibility for doing things on her own, even though this will mean rescheduling time, as it will take the child longer than it did the mother to accomplish certain routines. The parents were advised that this kind of handling was essential for the development of the child's self-confidence and independent functioning.

The eye defect was discussed as a likely area of sensitivity and as something which might occasion questions from other children. The parents were advised to discontinue denying the obvious and instead to give Kate a name for the condition, which would enable her to maintain a sense of personal dignity in dealing with the questions of peers.

The fear of cars was explained to the parents as an extension of the child's basic sensitivity to sudden and loud noises. They were told to reassure the child when she expressed her fears and to expect the problem to pass as the child had repeated experiences with cars.

SUBSEQUENT COURSE: At last contact, at 109 months, there had been gradual, moderate improvement in the child's functioning. At school, this was due in large part to separation from her faster moving twin and good handling by the teachers. Kate had advanced from being a remote, unresponsive, and uncomprehending child to one who made friends, was accepted and not teased by the other children, and was functioning academically in the middle group of her class. She has become a strongly motivated, diligent, and conscientious worker, takes great pride in accomplishment, and responds well to appeals to her self-esteem. Although she is still a slow learner, her persistence and diligence seem to compensate for this.

At home, an older sister has taken over much of the responsibility for the younger children and so the mother is less involved with Kate. Also, as the child has progressed, the mother's previous negative and complaining attitude has lessened; she takes some pride in Kate's accomplishments and does not fuss at her so much. As a result, negative interactions between mother and child are less frequent.

The child's basic temperamental characteristics are still present, but they no longer interfere, to any considerable degree, with her functioning. Each year she requires a shorter warm-up period at the start of the school term. Although she is participating more and is working at grade level, her teacher feels she is producing below her potential. Kate now responds to overtures from other children and exchanges visits, but she does not yet initiate friendships. She continues to be wary of cars, particularly of "exploding motors," still does not express her feelings easily, but has been able to tell her mother that she expects too much from her—"I'm not old enough." She shows no concern about her eye defect, for which treatment is continuing. The basic factor in the advances she has made is that some feeling of self-worth has replaced the demoralization that had been developing at the time of consultation.

Selective Extraction

Activity level

INTERVIEW I (eleven weeks): Doesn't move much in sleep. Plays actively with crib toys. Much less active than twin. (Observed at two days of age during physical examination. Baby was quiet—did not cry.)

INTERVIEW II (five months): Doesn't move much in sleep. Fairly active in daytime.

INTERVIEW III (eight months): Moves somewhat in sleep. More of an effort for her to turn over than twin (she is two pounds heavier).

INTERVIEW IV (eleven months): Reported "much less dextrous and fast" than twin (with regard to food grabbing). Moves less in sleep than twin; less active (weighs three pounds more).

INTERVIEW V (thirteen and one-half months): Reported not as dextrous as twin in self-feeding, but more adept with cup. Mother explains it took longer for vaccination scab to fall off because "she didn't wiggle as much" as twin. Now an active crawler, but never as active as sister.

INTERVIEW VI (eighteen months): Moves a lot in sleep. Still cautious in walking, takes small steps.

INTERVIEW VII (twenty-four months): Very active.

INTERVIEW VIII (thirty-two months): Quite active—doesn't move as fast as twin. Can sit for longer periods, is more cautious in play and running around.

INTERVIEW IX (thirty-nine months): Not very active. Prefers sedentary or quiet activity. Does not have good gross coordination. Does not run, climb, etc. as well as twin. Difficulty in opening and turning objects; can't turn knob on phonograph (mother feels this might be fear). Can't put on socks despite practice.

INTERVIEW X (forty-six months): Doesn't abide by rules so readily. Mother talks, but no response. "Goes about business."

TEACHER INTERVIEW (fifty-two months): On the whole prefers quiet play, less active than most children. Gross coordination (climbing) is poor, and teacher feels this due to inexperience and will improve.

INTERVIEW XI (fifty-three months): No mention.

INTERVIEW XII (fifty-nine months): "Does not rush herself." Sometimes mother is not sure if child hears her. Mother has to dress her. Takes a long time if she does it on her own, and pressed for time in morning. May put pants on backwards; can't pull up tights; can't put shoes on. Just sits until mother raises her voice, then may try; but mother usually does it for her. Also no effort to wash self in bath. Mother thinks she is afraid of doing things wrong and then being punished by mother, so she does nothing.

KINDERGARTEN TEACHER INTERVIEW (sixty months): Teacher does not think she is up to level of other children in use of large or small muscles. Awkward and slow in marching, running, pasting, cutting; unable to skip or jump. It takes her a long time for everything.

Reactions to new situations

INTERVIEW I (eleven weeks): Refuses pacifier—does seek finger or hand.

Vitamin drops: a little fussing the first time, took them well from then on. Cereal: took it well first few days, then took it with fussing, then fussing diminished and stopped after a few days. Bath: cries when put in, but quiets in a minute; lies quietly, somewhat tensed.

INTERVIEW II (five months): With new foods, makes face with first taste, then takes another taste and takes it well.

Dressing: little fussing.

"More serious" with strangers than twin. "She's less trusting." Cries after looking at some strangers, but with others will finally laugh in response to their overtures.

Only cried a few minutes with injection.

INTERVIEW III (eight months): Takes most food well. Sometimes will make a face, but takes it well. Egg introduced—taken well. Apparently little reaction or resistance to routines, such as cutting nails, washing hair, etc. Less willing to smile at strangers than twin, but she will.

INTERVIEW IV (eleven months): Very timid, afraid to get on her feet. Stands up a few minutes, then cries to be put down. Drinks from cup. Eats very well. Eats everything (except squash).

Some fussing and resistance to nail cutting and face washing; gets angry and cries with nose and ear cleaning.

To strangers: studies person a while, finally responds to overture. "You have to work at it." Traveled in car several times—no fussing.

INTERVIEW V (thirteen and one-half months): Takes new food in mouth, "and if she doesn't seem to trust it, takes it out and puts it on the tray and will later take it up herself and eat it." Will swallow food if commanded to—even with wry face. No difficulty in transition to cup. Plays with bottle now.

After no bath for one month due to vaccination, she cried at first attempt. Crying lessened with further exposure and now plays with sister in tub. "She isn't too trusting and holds on tight." With crawling, at first would stay very much in one place on floor—now active crawler. Took long time to stand, preferring knees. Always cautious with walking, even with help.

Cautious acceptance of new toys, but later plays with them more persistently than twin. Used to cry when twin took things from her— now will take twin's things.

Needs warm-up with strangers, then will accept them.

INTERVIEW VI (eighteen months): "She has changed more than twin." Is more lovable, more willing to be kissed. Eats very well—"Seems to like everything, whatever I give her." Takes new foods easily though often "makes a face."

After bath-free interval of a few weeks, mild negative reaction to bath for a few days. Not responsive to "no"—"Stubborn."

Wary of strangers—five-to-ten-minute warm-up, then friendly.

INTERVIEW VII (twenty-four months): Slow to make friends—examines them first. Cautious with strangers. Examines other children carefully— but hasn't had much contact. Sits on toilet willingly then starts to fuss. Training not successful. Obeys "no," but is "insulted" and cries briefly.

INTERVIEW VIII (thirty-two months): Feeding continues "very fine." At twenty-four months, mother lost nipple of bottles—announced "no more bottle"—Kate accepted it without fussing.

When mother started putting her on potty after meals, she cried, tried to get off. "I made her sit there and she finally gave in." Less time to train her than twin, "came quickly." Dry during day since then (age twenty-five months), and dry at night since age twenty-eight months.

"Not as trusting of people" (as twin). Timid with strangers, clings to mother. Takes warm-up time with new child, but not as long as with adult. Mother comments that in general she is slow to adapt to new situation or people.

When taken to beach ran in water at once, no resistance. Didn't want to go in wading pool, but did enjoy sprinkler from the first time it was set up.

Family moved to house in suburbs eight months ago. Immediate adjustment, including sleeping in strange room, from first day.

INTERVIEW IX (thirty-nine months): When going-to-bed routine is changed at times, she fusses, whines, but finally goes to bed. No problems in putting her to bed at grandmother's house where she slept in room with other members of family.

If bath is omitted, she asks for it. Loves to take medicine, cooperative with temperature taking. Friendly and eager to greet physician. Cries a bit with examination; with injection, starts crying when needle is removed, stops when mother cuddles her.

Tends to stand and watch children play. Needs long warm-up before she will join. Usually follows twin. For past month tends to initiate some play with twin.

Fear reaction to first use of glider in playground. Now Kate likes it—took two to three times to overcome. Liked high slide when older sister took her (mother was afraid). Refused all rides (in amusement park) but one. Seemed frightened.

In new endeavor, asks for help. If can't do it on her own may lose interest. Likes encouragement. Won't push herself; must be reminded and encouraged to participate.

With strangers, stands near mother, waits and watches. Remained at mother's side during entire afternoon visit to mother's friends she didn't know. Refuses interaction initiated by stranger at first meeting. Does not accommodate to strangers. Would not speak to interviewer and appeared angry because she had inadvertently sat on Kate's chair, even though chair was vacated. In new situation, hangs back, waits, watches. In friendly atmosphere, will get involved after sufficient exposure—may take more than one.

INTERVIEW X (forty-six months): Protested removal of crib, although she seemed to want new bed. Wanted crib for dolls. After several days, no objection when crib was removed. If someone takes her place at table she may have tantrum, throw herself, or scream. Will use bathroom facilities anywhere.

Nursery school started two days ago. Went without adult first day. Reluctant regarding noise of bus, but when door was opened, she ran in. On return was happy, sang; not so fussy, more alive. Brought drawings home.

In play, tends to watch when others are engaged in activity, does not run right in. Prefers to go out if twin and friend are out. In own house may sometimes participate and play when outsiders are visiting.

In new endeavor, watches when mother demonstrates, then attempts. Asks for mother's help when she can't do it alone. (Still poor results with putting on socks—mother still "making a point" of it.) Tries to learn new activities; persists.

Needs warm-up with strangers—not so long as formerly. Does not get involved in interaction with stranger at first meeting—watches and waits. With new situation is cautious, holds back, watches, but not so long as formerly.

When mother returned to work, twins were left with grandmother. They asked for mother several times, seemed cranky, and on her return followed her about house more than usual.

No longer abides by rules so readily—lets mother talk, but makes no response; "Goes about her business."

TEACHER INTERVIEW (fifty-two months): Attitude on arrival, consistently neutral. Waits for teacher to greet her and may or may not respond. Will respond to smile of another child. Tends to stay apart from other children at playground (first activity of day), but joins more now at teacher's suggestion.

At first needed to be started off with undressing. When she wants help doesn't ask directly, but stands silently in front of teacher. No talking during this period.

She used to cry and hang back from entering bus to go home. Now she is ready—does not linger or anticipate.

Follows instructions well and is not negative. With new experience, hangs back and holds teacher's hand—then able to participate. Can be counted on completely to carry out and know routines and "could lead the class in these, if necessary." Does not talk during routines, but will answer if spoken to. May talk to children about some of the activity—minimal talk, but does not appear shy. Immediately cooperative, quieter than most, does not require special routines.

In structured play, watches and listens and is slow to participate. Beginning to join in more. In free play, seems most relaxed when on her own, although beginning to have some involvement with other children. At start of school, didn't seem to know anything—seems to have taught herself. Is busy—prefers crafts, painting, puzzles.

Seemed freer indoors than outdoors where everything seemed new to her. Outdoors she was cautious, hesitant, and even fearful. Is beginning to try some of the outdoor equipment at teacher's suggestion. More participating in some of the silly play outside. For past few weeks has been joining group in (optional) trip to woods and seems to enjoy it. At first always stayed out. Began to participate in sleigh riding only after teacher went with her. At first, expressed fear of going up a hill, slides, and equipment. It seems rather a disinterest, and that she would have approached nothing on her own, but she was willing to try with firm approach and help from teacher.

Undemonstrative expression, but apparently aware of everything that is going on. Does best learning if teacher will instruct child next to her so Kate may watch and go at her own pace.

Tends to avoid new things and doesn't ask for but will accept help. Usually persists until she masters it.

Speaks little, but more to children than adults, with whom she is likely to hang head and mumble. Wary and cautious with teacher at first—several months before she became more receptive. Also several months to establish relationship with children. Now plays with children in her group, especially two girls who are also interested in her.

Difficult to assess her feelings, though she will indicate pleasure by a smile, and displeasure by head-hanging, whining, tears, and non-cooperation. No evidence of anger or hurt feelings.

INTERVIEW XI (fifty-three months): Began to vomit every morning before going to school—not on weekends. Vomiting stopped within a week after mother reprimanded her. Likes to see mother off for work before she finishes breakfast.

Visits neighbors infrequently although sister goes readily (has to cross street). When family visited another city, it took three days for her to get used to relatives. Did not answer when spoken to or have anything to do with adults. She was willing to go with neighbor and her children.

INTERVIEW XII (fifty-nine months): Doesn't talk about school. May give some information on repeated questioning from mother. Doesn't get upset—just doesn't answer. Teacher called mother for conference a week ago because Kate has not seemed to warm up. It happened this same day was first time Kate came to teacher spontaneously to ask about something. Teacher's concern about absence of speech led to referral to speech therapist and psychologist. Teacher thought child was unable to talk.

When taken to movies, older sister reports she "sits through quietly."

Casual greeting to mother when she arrives home from work; if she is interested in T.V., no greeting at all. (Contrast to behavior in Interview XI where she interrupted breakfast to see mother off for work.)

Apparently not interested in dates, although she is left alone when twin visits friends. Reluctant to go outside alone. When mother gives her individual affection she "cuddles up." When stranger comes to house she does not run away. May not talk, may not answer, just disregards strangers.

More than a week or two before she "accepted" housekeeper, i.e., allowed her to do things or responded to her overtures. Her "acceptance" consists in responding when they initiate—does not initiate herself.

At family get-togethers doesn't talk to children, doesn't play readily. Will follow if asked, but does not participate in activity.

No longer comes to meals as quickly—still insists on own special place and chair similar to twin's. No effort to wash self in bath. Mother thinks she is afraid she will do things wrong and mother will punish her, so she does nothing.

KINDERGARTEN TEACHER INTERVIEW (sixty months): Teacher, who had had no information from previous nursery school, was guided only by child's present behavior in kindergarten. Complete absence of speech gave teacher and other children impression that Kate was unable to talk.

Outstanding characteristics of child: passive reactions and lack of emotional response; inability or unwillingness to follow class project or instructions; lack of reciprocal relationship with any child. When group instructions are given, she looks about, but there is no indication that she has heard or understood. When her table is called for structured play, she does not respond and even appears unaware of other children having left. When finally she is called individually, she will look up and approach teacher hesitantly. With encouragement she may join group physically. Her answers to teacher's questions are given by nodding her head, or silence if question is not so phrased as to make this possible.

She has had no conversation with any child. Her "play" in class doll corner (which she seems to favor) consists in sitting at table and being served by others. She is passive. At times when a partner is necessary, she stands at the end of line until someone takes her hand, and she becomes a "partner." When she finally brought something for "show and tell," she raised her hand and pushed object toward the teacher, but would not describe it (as is usual procedure). Answered teacher's questions with nods.

Marked absence of emotional response to failure (can't even tell if she is aware of not having done task properly or completed it), and there is no sign of pleasure with accomplishment. When things go wrong in an activity she is involved in, she just leaves the scene. If another child takes something from her, she just lets it go. There is no crying, no anger, and no affection.

On her birthday she tore the birthday crown off her head. When teacher questioned her, she looked embarrassed, backed away, lowered head, held hand near face. (Other children have commented about her absence of speech, and eye defect.)

Very recently there have been some changes in behavior: 1] She has come to the teacher with complaints about children who are not letting her "play." 2] She held hands, while walking with another child who had approached her. 3] She played with trains sitting next to another child. 4] On day of school observation, there were indications of increased interaction with other children. Also, there were indications that she was watching the activities of other children and listening to their interaction with teacher—"Kate watches teacher"; "She turns to listen to conversation between teacher and her assistant"; "listens to teacher talking to children at table behind her"; "glances at girl"; "watches boy pass her"; etc.

Fears

INTERVIEW I (eleven weeks): Startles and cries at loud noises. Blinks with bright light, doesn't cry.

INTERVIEW II (five months): Startles with loud noise. No reaction to bright light.

INTERVIEW III (eight months): No cry or startle with loud noise. Fusses with bright light. Brief cry with injections.

INTERVIEW IV (eleven months): Cried once at loud noise recently. At other times, "looks," can tell she is not so happy.

INTERVIEW V (thirteen and one-half months): Awakening during night. When much fussing, parents go to her and she goes right back to sleep.

INTERVIEW VI (eighteen months): Doesn't let mother "out of her sight." Screams when mother leaves, cries until she comes back.

INTERVIEW VII (twenty-four months): Rarely awakens at night, but did a few nights ago and started to cry. Mother thinks crying due to seeing a new strange picture on wall.
    She is "frightened" of and cries with noise of wind, rain on window. Stops when held or talked to. Startles with sudden noises. When there is heavy traffic, mother has to take her inside a store. She cries and clings if left outside alone. (In clinical study when child was sixty-one months of age, parents dated onset of car phobia as eighteen months on specific occasion when very loud truck suddenly approached and Kate was startled and frightened—cried and bolted.)

INTERVIEW VIII (thirty-two months): Not generally awakened by sound. Cries briefly when hurt, quiets when kissed. Still cries with sound of motor of any car, especially truck. However, will ride in car and shows no reluctance.

INTERVIEW IX (thirty-nine months): For a brief period (week or two at thirty-one and one-half and thirty-nine months) awakened and cried at night, pointing to reflection on wall made by light from lamppost. Mother pulled down shade and crying at night stopped.

Six months ago began to exhibit fear of hair washing (twin had exhibited fear first—mother not sure what started it). She fussed and cried, but mother went ahead anyway. Fear is diminishing.

Fear reaction to first use of glider in playground. Now likes it— took two or three times to overcome.

Frightened by loud, sudden noises. Has become accustomed to, and no longer reacts to ring of oven timer, which used to frighten her. Frightened by thunder, which also awakens her—runs to mother crying, is easily soothed. When large trucks stop suddenly in street, runs to mother and cries if not picked up. Showed fear of friendly dog in neighborhood (huddled near mother)—not afraid of dogs she knows.

In discussion of difficulties in turning and opening objects, putting on socks, etc., mother comments that she can't turn knob of phonograph. "Mother feels this latter might be fear."

Asks for tricycle more often. If large truck is near, gets off tricycle and runs crying to mother. Quiets with explanation, but will not go back. When walking outside, will not walk near curb.

Will only go on one ride in amusement park. Formerly went on several with twin, but seemed frightened during summer (thirty-two to thirty-three months) and now refuses all but one, horses that move up and down.

Mother thinks Kate is afraid of her, and tries to please her. Persists in trying to put on socks, crying as she attempts it, and does not call for help because mother insisted she do it on her own.

May cry if hurt—comes to mother to be kissed and returns to activity if not severe. Accepted soaking routine for sore toe.

INTERVIEW X (forty-six months): Was frightened by rushing of water in strange bathroom and did not want to sit on toilet.

Fears noise from cars, trucks. No fear of dark or shadows or light. Both twins show fear of storms, which awaken them at night, crying, but mother able to calm them, talk to them, and they return to sleep.

When hurt, cries, comes to mother for medicines, bandages, and cuddling.

TEACHER INTERVIEW (fifty-two months): School bus driver reports he must make complete stop and turn off motor when picking her up at her home or she will cry and refuse to get into bus. Child "will not explain" why she feels this way. Teachers feel that her fear reaction to bus persists more to conform to what is expected of her, than because it is an expression of real fear. They cite as example grandmother calling instructions from porch to driver to turn motor off because Kate is frightened. Further, teacher reports that Kate has joined other children in getting into her car, without requesting that motor be turned off. However, on departing from school she used to cry and complain and hang back from entering bus for return home. Cried at sight of cars and buses while sitting on hill with teacher and children. When teacher told her to stop nonsense or explain what it was about, she stopped immediately and smiled.

Seemed somewhat fearful of outdoor equipment that appeared to be new to her. Mother took children to playground infrequently, as they might get hurt. Still has not tried the big slide after six months in school. She did express fear about going up a hill, slides, and equipment. No indication of fear of people.

INTERVIEW XI (fifty-three months): Appears less fearful of cars. Sometimes it gets worse, then gets better again. Grandmother reports she was about to cross street to join boy on other side when a car passed. She waved to it, but then didn't cross.

Neighbor reports she is afraid of her (neighbor's) dog.

Will not stay outside without sister.

May or may not cry if hurt, and may be satisfied with a kiss.

INTERVIEW XII (fifty-nine months): Walks to school with housekeeper and twin. Housekeeper tries to play a game while crossing street. Kate tries to get across quickly—pulls housekeeper to go faster. Mother thinks fear of crossing street may have been aggravated by fact that mother spanked her for not putting on socks correctly (a long standing area of conflict between them). Kate cried, but now puts on socks. Now crosses street to seek out children she knows from school.

Sensitivity about her eye

INTERVIEW X (forty-six months): First time eye is mentioned in histories. Has had recurring sties on her eye, and has some neurological problem with it—mother hasn't had it checked (seems to have neglected it).

In discussion of outdoor play: "Kate holds hand over eye."

TEACHER INTERVIEW (fifty-two months): Eyedrops administered in school. Child is cooperative, matter of fact about it; comes to director, whenever indicated, to get it done.

INTERVIEW XI (fifty-three months): At doctor's office little boy asked Kate, "What is the matter with your eye?" She answered, "Nothing. Are you a little boy?" Received no answer and did not pursue.

Asks for medication for eye, but does not talk about it otherwise. At forty-eight months she complained of pain (fluid accumulates in back of eye causing eye to bulge). Drops reduce pressure. Mother says medication will need to be continued perhaps several years.

She goes willingly to physician, but mother has to hold her in chair during examination. Talks more and is more active than formerly.

INTERVIEW XII (fifty-nine months): A child in her class asked what is the matter with Kate's eye. She did not answer. Mother doesn't know details of incident.

Recently Kate says, "I look pretty," "I am pretty." Older sister always says Kate is very pretty—looks in mirror when wearing dress.

"The whole family feels she has an affliction." Housekeeper and father speak of her in lowered voices.

Medication apparently does not completely control pressure—difference of opinion on surgery. She accepts medication (eyedrops) and going to physician. Does not move toward examination chair, but sits quietly when mother holds her. There has been no attempt to put her in chair without mother.

KINDERGARTEN TEACHER INTERVIEW (sixty months): Refused to wear birthday crown—tore it off her head. When questioned by teacher, looked embarrassed, backed away, lowered head, hand near face. Usually some "little busybody" makes a comment about her—remarks directed to fact that she does not talk, and what's the matter with her eye.

Subsequent course

KINDERGARTEN TEACHER INTERVIEW (sixty-four months): Improvement in relations with teacher—none with children. Little response to reading readiness, does not follow or respond to group instructions.

Parents have not responded to teacher's request for conference. Mother reports school does not want to promote Kate to first grade. Parents are working with her on reading readiness—withholding dessert if she does not buckle down and learn.

INTERVIEW XIII (seventy-two months): (Kate apparently is in first grade —details not given.) Explosive crying when she can't have her way.

Mother tries to get her to speed up dressing—she will sit there and seems to get lost. Mother spanks, yells, helps. Now improved—seems more able, gets ready. Has worked on tying a bow; stayed with it, but cried—unable to learn. What she learns she retains—but takes her longer to learn. Hard to manipulate things with her fingers. Won't practice on own. Mother helps with clothes that are tight.

Frightened when asked to do something out of ordinary. Has run across street by self—if she wants something enough, will disregard her fears.

Eyes: Has asked why she goes to eye doctor and why she needs drops. Mother tells her it is to keep her well.

Older sister is mother substitute.

FIRST-GRADE TEACHER INTERVIEW (seventy-nine months): Has shown greater growth and progress in first grade than any child teacher has ever known. At first, uncomprehending, remote from school situation, unresponsive, totally incapable, made no attempt to involve self with other children. Now a different child. Has moved from bottom of class to middle group in almost all subjects. Strongly motivated, works diligently and conscientiously, great pride in accomplishment, has made friends and been accepted by group, is not teased. Strongly motivated by appeals to self-esteem and pride in accomplishment. Slow learner, but diligence and persistence will go a long way.

Teacher feels child was made to feel inadequate, especially in relation to twin, by mother's negative attitude, constant complaints as to extra care she required, heavy-handed and unloving way. Kate expected everything to be done for her at first, including things she was able to manage. In spite of remarkable change in attitude and ability, she regressed dramatically on the one occasion sister's class joined her own for a day—became passive, did no work, constantly looking at twin.

Now mother's attitude has changed—overtly proud of child's accomplishments. Kate has become active volunteer, raises hand frequently, smiles when called on. Loves homework—responsible in getting it done. Has begun to participate in group games—clumsy and inept, but tries. Now accepted by group—but not particularly sought out.

INTERVIEW XIV (eighty-three months): Vision is 20/50 in one eye and 20/200 in other. May need glasses in next year. Reading second-grade level, in top group in class (mother later changed her statement—said child was in lowest group).

Surprises mother and gets dressed before twin. Now able to tie laces, do buttons. Can't be rushed—gets rattled and cries, tries to continue what she is doing, but mother feels sorry and does it for her.

SECOND-GRADE TEACHER INTERVIEW (eighty-nine months): Most marked change has been in communicativeness. Is average in subjects—needs more help in arithmetic. She plugs, pushes. Teacher feels she is working up to ability. Participates in everything. Seems accepted by other children.

Has been having speech therapy this year—"th" sound.

FOLLOW-UP INTERVIEW WITH MOTHER (eighty-nine months): Fear of cars and exploding motors continues to be present—will "bolt" across street even if car is distance away, seems not to know what to do. If someone is walking with her, she will drag person by arm. In unfamiliar shopping center parents have had to hold her—might run in path of car; mother has had to warn teacher about this before school trips.

More outgoing, speaks more, but takes time to warm up. Same thing every year at beginning of school.

Eye: Mother claims that in accordance with psychiatrist's advice at the clinical evaluation, they gave Kate a name for her condition, "sightitis." Interpretation of need for drops given to child is "to keep eye well."

INTERVIEW XV (ninety-five months): Mother feels Kate isn't interested enough in school work, in reading needs better work habits.

Now dresses herself—still very slow, needs help with back buttons and tying. When ready (capable) to do something, she can be trusted to do it properly.

Is not invited by friends, not part of neighborhood group. Mother concerned because child is heavy.

Fear of insects—if she sees them or thinks she sees them, she screams.

Mother seems to have less contact with twins—older sister takes over. Parents in weekly therapy group recommended by psychologist of older son.

TELEPHONE CALL FROM MOTHER TO INTERVIEWER (ninety-eight months): Teacher reports Kate seems to be day dreaming—yet when called on teacher is surprised that she "knows as much as she seems to." Teacher feels she needs pressuring. Mother has been helping her. Current report card was one of the top report cards (apparently of class). Mother will check on child's progress.

INTERVIEW XVI (one hundred and nine months): Still seems afraid of cars—"bolts" across the street. No other fears mentioned. Shorter warm-up required at school this year. Responds to overtures from children—doesn't initiate. Exchanges visits with one child.

About six months below "potential," but at grade level. In middle group in reading and spelling. Always difficulty with math—parents help, but mother feels she doesn't pay attention.

Doesn't show feelings. Likes and dislikes mild. May tell mother she expects too much—"I'm not old enough."

New medication for eyes—no concern—no glasses. Things going smoothly this year.

ROY—CASE 17

SUMMARY

AGE AT REFERRAL: Seventy-six months.

PRESENTING COMPLAINTS:
1] Refuses to carry out parental requests.
2] Hesitates to try new things; gives up easily.

ONSET OF PROBLEM: Forty-eight months.

CLINICAL INTERVIEW: The child entered the room immediately and began playing with the toys. He initiated an active conversation with the examiner; his spontaneous talk consisted of gentle derogatory comments about the equipment, refusals to comply with a request, and orders to the examiner to do something. He occasionally used improper language ("shit"), tentatively at first and then, when the examiner made no comment, without hesitation. Despite these negative verbalizations, his mood was predominantly positive.

He constantly involved the examiner in play and in verbal interchange, demanding assistance (whether needed or not) either politely or in terms of an order. When the examiner did not comply or when she gave him instructions as to how he could do a task himself, he usually did so, pausing slightly at times to be sure she would not finally comply. When he flatly refused to do a drawing, he continued to mention the fact and to plan how he might comply with the examiner's request at his own chosen time and place. (He spontaneously promised to send her a drawing by mail.) Although he initially did not participate in cleaning up at the end of the session, he finally joined in, even though no persistent request for his aid was made.

The child's selection and use of toys was appropriate, and his verbalizations, facial expressions, and tonal variations were relevant. His language reflected the high cultural level of his family, but was not outstanding. His motility was average.

DIAGNOSIS: Reactive Behavior Disorder, mild.

TEMPERAMENT: This child's outstanding temperamental characteristic is his high degree of distractibility. His basic pattern also includes low persistence, mild intensity, low activity level, and predominantly positive mood. In infancy he tended to have initial withdrawal reactions to the introduction of new things, such as new foods. His reactions to new situations, such as a change in bed or sleeping at a different house, were less negative, and his initial responses to people were positive. Because he was very adaptable and could easily be distracted, his negative reactions were replaced by positive acceptance once he had had some exposure to the new. However, by the time of the psychiatric examination, his initial negative reactions were more pronounced, more persistent, and less adaptable to change.

PARENTAL FUNCTIONING: The mother is rigid and compulsive. She tends always to urge the child, to scold him, and to find fault with his behavior. By her own description, she is prone to react intensely, to fuss, and to scream. She has always pressured the child in an attempt to get him to meet her own standards, which were not always realistic. She sang to him and diverted him during infancy to make him eat more, even when he actually was eating well; she discouraged his early attempts to do things for himself (it made a mess and took extra time), yet later, when he grew older, she fussed because he continued to be dependent on her servicing him.

The father who is more even-tempered, had a positive involvement with the child in his early years. Later he reacted to the deteriorating family interaction by withdrawing and became ineffectual in routine handling of his son. When the mother tries to involve him (usually on her own terms), active quarreling results. The parental friction is observed by the children who sense the mother's deep hostility and have expressed their feelings that the mother does not like them or their father.

DYNAMIC FORMULATION: The mother made use of the child's high distractibility and nonpersistence in infancy to manipulate his behavior according to her demands. At that time, her handling and his temperamental qualities were consonant with each other. However, as he grew older and she required that he carry through to completion all tasks, a dissonant demand on a distractible child, his temperamental traits were no longer an asset in their relationship, and a negative interaction developed. This was exacerbated by the mother's pressuring and screaming insistence that Roy meet all her expectations, handling that served to reinforce the child's negative reactions. Moreover, as a result of his mother's early deterrence of his initial steps toward independence, plus his own tendency not to work at anything until he could be sure of success, Roy has gradually come to refrain from attempting anything new. The mother's intolerance of her son's distractibility combined with his negative reactions to her demands has maintained the destructive interaction between them.

RECOMMENDATIONS: The parents were told to modify their handling so that the child's noncompliance with routines would be dealt with in a cause-and-effect manner, with a minimum of nagging and exploding. Thus, the child is to be shown what will happen if he doesn't comply with parental demands—if he dawdles, he will be late for school—and the specific situation is not to be clouded by parental nagging, which so far has enabled him to escape the objective effects of his behavior: He has never been late for school as his mother keeps at him every morning to get ready.

The parents should praise the child for his attempts in endeavors he is trying to master instead of pushing and reacting negatively to his temporary lack of success. They should deal with his distractibility patiently and without pressure. Demands should be limited to only important issues, and the mother should disengage herself from the child's minor routine activities.

SUBSEQUENT COURSE: Between 76 and 107 months, the child's symptoms became increasingly severe. There was a continuous battle over all home routines, and the child began to tune out his mother and to resort to protective lying. In school, he had difficulty understanding his work and failed to complete assignments. In addition, he developed a tic. The diagnosis was changed to neurotic behavior disorder because of the marked extension of his problem behavior, and weekly guidance sessions with the mother were recommended. These were held for six months, but at 120 months, when the child was seen again, his symptoms persisted. During this second clinical interview, the child showed some awareness of the negative interaction between himself and his mother, although he did not acknowledge this openly. He tended to place all problems in the past or in a minor key.

Because the destructive parent-child interaction remained unchanged and the mother was unable to follow guidance directions, the child's problems have become increasingly severe; his inattention to his mother has been extended to his teachers, and the deteriorating interparental relationship has had a further negative effect on his development. At last contact, the parents were advised to declare a moratorium and handle the child permissively.

Selective Extraction

What he will try and under what circumstances

INTERVIEW I (four and one-half months): First week he had difficulty getting milk from nipples with small holes; his reaction was to fall asleep.

Grimaced first two to three times with each new food, but took it well—then no grimacing. When getting full, starts to wiggle—pushes food out of his mouth—can be diverted by singing—stops wiggling and finishes food. Occasionally he is not diverted—tightens lips and refuses more food. Takes three-fourths of a bottle before solids; if bottle taken away before this, he cries violently. If solids given first, he starts to wiggle and, after a few spoons, starts to cry.

Sleeping through night accomplished by waking him at 11 P.M. for feeding.

If playing on back and put on stomach to sleep, he will prop himself up a few minutes, then whimper until returned to back. In evening he is not returned to his back—stops whimpering after a few minutes and goes to sleep.

Smiles at pictures on wall; smiles and talks to mother; seems to recognize father by smiling; smiles if his head is rubbed. Mother afraid she picks him up and talks to him too much. However, he never cries when put down.

Loved bath from first time he was given one. Kicks, laughs, gurgles, never cries. Doesn't cry when taken out.

INTERVIEW II (six months): Whimpering when put in crib on stomach stopped in last three weeks when he became active thumb-sucker. May awaken at 6:30 A.M., put thumb in mouth, and then sleep until 8:30. Mother put him down to get something, he started to cry—put thumb in mouth and stopped crying immediately.

Stayed five to six weeks with aunt while parents on vacation. Four children and dog in the house, television going constantly. Adjusted very well—startle reaction to noise is much diminished since then. On visit to strange house, he slept in car bed—adjusted same as if he were home.

First two to three days in playpen would whimper if mother left room—no longer whimpers—plays actively in it a half hour. Doesn't cry if mother leaves him alone in crib. Sometimes "shrieks," apparently for joy, in playpen when he is alone.

Several times father has gone to child's room at 6:30–7 A.M. and found him awake—talked to him. Baby smiles—doesn't fuss if father walks out, then fifteen minutes later he is asleep.

Meat and egg added to diet—didn't grimace as he had with previous new solids. Four refusals of orange juice in past month—grimaces, wriggles, turns head, pushes nipple out, but doesn't cry.

INTERVIEW III (ten months): Some days rejects meat—turns head away, makes face but doesn't cry. Takes orange juice every day, but very little, pushes it away. Cup tried at five months—didn't drink from it; tried again at seven months—played with it, made bubbles, drank very little; tried again at ten months—still played with it, but drank more. Junior foods added at eight months. He took all well from the start. No crying on awakening. Feedings have sometimes been delayed fifteen to thirty minutes—no fussing. Feeding table introduced at six and one-half months. Ate well in it from beginning.

Kicks and laughs in bath, no reaction to coming out. No reaction to being wet; no reaction to first tooth a month ago.

Lack of perseverance—doesn't try to sit up by himself—no struggle with turning over (did it at seven months). Tries once or twice to get something out of reach, then gives up without fussing.

No reaction to different cribs or different surroundings, e.g., seashore in summer, week's visit to grandmother, new apartment.

Bounces and laughs a lot in teeter chair; he "shrieks." Will stay in playpen alone thirty minutes—longer if mother is in room.

INTERVIEW IV (twelve months): Father plays with him very actively after supper—he gets "all wound up," but still goes to sleep quickly.

Started bathing in sink two months ago. Looked around, touched sink in various spots, didn't cry. Quickly began to play in sink as he had in bathtub. Put on toilet seat two weeks ago. (Has bowel movements regularly after breakfast and lunch.) Mother made a game of it. Evacuates there regularly.

Mother can leave without his crying. Occasionally a moment's mild fussing.

Cold—stuffy nose—not cranky in daytime. Up once a night for a week—right back to sleep for rest of night after drops were put in his nose.

Very little fussing with three new teeth. First haircut—liked it, didn't cry.

Doesn't sit up himself—if put in sitting position, will stay until he quietly falls over. Doesn't try to stand except in teeter chair.

Sometimes eats well, sometimes little. Towards end of each meal has to be distracted in order to get him to finish. No foods he clearly and consistently refuses. No attempt to feed himself. Doesn't usually grab at spoon; if he does, is easily distracted, especially by singing.

"He rarely cries; if he starts we distract him and he stops."

Turns and twists with diapering—distracted by singing.

INTERVIEW V (fifteen months): Sitting and standing came without much effort or struggle. "He's not a keeper-afterer." Tried to crawl two steps to living room once, didn't succeed, didn't try again.

Wakes at 6 A.M.—talks to himself about thirty minutes, then starts to call. Often goes back to sleep if he is not answered. Sometimes awakens at night; goes back to sleep quickly with patting. Moved to parents' room two and a half months ago. No change in sleeping pattern. Back to own room tonight—much company, moving of furniture. Cried only few minutes before going to sleep.

Doesn't fuss if mother leaves—waves bye-bye. Several visits to strange homes—adjusts immediately.

Eats but must be distracted for past two months. Must give him toys or sing to him. If not distracted, doesn't eat—plays, stands up. With distraction eats a great deal. When really satiated, just stops eating—distraction doesn't work. Juice from cup. Mother has to hold it. Now takes orange juice. He holds bottle for one-half bottle then plays with it. Mother thinks he would rather she hold it, but she insists he do it. Won't even taste two new foods introduced—just throws them off tray—doesn't fuss.

No objection to toilet seat, but nothing happens now. Formerly had two regular bowel movements a day—sat on toilet then and had them there.

"Tried to arrange house so I have minimum of 'no's'—He pays no attention to them anyway." When slapped, he laughs. "Thinks it's a game. Cried for a moment with a few slappings."

GESELL TEST (sixteen and one-half months): Not disturbed by strange surroundings—no warm-up period needed. Positive responses definitely dominate—no fussing when told not to touch drawers. Only frowned when he did not like something or he was not understood. Only time he cried was when mother put his sweater on. Cry was of mild intensity and over in a minute. Absence of negative responses. "He was active in a very quiet sort of way."

INTERVIEW VI (twenty-one months): Almost every night he awakens between 9 and 12 o'clock. Cries moderately, as if he's scared. Calls, "Mommy, come." Picked up and held about five minutes. "He cuddles up," then goes right back to sleep. Sometimes wakes up once or twice more before midnight—same routine. Rarely falls asleep after a few minutes of crying. Sleeps through night.

During hot spell in summer ate very little—took bottle well. Stopped eating eggs altogether. Closed mouth, spit food out, threw food on floor, refused to try anything new. Eating better now. Drinking all liquids from cup regularly, except morning bottle. Both he and mother hold cup. He will try to hold it alone, but he spills a lot, so mother takes over. Even when eating well, mother usually distracts him to get him to eat more.

Dressing: cooperates—often wiggles, doesn't cry. No objection to face and ear washing. Nails: cried—had to be held. Last two times mother asked him first—he cooperated.

Walked at eighteen months. Came very quickly. "He doesn't work at things."

Wakes up 7–7:30 A.M.—doesn't call—sometimes falls asleep again. At 8–8:30 calls, "Mommy, come." Father gives him bottle, which he holds by himself in crib. Throws it out when he's finished.

Taken to restaurant first time. Sat an hour, said "hello" to waiter, ate moderately, behaved well.

Learns prohibitions quickly and obeys quite well. Sometimes "teases."

"Likes people. Very friendly; talks to everybody in park, even strangers trying to read." Several months ago he went through a period of shyness with strangers—put his head in mother's lap and just looked at them. Responded in five minutes to overtures. Initial shyness now very brief or absent. Responds to smile at once. Doesn't really play with other children; will play with older children. If toy pulled away, he calls mother, whines, or does nothing.

Mother practices new words with him—he responds eagerly, learns new words quickly. Doesn't practice new words much by himself.

HOME OBSERVATION (twenty-four months): When observer first arrived he hid, but quickly turned this into a friendly game of peek-a-boo.

Mother gave him a piece of candy, prompted him to say "thanks." Later he uncovered candy dish and helped himself to another piece. Went back for a second, and after that, a third, at which point mother told him "no," and he did not take a third piece.

Mother plied him with questions about music—"Who wrote Carmen?" "Who wrote Faust?" He answered mechanically. Sometimes he answered, "no, no," but later answered correctly when mother insistently asked again.

He was distracted by any sounds outside—fire siren, dog barking, cat mewing, auto horn. He identified sounds correctly, then usually went back to what he was doing. At one point he put his rocker upside down, but immediately turned it rightside up again when mother told him to.

INTERVIEW VII (twenty-six months): "He's changed now—getting very balky; a fight to get him dressed at times; discipline is a problem. I can usually divert him, except in getting him dressed."

To bed at 7 P.M.—not as easily as before; may start to cry unless a game is played with him. If he cries, mother goes out of room, shuts door, and he stops in one to two minutes. Still awakens in evening—cries or calls, mostly for "daddy"—picked up, held few minutes, back to sleep. Sometimes accepts mother, sometimes insists on father. Up at 8 A.M., calls for "daddy," who gives him bottle. If his call is ignored, he may go back to sleep until 9 A.M.

Eating "terrible"—skips many meals, eats much less, irregular intake, inconsistent likes and dislikes. Won't try anything new unless he sees his parent eating it. Eats a good deal between meals: mother gives him crackers, fruit, raisins. He rejects food by saying "no" and shoving plate away. Finger feeds himself—doesn't use utensils—"messy," so mother feeds him.

Refuses medicine by closing mouth—cries if forced—stops crying as soon as medicine is swallowed.

Bath: "Sometimes I have to force him in, then force him out." Cry each time is brief; he is easily diverted, can easily be made to laugh loudly. Very resistant to diapering—squirms, tries to stand up, cries. Mother gets angry. His crying subsides when she spanks him. "That's the only spanking that means anything, the others don't." Doesn't try to dress or undress himself—a little resistant but not as much as with diapering. Says "no" to nail cutting, starts to cry. Sometimes allows it, sometimes has to be forced. Doesn't fuss much with hair brushing or hand washing. Cries when hair is washed; stops when mother finishes. No objection to haircut, except when trimmed behind ears—distracted with lollipop. Won't sit on potty—fusses.

Will play by himself fifteen minutes if mother in room; five to six minutes if she is not there. Often asks parents to play with him. Likes records playing continuously—tried to put on records once, broke them—didn't object to their being put out of reach. Asks for help quickly if he drops something. Takes to new toy only if it's a truck or car—if toy too difficult, quits quickly, tenses, clenches fist, and cries.

Doesn't climb out of crib. Very cautious—holds on to mother or railing in going up or down even two steps.

Always responded easily to discipline until two weeks ago. Still obeys various prohibitions easily—is more insistent about some things he wants, stamps foot, and says "no" to substitute. Will throw a few things; has hit mother once. "It's really mild, compared to other children."

Cries throughout physical exam and injection. Stops as soon as finished. Hides behind chair when he sees physician.

Mother goes out two mornings a week; he never cries. Can be left with new baby-sitter at night. "Not a prolonged crier for anything. Cries for the moment." Easily diverted—can easily be made to laugh loudly.

INTERVIEW VIII (thirty-three months): Father plays with him and reads to him at bedtime. Child fusses some if this routine is omitted. At home, and more frequently in country, woke up several times during night crying or calling. Asked to be put "one minute on couch." This was done, then he went back to sleep easily. Second night home, asked to sleep on studio bed in his room—has slept there ever since and now awakens at night very rarely. Fell out of bed two to three times first week—cried, but stopped immediately on being comforted and went right back to sleep.

Eating is "terrible"—eats practically nothing—decent meal perhaps twice a week, yet he nibbles a lot between meals—mother lets him have crackers, juices. Eats no better with parents or in restaurant. Preferences inconsistent, rarely tries new food. Rejects food by saying "no"—may throw the food. If eating, accepts help and now asks for it. Doesn't use utensils much, mostly fingers. Mother tries to increase his intake by distracting him. Doesn't force him—"Can't anyway, he wouldn't take it, he'd turn his head and throw the food."

Bath: likes it—sometimes objects to coming out. "Doesn't cry much, only if I force him." Can be persuaded to come out by making game of pulling plug. Cries and struggles with hair washing. Balky about dressing and undressing, and worst with diapering. Tries to run away or get off bathinette. Mother often gets him to quiet down with a mild spank. Less resistance with father. Nails: pulls hand away, says "no"— if forced, he cries. Stops crying as soon as procedure is finished. Hair brushing: pulls head away, fusses. Hand washing: cooperates. Doesn't try to do it himself.

Not a climber, cautious, doesn't go on sliding pond. Mother says she doesn't go near it in park, "Makes me nervous."

Training: mother tried irregularly—"I've done literally nothing." (Note: This contradicts mother's previous statements.) Refuses to sit on seat. If mother makes fuss, he sometimes will stand on step stool to urinate successfully. Many other times he resists. Never asks. Bowel movements irregular—no fussing with wet or soiled diaper except in morning when he asks to be changed.

Negative reaction to pediatrician—shrieks from minute he sees him until he leaves. Resists examination, cries throughout.

Discipline: "Lately it's like talking to the wall." Fairly good until past two weeks. (Note: Mother made same comment in last interview.) Teases a lot—mother is driven to yell or spank to get results. Father more patient—takes a lot of time, "cajoles"—finally successful. "You can reason with him; if you say 'one more time,' he'll agree. Lives up to promise." In past few weeks not as good about not touching prohibited objects. When frustrated, screams and throws whatever is in his hand— he is distractible, so his reaction subsides quickly.

INTERVIEW IX (forty months): "He's contrary, perverse, and negative. But he's cute anyway. The biggest chatterbox in the whole park. He wants his way."

To bed at 8–8:30 P.M. Prolonged routine—"Everything is a struggle." If read to, he keeps asking for more. "He asks in a very nice way, it's hard to say no." If refused, he fusses and persists. Gets his way more easily with father who says, "I don't feel like upsetting him before bed." Father then lies down with Roy for few minutes, then goes out. Some nights Roy goes to sleep quickly, other nights he stays awake till 10 P.M.—keeps calling or playing in room; doesn't come out of room. Mother scolds him for calling, but he pays no attention. Had been calling one to two times a night, went back to sleep with patting. No more calling since night-light put in his room three months ago. Wakes up 8–9 A.M.: plays by himself until he hears someone, then comes out of his room.

Eating "terrible." Limited diet. Drinks a lot of milk—two bottles plus several cups. Nibbles a lot between meals. Mother tried to refuse but gave in—"I couldn't stand the nagging and he has to eat something." Won't try anything new unless he sees another child eating it, but won't continue taking it. Rejects food by pushing it away, announcing, "Don't want anymore." Uses some utensils—"messy"; mother feeds him. Mother gave up distracting him, it took too much time and sometimes actually distracted him from eating, though sometimes it did help a little. Persuasion and bribery have been used—no success. "He's consistently negative about everything."

Bath: "When we finally get him in, he loves it." Many times he says "no," and there is a big fight. He screams while he's being undressed and put in; then he stops, plays in tub. Dressing was a battle each time. Past weeks less resistant. Nails: may cry or fight. Mother bribes him with candy and he becomes more cooperative. Haircuts: goes with father— very cooperative.

Not careful of toys—breaks them, is not upset. Only takes to new toys if they have wheels. Will play with toy car for thirty minutes; listens to records an hour or more, sitting quietly. With difficult toy, gives up very quickly or calls for help. "No perseverance at all."

No play with children his own age—ignores them if they visit. If toy is grabbed, doesn't fight. Asks for it back or comes to mother to get it. They tell him to ask child. He doesn't, continues to nag parent to get it for him, parents refuse.

Started nursery school. Walked there by mother, father, or maid. Routine interrupted first week because of illness. When he recovered, he did not mind returning, but had not fussed about staying home when ill.

Training pants now—doesn't go himself. Mother reminds him. Sometimes he refuses and wets himself. Had bowel movement on toilet only twice. Has two bowel movements a day—irregular; has bowel movements in pants. Mother not successful in bribing him with new truck. Will announce he has had a bowel movement only in past few days. Before he announces it, may go into his room and shut the door. Keeps repeating "I don't do it anymore, I'll tell you when I have to go." Mother is annoyed. There have been many battles.

New baby brother (born three months ago). First few days when baby was being fed he asked for a bottle himself. Now, when mother is busy with baby, he may dash around slamming doors. In general, parents say he shows very positive response to baby, pats and kisses him often. No negative reaction. Seems very interested in baby.

Same negative reaction to pediatrician as previous interview.

Discipline: Mother says he "doesn't pay any attention to either of us." Father says, "not so bad." Mother says he used to be very good— now she has to yell to get any obedience. (Note: Mother made similar statement in previous interview.) Father says, if child says no and you wait awhile and ask again, he will do it. If something is taken from him he will scream and throw things for two to five minutes. Not so easily distracted as before, but his reaction subsides quickly. Doesn't climb— no interest in trying tricycle, skating, or riding fire engine.

INTERVIEW X (forty-seven months): Sleep routine: Two books are read to him and then parent lies down with him for five to twenty minutes. If he had no nap, he goes right to sleep; otherwise, plays, comes out, asks questions, no real fuss. Father does doutine if he is at home. Night awakening rare since he was given night-light. Cries; goes back to sleep with patting. Asks for "blanket" (diaper), which he chews. Back to sleep as readily for either parent now.

Plays records on awakening. Complies with parents' request not to come into their room until they are awake.

Mother still dresses and undresses him. He just sits and lets her do it. If asked to dress himself, he dawdles, is uncooperative. "Hopeless."

He can do certain things, but doesn't, despite mother's pressuring. Mother thinks he purposely puts two feet in pants leg, then becomes frustrated and howls—"He knows how he can get a rise out of me." When mother has time on weekends, she tries to get him to dress himself. He prefers father to do it—insists on father on weekends. Does a little more himself than he used to.

Bath: does not resist it since nursery school—it's a play situation. Does not wash himself, even when asked—permits and expects mother to wash him. Screams with hairwashing.

Illness: "Worst patient." Now takes one kind of medicine since grandmother introduced it. Formerly would not take medicine and mother could not give it to him alone. Mother and father held him down, held his nose and poured it down when necessary. Fusses, whimpers with temperature taking. Father does it better. When ill at grandmother's home when baby was born, he was a much better patient— quiet, apathetic.

Strong negative reaction to foods he dislikes—there are many. Mother does not offer them. Eating habits unsatisfactory—"Terrible." Mother thinks he is a feeding problem.

Toilet trained by three and a half years. Training started when baby was born. Would not go on any seats or potty chair. Very irregular. Mother used bribery. One day he asked to go to toilet, and soon began to go on his own. Does not demand servicing. Closes door. Diapers were removed at night at about forty-four months—since then he has stayed dry and had only one accident at night. When it happened, he became upset, uncomfortable, asked to be changed.

He is reluctant to tackle a new experience for the first time— hangs back, complains. When he finally does participate, either by being cajoled or when it is brought up a second time, he enjoys it tremendously and participates enthusiastically. With new situations, accepts person or place immediately. A new activity or new food not accepted the first time may be accepted on subsequent presentation, e.g., painting at school.

Pays no attention to most prohibitions, especially keeping trucks out of living-room, but doesn't turn on television before dinner or lock bathroom door. When told to stop activity, he continues very obviously "to show negativism." Sometimes argues about prohibitions, but soon disregards them and continues forbidden activity. "His response to rules doesn't depend on person making them. He can be cajoled into obeying, but will not follow a rule stated directly."

Doesn't ride or climb easily; not able to ride bike; cautious.

I.Q. OBSERVATION (fifty-one months): Complied with examiner's requests, but continually interrupted to ask if he could play with the toys. In play period, resisted putting toys away (examiner had made this a condition for playing with the stove). He finally complied. Made many demands on examiner for fixing or adjusting toys; repeatedly interrupted conversation between mother and examiner. Resisted leaving. Mother pushed him out of playroom, and he began to hit mother, who made no move to stop him.

NURSERY SCHOOL OBSERVATION (fifty-one months): When a block didn't fit easily on structure he had made, he said, "We don't need it." Another child showed him how to fit it on.

Asked teacher for help with fitting cars together several times—also requested help with clay and with removing smock. Refused to put clay material away when teacher requested, but did help with putting away blocks.

Asked boy for truck several times—sulked when refused, but was soon smiling again.

INTERVIEW XI (fifty-three months): "Extremely disobedient, can't get him to do anything. If you tell him to do something, he does something else."

When father is home, Roy whines, asks for books, delays going to sleep. If he had nap (rare), comes out of room on pretenses, though parents tell him not to.

Bottles discontinued two weeks ago. Accepted fact that nipple was stopped up (mother had purposely put an egg into his milk for three days). Gave up chewing rag; hides it when he sees mother. Sucks thumb only on going to sleep. On awakening, stays in his room with the door shut and plays records, after "I really drummed it into him."

Mother has to dress him. He dawdles, won't try, says he can't do certain things. Mother gets impatient and, after pressuring him unsuccessfully, takes over. Mother considers eating a problem—limited variety and intake. Has to be called several times, distractions reduce consumption. Toileting on his own. Bath: goes eagerly. Mother washes him. Grandmother gets him to wash himself. He ignores mother's request. Screams with hair washing. Improved reaction to physician. No longer screams, permits temperature taking, accepts medicine without fuss. Rarely hurts self (very cautious). When gets scratched and he notices it, he comments about it for a long time. Comforted by being held.

Is eager to get to nursery school. Asks for it and is at loose ends on holidays. "Does not want to go enough to dress without (mother's) help." Teacher reports he does not conform. Wrestles with two other children, makes noise, clowns, disrupts class, and is sent out of room. He does not object, as he then engages director, or whoever will listen, in conversation. He does not readily enter activities; will observe and when all other children are involved, he can then be interested. Tends to lead. When he wants to, he orders children, assigns them tasks. School reports he usually must have his way. Does not accommodate to other children as a rule, particularly those he knows.

Very demanding—needs many reminders to obey, delays completing necessary tasks. Mother often must nag and yell to get him to do something. If person takes time and patience, he will do what he has to do eventually. If he can't do something he undertakes, he doesn't try—screams, knocks something over. Stops screaming when he gets help.

Resists new situations, except new people—several exposures needed before he accepts.

NURSERY SCHOOL TEACHER INTERVIEW (fifty-three months): First one and a half weeks, mother had to stay in "Mother's room" at school. Then he became eager to join in, and now, taken by father, he ignores father's departure. Asks for much help—more than necessary—with dressing and undressing. Chatters constantly while being helped. Teacher thinks this is an effort to distract her from knowing she's dressing him.

At beginning, he hung back; had hard time adjusting. Behavior to requests is variable, but he must be spoken to individually. When he doesn't comply, which is frequent, he acts silly—other children laugh.

Resistant to change in routine. Never participates in new activity the first day, seems disturbed by it. He will enter the second day, but only for a short time.

Even though he often is apparently not listening, he will remember stories better than anyone else in class. In singing, may substitute "yah yah" for words, become silly, but keeps perfect rhythm and pitch, never even misses half notes. Teacher frequently has to ask him to leave room because of noise he makes—throws things. Not generally silly during snack time—eats well.

Couldn't fold his mat, though others could. Girls would compete for folding his mat, but at teacher's insistence, he began to do it himself.

Erratic play behavior—wants songs he asks for, but sometimes is silly even with those. In dramatic play, always takes role of the infant directing others as to what to do about the baby. Can't sit and listen to stories. Acts parts—may try to usurp teacher's role.

In learning, doesn't try or persist. After four to five weeks of constant teacher encouragement, learned to ride smallest bike. Seemed anxious—repeated "I can't." Teacher feels he is not dextrous, can't put things together, doesn't hold paintbrush skillfully, never climbs, and refuses help with this. He is very careful.

INTERVIEW XII (sixty months): School: more accepting of rules and working within limits. Says "I can't" when asked to participate in activities in which he is not sure.

At home, won't let friends share toys; in playground may go out without a toy, but ends up playing with everything. Does not use playground equipment in park; usually finds playmates.

Difficult endeavors, block building, or drawing, he will do with an adult, but not on his own until he masters the activity. Doesn't readily participate in new activity.

"Disobedient." Needs to be reminded many times. Delays completing tasks. Screams with something he can't do until he gets help.

In summer (fifty-five to fifty-six months), more eager or willing to go in water if mother or father went. (Kept out good part of time because of sore throat.)

Below average in coordination.

Generally dresses himself now; puts clothes away on own, puts toys away on instruction. In bath, mother washes him. Gets out and dresses on his own.

Father takes him to school and mother calls for him. He waits alone downstairs for bus for after-school activities.

No screaming with new physician. Permitted dental work only after asking many questions and obtaining explanations from dentist. When visiting, or on trips with other people, is reported to be cooperative, obedient, pleasant. Very fond of grandparents. Will stay with them. Mother says, "They expect more than we do."

SCHOOL OBSERVATION (KINDERGARTEN) (sixty-four months): Announced intention of making clay ashtray. Then clay fell on floor, and he started playing with it; ended up without making ashtray.

He tends to ignore demands of other children when involved in his own dramatic play. Not willing to share toys with which he is playing.

Continued to play after teacher announced clean-up. Stopped after second reminder. Didn't clean up, although after additional reminder, put a few toys on shelf, but played with them. Needed individual reminder for "rest," then talked and ignored teacher's reprimand. Responded quickly to milk and cookies.

KINDERGARTEN TEACHER INTERVIEW (sixty-five months): Didn't dress and undress himself at beginning of year. Would come for help without trying to do it himself. Now he does it himself, except for rubbers. Now faster and more capable. Now has to be reminded 50 per cent of the time to dress and undress, as he gets involved in conversation and in teasing others.

Reluctant to start new activity. Says, "I don't want to"—appears inattentive. When he decides to participate, he will follow instructions, which must be given individually, because he starts later than the others. Doesn't stick to activity. Has to be brought back. Recently did good job in making puppet. Worked on it day after day.

Followed routines more readily at beginning of term; is more resistant in past month, as if he is not listening. At clean-up time he looks as if he's cleaning up, but is actually playing. Talks during rest—rarely puts head down. Has to be reminded. Spills milk a lot—not intentionally. Willing to clean up. One of last to be seated.

No longer as cautious in climbing. Follows rules in singing and rhythms, which he loves. Teases about prohibitions. Often follows lead of others in complying or not. With firmness he obeys.

At beginning he said "I can't" to skipping, hopping, jumping. It took two months, with teacher's help and mother's coaching, for him to master. Now he joins and tries, even though he doesn't do well. Loves rhythmic dramatization of animals—initially wouldn't try.

Needs close supervision for completion of projects. Avoids areas where he thinks he will not succeed. Prefers play with cars—is persistent in this—shifts quickly from areas in which he is not competent. Grabs toys. Always has a good reason why he needs them. Will give some up at teacher's insistence.

Coordination below average. Tries to work out new endeavor himself rather than ask for help; if it is too difficult, he leaves it. Now more willing to try new activity with assurance of teacher's help. If he is successful, is very proud. Leader in dramatic play. Uses words and gestures rather than motor activity. Imaginative. In altercation, usually asks for help. Doesn't hit. Demands for teacher's help are moderate.

INTERVIEW XIII (seventy months): Refused to go to "Y" group when mother worked for three weeks and couldn't pick him up at school as usual. Mother said he didn't have to go. Went willingly when mother stopped working.

Twice refused to go to day camp group at summer hotel. Mother made him stay alone in bungalow all morning. He did not seem happy, went in afternoon.

Seems to accommodate to desires of friends.

Does not obey, needs to be reminded. Two rules that have been enforced all along he does not violate; does not play in living-room, and does not use mother's record player. Three-fourths of the time he will not turn on television during forbidden hours; if he does, mother turns it off with no comment from him. When given instructions, does not seem to listen or hear—may say O.K. and continue with activity.

In new situation, is reluctant to start, but can be talked into going; then has wonderful time.

Holds hands over ears for certain sounds, certain music, or when he doesn't want to hear something taught to him.

Tonsillectomy: He was prepared for it. Showed no fears. Asked father to stay with him, but father did not. Did not talk about hospital experience afterward. No longer resists visits to physician; is told in advance whether he will have injection or not. Talks about not liking injection, whimpers a little when needle goes in.

When he goes to school, mother takes him to corner and watches him cross with the lights. Same on return. Once when mother could not meet him, she had someone else watch him cross, and he came home alone.

He was permitted out alone last spring. Once mother could not find him, and he later told her he was up on the roof. May not come right home from "Y" activities, although he has been instructed to do so. Stays downstairs. Is allowed somewhat more freedom in the country; only one road was prohibited. He reported that someone crossed him on that road several times. He does not tell mother when he is not going to come home as planned.

Needs to be amused when he has no planned activity. Destructive of toys. Does not use toys other than cars without outside stimulation.

After he learned to ride two-wheeler with training wheels during summer, mother asked if he would like to join a bike-riding group. He would not go because they didn't have training wheels. Feels he cannot succeed on bike without them.

Not shy. Always gets up in "show and tell," brings something every day. Teacher says she knows everything that goes on at his home. He gets up and talks with great authority, whether he knows about subject or not.

PSYCHOLOGICAL TESTING REPORT (seventy-two months): Functioning on Stanford-Binet was in the bright-average range. However, this was achieved through continuous efforts of the examiner to keep him at the task and to motivate him to work at the peak of his capacity.

FIRST-GRADE TEACHER INTERVIEW (seventy-five months): At first he had no work habits—"felt it was acceptable to do anything he wanted." There has been a big improvement, although he is still immature in relation to the group.

Very good in music—will listen for a long time. He says other children don't know how to listen.

No problem with learning—needs to be told only once—problem is with carrying through. Has to be told several times to pay attention—ultimately completes his work with no protest. Needs lots of encouragement to carry through in all areas. Would play with something he had brought when it was time to work on his own. He works when teacher insists, but needs constant reminders. In reading, which he likes and does well, he listens attentively. He is the best reader in the class. He is easily distracted and has a short attention span.

At first, he did not appear to understand homework and did not do it. Teacher had conference with mother, who has taken responsibility for getting him to do it. Mother has to watch him at home in same manner teacher does at school. There have been some fights about homework. Roy had to be kept in several times after school to finish—

took a long time, but now does homework. While parents were on vacation, Roy's school work seemed to improve—he paid more attention, his homework improved, and he seemed more settled. This continued for about a week after his parents returned.

CLINICAL INTERVIEW WITH PARENTS (seventy-six months): Almost any request by either parent will be refused. Mother repeats until she is nagging, and finally there is a "battle royal"; father repeats demands more patiently, but gets no better results.

Last year his teacher remarked that he was afraid to try to learn certain activities (e.g., skipping) in class. Roy asked his mother to teach him to skip at home. Mother was patient and made a game of it as teacher had suggested. He was very hesitant at first, but did learn. From this experience, parents began to make the point that he should at least try to learn new things, and that there is nothing wrong with failing as long as one has done one's best. He is beginning to use this concept with some endeavors.

At school, Roy is working at a high level, participates at a high level, and his teacher has commended him for this.

He puts off homework, often does it in a sloppy manner. At teacher's request, mother has insisted he make it neat. Father sits with him while he works. Roy now shows less resistance to starting to work and to correcting the paper.

Roy dawdles, loses things such as a jacket, a record, his homework book, and he is indifferent to these issues. Mother complains that Roy cannot or will not follow an instruction. If told to come home straight from school for piano lesson, he will first go to the library and keep teacher waiting; if told to meet her in a specific place, he will never be there, and she has to hunt for him. When he lost the key to his locked school bag, he said to her, "We have a problem; you have to get another key."

Reactions to people

INTERVIEW I (four and one-half months): No mention.

INTERVIEW II (six months): If stimulated by people talking to him or playing with him, he "shrieks," apparently for joy. Never cries at a strange face. If person talks to him, he smiles back. Smiles spontaneously at both parents.

INTERVIEW III (ten months): Looks at strangers five minutes, then smiles. Never cries at strangers. When father arrives, he's "frantic," kicks, jumps, and shrieks.

INTERVIEW IV (twelve months): Smiles after little while in response to strangers. "Shrieks and jumps" with father's arrival.

INTERVIEW V (fifteen months): Initiates advances to many strangers—looks, smiles, waves. Responds quickly to overtures. With other children, gets noisy, smiles at them for a few minutes, then ignores them.

INTERVIEW VI (twenty-one months): Friendly, talks to strangers in park. Short period of shyness initially—now initial shyness very brief or absent. "Gets practically hysterical with joy when he sees someone he knows." Runs around laughing, calling the person's name.

HOME OBSERVATION (twenty-four months): Friendly to observer. Hid, but developed this into a game of peek-a-boo and entered into play with her.

INTERVIEW VII (twenty-six months): Positive response to stranger's overture within few minutes. Can be left with new baby-sitter at night.

INTERVIEW VIII (thirty-three months): Immediate positive response to strangers. Lets almost anyone pick him up. Friendly with new baby-sitter. More positive reactions to men.

Doesn't grab toys; lets toys be grabbed from him. Doesn't cry. Does hold on a bit if a familiar child is pulling toy. Plays better with older children and adults than with children his own age. Older children don't push him away. If child his own age pushes him, he comes running to mother—doesn't cry.

INTERVIEW IX (forty months): Immediate positive response to all strangers, initiates conversations with all strangers he meets. Does not play with children his own age. Ignores them if they visit. If his toy is grabbed, he doesn't fight. Asks for it back or comes to mother for help. If he sees toy he wants, may ask mother or father to get it for him—parents refuse.

INTERVIEW X (forty-seven months): Plays with other children—joins groups. Walks up to other child or group and asks if they want to play. Offers his own toy in exchange for others' toy—"makes a deal." No warm-up needed.

Does not easily accommodate to others' ideas. If suggestion appeals to him, he follows it. Otherwise he insists his idea be followed; tries to get other children to comply or leaves the activity. With other children, needs supervision—pushes, pinches (recent). When disagreement arises, he comes to mother or supervising adult, cries when his toy is taken, stops when it is given back.

Friendly to people, initiates interaction. Excited about relatives (except aunt). Prefers men. Ignores mother's attempts to restrict his questioning of strangers. When strangers initiate conversation, he does not answer readily.

INTERVIEW XI (fifty-three months): At nursery school, tends to lead when he wants to—orders children, assigns them tasks. Plays differently with different children, depending on whether they respond to his orders. With those who do not accept his orders, he plays better, on a more organized and give-and-take basis. Most children go along with his orders—no quarrels; if not, he generally leaves them. Initiates play with strange children; usually accepted—not distressed if not accepted. He does not accommodate to other children as a rule, particularly those he knows. Not so ready to share. Does not grab. Does not ask for aid, hangs on to own toys.

With strangers, he is immediately at ease, asks any question, makes any request, even unreasonable. Asked man on bus to move from window so he and mother could sit there; when mother said she had no change for something he wanted, he asked a strange woman if she had money. Very demanding. Asks anyone for what he wants, including mother and father.

NURSERY SCHOOL TEACHER INTERVIEW (fifty-three months): Very popular at school—all girls want to marry him, vie for folding his mat. "Charming, bright, quick to smile." Relations with teacher: strictly attention-getting. Not a follower—potential leader.

INTERVIEW XII (sixty months): Eager for school, makes friends, exchanges visits in afternoon. Attends ice-skating group two afternoons; "Y" play group two afternoons. Reported to be excellent visitor in friends' homes. When others visit him, he will not share his toys. No altercation with other children, except that he doesn't let them play with his toys. In playground may go out without toy, but ends up playing with everything.

Initiates much activity. When with another child who also initiates, seems to play on more organized level. He does not accommodate generally.

At summer day camp, was ready to accept role of leader, initiated play, told other children what to do—seemed to imitate counsellor. Part of summer was in nursery group (one year younger), and mother changed him against his wishes, but he was happy balance of summer.

Very fond of grandparents. Will stay with them. Mother says, "They expect more than we do."

If younger brother takes his toys, Roy hits him, yells. When brother cries because Roy pinched or pushed him and mother asks what happened, Roy will say, "I don't know," "Nothing," or "He fell."

INTERVIEW XIII (seventy months): Has many friends with different interests and when he is with them plays the way they want. Will accommodate more often in others' homes. (Mother hears reports from other mothers.)

May play on brother's level. Fights start because of brother's teasing and Roy's unwillingness to share. When they greet each other after school, there is genuine fondness; they hug each other, speak differently to one another than to others.

With strangers, he must be the initiator. If mother introduces him to someone, he may be shy about shaking hands, but he will walk up to strangers and start a conversation with no hesitancy. Will also join in with strange groups of children.

Although he does not obey at home, he will obey immediately if asked by someone not with him all the time, e.g., grandmother. If grandmother brings each boy a different toy, Roy will not even look at his but wants whatever his brother has, and a fight ensues.

FIRST-GRADE TEACHER INTERVIEW (seventy-five months): Talks to adults and children in the same manner; has "no respect for adults." Teacher discussed this with him and he agreed. He is "receptive" to teacher. Has many friends in class—relates well to other children, and they to him. Not a leader—sees what other children are doing and joins in. Sometimes he is bossy—tells others what to do. If child says "no," he accepts the refusal.

Parent-child relationship

INTERVIEW I (four and one-half months): First three weeks, sleep was irregular. Slept short periods at night—one and a half to two and a half hours; during day he slept as long as five to six hours. Fed whenever he awoke. Sleeping through night accomplished by waking him at 11:00 P.M. for feeding.

Is picked up and fed as soon as he cries. Grimaces with new foods. Mother "would not force it if he grimaced." When he indicates he is getting full by wiggling and pushing out food, he can be diverted by singing, then he finishes food. Mother thinks he eats a lot.

After bowel movement he usually is changed right away.

"He doesn't get a chance to cry. I'm always jabbering at him." "Never screams with anything unless I let him build up."

Cried a little when hi-fi speaker was first turned on, but stopped when picked up. Mother accustomed him to it by turning it on softly, while he was being held; now he doesn't cry when he hears it, even if he is not held.

Fondled a lot by mother. "He takes it"—no smile or crying. Mother afraid she picks him up and talks to him too much; tries to restrain herself. However, he never cries when put down.

Occasionally a little restless with nail cutting—usually not, maybe because mother talks to him.

Sick with bronchitis—moderately fussy, "but for being sick I expected more trouble."

In evening, mother does not turn him from stomach to back when he whimpers—he falls asleep in a few minutes.

INTERVIEW II (six months): "I talk to him all the time. I maul him. He seems to like it. I guess he'd better."

INTERVIEW III (ten months): When losing interest in meal, toward end, he will eat more if he is distracted by talking or banging spoon. (Mother says he eats well.)

INTERVIEW IV (twelve months): Father plays with him very actively after supper—he gets "all wound up," but still goes to sleep quickly.

No attempt to feed himself. Doesn't usually grab at spoon; if he does, is easily distracted. In general is easily distracted, especially by singing. "He rarely cries; if he starts to cry we distract him and he stops." Towards end of each meal, he has to be distracted before he will finish. Sometimes eats well, sometimes little.

Bowel movements regular—after breakfast and lunch. Put on toilet seat two weeks ago—mother made game of it. Has bowel movements regularly.

INTERVIEW V (fifteen months): Sometimes cries in sleep or wakes up—goes back to sleep after parents pat him. Past two months he won't eat unless he is distracted by singing or toys; then he eats a great deal. Holds bottle until it is half finished, then he begins to play with it. Mother feels he'd rather she held bottle, but she insists he hold it. Drinks juice from a cup—mother has to hold it. "Eating not as pleasant as it used to be—he's a pest."

Still placed on toilet seat—doesn't object, but nothing happens.

"Tried to arrange house so I have a minimum number of 'no's'—he pays no attention to them anyway." When slapped, he laughs—"Thinks it's a game." Cried for a moment with a few slappings.

INTERVIEW VI (twenty-one months): When put to sleep, if he has been excited by previous play, mother will hold him and sing to him before putting him down. Otherwise, she puts him right in the crib and he goes to sleep with only mild fussing.

Getting up in early part of evening becoming almost nightly pattern. Calls, "Mommy, come"—is picked up, held five minutes. He cuddles up, then goes back to sleep. May happen once or twice more. If he awakens a fourth time, mother does not go in—he falls asleep after few minutes crying. When he calls, "Mommy, come" in morning, father gives him bottle, which he holds himself, in crib.

Feeds self with hands—also allows himself to be spoon-fed. Mother and he both hold cup—tries himself, but spills a lot, so mother then takes over. Even when eating well, mother usually distracts him to get him to eat more.

Toilet training not attempted. (Note: this is contradiction of mother's previous statements.)

Mother practices new words with him—he responds eagerly, learns quickly. Walked at eighteen months. Had positive reaction. Mother made game of his success.

HOME OBSERVATION (twenty-four months): When observer rang bell on arrival, she could hear mother say to him, "Say 'hello' to the lady." While he was playing ball with observer, mother plied him with questions about music, e.g., "Who wrote Carmen?" "Who wrote Faust?" He answered mechanically. Sometimes, he would say "no, no" to question, but when mother asked insistently, he would give correct answer. Mother also asked him to name objects in book.

INTERVIEW VII (twenty-six months): To bed at 7:00 P.M.—not as easily as before. May start to cry unless a game is played with him. If he cries, mother leaves room, shuts door; he stops in one to two minutes. Still wakes up in evening—calls for "daddy." Father picks him up, holds him for a few minutes, then Roy goes back to sleep. If mother goes in, Roy sometimes accepts her, and sometimes insists on father. Up at 8:00 A.M.—calls "daddy" who gives him bottle. If his call is ignored, he may go back to sleep until 9:00 A.M.

Eating "terrible"—skips meals, eats less, asks for crackers, fruit, raisins, between meals—mother obliges. Finger feeds himself, doesn't use utensils—"messy," so mother feeds him.

Sometimes mother has to force him in bath and then force him out. Crying brief—easily diverted. Can easily be made to laugh loudly. Very resistant to diapering—squirms, tries to stand up, cries. Mother gets angry. His crying subsides when she spanks him. "That's the only spanking that means anything—the others don't." Doesn't try to dress or undress himself.

When father is home, Roy always goes to him in preference to mother. Always responded well to discipline until two weeks ago. More insistent on something he wants—stamps foot, says "no" to substitute—will throw a few things, hit mother once. "It's really very mild, compared to other children."

INTERVIEW VIII (thirty-three months): "In general he's wonderful, in most respects. He has mind of his own."

At bedtime father plays with him, reads to him; child fusses some if this activity is omitted.

Eating is "terrible"—eats practically nothing. Decent meal perhaps twice a week. Yet he nibbles a lot between meals—mother lets him have crackers and juices. If eating, he accepts help and now asks for it. Mother tries to increase his intake by distracting him. Doesn't force him—"can't anyway, he wouldn't take it, he'd turn his head or throw it."

"Doesn't cry much, only if I force him" into bath. If he wants to stay in tub he can be persuaded to come out by making a game of pulling the plug out. Doesn't try to wash himself. No objection to being washed. Balky about dressing, undressing; worst with diapering. Tries to run away—cries—mother often gets him to quiet down with mild spank. Less resistance with father. When father around, Roy prefers him. If he awakens at night, always calls father, pushes mother away when she comes.

Discipline: Mother says he used to be fairly good until past few weeks. (Note: mother made same comment last interview.) He teases. Mother is driven to yell or spank to get results. Father more patient— takes a lot of time, "cajoles."

Not a climber—doesn't go on sliding pond—mother says she doesn't go near it in park—"makes me nervous."

INTERVIEW IX (forty months): "He's contrary, perverse, and negative. But he's cute anyway. The biggest chatterbox in the whole park. He wants his way."

Now prolonged bedtime routine—"everything is a struggle." Read to, keeps asking for more. "He asks in very nice way, it's hard to say 'no.' " If refused, he fusses and persists. Gets his way more easily with father who says, "I don't feel like upsetting him before bed." Father lies down with him for a few minutes, then goes out. Some nights Roy keeps calling or playing in room till 10:00 P.M. Mother scolds, he pays no attention. No calling during night since night-light put in his room three months ago.

Eating "terrible"—limited diet, drinks a lot of milk. Much nibbling between meals. Mother tried to refuse, but gave in. "I couldn't stand the nagging and he has to eat something." Uses some utensils—messy, mother feeds him. Mother gave up distracting him, it took too much time, and sometimes actually distracted him from eating, though some-times it did help a little. Persuasion and bribing used—no success. "He's consistently negative about everything."

In bath (battle to get him in), sometimes washes himself, but not well, and "I have to do it over." Washes hands in sink himself, likes to do it. Allows mother to wash him. Cries and fights with her washing, "But I do it anyway." Nail cutting: may cry or fight. Mother bribes him with candy, and he becomes more cooperative. Goes with father for haircuts. Very cooperative. Likes to "roughhouse" with father. If a toy of his is grabbed, he asks mother for help. If he sees a toy he wants, he asks mother or father to get it for him. They tell him to ask child—he doesn't—nags parents about it—parents refuse.

Mother gets impatient and annoyed with difficulties in toilet train-ing—she knows she shouldn't. Roy had bowel movements only twice on toilet. Mother reminds him about urination—sometimes he complies; sometimes he resists. About bowel movements he keeps repeating, "I don't do it anymore, I'll tell you when I have to go" just before he announces he has evacuated in pants. There have been many battles.

Baby brother born three months ago. Roy stayed with aunt and grandmother two weeks—was ill—father slept there. Mother visited Roy—he cried a lot that night. She didn't visit him again next week— he was fine. Told him new fire engine was brought by baby—"Made big hit with him." Asked for bottle when mother fed baby. Now when mother busy with baby, he dashes around, slams doors. Parents say he had positive response to baby—pats, kisses baby often. Since birth of baby, he is more affectionate toward mother—doesn't push her away when father comes home as he used to. "He doesn't reject me."

Doesn't fuss when parents go out—asks, "Will you come back?" Very positive reaction to father. Very demonstrative to both parents.

Discipline: Mother says he "doesn't pay any attention to either of us." Used to be very good, but now she has to yell to get any obedience. (Note: contradiction with statements in previous interviews.) Father says, "Not so bad—if he says 'no' and you wait a while and ask again he will do it. Outside of this negative thing he's a darling."

INTERVIEW X (forty-seven months): Parents say, "Basically he is a very sweet, friendly, very bright youngster. For past few months he has been going through a stubborn and contrary phase. Improved since mother calmed down. He is more cooperative since he started school. Great talker, very sociable. Cautious."

When he awakens at night (rarely since night-light), he goes back to sleep readily for either parent. When father not home, mother gets him to bed easily; he dawdles more with father because father "is too patient." Father takes over when he is home. Routine is two books, then a parent lies down with him for five to twenty minutes. In country in summer, father not available for this—reading a must, and mother arranges life so it can be done as Roy expects.

Dressing and undressing: On weekends, when mother has time, she tries to get him to dress and undress himself. He can take off shoes, socks, pants, and put on pants, but does not do so despite mother's pressuring. Mother finally does it. Roy is not involved—just sits and lets her do it. If asked to do it himself, he dawdles, is uncooperative—"hopeless." When mother asked him to do it, she thinks he purposely put two feet in one pants leg just to show he couldn't do it, howled, and then became frustrated. "He knows how he can get a rise out of me." Many times mother gives a little help, and then he will finish; other times she is impatient and takes over and finishes the job. Many times he will undress, except for shirt, as mother asks—formerly mother always did it. Prefers father to dress him; on weekends, insists on it. Is dressed for school while he eats his breakfast. Won't brush teeth. Mother persistently reminds him, but in the end he does not do it.

Bath: no resistance since nursery school. Does not wash self—permits and expects mother to do it. Grandmother can get him to wash self. Screams with hair washing, but mother goes ahead. When taken out in towel, becomes very affectionate. Mother thinks he is cute and takes advantage of this period. Roy is happy at this.

Struggled over medication during illness. Mother and father held him down, held nose, poured it down when necessary. Now takes one kind of medicine since grandmother introduced it. Was better patient when ill at grandmother's house when baby was born. Fusses, whimpers with temperature taking. Father does it better. Mother says she doesn't really attempt to get him to eat during illness. When he gets hungry enough, he will eat.

Enjoys shopping with mother. Prefers to sit in basket and be pushed. Mother does this.

Eating: Mother helps him by reading or feeding him when he seems tired. Mother thinks he is a feeding problem—eating habits are unsatisfactory—"terrible." Many dislikes. Permits mother, father, grandmother to help him.

Mother says it has been reported that his behavior is very delightful with people other than herself. With them he eats well, is compliant, goes along with plans adults make, is able to walk for long periods without complaining. With mother, he is not obedient, dawdles, runs about.

In new endeavor, he frequently needs and accepts help. Doesn't work at it long. If car is stuck under bed, he doesn't patiently try to get it out, instead he becomes frustrated and screams. Stops when mother gets it out. When he is frustrated, mother always "comes to rescue."

Cries hard if physically hurt—parents try to tease him out of it—may accept or react with violent resentment.

Mother hugs him a great deal, which he likes. Prefers father to mother when both are present. Extremely fond of father and reacts obediently and positively. Later statement: "He pays no attention to prohibitions; his response doesn't depend on the person. Can be cajoled into obeying, but will not follow a rule stated directly."

I.Q. OBSERVATION (fifty-one months): Resisted leaving—mother pushed him out of playroom; he began to hit mother, who made no move to stop him.

INTERVIEW XI (fifty-three months): "Extremely disobedient, can't get him to do anything. I shouldn't be so negative about him he's really a wonderful child."

Father permits him to take nap at 5:00 P.M., despite mother's objections; he then goes to sleep at 11:00 P.M. Father gives in to Roy, does not limit him. When father is home, Roy whines, asks for books, delays routines. Mother feels he sets too few limits. Roy does not listen to mother unless she screams. Father asks him calmly, but he does not listen.

Mother considers eating a problem. Limited menu. Distractions reduce consumption. He has to be called several times. Does not eat with family—mother feels her meal would be ruined if he did. About two weeks ago mother said no more bottles. For three days she purposely put an egg in bottle to stop up nipples—she showed them to Roy, and he accepted her decision.

Chews rag, but hides it when he sees mother.

On awakening stays in room with door shut and plays records, after "I really drummed it into him."

Mother washes him in bath—he ignores request to do it himself, though grandmother can get him to do it. Very affectionate when mother takes him out.

Started nursery school. "Eager to go but not eager enough to dress himself." Looked forward to going when he started, but didn't want mother to leave. Has to be told in advance if maid is to pick him up instead of mother—even then he may become angry.

Very demanding—asks anyone for what he wants, including mother and father.

Needs to be reminded many times to obey. Usually delays completing any necessary task. Mother finally gets him to do it only after repeated nagging and yelling. One of mother's major complaints is his many interruptions of adults' conversations. Mother is constantly correcting him for this. Mother concerned at lack of limits imposed by father, who "gives in and has so much patience."

INTERVIEW XII (sixty months): Mother taught him to cut with scissors at request of teacher. He was willing to be taught, but would not try continuously and wouldn't work on his own until he was successful.

Prefers father—no difference in obedience to parents although generally he does not obey unless mother yells. Father now more strict—scolds him more. "When I tell you, you have to obey." Example: Roy wanted radio, father wanted to finish lunch and asked him to wait. Roy said, "Go soak your head." Father put him in bathroom. Mother tried to get him to say, "I'm sorry." Roy was nearly asleep, but would not come out to apologize.

Generally dresses self, except tying shoes. Threatens mother he will put clothes on backwards, which used to get a rise out of her. Once she said, "O.K. others will laugh," he put clothes on correctly. Puts away clothes on own, toys on instruction. Mother washes him in bath; he gets out and dresses on own.

INTERVIEW XIII (seventy months): Recently not as much of a hassle in morning to get him dressed and going to school. Somehow he gets dressed himself, though he needs to be reminded many times to get started. Mother puts clothes out on a chair.

When he refused to go to "Y" for three weeks while mother was working and couldn't pick him up after school, mother agreed that if he did not want to go, he didn't have to. Next week when mother stopped working, he went willingly. When he refused to go to day camp twice, mother said he would have to stay in bungalow. She left him alone in the morning—he did not seem happy and he went in the afternoon.

Mother tries to allow him more freedom. Walks to corner with him and watches him cross to and from school, lets him return home from "Y" alone, permits him downstairs alone, gives him freedom in country. But he does not show "reliability"—does not come into house on return from "Y," but stays outside; when supposed to be downstairs, was up on roof; in country said he had crossed the one forbidden road; did not report change in plans, such as having lunch with friend and not coming home.

Does not tell what happens at school, except indirectly—"Want to hear a song?" etc. If mother asks, then he does not tell her anything.

Is "mad about father." Father also is devoted. Spends much time and encourages him in use of manipulative toys, reads to him. Roy is disappointed if father comes home late, asks for father if he is hurt or unhappy. Father still will not discipline him—hard to refuse him anything, doesn't raise voice, but will repeat request five to six times until Roy obeys. Mother finds it impossible to deal with him this way. Mother begins to yell if Roy does not obey after several requests. He really does not obey father any better. Seems not to pay attention until mother yells. Whines when mother says "no" to a request of his. Usually she does not give in and now, since she says she will not listen to the whining, she thinks he is whining less, even when not reminded. Mother usually "wins" when he whines for something she feels he should not have.

Very affectionate with mother—affectionate with everyone.

With tonsillectomy, asked father to stay at hospital, but father did not. Two evacuation accidents this summer—at neighbor's house. Mother scolded him and talked to him—he did not comment. Didn't seem embarrassed.

FIRST-GRADE TEACHER INTERVIEW (seventy-five months): Teacher had conference with mother because Roy didn't do his homework. Now mother has taken responsibility for this—has to watch him at home in same manner teacher does in school. There have been fights about it. While parents were on vacation, Roy's schoolwork seemed to improve, he paid more attention, his homework improved, and he seemed more settled. This continued for about a week after parents returned.

Mother says he is difficult at home—"ornery." Had difficulty establishing homework routines. Behavior at home different from that at school—"does not listen" at home.

CLINICAL INTERVIEW WITH PARENTS (seventy-six months): Problems with which both parents are concerned center most prominently around the daily multiple fusses, which are precipitated by routine requests. Almost any request made by either parent will be refused by Roy. Mother repeats until she is nagging, and finally there is "a battle royal"; father repeats more patiently, but gets no better results.

Roy puts off his homework, often does it in a sloppy manner. Teacher told mother to insist that he make it neat. Roy has resisted, mother has coaxed, conned, and coerced; father sits with him while he works. Child now works with less resistance.

Roy and his brother constantly wrestle and play. Mother finds this intolerable in the morning when Roy should be getting dressed for school and in the evening when he should be preparing for bed. Her typical handling is to make a long speech. When the study psychiatrist suggested that there be a minimum of speech-making and that the boys be separated unpunitively until her requests were fulfilled, the mother objected to the fact that this would not be regarded by Roy as a punishment. The father was immediately clear that it was not punishment that was advocated, but structuring the situation so that it would be easier for Roy to complete the few mandatory acts with a minimum of distraction. The mother feels that the boys' annoying acts are deliberately aimed at causing her discomfort. While the younger boy is the "instigator," the mother's greatest wrath is expressed against Roy.

The mother reported that the parental relationship was very poor —there is "great hostility." She states that she frequently makes negative remarks, such as "I just can't stand this family; I just want to leave." Roy has been heard to say to his brother, "She hates us . . . She doesn't like daddy." Both children prefer the father, and the mother considers this justified since she considers herself a nag.

Mother continued her description of Roy's behavior by saying, "He just wants to play, he has no feeling of responsibility unless you're pounding at him." Their relationship is never pleasant, mother is constantly irritated with him. Mother has to check up on his homework and then forces help on him. "It is very messy—you will have to do it again"; if his arithmetic is poor, she insists on drilling him. Once, after a terrible fight, mother refused to drill him on his spelling words for a test the next day, and he then got 100 per cent, whereas he usually gets 90 per cent. She presented this as an illustration of how things happen so he does not learn from experience.

The attempt was made to show the mother the inevitability of the child's assuming that all problems were hers rather than his, in view of her tendency to take so much responsibility for everything he does, and her unwillingness to let him face the possibility of his actions having unpleasant consequences.

Subsequent course

INTERVIEW XIV (seventy-eight months): Mother has to remind child at each step in routines—has to tell him to get up, get dressed, brush his teeth, etc., otherwise he dawdles and plays with his brother. The advice given to her at the clinical consultation "has not worked." Mother warns Roy, "If you are not ready, you'll be late," but this makes no difference. Yesterday she was furious, yelled at him, said everyone would leave without him. He went alone and just made it to school. He is not late because mother nags him.

Mother has to function in accordance with routines, is very compulsive about getting everything ready and being on time. She scolds a lot about everything and can always get her way, but only after a lot of screaming and aggravation. She has a great need to have everything done right—is inclined to keep after Roy for every little thing. Father will announce a punishment when Roy has been fresh to him, will be firm in the face of pleading and arguments, then will retract with the statement that Roy will not be given another chance next time.

There are still many objections from Roy when his mother tries to help him with his homework and drill him in arithmetic. Yet she feels that he doesn't do so well in arithmetic, that he needs help, and that she should work with him.

The child still cannot be relied on to do as instructed—he goes off with other children, plays where he has been told not to, talks to strangers. He is very uncooperative. He likes to dress himself, although he has to be reminded constantly; if his mother tries to dress him, he says he can do it himself—he has to have his own way. He would rather deny himself something he wants rather than comply with a demand—as refusing to put on socks so he could play tennis with his father.

INTERVIEW XV (eighty-three months): He resists everything—will refuse verbally then, after a struggle in which he and mother argue, he may comply with what was requested. When he doesn't want to comply, he doesn't answer, seems not to hear. Mother repeats until she gets upset and yells—then he does what she wants. He is scolded a great deal—mother doesn't know if he is listening unless she "tricks" him and asks him what she has said. Sometimes he doesn't know and says "what?"

He now does homework according to a set routine and doesn't

have to be reminded. Mother reminds him, but admits this is not necessary. She makes him do his work over because it is not clear. He fusses, but eventually she wins, after a struggle each time. He made sentences out of new words, did it quickly. Then mother made suggestions about how to make them more interesting. He complained a bit, then rewrote them.

When father is home, children go to bed later than usual because he has patience, talks, makes requests a number of times, plays with them, and forgets the time. Children keep running out of bedroom, and father does nothing; even when he gets stern they pay no attention. Mother has to step in and yell—then they comply. Roy complies more readily away from home; mother always gets good report about his behavior. Mother wishes she had the assurance he has with people.

Teacher told mother Roy is very bright, "but you have to sit on him to make him do anything." Mother insists on hearing spelling words—he fussed at first, but now accepts—gets 100 per cent on the tests. The mother feels she must make her children achieve so she can show their grandmother that they do as well as her other grandchildren.

Relations between parents are deteriorating—they have nothing in common except fighting about the children. Mother realizes she does a lot of yelling, makes demands that are not necessary. Yet father has infinite patience and children take advantage; they do not comply or feel at all responsible for doing so.

SECOND-GRADE TEACHER INTERVIEW (eighty-seven months): Roy is "a born salesman." "He has a charming manner, and is very likeable."

Teacher pleased with progress he has made since the beginning of the year. At the beginning he was lackadaisical and needed to be prodded. Often he didn't finish an assignment, and his papers were slipshod and careless. When the teacher criticized him, he cringed "like a puppy." She then decided to become more firm, not to let him get away with so much. He changed his attitude toward his work; now does it willingly, finishes, shows much progress. Teacher thinks the change results from her sterner approach, plus maturation on Roy's part. He tries much harder than before. His behavior in school is excellent. "All you have to do is speak to him and he complies."

He is attentive to anything new that is presented. Math comes more slowly. At first he had to be prodded. Teacher called on him continually, gave him almost personal instruction. Now he surprises teacher by solving the problems on his own.

He is in the top reading group and is a colorful speaker. Has had to work on handwriting because his coordination was below average. He also had to work on creative writing and now can do a piece which is average for class.

Has many friends, is a leader, a happy child.

FOLLOW-UP DISCUSSION WITH PSYCHIATRIST (S.C.) (ninety months): Mother says the "major part of the year has been one fight from beginning to end." Problems continue: Roy balks at every routine, dawdles, loses things, is indifferent to losses. Mother continues to nag, quarrels ensue. Parental relationship is very poor.

Recommendations given to the parents focused on eliminating the daily hassles, starting with the morning. Roy should be allowed to dawdle with no admonitions. If he can dawdle and still get to school on time, there is nothing wrong with his way of getting ready.

FOLLOW-UP DISCUSSION WITH MOTHER (HER REQUEST) (ninety-five months): "It's just as bad as it ever was. He just wants to play, has no feelings of responsibility unless you're pounding at him."

Mother says there is "no nagging" about getting him dressed for school, but there are four to six reminders during the process. He has not been late to school. Homework is done immediately after school— it's "the only time to chain him down." It's a constant hassle, he does it in the sloppiest way, and mother has to insist that he get started. Mother checks up on him—makes him do it over because it is messy, drills him. Mother is constantly irritated.

Advice again focused on telling the mother to allow the child to assume responsibility for his actions and their consequences.

INTERVIEW XVI (ninety-six months): Roy is the youngest child in his third-grade class. Teacher says he is bright, but he talks too much. He does good work. However, mother finds it very hard to get along with him. It makes no difference what mother does or says—Roy can't go along with it. Nothing gets done with ease. In the end mother always wins, but she has to argue and yell until he finally does it.

Mother has to call him about twelve times for bed or meals, and then he comes, sulking, but gets over it easily in a few minutes. Mother and he have had terrible scenes when she makes him redo his homework, and she literally beats him.

He constantly breaks things, pays no attention to rules—"it is pointless to have rules."

Does very good work in school, but math is on the weak side. Mother makes him do extra homework for math, scolds him either for not doing homework, or for not doing it neatly. He doesn't answer, seems not to hear. Mother says, "Do you feel better now that you ate my heart out?" and he answers "Yes."

He always gets 100 per cent in spelling and 80 per cent or 90 per cent in math. Once got 60 per cent in math—teacher said he seemed embarrassed.

Has many friends, gets along well with children, is well liked.

Mother feels it is impossible for her to have any smooth interaction with Roy, primarily because she does not get along with the father, who exhibits many of the same traits as the child. Father doesn't come when called, he ignores her, thinks that anything the children do is permissible, that she demands too much, and has too high standards and expectations.

FOLLOW-UP DISCUSSIONS WITH BOTH PARENTS SEPARATELY (AT MOTHER'S REQUEST) (one hundred and seven months): Mother is "terribly frustrated" about Roy. Her eyes fill with tears as she describes the fact that he does not function outside of playing unless she is constantly at him. Now, to make matters worse, father is also at him constantly. While mother reiterates her deep feelings of inability to modify her approach to the child, she wishes the father to be seen for the purpose of modifying his approach, and sees no reason why he should not change if it is best for the child.

Roy spends up to three hours on his homework during which period his mother wanders in and out reminding Roy to do his work, checking his work, making him correct it, and finally approving it, although it may not be as perfect as she would wish. The father then comes home and asks to see Roy's work. He often has the child do it over again because he thinks it is too sloppy. There is a second commotion, often a duplication of drilling, too, and the mother feels it is not fair to the child for the father to make him do the work over after she has already approved it.

The mother says the differences between the parents are intense. The father makes issues about things that the mother considers unimportant, such as neatness. He refuses to discuss issues, listens to his wife in silence, or buries his head in a newspaper while she talks. The family cannot do anything smoothly—a simple plan of going to the park on Sunday easily turns into a nightmare—the father objects to something Roy is wearing, a battle about changing ensues, and finally the child complies. In the end, everyone goes out feeling sulky and angry.

Morning routine is "not too bad," but still a problem.

Teacher complains that Roy talks in class, doesn't pay attention. He may "happily" remark to mother that he has gotten 39 per cent on a math test.

The child now not only refuses to comply with requests, but he tunes out his mother and resorts to protective lying. His teacher says he doesn't understand his work and is generally tense. He has also developed a tic.

SECOND CLINICAL EVALUATION (one hundred and twenty months): The child tended to place all problems in the past or in a minor key. He stated that he was sure he had problems, but "right now I can't think of which." He had some awareness of the negative interaction between himself and his mother, although he did not acknowledge this openly.

BONNIE—CASE 18

SUMMARY

AGE AT REFERRAL: Fifty-three months.

PRESENTING COMPLAINTS:

1] Tantrums. These were precipitated by a parental request to which the child objected or the failure of a self-initiated endeavor.
2] Sensitivity to tightness or roughness of clothing.
3] Demands unnecessary servicing.
4] Demands to be center of attention; insists on being listened to when she has something to say, without regard to the needs of others.

(None of these problems characterized her behavior outside the home.)

ONSET OF PROBLEM: Forty-eight months.

CLINICAL INTERVIEW: Bonnie, a well-built, nice-looking girl, did not hesitate to enter the playroom, nor did she give any objection or indication of concern at her mother's leaving. She related to the examiner positively in terms of her attention, interest, and verbalizations.

Her play with the toys was appropriate and organized, and she expressed her interests clearly. Her discussion was related to the ongoing activity, and she became more talkative as the session progressed, although at no time could she have been termed loquacious. The quality of her play, its content, and her verbalizations were all appropriate to sex and up to or superior to age. She was cooperative, followed directions, and serviced herself appropriately.

At the conclusion of the session, Bonnie asked her mother if on the way home she could wear the new shoes they had just purchased, a request which the mother had previously denied with an explanation. At her mother's continued refusal, Bonnie whined and fussed briefly, but when she said good-bye to the examiner, she again was happy and smiling.

COMMENT: It should be noted, as documented in the histories, that the child's behavior outside the home has almost always been socially acceptable.

DIAGNOSIS: Reactive Behavior Disorder, moderate.

TEMPERAMENT: From early infancy, the child's behavior has been characterized by extremely intense reactions that, in the first months of life, were predominantly negative. The mother's summary of the first nine months was, "That child was always fussing and screaming every minute." Positive reactions were equally intense. She was "very thrilled" with learning to walk, then resisted being put into her carriage, "struggled to get out," "bellowed." When finally taken out, she "laughed and ran," and if her mother pulled her back, "She threw herself on the floor and screamed."

In the early years, she also displayed irregularity of physiological functioning, initial negative reactions, very little tolerance for frustration, and very slow adaptability. Noted throughout was a low sensory threshold. This was indicated in her reactions to being wet and her startling to noise, easy awakenings, and frequent rashes. With increasing age, it became evident that she was sensitive to the textures of fabrics.

PARENTAL HANDLING: Before consultation, parental handling had, in large part, been shaped by the intensity of the child's reactions. The parents stated at nineteen months, "She has everyone terrorized." They were intimidated by the violence of her responses and the tension, stress, and difficulty that resulted from the child's persistent and consistent challenging of all rules that did not fit her desires. For the most part, the decision to make a demand on the child or to impose a limit was based not only on the specific issue itself, but also on the number and kind of interactions that had immediately preceded it. On the whole, the parents tended to avoid scenes by giving in to or by appeasing the child.

While these parents appeared to feel less personal involvement with and to have fewer feelings of responsibility for the child's behavior than is usual in middle-class families, there was still the assumption, particularly by the mother, that the child's problems stemmed from insecurity and that this must be related in some way to parental handling. Both parents exhibited an unusually high threshold of tolerance for Bonnie's difficult behavior.

DYNAMIC FORMULATION: The child's temperamental characteristics have made for great difficulty in managing her. Her negative and intense responses, in combination with the irregularity of her functioning, made it almost impossible for the mother to be consistent and to respond appropriately to the baby's needs. When the child was six and a half months old, the mother said, "You know babies . . . they're always screaming and you never know why. . . . Most of the time I can't figure out what she wants." Moreover, the parents' tendency to modify their demands on the basis of the amount of stress the child's anticipated reaction would add to a situation served to confuse the child as to what was appropriate behavior, since the same activity might be permitted on one occasion and interdicted on another. Similarly, the parents' tendency to capitulate in the face of her violent outbursts taught her that success in obtaining her desires often depended on the vigor of her expression, and thus led to the intensification of the tantrums and increased persistence in her demands.

The parents' complaint that the child demanded unnecessary servicing was not borne out in the histories, which showed steady progress toward independence, exhibited largely in the child's taking over an area such as feeding or dressing through violent and insistent refusal to permit the mother to service her. It is true that initially there was irregularity and inconsistency on the child's part so that at times she would accept or insist on being serviced, but eventually she came to reject all aid in the given area. During the clinical observation there was no indication of dependency.

The data also suggested that there might be a linkage between the child's low threshold to sensory stimulation, which was well documented, and her low threshold to other awarenesses, such as frustration.

RECOMMENDATIONS: Parents were told that evaluation of the antero-spective data and direct examination of the child ruled out insecurity as a basis for the behavior problem. Rather, the issue was the very real and substantial difficulty of working out a method of management for a child who showed intense reactivity, persistence in her tantrum behavior, and low threshold to frustration.

They were advised to select initially a small quota of issues, preferably those having the greatest impact on family relationships, set up rules for these areas, and quietly and consistently request compliance. The inevitable stormy resistance from Bonnie would have to be waited out patiently. The parents were counseled to avoid involvement in her tantrums, either by appeasement or by any display of anger, to accept them as a response which she, at that point, was not able to control, and to recognize that while she was in the process of so reacting it was not possible to reach her. They were told to be even more persistent in following through on their demands than she would be in refusing to accept them. The parents were advised not to allow themselves to be drawn into any discussion or negative interchange with the child in the interest of keeping clear the basic issue, compliance with the stated rule.

At the same time, the parents were told to ignore for the present issues that were of lesser importance in terms of their effect on others, as it was important to avoid unproductive clashes and their resultant negative interaction between parent and child.

SUBSEQUENT COURSE: The last follow-up at age 118 months indicated that all problems had disappeared and Bonnie was considered to be "recovered."

Her tantrums had gradually become less intense and less frequent, until finally the child would only whine in response to frustration. Sensitivity to clothing was no longer a problem due to an increased threshold and the fact that the mother began to make automatic adjustments in Bonnie's apparel. There were no longer demands for unnecessary servicing or attention.

The marked improvement in this child is related to two factors. First, and of primary importance, is the fact that the parents were able to modify their handling of the child appropriately. With the assurance that Bonnie was not insecure and with the understanding of the dynamics of the problem which they gained from the consultation, they were able to be firm and consistent on important issues and to bypass other behaviors. As the mother expressed it in a follow-up discussion, "You helped me because I was able to relax with Bonnie, knowing that I wasn't the culprit and it wasn't all because of me." A secondary factor is the fact that with increasing age and competence, there were fewer activities in which Bonnie failed to perform at the high level she set for herself and, as a result, she has had less and less cause for nonproductive frustration. Thus, the child has been able to adapt and develop optimally, although her basic pattern of easy frustration and intense reactivity remains.

Selective Extraction

Intensity of reactions

INTERVIEW I (six and one-half months): No set behavior pattern. Goes along in one way for two weeks and everything wonderful, then she suddenly goes off.

Pretty cranky baby; cried a lot, screaming up to a half hour. Has to be rocked twenty to thirty minutes on first going to sleep—otherwise she cries.

Past month cries a lot during day—mother thinks it may be constipation or teething. "Most of the time I can't figure out what she wants."

Satiation: Stops sucking, sometimes cries. Always refused pacifier —screamed if put in her mouth. Past month mother offered bottle (child had been breast-fed). Didn't take it, chewed on nipple.

Three weeks ago bottle of juice offered at beginning of supper meal, when child was hungry. She screamed, rejected supper, had to be breast-fed. Didn't eat supper for two to three days. When bottle was offered again, didn't take it, but if hungry, she cried.

Took vitamins O.K. from two weeks to three months. Then started spitting them out and crying; continued this one to two months, then again took them. When cereal started, "Ate it like crazy, huge quantities." Now eats only half of what she used to, and less positive reaction. In general, eats much less solids in past month. Sometimes during meal stiffens out and cries—refuses more food. Sometimes as soon as she sees jar of food at lunch, starts crying. Usually takes only breast at lunch.

Cries when outer clothing put on. "Yells her head off."

"Used to be terrible" with nail cutting—pulled away. No crying. In past month, holds still and watches. Puckers face and struggles with face washing. Moans, doesn't scream.

Smiles at many strangers, takes initiative. Usually content in anyone's lap—sometimes screams when held by strangers, subsides when mother takes her.

Cried one to two minutes with first and second injections.

INTERVIEW II (nine and three-fourths months): Irregular nap in afternoon, outdoors. Will not sleep indoors in afternoon—"just screams."

At about seven months, took milk from bottle from father (had rejected it from mother). Gradually increased intake and accepted from mother also.

Eats pretzels or bread crusts by the dozen. ("Whenever she's moaning and groaning I give her something to eat.") Lusty appetite. "If you give her more than she wants she screams." Happens at end of almost every meal.

"That child was always fussing and screaming every waking minute up to a week ago."

"Big joke" to have clothes put over her head. With nail cutting, pulls hand away, pulls at scissors, finally starts to scream. With hair brushing, bats brush away. Fusses with face washing. Can be distracted.

Screams after few minutes in playpen. When she's unhappy or miserable, she throws herself and stiffens out. If mother leaves her outside with stranger even for a moment, she screams. (Can be left in house with known baby-sitter without crying.) If parents or sib leave her alone in room, she starts screaming right away.

Reaction to third injection same as to first two—screamed loudly one to two minutes. Given by uncle—when he visits, she eyes him suspiciously; if he touches birthmark on her cheek, she screams. Screams with slightest bang or hurt.

INTERVIEW III (fourteen months): At eleven and a half months, "suddenly out of nowhere" refused all baby foods—pushed them away and cried. Takes regular foods. Increasingly selective about foods, also violence of rejection increased. If given something she doesn't want, cries, tries to wipe it off tongue, spits. (Mother washes tongue off with washcloth.) If given more food than she wants, throws it back at mother.

Howls and struggles with diaper changing. No longer objects to hair brushing, nail cutting, face washing. Won't stay in playpen. If left alone, cries loudly.

After a week with aunt (where she adjusted well), was "divine" for first week at home. Played by self, demanded little attention—then reverted to not staying alone, demanding, crying for attention. Mother thinks due to teething.

Responds easily to smile from stranger. If many strangers thrust upon her, she "hides, wants to be protected."

If mother leaves her side in playground, even for a minute, she "cries bitterly." If another child takes something from her, she struggles and screams. Very upset at "no"; if something taken away she yells.

May cry loudly and long if hurt, but not a sound if hurt while playing.

INTERVIEW IV (sixteen and one-half months): Left with aunt ten days at fourteen and a half months. Aunt stayed with her until she was asleep, if not, she screamed. (Mother had been walking out—no screaming.) When mother returned, "She didn't know me." If aunt left room and Bonnie was alone with mother, she ran after aunt, screaming. O.K. after mother stayed overnight.

At home, returned to former pattern of going to sleep without fussing and mother walking out. Suddenly, one night (age sixteen months), she screamed when put to bed. Very loud screaming, "hysterical" for twenty minutes. Father then took her out; she was O.K. (Had been teething.) Then screamed every night for about two weeks (only one night exception to this), and had to be taken out or parents had to sit with her. No fussing since. (Mother thinks teething is better.) Also sometimes woke up during night screaming (usually when put to sleep earlier). Never permitted to scream more than thirty minutes. Taken into parents' bed and then returned to her own.

Rejection of disliked foods very definite—spits out, rubs tongue to get rid of taste. "She's very self-assertive, never any doubt about what she wants." Lets mother feed her at beginning of meal, then insists on taking over. If mother continues to try to feed her, she "howls, has a fit, everything goes flying."

About a month ago wouldn't sit down in tub, howled—"Maybe it was too hot." Bribed with lollipop each time since, O.K. now. No objection to dressing or diapering now, sometimes tries to dress herself. Only occasionally "explodes" when unsuccessful—throws everything around.

Started walking—"Very thrilled with it." Then resisted carriage, struggled to get out, cried, "wanted to walk." "Bellowed" in shopping cart; if put down, laughed and ran out of store. If mother pulled her back, she threw herself on floor and screamed. After two days, put in stroller—O.K. Several days ago put back in carriage—O.K.

Very possessive of toys. When another child is around, she howls if child even touches one. If brother or sister takes something she wants, she screams and throws herself on the floor. Easily distracted after mother picks her up. If toy is too difficult, she will scream and throw it.

When mother says "no" either she stops and cries, or laughs and does it even more. Spanking only intensifies her reaction.

If she falls and hurts herself, hardly cries if intent on something. At other times cries loudly, but not long.

INTERVIEW V (nineteen and one-half months): Sleeping "perfect" until last month. Began screaming at bed- and naptime (was teething). With upper respiratory infection, screaming was worse for one and a half weeks. Also awakens screaming during night—taken into parents' bed.

With minor cut, screamed at top of her lungs for half hour.

Rejects food by spitting out. If given more food than she wants, picks it up and throws it across room. Wouldn't let mother feed her (feeds herself). Gets "furious" if you touch her cup.

If she sees anyone going out, comes running with her snowsuit. If refused, throws self on floor and cries; can be distracted, sometimes not easily. Used to object violently to washing hands and face—less now. "Loves" hair brushing—bends head. Overtures to strangers—demands attention from whomever is around. If toy is pulled from her, she fights, screams, and hits. Tries to grab toys from other children, has tantrum if denied. Cries and screams when father leaves in morning—lasts up up to five minutes after he leaves. Violently objects to someone going into bathroom and closing door—screams and pounds on door.

About discipline, father says, "She has such a pair of lungs she has terrorized us. She's violent in her responses." If frustrated, screams and throws herself on floor. If spanked, only cries more loudly.

Has passion for books and being read to—asks many times daily. If refused, cries.

INTERVIEW VI (twenty-five and one-half months): "Same quality she's always had, of doing everything with her whole being."

If mother sees she's not sleepy, lets her stay up. "She's so strong-willed there's no sense insisting."

Terrified by thunderstorm—clings to mother.

May call parent during night for bottle of milk. If parent other than one she calls comes, she cries and refuses bottle. Insists on parent called.

If doesn't nap, calls in about twenty minutes. "If she won't sleep, one hundred horses won't make her."

Often insists on sitting on father's lap while feeding herself. "I give in, she screams so loud I can't bear it." When frustrated, throws herself on floor and screams until parents pick her up—they always do. "We do almost anything to keep her quiet, she has such a voice. Useless to try, she outlasts us." Insists on own choice of clothes. "Otherwise I can't get it on her." If unsuccessful in attempts to dress self, screams. Readily accepts help.

If rejected by brother, she lies down and screams. If toy is too difficult, lies down and screams. Accepts help and screaming stops. If sister pulls toy away, Bonnie fights hard. If another child pulls, she fights half-heartedly, cries.

If spanked for discipline, she cries loudly, but spanking has no effect on her behavior. To "no," she laughs, thinks it's a big joke.

INTERVIEW VII (thirty-two months): Disturbance in sleep again. "Screamed hysterically" when put in bed. Mother doesn't press new foods. "You can't make her eat." Screamed with hair washing until several months ago. When mother refused her choice of clothes, she screamed. More amenable last few months. If unsuccessful in dressing self, screams, accepts help. With hair brushing, yanks brush away, says, "I'll do it myself," messes hair. Mother lets her do it—"I'll let her do anything, so long as she doesn't yell." With hand and face washing, "Sometimes I have to drag her kicking and screaming." Likes rough play—diving off furniture.

Gets weekly book from library. Won't let anyone touch it or read it, even to her.

Screams if anyone sits on her chair or uses her dish or spoon until they give it up. If misses ritual of jumping from elevator into hall and from hall into street, insists on going back to do it.

"Still capable of throwing a fit anywhere, if she doesn't get what she wants or if someone walks in front of her." "When she's not screaming with frustration she's gay and happy." "When you tell her not to do something she turns around, does it and laughs." If frustrated and screams, sometimes easily distracted, sometimes not.

INTERVIEW VIII (thirty-eight months): Mother says, "Very bouncy child. Very happy when occupied; difficult when displeased—throws tantrums. Ebullient, full of life force."

Eats by self. Mother insists on cutting meat. If Bonnie has started and mother intervenes, she howls, collapses on floor. If stopped from taking liked foods from others' plates, she fusses, howls. Won't tolerate unwanted food on plate—pushes plate away or dumps specific food on table.

Wants to help others—may cry if rejected, but can be diverted. If she wants something, "if thwarted in any way," will howl and kick and carry on—continue until worn out. Mother can quiet her by picking up and cuddling.

INTERVIEW IX (forty-five months): Tantrums resuming once or twice a day.

Awakens at night and calls mother to come to cover her. Cries if mother doesn't come. Period of two weeks with four or five nightmares— screaming, eyes staring ahead, mother could not waken her. When mother held her, Bonnie kicked part of the time. Cries if three blankets not arranged in special order.

Intense battle about what to wear for past six to nine months. Very neat—things must be in certain place; snowsuit tied certain way; she must open door to aunt's house, shrieks in advance for fear someone else may do it.

All foods are either liked intensely, or she doesn't eat at all. Eats eagerly, concentrates on eating.

Must say good-bye to brother and father, cries if routine omitted— her feelings are hurt.

Accepts absolute and safety rules, not relative prohibitions—cries, screams, tantrums in response to latter. Mother leaves her screaming, crying on street or floor. Takes five to ten minutes, then Bonnie comes to mother—may continue to cry.

If refused gum before lunch, may have tantrum. Uses language little in argument, screams instead. If expressed desires are not met, al- most always has a tantrum.

INTERVIEW X (fifty-one months): Mother says she has "no more tan- trums."

Eats great quantities of what she likes, otherwise doesn't eat at all.

Gets lost easily in a crowd. At museum, screamed in terror when she didn't see mother, who was just a few feet away. If unsuccessful in activity, may cry or leave it—accepts help. Will come to mother crying if rejected in play.

No longer violent response to prohibitions. Still cries when request is refused and when unsuccessful, but not as extreme. Now uses language instead of crying, howling.

Threshold to sensory stimuli and to frustration

INTERVIEW I (six and one-half months): Grins when anyone looks at her.

Past month cries a lot during day. Mother thinks cause may be constipation or teething. "Most of the time I can't figure out what she wants." Whenever taken outdoors, stops crying—keeps looking at ob- jects around her.

With bath, up to one month ago, seemed bewildered, looked un- comfortable, fussed a little. More relaxed, moves and splashes now. (Only one bath per week.)

Cried when diaper was wet for first two months. Stopped crying as soon as changing started. Cries with bowel movement, stops as soon as changing starts. Constipated in past months—small, hard movement once a day. Doesn't cry during passage.

No crying with dressing except with outer clothing; then "yells her head off." Some startle to loud noise, sometimes cries. "Very sound-sensitive, turns in response to any sound, even in sleep. Averts head and closes eyes with bright light." Same reaction with first and second injection; cried one to two minutes.

INTERVIEW II (nine and three-fourths months): Cried, was always fussing and screaming up to week ago. Past two months sleeps through night. Mother thinks may be due to moving to room by herself so she is not awakened by sounds in the room. When ill, awakens once during night—stays up as long as an hour. Also awakens early in morning when ill.

No fussing when wet. Fusses with bowel movement if not changed within ten minutes. No longer constipated (given malt).

Screams after a few minutes in playpen. If left outside with stranger even for moment, she cries. If left alone in room by parents or sibs, she starts screaming right away.

As with first two injections, cried loudly one to two minutes for third. Given by uncle—when he visits, she eyes him suspiciously; screams if he touches birthmark on her cheek.

Anytime the slightest thing happens, bangs herself, etc. she screams.

No startle with loud noise. Reaction to noise when asleep unknown. "Holy law is if she's asleep, no one goes in." Averts head or cries with bright light.

INTERVIEW III (fourteen months): Doesn't fuss when wet or soiled. When nothing bothers her physically, she's happy. If anything bothers her the least bit, she's miserable.

If mother leaves her side in playground even for a minute, she "cries bitterly." If another child takes something from her, she struggles and screams. Very upset at a "no" or if something taken away. Yells. If hurts self while playing, doesn't make a sound. At other times may cry loudly and long.

No startle or reaction to bright light. Parents think she is very responsive and sensitive to sound.

INTERVIEW IV (sixteen and one-half months): For period of about two weeks, screamed hysterically up to twenty minutes on being put to bed unless parents took her out or stayed with her. Also sometimes awakened during night screaming and was taken into parents' bed for a while. Mother thinks due to teething. "When she has the slightest physical discomfort, she fusses a lot, she's up in arms." Continued until five nights ago. Mother thinks teething is better.

Rejection of disliked foods very definite—spits out, rubs tongue to get rid of taste. (True also in Interview III when mother would wash tongue with washcloth.)

For about a month, wouldn't sit in tub, howled—"Maybe it was too hot." Bribed with lollipop each time—since then, O.K.

Sometimes tries to dress herself. Only occasionally "explodes" when unsuccessful, throws everything around. Most of time doesn't show frustration.

After learning to walk, resisted carriage, struggled to get out. In shopping cart, "bellowed." If put down, she laughed and ran out of store. If mother tried to pull her back, she threw herself on floor and screamed. Put in stroller after two days—O.K. Back in carriage several days ago—O.K.

Very possessive of toys if another child is around, howls if child even touches one. If brother or sister takes something she wants, she screams and throws herself on floor. Easily distracted when mother picks her up. If toy is too difficult, she will scream and throw it.

INTERVIEW V (nineteen and one-half months): Sleeping perfect until last month. Began screaming at bed- and naptime (was teething). With upper respiratory infection, screaming was worse for one and a half weeks. "In declining phase," screaming much less, down to a few minutes, not taken out. Wakes up cranky after nap—wants to be held—lasts a half hour.

Very sensitive to pain—with minor cuts, screamed at top of lungs a half hour. Food and being read to are almost only things that distract her from pain.

Rejects food by spitting out. If given more than she wants, picks it up and throws it across room. Won't let mother feed her—gets "furious" if you touch cup.

Doesn't cry at unsuccessful attempts to put on own shoes. Lets mother do it. Gets snowsuit if sees someone going out. If refused, throws self on floor and cries—sometimes not easily distracted.

Rarely fusses when wet or soiled. Either constipated (one bowel movement every two days) or diarrhea (two per day, very loose). Seems happier with diarrhea.

Less violent objection to hand and face washing.

If toy is pulled from her, fights, screams, hits. Tries to grab toys from other children—has tantrum if denied.

Cries and screams when father leaves in morning.

Objects violently to someone closing bathroom door—screams and pounds on door. "She has to be part of everything."

"She has such a pair of lungs she has everyone terrorized." If frustrated, screams and throws self on floor. Mother says she doesn't attempt to touch stove or light plugs. If spanked, cries more loudly; "She gets insulted."

Asks to be read to many times daily. If refused, cries—can be diverted. Recently, if her crying is ignored, it stops more quickly.

Gets skin rash on face and arms in cold weather, keeps scratching at it—doesn't cry.

INTERVIEW VI (twenty-five and one-half months): Awakened and terrified by thunderstorm. Clings to mother.

Period of night awakening lasted until three months ago, then improved spontaneously. Parents think disturbance due to teething. "When she is in good shape, she sleeps O.K., nothing bothers her."

For several months resisted bath (only went if given lollipop). Even now wants to get out quickly. Parents think perhaps due to skin sensitivity, has skin eruption. Positive reaction to beach and wading pool. If unsuccessful in attempts to dress self, screams. Readily accepts help.

Lies down and screams if rejected by brother, or if toy is too difficult.

INTERVIEW VII (thirty-two months): Food intake irregular. Mother thinks related to teething. Rejects food by letting it drop out of mouth, "Then she holds tongue out and makes me scrape the rest off."

Takes bath fairly well—follows brother in. If unsuccessful in dressing self, screams, accepts help. Not upset when she wets bed—tells mother. Cries when falls, O.K. as soon as comforted.

No longer easily awakened by sound (as previously) or light.

Skin very sensitive, gets rash easily, complains about it.

Gets weekly book from library. Won't let anyone touch it or read it, even to her. Screams if anyone sits in her chair or uses her dish or spoon.

"Still capable of throwing a fit anywhere if she doesn't get what she wants or if someone walks in front of her." "When she's not screaming with frustration, she's gay and happy." When she is screaming with frustration she is sometimes easily distracted, especially by physical play, sometimes not.

INTERVIEW VIII (thirty-eight months): Won't tolerate unwanted food on plate—pushes plate away or dumps specific food on table. Showers instead of bathing now. Gets worried if scratched or hurt and won't get in bath until she's better. If she has scratch or rash or bumps, gets upset and cries. Is sensitive to wrinkles in socks—"The princess with the pea." Accepts physician.

When thwarted in any way (with something she wants), will howl and kick and carry on until worn out. Mother can quiet her by picking up and cuddling.

INTERVIEW IX (forty-five months): Easy to manage when not crossed in area in which she is touchy.

Sensitive skin, can't wear wool—thread or knot may "bother" her. Mother can't evaluate how much is really disturbing. No dermatitis from clothes. Dislikes tight clothes.

Very neat, used to demand that if something had been moved it be replaced. Snowsuit must be tied certain way or it must be retied; she must open door to aunt's house—shrieks in advance for fear someone else will do it. Insists plate be removed when finished eating; must sit in own chair; no table mat, though others use them—does not like feel of plastic mat—no objection to tablecloth.

Eats foods liked intensely—otherwise doesn't eat at all. Eats by herself; insists on doing what she can—will permit mother to help with grapefruit, which might irritate skin if it slips under lower lip. Chronic allergy and dermatitis under lips and right wrist (uses wrist to wipe mouth) only in winter—clears up in summer.

Takes a while to get over illness—requires nap and rest for week or more after illness (virus infection).

Must say good-bye to brother and father. Cries if omitted.

Frustrated if unsuccessful in new endeavor. Accepts help from mother and sibs. Frustration with unsuccessful endeavor or denial of request. More apt to happen when tired. Same situation may cause whining one day, and tantrum the next. Does not like to be crossed. Once she has stated a desire, she must win out, "must save face." If request is denied, she can sometimes be appeased by being given a choice of two other things—when denied gum before lunch, crying persisted after tantrum all the way home. Mother gave her choice of holding bundle or opening door, and crying stopped.

Crying when hurt may depend on involvement in play. A bandage cures everything.

Feelings easily hurt. If not given her turn when due, comes crying to mother in "agony."

Sensitive to smell. Leaves table until sister finishes foods Bonnie dislikes. Accepts absolute and safety rules. Cries, screams, and has tantrums with relative prohibitions—may have tantrum if denied gum before lunch.

INTERVIEW X (fifty-one months): Seems to require more sleep than older sibs. After nursery school may fall asleep at 4 P.M.

Sensitive skin. Can't wear wool, complains it's scratchy; can't tolerate folds, rumpled socks. Dislikes nubby materials, fusses, takes off clothes. Neat—notices rearrangements, what people wear. Must open door on visiting aunt. Must have clean plate (refuses bread and butter on same plate with eggs), same chair, no place mat.

Gets lost easily in crowds. In museum, only few feet away from mother, screamed in terror.

Gives up if can't achieve. Lets mother show her. If unsuccessful, may cry or leave activity. Pain comforted by medication, bandage.

Feelings hurt easily—if not given turn or rejected in play, will come to mother crying.

Sensitive to smell (especially foods).

No longer violent response to prohibitions. Still cries when request is refused, but not as extreme. When not successful with what she undertakes, cries. Not as frustrated as before—more so when tired.

Dependence and independence

INTERVIEWS I AND II: No mention.

INTERVIEW III (fourteen months): Left with aunt for a week—adjusted well. As soon as saw parents, refused to go back to aunt's arms. First week on return home played by herself, demanded little attention. Then reverted to crying for attention and not staying alone.

Doesn't actually cling to mother much. If mother leaves side in playground, even for minute, cries bitterly. If another child takes something from her, she struggles and cries.

INTERVIEW IV (sixteen and one-half months): Left with aunt ten days— screamed if not sat with until asleep (had not been so with mother). On mother's return, "didn't know me." Wouldn't stay alone in room with mother—if aunt went out, she followed her, screaming. O.K. after mother stayed overnight. Also reverted to former pattern of not screaming when put to bed. Suddenly, for period of about two weeks, began screaming on being put to bed unless taken out or parents sat with her. Mother thinks due to teething.

Takes liquids from cup. Milk offered only in bottle. "No special reason." Lets mother feed her at beginning of meal, then insists on feeding herself. If mother continues to try to feed her, she "howls, has a fit, everything goes flying."

In bath, washes herself, lets mother wash her. Sometimes tries to dress herself. Only occasionally "explodes" when unsuccessful, throws everything around.

Started walking five weeks ago. Came quickly without much effort. "Very thrilled with it, we made a big fuss over it." Then resisted carriage, struggled to get out, cried, "wanted to walk." If put down when shopping, laughed and ran out of store.

INTERVIEW V (nineteen and one-half months): Uses cup at mealtime— "gets furious if you touch it." Wouldn't let mother feed her at all—past few weeks occasionally accepts mother's help.

Tries to wash self and brother in bath. Permits mother to wash her. Tries to put on own shoes—if unsuccessful, lets mother do it. If toy is pulled from her, fights, screams, hits.

INTERVIEW VI (twenty-five and one-half months): If very hungry, may let parent help with feeding, otherwise refuses help. In bath, washes self somewhat, allows mother to wash her. Sometimes tries to dress self—

if unsuccessful, screams. Accepts help readily. Wants nails cut when sibs' are done—true in past several interviews. Also imitates sibs in taking foods formerly disliked.

When sister pulls toy, fights hard; if another child pulls, fights half-heartedly, cries.

INTERVIEW VII (thirty-two months): Feeds self, uses utensils well. Will let mother help her if it's food she likes. In bath, does fair job of washing self, no objection to mother washing her. Period when she insisted on dressing self and refused help. Now doesn't dress self much, accepts mother's help. If unsuccessful, screams, accepts help.

Toilet trained suddenly two months ago. Had resisted toilet, mother tried again, she agreed, and was trained for both urine and bowel movements in few days. Wets at night 50 per cent of time, rarely during day.

With hair brushing, yanks brush away saying, "I'll do it myself." If toy taken, shrieks wildly. Fights back if taken by sib; doesn't fight, cries, if taken by strange child.

Sits on mother's lap if strangers around. With one stranger, warms up quickly.

INTERVIEW VIII (thirty-eight months): Mother says, "Pretty self-sufficient." Eats by herself; wants to serve self. Completely toilet trained now. Mother says training was accomplished when Bonnie heard another child was "trained" and then asked to go on toilet and was trained in two to three days. Also pattern of staying dry at night established at same time.

Likes to help others.

Undresses and attempts to dress self. Permits mother to wash hands and face, prefers doing it herself.

INTERVIEW IX (forty-five months): Awakens on own, climbs out of crib—does not demand attention or help until mother is ready. This was routine for sibs, and she slipped into it.

Able to put on shirt, underpants, and skirt alone, but mother dresses her—she has not asked Bonnie to do this. Undresses self, puts on own pajamas. Used to put clothes away, now may leave them in heap.

Eats by herself, insists on doing what she can for herself. Asks to set and clear table—can set table exactly so. Eats neatly. Toilets self except for mother wiping. Imitates brother on closing bathroom door. Washes self in bath.

Not aggressive with playmates, does not grab toys; if playmate is rough, comes to mother for comfort. May need a little warm-up with strange children. Apt to follow interests of older sibs.

Does not cling to mother on initial visits to friends. Stayed without mother for story hour at library.

INTERVIEW X (fifty-one months): Mother says child is "very mature." When mother said she was not taking a bottle to the country, Bonnie said, "Yes, I won't need it anymore."

Partially dresses self. Can't do back buttons. Undresses, puts on own pajamas. Permits mother to help her, but not feed her. Best table manners in family. Likes to help with setting, cleaning. Toileting on own—mother wipes. Washes self in bath—mother washes.

Plays alone very short periods—follows mother with toys. O.K. with another child. Follows somewhat more than initiates. In playground altercation (rare), comes to mother.

Lost easily in crowds. In museum, only few feet away from mother, screamed in terror. Now afraid, must hold mother's hand. No objection to mother leaving her at home. Accepted school first day.

Handling by parents and relationship

INTERVIEW I (six and one-half months): Pretty cranky baby—cried a lot. Mother let her cry and breast-fed her at "reasonable" intervals of three to four hours. No success with attempt to wake her at 10 P.M. to eliminate 2 A.M. feeding. Would refuse to nurse at 10 P.M., and then get up at 2 A.M. anyway.

Wakes up 6–7 A.M. Plays by herself up to twenty minutes, then starts to cry; then has to be diverted again every twenty to thirty minutes with change of position. Finally fed at 9 A.M.

Cries a lot during day. Mother thinks it's constipation or teething. "You know babies. They're always screaming and you never know why." "Most of the time I can't figure out what she wants. I breast-feed her and that keeps her content for a half hour."

Breast-feeding: At present, "I'm sloppy on that—feed her whenever she cries." This is the only of three babies mother has breast-fed. Mother says she never tried giving her water or juice from a bottle—"I don't know why. Guess I was too lazy. Just couldn't figure out when you're supposed to." Then mother says she did try several times, and it didn't work. Mother has offered bottle of milk several times in past month. Child chewed on nipple, didn't take it. About three weeks ago was given bottle of juice at beginning of supper when she was hungry. She screamed, rejected supper, had to be breast-fed. Rejected supper two to three days. Bottle not offered for a week—just a few times since. She doesn't take any if hungry. She cries.

Took vitamin drops O.K. from two weeks. At three months, began to spit them out and cry. Mother kept giving them, then Bonnie again started taking them O.K. after one to two months. Rejects vegetables— closes mouth, makes face. "I don't knock myself out giving it to her."

Only bathed once a week—"She doesn't get so dirty." (First baby had daily bath.) Mother says she fussed more with first baby, by third, she realizes this isn't necessary.

Mother has to rock her for ten to thirty minutes on going to sleep or she cries. "I've been doing that since she's born, but it's all wrong. I didn't want to wake the other children." Wakes every night between 3–5 A.M. Mother nurses her.

INTERVIEW II (nine and three-fourths months): Rocking on going to sleep was stopped two and a half months ago. Parents vague as to how it was stopped—"Didn't seem to make any difference"—Maybe due to change to bigger bed, "which doesn't rock." Child sleeps through night. "That just happened, I didn't do anything." Maybe due to moving to own room so not disturbed by noise.

At two and a half months, accepted milk in bottle from father (had rejected it from mother). Thereafter took it from mother also, increasingly larger amounts, and then breast was discontinued. "Whenever she's moaning and groaning I give her something to eat. Until last week was moaning and groaning every waking minute all her life. I figure if she has food in her mouth she can't cry." "That child was always fussing and screaming every waking minute up to a week ago. She's sweet and adorable; has a wonderful time with the other kids."

Father participates in care. More precise and definite memory for events; mother indefinite about many points.

INTERVIEW III (fourteen months): Usually doesn't take milk with meals—"I guess I don't try very hard." If given something she doesn't want, cries, tries to wipe it off tongue, spits. Mother washes tongue off with washcloth when this happens. If given more food than she wants, throws it back at mother.

Left with aunt for one week, adjusted well. As soon as she saw parents again, wouldn't go back to aunt's arms. For a week after return home she was "divine." "The way they're supposed to be, the way I've never had them." Played by herself, demanded little attention, then reverted to former pattern—crying for attention, not staying alone. Doesn't actually cling to mother much. If mother leaves her side in playground, even a minute, "Cries bitterly." Gets very upset at "no" or if something is taken away. Yells, but is easily distracted. "I don't tell her 'no' much."

INTERVIEW IV (sixteen and one-half months): While with aunt for ten days, would scream unless sat with until asleep. On return home, reverted to former pattern of allowing mother to leave after putting her in bed. About a month later, suddenly started screaming on being put in bed. Allowed to scream twenty minutes, then father took her out and she was O.K. For two weeks, parents either had to take her out or sit with her. Sometimes awakened at night screaming—taken into parents' bed. Mother thinks due to teething, which is now better.

Takes liquids from cup. Mother gives milk only from bottle—no special reason. Child lets mother feed her at beginning of meal, then insists on taking over. If mother continues to try to feed her, she "howls, has a fit, everything goes flying."

Wouldn't sit in tub, howled—"Maybe it was too hot." Bribed with lollipop each time since, then O.K. Washes self, lets mother wash. Put on toilet seat once, no result—"Typical me, I tried it once, nothing happened, I gave up."

Learned to walk—"Thrilled with it, we made a big fuss over it." Then resisted carriage, struggled to get out, cried, "wanted to walk." Mother couldn't go shopping with her—"bellowed" when put in shopping cart. If put down, laughed and ran out of store. If mother tried to pull her back, she threw herself on floor and screamed. After two days, put in stroller—O.K. Put back in carriage several days ago—O.K.

Left with aunt several times, cries briefly as mother leaves, then O.K. Mother once left her for five hours in afternoon—fussed a lot. If brother or sister takes something, she screams and throws self on floor. Mother picks her up—she is easily distracted.

"I'm not a very hot one at discipline." When mother says no, either child stops and cries, or laughs and does it even more. Spanking only intensifies her reaction.

INTERVIEW V (nineteen and one-half months): Sleeping was "letter perfect" until one month ago—would go to bed smiling, slept all night. "Then the whole thing went to pieces." Began screaming at bed- and nap-time (was teething). Was taken out and put to bed later on (as in previous episodes). Also awakened at night, screaming. Usually ended up being put in parents' bed. Screaming worse for one and a half weeks with upper respiratory infection. Last week in "declining phase," scream-ing much less, down a few minutes—not taken out. Says good-night to rest of family cheerfully, kisses them, is put in bed and starts to scream. Bottle given only at bed- and naptime. Cup at mealtime—"Gets furious if you touch it." Feeds herself. Wouldn't let mother feed her at all—in past few weeks occasionally accepts mother's help. Jumps up and down, makes a game of avoiding mother while being dressed. Will co-operate when mother tells her shoes will be put on. Doesn't cry at un-successful attempts to put on shoes—lets mother do it.

About discipline, mother says, "Of course I do very little about that." Father says, "She has such a pair of lungs, she has everyone terrorized." If spanked, only cries louder—"She gets insulted." Mother notes she does not attempt to touch stove or light plugs. Recently, if crying is ignored, it stops more quickly.

INTERVIEW VI (twenty-five and one-half months): If mother sees she's not sleepy, lets her stay up—"She's so strong willed, there's no sense insisting." May call parent during night for bottle of milk. Insists on parent she has called. If the other comes, she cries and refuses bottle.

Night awakening improved spontaneously three months ago. Parents think it was due to teething. "When she's in good shape, she sleeps O.K. Nothing bothers her." Calls in about twenty minutes if doesn't nap. "If she won't sleep, one hundred horses won't make her."

Often insists on sitting in father's lap while eating. "I give in, she screams so loud, I can't bear it." When frustrated, throws self on floor and screams until picked up—parents always do—"We do almost anything to keep her quiet, she has such a voice." If very hungry, may let parent help with feeding, otherwise refuses help.

At twenty-one months, undressed self completely as soon as dressed. Went on all day long about one month, then "got over it." Insists on own selection of clothes, "Otherwise I can't get it on her." Screams with unsuccessful attempts to dress self—accepts help readily. Put on toilet several times, presses hard, then says, "I can't." Asks for diaper with bowel movement, says "no" to suggestion of toilet. Mother comments she is not one to push this issue.

Constant demand on father's time, fusses when he leaves—fuss is minimal unless good-bye kiss is omitted. Frequently same with mother.

Plays more by self—demands less of parents' time. Usually plays with sister. Content to be read to indefinitely—if refused, can be distracted easily. If toy is too difficult, lies down and screams; accepts help, screaming stops. "That's the only way to stop it."

Unresponsive to discipline—"She thinks it's a big joke." Cries loudly if spanked, but no effect. "Probably I'm not adamant enough, she doesn't seem to do any vital thing wrong."

INTERVIEW VII (thirty-two months): Disturbance in sleep again. "Out of the blue," screamed "hysterically" and tried to come out when put to bed. Handled at first by starting her in parents' bed and then returning her to her own. Began awakening more and more frequently during night with necessity of repeating procedure until she finally slept in parents' bed all night, with one parent sleeping in living room. This continued several months. Then put to bed in living room, but would follow parents to bed when they retired. Finally, "all were worn down to last frazzle," parents put her in her own bed firmly and mother stayed until she went to sleep. Same procedure when she awakened at night. After a week, didn't object to mother's not staying. Now "perfect." If awakened (rarely), returns to sleep with covering or bottle. Mother thinks problem may have been started with late afternoon naps—"Nothing I could do about it." Now naps only once a week, goes to bed later at night.

Feeding is fine—"When she's hungry she eats and when she's not I don't care if she doesn't eat." Mother doesn't press new foods. "You couldn't make her." Rejects food by letting it drop out of mouth, "then she holds her tongue out and makes me scrape the rest off." Feeds self—will let mother help her if it's food she likes.

With hair brushing, yanks brush away, "I'll do it myself," messes up hair. Mother lets her—"I let her do anything, so long as she doesn't yell." Lets father brush her hair. With hand and face washing, usually cooperative. "Sometimes I have to drag her kicking and screaming."

Screaming with hair wash until several months ago. "I didn't do it when she screamed."

If mother refused her choice of clothes, she screamed. Mother gave in unless going visiting—screamed, finally subsided. More amenable last few months. Had a period when she insisted on dressing self and refused help. Doesn't dress self much now—accepts mother's help. If unsuccessful in dressing self, screams, accepts help.

Trained two months ago—came suddenly. Had resisted sitting on toilet—mother tried again, she agreed, and was trained for both urine and bowel movements in few days. Still wets 50 per cent of time at night, rarely during day.

Rapid shifts of occasional preference for one parent over the other. "If you tell her not to do something, she turns around, does it, and laughs."

INTERVIEW VIII (thirty-eight months): Eats by self—wants to serve self. Mother insists on cutting meat. If Bonnie started and mother intervened, would howl, collapse on floor. Mother cuts meat in kitchen. With food she likes, wants to eat all portions prepared for entire family; will try to take food from others' plates if mother does not watch. Fusses, howls if stopped. Mother stops her anyway, but tries to avoid.

To bed with bottle of milk—recently may have cereal and chocolate milk with brother instead. May call for bottle of milk at night, which mother gives her. No sleep problem—may talk or come out if had occasional nap—soon settles down. Completely toilet trained. "Perfect in every respect." Mother helps by wiping.

Enchanted with father. When he is home, she wants him to do everything for her. May say, "I like daddy better" to tease mother. Snuggles up to mother when tired or wants comforting. Warm-up needed with new people—clings to mother for a while.

INTERVIEW IX (forty-five months): Goes to bed willingly. Mother feels she is indulgent; feels Bonnie needs something to take to bed, gives her night bottle. Wakes at night, asks to be covered. Mother asks her to cover herself, but she cries, and since mother does not want other children awakened, mother gives in and covers her. Either father or mother can quiet her at night. Wants three blankets arranged in definite order (otherwise cries). Mother makes sure they are arranged and dried same day as washed. Otherwise, although Bonnie will be reconciled, "it is with a heavy heart." Awakens on own, does not demand attention in morning until mother is ready.

Can put on some clothing herself, but mother has not asked her to dress self—mother does it. Intense battle about what to wear for past six to nine months. Much arguing back and forth and nagging—then mother says, "this is it." Will finally accept skirt or pants instead of party dress, but not the particular one mother selected. Father somewhat more successful in getting her to accept clothes—child more negative with mother.

Insists plate be removed when finished eating (mother does this). Eats only foods liked intensely or doesn't eat at all. Goes on food jags. Mother usually doesn't serve disliked foods. Father has more success with getting her to accept different foods. Eats by herself; insists on doing what she can for herself (mother cuts food). Mother considers intake satisfactory, but is not happy with selection of food.

Father is for fun in play; mother is for service. Will obey, give in more readily to father. If tantrum arises with him, it lasts a short time.

Obeys absolute and safety rules. Does not accept relative prohibitions—cries, screams, eventually will give in. Mother leaves her when she is crying, screaming, on street or floor. Takes five to ten minutes, then comes to mother, though may continue to cry. If denied gum before lunch, may have tantrum and cry all the way home; then mother gives her choice of holding bundle or opening door. This opportunity to make selection is "face saving" and stops the crying and tantrum.

INTERVIEW X (fifty months): "Cute, responsive, no more tantrums, very mature, quite bearable." Still demands mother or father cover her during night—otherwise won't go back to sleep.

At birthday, mother said bottle would not be taken to country—Bonnie said, "Yes, I won't need it anymore." Father said ridiculous to have three blankets (after return from country)—she accepted. Now only two blankets, no special order.

Partially dresses self—can't button back buttons. Mother or Bonnie selects clothes. Mother permits Bonnie's selection even if not too appropriate.

Eats great quantities of what she likes, otherwise doesn't eat at all. Other children like same things so mother prepares. Used to run away if didn't like supper, now must ask father to excuse her. (He always does.) Permits mother to help her, but not feed her.

Plays alone very short periods. (O.K. with another child.) Carries toys around following mother.

Mother intercedes in fuss with sister, not necessarily at Bonnie's request. In rare playground altercation, comes to mother—mother distracts her. Will come to mother crying if rejected in play. Mother holds her in lap a short time, crying stops.

Says she likes father best. Permits him to service her, wants to accompany him on trips. Elaborate morning leave-taking. Seeks mother when hurt. No objection to mother leaving—likes sitter.

No longer has tantrums when crossed. Father firm, sticks to statement. Mother not very exacting. Mother may spank if child disobeys, teases. Still cries when request is refused, but not as extreme.

Subsequent course

INTERVIEW XI (fifty-seven months): Helps mother put bundles away. In writing numbers, one was crooked. She screamed, had to have clean paper and start over. May erupt on occasion. Reacts violently when she loses to her sister. Accepts losing to a friend. Mother promised her game she wanted if she did not scream for four days. Child would stop herself with and without reminding—earned the game.

INTERVIEW XII (sixty-three months): Mother states they "have just gone into a slightly difficult phase."

Was out for first week of school with ear infection; balked when taken back—would not enter and returned home. Later said she had seen no girls in line, only boys. After following two days, which were holidays, mother got her ready matter-of-factly, and she returned to school without comment—has gone since then.

At home, when she wants something, she must have it immediately or she screams. Feelings are easily hurt—will cry, scream, throw, hit. Outside the home, she is meek, shy—plays with other children, accommodates.

Must be physically forced to do what she doesn't want to do, or to stop a prohibited activity. Father is better at disciplining child—he persists at it; mother realizes that there are times when she lets Bonnie do as she wants because it is easier at the moment.

She likes mother to dress and undress her, and mother obliges. Not true during the summer when she did it on her own. Continues to refuse tight, itchy clothing.

INTERVIEW XIII (seventy-one months): Tantrums less intense—now "whining sulk." Less clothing sensitivity. In some ways wants unneeded help.

KINDERGARTEN TEACHER INTERVIEW (seventy-one months): Child does not show easy anger.

FIRST-GRADE TEACHER INTERVIEW (eighty months): No extreme emotion. Teacher would like to "spark her with enthusiasm." Child is very calm, never ruffled. Not attention-seeking.

INTERVIEW XIV (eighty-two months): Reported to be quiet at school, but when upset at home, cries loudly.

SECOND-GRADE TEACHER INTERVIEW (ninety-three months): Great change, more enthusiasm—still placid, not excited enough to argue, but will on rare occasions get angry. Defends self, something she did not do before.

INTERVIEW XV (ninety-five months): Mother was in despair—ready to call study psychiatrist. Child showing much frustration, crying and moaning. Slightest thing causes frustration. Goes in cycles.

Has disliked school this year and last—dislikes teacher. For months, cried every morning—did not want to go. Brought home good report card, but not as good as sibs.

Outside she is shy, conforming; at home, unreasonable, moans at slightest thing. Will continue for twenty minutes, but when age three, would lie on floor and kick. No explosive anger as there used to be.

INTERVIEW XVI (one hundred and six months): Has done very well in school; teacher says she is outstanding. Bonnie still says she doesn't want to go to school.

Still has tantrum once in a while when can't learn poem in five minutes. Frustrated at not getting what she wants immediately. Tantrums less frequent. Mother and sister will say, "I'll listen if you don't cry."

INTERVIEW XVII (one hundred and eighteen months): No tantrums, less whining. Less compulsive about routines, eats more foods, has less sensitivities. Can be talked out of things more easily. Resistance to school not mentioned. Not as good a report card as sibs, but she didn't seem bothered.

INDEX

A

Ackerman, N., 200
Activity level, 20, 116–23
  data analysis, 54, 57, 59, 60, 61, 63, 65, 69
  high, 116–19
    distractibility and, 117, 118
    intensity of reactions, 117
    management problems, 116–18
    play space needed, 116, 118
  hyperactivity, 116
  hyperkinesis, 131, 135
  illustrations, 20
  low, 119–23, 202
    intellectual potential, 120–21
    misinterpretation of behavior, 122–23
    parental handling, 120–22
    persistence and, 121–22
    results of parent guidance, 181
    results of treatment, 176
    slowly moving child, 120
    temperamental characteristics, 20, 119–20
  questions for evaluating, 193, 196
  relation to disturbance, 57
  temperamental characteristic of, 20
Adaptability, 17
  data analysis, 54, 57, 59, 60, 61, 63, 64, 65, 69
  illustrations, 21
  nature of, 21
  questions for evaluating, 193, 196
  temperamental characteristic of, 21
Age of onset of behavioral disturbance
  clinical case group, 67–69
  definition, 35
American Handbook of Psychiatry, 185
Anger, explosive, 150
Anterospective studies, 7–8
  need for, 7–8
  review of, 34
  selective extraction, 50–51
  value of, 4
Anxiety, 34, 185
  role of, 186–90
  symptom formation, 188
Approach/withdrawal, 21
  data analysis, 54, 57, 59, 60, 61, 63, 65, 69
  illustrations, 21
  questions for evaluating, 193, 196
  relation to disturbance, 57
  temperamental characteristic of, 21
Approval of child, 26
Association for Aid to Crippled Children, vi
Attention span and persistence, 23–24, 155–56
  illustrations, 23–24
  nature of, 23–24
  questions for evaluating, 195, 196–97
  temperamental characteristic of, 23–24
Autism, 183
Avoidance mechanism, 166–68, 170

B

Baby and Child Care (Spock), 13
Baths, response to first, 15
Behavior disorders
  cases of early onset, 67–68
  causes, 3, 182–90
    theoretical formulations, 182–90
  interactions between child and environment in development of, 71–74, 82–85, 86–91, 96–99, 103–108, 111–15, 118–19, 120–23
  prevention of, 202–203
  severity of, 43–44
  temperament and, 3–9, 53–70, 133, 134–35
    quantitative analysis, 53–70
    traits most frequently identified with, 71
Behavioral development
  brain-damaged children, 124–36
  concept of temperament, 3–9
  longitudinal data on, 7–8
Bibring, G. L., 201
Birth of younger child, effect of, 27
Bowel problems, 150–52, 163–66
  symptoms, 45, 205
Bradley, C., 135
Brain damage, 34, 116, 124–36, 153
  behavioral development, 124–36
  case studies, 124–33
    Barbara (case 1), 130–33
    Bert (case 42), 124–28
    Kevin, 128–30
  difficult child pattern, 134
  divergence in development, 133
  environmental demand, 134
  hyperkinetic syndrome, 126, 135
  intellectual functioning, 133
  language comprehension, 125, 128, 130, 131